West's Federal Taxation

Corporation, S Corporation, & Partnership Practice Sets

William H. Hoffman, Jr.
University of Houston

Eugene Willis
University of Illinois at Urbana

James E. Smith
College of William and Mary

William A. Raabe
Samford University

David M. Maloney
University of Virginia

Prepared by

Donald R. Trippeer
Lehigh University

WEST/SOUTH-WESTERN College Publishing

An International Thomson Publishing Company

Accounting Team Director: Richard K. Lindgren
Acquisitions Editor: Alex von Rosenberg
Developmental Editor: Esther Craig
Production Editor: Rebecca Glaab
Production House: Mary Hartkemeyer
Marketing Manager: Maureen L. Riopelle
Manufacturing Coordinator: Gordon Woodside

ISBN: 0-538-88915-2

1 2 3 4 5 6 7   WST   4 3 2 1 0 9 8

Printed in the United States of America

International Thomson Publishing
West/South-Western College Publishing is an ITP Company.

TABLE OF CONTENTS

PREFACE

Although these practice sets are designed for use with West's Federal Taxation Series, they can be used effectively with most introductory textbooks on taxation. The practice sets should be assigned after coverage of the related materials, as they are comprehensive and require substantial text coverage for successful completion.

The practice sets include the common forms that would be used. Practice sets for corporation, S corporation, and partnership returns are enclosed. Practice sets for individual returns are published separately.

To facilitate completion of the returns, selected instructions for tax forms are provided.

All comments or suggestions will be appreciated.

Donald R. Trippeer
Lehigh University
drt2@lehigh.cdu

CORPORATION PRACTICE SET

Monarch, Inc.

Federal Tax Return

FACTS

Monarch, Inc. is owned by Sarah T. Johnson and her husband, John J. Johnson. The corporation manufactures butterfly-theme novelty products that are sold to boutiques (business activity code number 1883), and has reported positive financial and taxable incomes since inception. The company is located at 311 Center Street, Bethlehem, Pennsylvania 18015. The company's employer identification number is 46-5687713, and the calendar year is used for tax purposes. The date of incorporation was February 1, 1993.

Sarah T. Johnson (social security number 563-14-0208) is an 80 percent shareholder and president of the company. John J. Johnson (social security number 432-10-8765) is a 20 percent shareholder and vice president of the company. Both persons devote 100 percent of their time to the corporation. Sarah's compensation is $129,600 per year, and John's compensation is $72,000 per year.

The corporation is not a personal holding company. While the corporation is a 'closely-held C corporation,' it does not engage in activities to which the at-risk or passive activity loss limitations apply.

The corporation files its tax return on the accrual method. Inventory has been consistently valued at cost under the FIFO method using the full absorption procedure. Inventory capitalization rules of Internal Revenue Code Section 263A do not apply due to the 'small business exception' (average annual gross receipts for the three preceding taxable years do not exceed $10 million). The accounting records are computerized.

The corporation's audited income statement and balance sheet for the current year, prepared by the accounting firm of Down & Dirty, CPAs, follow:

MONARCH, INC.
INCOME STATEMENT
For the Year Ending December 31, 1997

Revenue:

Sales (net)	$ 5,784,381	
Cost of goods sold	(4,819,257)	
Gross profit		$ 965,124

Operating expenses:

Compensation of officers	$ 201,600	
Other salaries and wages	443,470	
Rental expense	30,384	
Interest expense	76,873	
Fines for improper disposal of waste	2,448	
Advertising	7,747	
Contributions	32,400	
Bad debt expense	2,880	
Depreciation expense	99,294	
Taxes	69,840	
Repairs and maintenance	6,489	
Miscellaneous expenses	17,533	
Total operating expenses		$(990,958)
Net Income from Operations		$ (25,834)

Other income and loss:

Dividend income	$ 96,254	
Interest income	2,106	
Loss on sale of investment in stock	(2,304)	96,056
Net Income (Loss) before income tax		$ 70,222
Income tax expense		(2,880)
Net Income		$ 67,342

MONARCH, INC.
STATEMENT OF FINANCIAL POSITION
December 31, 1997

ASSETS	Beginning of Year	End of Year
Current Assets:		
Cash & Marketable Securities	$ 423,600	$ 411,155
Accounts receivable	204,552	230,814
Allowance for Doubtful Accounts	(12,960)	(14,220)
Inventory	468,690	567,395
Total current assets	$1,083,882	$1,195,144
Machinery, Building, and Land:		
Machinery	$ 280,800	$ 320,760
Less: Accumulated depreciation	(86,400)	(157,392)
Building	990,622	990,622
Less: Accumulated depreciation	(119,108)	(147,410)
Land	72,000	72,000
Total equipment, building, and land (net)	$1,137,914	$1,078,580
Other assets:		
Goodwill	–0–	21,060
Total Assets	$2,221,796	$2,294,784

LIABILITIES AND SHAREHOLDERS' EQUITY

	Beginning of Year	End of Year
Current liabilities:		
Accounts payable	$ 184,610	$ 198,626
Notes payable (less than one year)	148,320	131,040
Total current liabilities	$ 332,930	$ 329,666
Notes payable (one year or more)	698,400	751,229
Total Liabilities	$1,031,330	$1,080,895
Common stock (10,000 shares authorized, 10,000 shares issued and outstanding, $72 par)	$ 720,000	$ 720,000
Additional paid-in capital	144,000	144,000
Retained earnings	326,466	349,889
Total Shareholders' Equity	$1,190,466	$1,213,889
Total Liabilities and Shareholders' Equity	$2,221,796	$2,294,784

STATEMENT OF RETAINED EARNINGS

Beginning Retained Earnings	$326,466
Net income for the year	67,342
Dividends paid in cash	(43,919)
Ending Retained Earnings	$349,889

ADDITIONAL INFORMATION ███████████

1. Monarch, Inc. made estimated tax payments attributable to 1997 of $4,320. The corporation also had a credit from an overpayment of its prior year Federal income taxes of $389 that it elected to apply against its 1997 tax liability.

2. All notes payable were issued at par and provide market interest rates.

3. Ignore state income taxes.

4. Dividend income is from the following sources:

Walmart	$56,654
Netscape	21,600
Cocoon Corp. (Monarch, Inc. owns 85% of Cocoon Corp.'s stock)	18,000
Total	$96,254

5. An analysis of the Allowance for Doubtful Accounts reveals:

Balance, 01/01/97	$12,960
1997 Transactions—	
Provision for bad debts	2,880
Recoveries on bad debts	(612)
Accounts written off as uncollectible	(1,008)
Balance, 12/31/97	$14,220

6. Goodwill of $21,600 arose on purchase of another business on 01/01/97. Amortization for financial purposes is over the maximum allowable period (40 years) and is included in Miscellaneous Expenses.

7. Assume that deductions for tax depreciation (i.e., Modified Accelerated Cost Recovery) for the year total $117,617. For this practice set do not complete Form 4562 (Depreciation and Amortization).

8. Meals and entertainment costs of $1,440 included in Miscellaneous Expenses are subject to the 50% disallowance rule.

9. Contributions included:

Salvation Army	$27,792
Government of Zaire, for African hunger relief	3,168
Humane Society	1,440
Total	$32,400

All contributions were paid in cash during the year except for the Humane Society contribution which was pledged by the corporation (i.e., approved by the Board of Directors) on December 15, 1997 and paid on May 1, 1998.

10. Included in interest income is $1,188 from $9,000 of City of Bethlehem, Pennsylvania General Obligation Bonds held throughout the current year. These bonds are included in the marketable securities account.

11. On 06/15/97 the corporation sold 100 shares of Loser Corp. common stock for $7,920. The stock had been purchased on 08/14/93 for $10,224.

12. Cocoon Corp. is a subsidiary of Monarch, Inc., formed in 1991, and operated in Bethlehem, Pennsylvania for the purpose of manufacturing butterfly houses. Historically Cocoon Corp. has been profitable and had a taxable income of $73,670 and an Alternative Minimum Taxable Income [Form 4626, Ln. 7] of $74,150. Monarch, Inc. and Cocoon Corp. have agreed to share equally any limitations on item(s) that the income tax law restricts across the corporations so long as the equal allocation results in utilization of maximum benefits available. However, if a corporation does not have sufficient investment, income, or tax to realize benefit of an item so allocated, any excess limitation shall be re-allocated to the other corporation to the extent that other corporation has sufficient investment, income, or tax liability to realize the benefit of the additional limitation. Sales by Cocoon Corp. to Monarch, Inc. are at "arms-length" prices (i.e., fair market values). Monarch, Inc. has not elected to file a consolidated income tax return with Cocoon Corp.

13. Form 4626 (Alternative Minimum Tax—Corporations) must be included in the return. For that purpose, assume the adjustment for depreciation of tangible property placed in service after 1986 (Form 4626, Line 2a) is a $21,485 positive adjustment. Assume the Adjusted Current Earnings (ACE) Adjustment on Line 4e is $-0-. [This assumption removes the ACE adjustment from this practice set].

14. Disregard any penalty on underpayment of estimated tax.

REQUIRED

From the above information, prepare Monarch, Inc.'s 1997 Federal income tax return (Form 1120), including all needed supporting statements, schedules, and forms. Unless otherwise noted, assume Monarch, Inc. follows the policies of making all elections to minimize its current income taxes and, to the extent possible, of conforming procedures for financial and tax accounting. Round amounts to the nearest dollar. If additional information is needed, make realistic assumptions and fill in all required data.

CORPORATION PRACTICE SET

Monarch, Inc.

FORMS

Form **1120**

Department of the Treasury
Internal Revenue Service

U.S. Corporation Income Tax Return

For calendar year 1997 or tax year beginning ...., 1997, ending ...., 19 ...
▶ Instructions are separate. See page 1 for Paperwork Reduction Act Notice.

OMB No. 1545-0123

1997

A Check if a:

1 Consolidated return (attach Form 851) ☐
2 Personal holding co. (attach Sch. PH) ☐
3 Personal service corp. (as defined in Temporary Regs. sec. 1.441-4T— see instructions) ☐

Use IRS label. Otherwise, **print or type.**

Name

Number, street, and room or suite no. (If a P.O. box, see page 5 of instructions.)

City or town, state, and ZIP code

B Employer identification number

C Date incorporated

D Total assets (see page 5 of instructions)

E Check applicable boxes: (1) ☐ Initial return (2) ☐ Final return (3) ☐ Change of address $

Income

1a Gross receipts or sales _______ **b** Less returns and allowances _______ **c** Bal ▶	**1c**	
2 Cost of goods sold (Schedule A, line 8)	**2**	
3 Gross profit. Subtract line 2 from line 1c	**3**	
4 Dividends (Schedule C, line 19)	**4**	
5 Interest	**5**	
6 Gross rents	**6**	
7 Gross royalties	**7**	
8 Capital gain net income (attach Schedule D (Form 1120))	**8**	
9 Net gain or (loss) from Form 4797, Part II, line 18 (attach Form 4797)	**9**	
10 Other income (see page 6 of instructions—attach schedule)	**10**	
11 **Total income.** Add lines 3 through 10 ▶	**11**	

Deductions (See instructions for limitations on deductions.)

12 Compensation of officers (Schedule E, line 4)	**12**	
13 Salaries and wages (less employment credits)	**13**	
14 Repairs and maintenance	**14**	
15 Bad debts	**15**	
16 Rents	**16**	
17 Taxes and licenses	**17**	
18 Interest	**18**	
19 Charitable contributions (see page 8 of instructions for 10% limitation)	**19**	
20 Depreciation (attach Form 4562)	**20**	
21 Less depreciation claimed on Schedule A and elsewhere on return **21a**	**21b**	
22 Depletion	**22**	
23 Advertising	**23**	
24 Pension, profit-sharing, etc., plans	**24**	
25 Employee benefit programs	**25**	
26 Other deductions (attach schedule)	**26**	
27 **Total deductions.** Add lines 12 through 26 ▶	**27**	
28 Taxable income before net operating loss deduction and special deductions. Subtract line 27 from line 11	**28**	
29 **Less:** **a** Net operating loss deduction (see page 9 of instructions) **29a**		
b Special deductions (Schedule C, line 20) **29b**	**29c**	

Tax and Payments

30 **Taxable income.** Subtract line 29c from line 28	**30**	
31 **Total tax** (Schedule J, line 10)	**31**	
32 Payments: **a** 1996 overpayment credited to 1997 **32a**		
b 1997 estimated tax payments **32b**		
c Less 1997 refund applied for on Form 4466 **32c** ( ) **d** Bal ▶ **32d**		
e Tax deposited with Form 7004 **32e**		
f Credit for tax paid on undistributed capital gains (attach Form 2439) **32f**		
g Credit for Federal tax on fuels (attach Form 4136). See instructions **32g**	**32h**	
33 Estimated tax penalty (see page 10 of instructions). Check if Form 2220 is attached ▶ ☐	**33**	
34 **Tax due.** If line 32h is smaller than the total of lines 31 and 33, enter amount owed	**34**	
35 **Overpayment.** If line 32h is larger than the total of lines 31 and 33, enter amount overpaid	**35**	
36 Enter amount of line 35 you want: **Credited to 1998 estimated tax** ▶ **Refunded** ▶	**36**	

Sign Here

Under penalties of perjury, I declare that I have examined this return, including accompanying schedules and statements, and to the best of my knowledge and belief, it is true, correct, and complete. Declaration of preparer (other than taxpayer) is based on all information of which preparer has any knowledge.

▶ _________________________   _________________________
Signature of officer   Date   Title

Paid Preparer's Use Only

Preparer's signature ▶	Date	Check if self-employed ☐	Preparer's social security number
Firm's name (or yours if self-employed) and address ▶		EIN ▶	
		ZIP code ▶	

Cat. No. 11450Q

Schedule A	**Cost of Goods Sold** (See page 10 of instructions.)		

1	Inventory at beginning of year	**1**		
2	Purchases	**2**		
3	Cost of labor	**3**		
4	Additional section 263A costs (attach schedule)	**4**		
5	Other costs (attach schedule)	**5**		
6	**Total.** Add lines 1 through 5	**6**		
7	Inventory at end of year	**7**		
8	**Cost of goods sold.** Subtract line 7 from line 6. Enter here and on page 1, line 2	**8**		

9a Check all methods used for valuing closing inventory:

    (i) ☐ Cost as described in Regulations section 1.471-3

    (ii) ☐ Lower of cost or market as described in Regulations section 1.471-4

    (iii) ☐ Other (Specify method used and attach explanation.) ▶ ....

  b Check if there was a writedown of subnormal goods as described in Regulations section 1.471-2(c) . . . . ▶ ☐

  c Check if the LIFO inventory method was adopted this tax year for any goods (if checked, attach Form 970) . . . . . ▶ ☐

  d If the LIFO inventory method was used for this tax year, enter percentage (or amounts) of closing inventory computed under LIFO **9d**

  e If property is produced or acquired for resale, do the rules of section 263A apply to the corporation? . . . . . ☐ Yes ☐ No

  f Was there any change in determining quantities, cost, or valuations between opening and closing inventory? If "Yes," attach explanation . . . . ☐ Yes ☐ No

Schedule C	**Dividends and Special Deductions** (See page 11 of instructions.)	**(a)** Dividends received	**(b)** %	**(c)** Special deductions (a) × (b)
1	Dividends from less-than-20%-owned domestic corporations that are subject to the 70% deduction (other than debt-financed stock)		70	
2	Dividends from 20%-or-more-owned domestic corporations that are subject to the 80% deduction (other than debt-financed stock)		80	
3	Dividends on debt-financed stock of domestic and foreign corporations (section 246A)		see instructions	
4	Dividends on certain preferred stock of less-than-20%-owned public utilities		42	
5	Dividends on certain preferred stock of 20%-or-more-owned public utilities		48	
6	Dividends from less-than-20%-owned foreign corporations and certain FSCs that are subject to the 70% deduction		70	
7	Dividends from 20%-or-more-owned foreign corporations and certain FSCs that are subject to the 80% deduction		80	
8	Dividends from wholly owned foreign subsidiaries subject to the 100% deduction (section 245(b))		100	
9	**Total.** Add lines 1 through 8. See page 12 of instructions for limitation			
10	Dividends from domestic corporations received by a small business investment company operating under the Small Business Investment Act of 1958		100	
11	Dividends from certain FSCs that are subject to the 100% deduction (section 245(c)(1))		100	
12	Dividends from affiliated group members subject to the 100% deduction (section 243(a)(3))		100	
13	Other dividends from foreign corporations not included on lines 3, 6, 7, 8, or 11			
14	Income from controlled foreign corporations under subpart F (attach Form(s) 5471)			
15	Foreign dividend gross-up (section 78)			
16	IC-DISC and former DISC dividends not included on lines 1, 2, or 3 (section 246(d))			
17	Other dividends			
18	Deduction for dividends paid on certain preferred stock of public utilities			
19	**Total dividends.** Add lines 1 through 17. Enter here and on line 4, page 1 ▶			
20	**Total special deductions.** Add lines 9, 10, 11, 12, and 18. Enter here and on line 29b, page 1 . . . . . . ▶			

Schedule E	**Compensation of Officers** (See instructions for line 12, page 1.)				

Complete Schedule E only if total receipts (line 1a plus lines 4 through 10 on page 1, Form 1120) are $500,000 or more.

(a) Name of officer	**(b)** Social security number	**(c)** Percent of time devoted to business	**(d)** Common	**(e)** Preferred	**(f)** Amount of compensation
1		%	%	%	
		%	%	%	
		%	%	%	
		%	%	%	
		%	%	%	

2	Total compensation of officers			
3	Compensation of officers claimed on Schedule A and elsewhere on return			
4	Subtract line 3 from line 2. Enter the result here and on line 12, page 1			

Schedule J — Tax Computation (See page 12 of instructions.)

1   Check if the corporation is a member of a controlled group (see sections 1561 and 1563) . . . . . ▶ ☐

     Important: Members of a controlled group, see instructions on page 12.

2a   If the box on line 1 is checked, enter the corporation's share of the $50,000, $25,000, and $9,925,000 taxable income brackets (in that order):

     (1) ☐ $ (2) ☐ $ (3) ☐ $

b   Enter the corporation's share of:

     (1) Additional 5% tax (not more than $11,750) ☐ $

     (2) Additional 3% tax (not more than $100,000) ☐ $

3   Income tax. Check this box if the corporation is a qualified personal service corporation as defined in section 448(d)(2) (see instructions on page 13). . . . . ▶ ☐   **3**

4a   Foreign tax credit (attach Form 1118) **4a**

b   Possessions tax credit (attach Form 5735) **4b**

c   Check: ☐ Nonconventional source fuel credit   ☐ QEV credit (attach Form 8834)   **4c**

d   General business credit. Enter here and check which forms are attached: ☐ 3800

     ☐ 3468   ☐ 5884   ☐ 6478   ☐ 6765   ☐ 8586   ☐ 8830   ☐ 8826

     ☐ 8835   ☐ 8844   ☐ 8845   ☐ 8846   ☐ 8820   ☐ 8847   ☐ 8861   **4d**

e   Credit for prior year minimum tax (attach Form 8827) **4e**

5   **Total credits.** Add lines 4a through 4e **5**

6   Subtract line 5 from line 3 . . . .   **6**

7   Personal holding company tax (attach Schedule PH (Form 1120)) **7**

8   Recapture taxes. Check if from: ☐ Form 4255   ☐ Form 8611 . . . .   **8**

9   Alternative minimum tax (attach Form 4626) **9**

10   **Total tax.** Add lines 6 through 9. Enter here and on line 31, page 1 . . . .   **10**

Schedule K — Other Information (See page 14 of instructions.)

	Yes	No

1   Check method of accounting: **a** ☐ Cash   **b** ☐ Accrual   **c** ☐ Other (specify) ▶ ....

2   See page 16 of the instructions and state the principal:

a   Business activity code no. ▶ ....

b   Business activity ▶ ....

c   Product or service ▶ ....

3   At the end of the tax year, did the corporation own, directly or indirectly, 50% or more of the voting stock of a domestic corporation? (For rules of attribution, see section 267(c).) . . . .

     If "Yes," attach a schedule showing: **(a)** name and identifying number, **(b)** percentage owned, and **(c)** taxable income or (loss) before NOL and special deductions of such corporation for the tax year ending with or within your tax year.

4   Is the corporation a subsidiary in an affiliated group or a parent-subsidiary controlled group? . . . . . .

     If "Yes," enter employer identification number and name of the parent corporation ▶ ....

5   At the end of the tax year, did any individual, partnership, corporation, estate or trust own, directly or indirectly, 50% or more of the corporation's voting stock? (For rules of attribution, see section 267(c).) . . . .

     If "Yes," attach a schedule showing name and identifying number. (Do not include any information already entered in **4** above.) Enter percentage owned ▶ ....

6   During this tax year, did the corporation pay dividends (other than stock dividends and distributions in exchange for stock) in excess of the corporation's current and accumulated earnings and profits? (See secs. 301 and 316.) . . . .

     If "Yes," file Form 5452. If this is a consolidated return, answer here for the parent corporation and on **Form 851,** Affiliations Schedule, for each subsidiary.

7   Was the corporation a U.S. shareholder of any controlled foreign corporation? (See sections 951 and 957.) . . . .

     If "Yes," attach Form 5471 for each such corporation. Enter number of Forms 5471 attached ▶ ....

8   At any time during the 1997 calendar year, did the corporation have an interest in or a signature or other authority over a financial account (such as a bank account, securities account, or other financial account) in a foreign country?

     If "Yes," the corporation may have to file Form TD F 90-22.1. If "Yes," enter name of foreign country ▶ ....

9   During the tax year, did the corporation receive a distribution from, or was it the grantor of, or transferor to, a foreign trust? If "Yes," see page 15 of the instructions for other forms the corporation may have to file . . . .

10   At any time during the tax year, did one foreign person own, directly or indirectly, at least 25% of: **(a)** the total voting power of all classes of stock of the corporation entitled to vote, or **(b)** the total value of all classes of stock of the corporation? If "Yes,"

a   Enter percentage owned ▶ ....

b   Enter owner's country ▶ ....

c   The corporation may have to file Form 5472. Enter number of Forms 5472 attached ▶ ....

11   Check this box if the corporation issued publicly offered debt instruments with original issue discount . . ▶ ☐

     If so, the corporation may have to file Form 8281.

12   Enter the amount of tax-exempt interest received or accrued during the tax year ▶ $ ....

13   If there were 35 or fewer shareholders at the end of the tax year, enter the number ▶ ....

14   If the corporation has an NOL for the tax year and is electing to forego the carryback period, check here ▶ ☐

15   Enter the available NOL carryover from prior tax years (Do not reduce it by any deduction on line 29a.) ▶ $

Schedule L — Balance Sheets per Books

Assets	Beginning of tax year (a)	(b)	End of tax year (c)	(d)
1 Cash				
2a Trade notes and accounts receivable				
b Less allowance for bad debts	( )		( )	
3 Inventories				
4 U.S. government obligations				
5 Tax-exempt securities (see instructions)				
6 Other current assets (attach schedule)				
7 Loans to stockholders				
8 Mortgage and real estate loans				
9 Other investments (attach schedule)				
10a Buildings and other depreciable assets				
b Less accumulated depreciation	( )		( )	
11a Depletable assets				
b Less accumulated depletion	( )		( )	
12 Land (net of any amortization)				
13a Intangible assets (amortizable only)				
b Less accumulated amortization	( )		( )	
14 Other assets (attach schedule)				
15 Total assets				
Liabilities and Stockholders' Equity				
16 Accounts payable				
17 Mortgages, notes, bonds payable in less than 1 year				
18 Other current liabilities (attach schedule)				
19 Loans from stockholders				
20 Mortgages, notes, bonds payable in 1 year or more				
21 Other liabilities (attach schedule)				
22 Capital stock: **a** Preferred stock				
b Common stock				
23 Additional paid-in capital				
24 Retained earnings—Appropriated (attach schedule)				
25 Retained earnings—Unappropriated				
26 Adjustments to shareholders' equity (attach schedule)				
27 Less cost of treasury stock		( )		( )
28 Total liabilities and stockholders' equity				

Note: *You are not required to complete Schedules M-1 and M-2 below if the total assets on line 15, column (d) of Schedule L are less than $25,000.*

Schedule M-1 — Reconciliation of Income (Loss) per Books With Income per Return (See page 15 of instructions.)

1 Net income (loss) per books

2 Federal income tax

3 Excess of capital losses over capital gains

4 Income subject to tax not recorded on books this year (itemize): ____________

5 Expenses recorded on books this year not deducted on this return (itemize):

  a Depreciation . . . . $____________

  b Contributions carryover $____________

  c Travel and entertainment $____________

6 Add lines 1 through 5

7 Income recorded on books this year not included on this return (itemize):

  Tax-exempt interest $____________

8 Deductions on this return not charged against book income this year (itemize):

  a Depreciation . . . . $____________

  b Contributions carryover $____________

9 Add lines 7 and 8

10 Income (line 28, page 1)—line 6 less line 9

Schedule M-2 — Analysis of Unappropriated Retained Earnings per Books (Line 25, Schedule L)

1 Balance at beginning of year

2 Net income (loss) per books

3 Other increases (itemize): ____________

4 Add lines 1, 2, and 3

5 Distributions: **a** Cash

  b Stock

  c Property

6 Other decreases (itemize): ____________

7 Add lines 5 and 6

8 Balance at end of year (line 4 less line 7)

<table>
<tr><td>

SCHEDULE D
(Form 1120)

Department of the Treasury
Internal Revenue Service

</td><td>

Capital Gains and Losses

**To be filed with Forms 1120, 1120-A, 1120-IC-DISC, 1120-F,
1120-FSC, 1120-H, 1120-L, 1120-ND, 1120-PC, 1120-POL,
1120-REIT, 1120-RIC, 1120-SF, 990-C, and certain Forms 990-T**

</td><td>

OMB No. 1545-0123

1997

</td></tr>
</table>

Name	Employer identification number

Part I — Short-Term Capital Gains and Losses—Assets Held One Year or Less

(a) Kind of property and description (Example, 100 shares of Z Co.)	(b) Date acquired (mo., day, yr.)	(c) Date sold (mo., day, yr.)	(d) Sales price (see instructions)	(e) Cost or other basis (see instructions)	(f) Gain or (loss) ((d) less (e))
1					

2 Short-term capital gain from installment sales from Form 6252, line 26 or 37	**2**	
3 Short-term gain or (loss) from like-kind exchanges from Form 8824	**3**	
4 Unused capital loss carryover (attach computation)	**4**	( )
5 Net short-term capital gain or (loss). Combine lines 1 through 4	**5**	

Part II — Long-Term Capital Gains and Losses—Assets Held More Than One Year

(a) Kind of property and description (Example, 100 shares of Z Co.)	(b) Date acquired (mo., day, yr.)	(c) Date sold (mo., day, yr.)	(d) Sales price (see instructions)	(e) Cost or other basis (see instructions)	(f) Gain or (loss) ((d) less (e))
6					

7 Enter gain from Form 4797, line 7 or 9	**7**	
8 Long-term capital gain from installment sales from Form 6252, line 26 or 37	**8**	
9 Long-term gain or (loss) from like-kind exchanges from Form 8824	**9**	
10 Net long-term capital gain or (loss). Combine lines 6 through 9	**10**	

Part III — Summary of Parts I and II

11 Enter excess of net short-term capital gain (line 5) over net long-term capital loss (line 10). . .	**11**	
12 Net capital gain. Enter excess of net long-term capital gain (line 10) over net short-term capital loss (line 5)	**12**	
13 Add lines 11 and 12. Enter here and on Form 1120, page 1, line 8, or the proper line on other returns.	**13**	

Note: If losses exceed gains, see **Capital losses** in the instructions below.

Instructions

Section references are to the Internal Revenue Code unless otherwise noted.

A Change To Note

Constructive Sales Treatment for Certain Appreciated Financial Positions.—The Taxpayer Relief Act of 1997 changed the treatment of certain appreciated financial positions. If the corporation holds an appreciated financial position in stock or certain other interests, it may have to recognize gain if it enters into a constructive sale after June 8, 1997 (such as a "short sale against the box"). See **Pub. 550,** Investment Income and Expenses, for more details.

Purpose of Schedule

Use Schedule D to report sales and exchanges of capital assets and gains on distributions to shareholders of appreciated capital assets.

Report sales, exchanges, and distributions of property other than capital assets on **Form 4797,** Sales of Business Property. Include on Form 4797 a sale, exchange, or distribution of property used in a trade or business; involuntary conversions (from other than casualties or thefts); gain from the disposition of oil, gas, or geothermal property; and the section 291 adjustment to section 1250 gains. See the instructions for Form 4797 for more details.

If property is involuntarily converted because of a casualty or theft, use **Form 4684,** Casualties and Thefts.

Parts I and II

Generally, a corporation must report sales and exchanges even if there is no gain or loss. Use Part I to report the sale, exchange, or distribution of capital assets held one year or less. Use Part II to report the sale, exchange, or distribution of capital assets held more than one year. Use the trade dates for the dates of acquisition and sale of stocks and bonds on an exchange or over-the-counter market.

What is a capital asset?—Each item of property the corporation held (whether or not connected with its trade or business) is a capital asset **except:**

1. Assets properly included in inventory or property held mainly for sale to customers.

2. Depreciable or real property used in the trade or business.

3. Certain copyrights; literary, musical, or artistic compositions; letters or memoranda; or similar property.

4. Accounts or notes receivable acquired in the ordinary course of trade or business for services rendered or from the sale of property described in **1** above.

5. U.S. Government publications, including the Congressional Record, that the corporation received from the Government, other than by purchase at the normal sales price, or that the corporation got from another taxpayer who had received it in a similar way, if the corporation's basis is determined by reference to the previous owner's basis.

Capital losses.—Capital losses are allowed only to the extent of capital gains. A net capital loss is carried back 3 years and forward 5 years as a short-term capital loss. Carry back a capital loss to the extent it does not increase or produce a net operating loss in the tax year to which it is carried. Foreign expropriation capital losses cannot be carried back, but are carried forward 10 years. A net capital loss for a regulated investment company is carried forward 8 years.

Special Rules for the Treatment of Certain Gains and Losses

Note: *For more information, get **Pub. 544**, Sales and Other Dispositions of Assets, and **Pub. 542**, Corporations.*

- **Loss from a sale or exchange between the corporation and a related person.**—Except for distributions in complete liquidation of a corporation, no loss is allowed from the sale or exchange of property between the corporation and certain related persons. See section 267 for details.

- **Loss from a wash sale.**—The corporation cannot deduct a loss from a wash sale of stock or securities (including contracts or options to acquire or sell stock or securities) unless the corporation is a dealer in stock or securities and the loss was sustained in a transaction made in the ordinary course of the corporation's trade or business. A wash sale occurs if the corporation acquires (by purchase or exchange), or has a contract or option to acquire, substantially identical stock or securities within 30 days before or after the date of the sale or exchange. See section 1091 for more information.

- **Like-kind exchanges.**—An exchange of business or investment property for property of a like kind is reported on **Form 8824**, Like-Kind Exchanges.

- **At-risk limitations (section 465).**—If the corporation sold or exchanged a capital asset used in an activity to which the at-risk rules apply, combine the gain or loss on the sale or exchange with the profit or loss from the activity. If the result is a net loss, complete **Form 6198**, At-Risk Limitations. Report any gain from the capital asset on Schedule D and on Form 6198.

- **Gains and losses from passive activities.**—A closely held or personal service corporation that has a gain or loss that relates to a passive activity (section 469) may be required to complete **Form 8810**, Corporate Passive Activity Loss and Credit Limitations, before completing Schedule D. A Schedule D loss may be limited under the passive activity rules. See Form 8810 for more detailed information.

- **Gain on distributions of appreciated property.**—Generally, gain (but not loss) is recognized on a nonliquidating distribution of appreciated property to the extent that the property's fair market value exceeds its adjusted basis. See section 311 for more information.

- **Gain or loss on distribution of property in complete liquidation.**— Generally, gain or loss is recognized on property distributed in a complete liquidation. Treat the property as if it had been sold at its fair market value. An exception to this rule applies for liquidations of certain subsidiaries. See sections 336 and 337 for more information and other exceptions to the general rules.

- **Gains and losses on section 1256 contracts and straddles.**—Use **Form 6781**, Gains and Losses From Section 1256 Contracts and Straddles, to report these gains and losses.

- **Gain or loss on certain short-term Federal, state, and municipal obligations.**—Such obligations are treated as capital assets in determining gain or loss. On any gain realized, a portion is treated as ordinary income and the balance as a short-term capital gain. See section 1271.

- **Gain from installment sales.**—If the corporation has a gain this year from the casual sale of real or personal property (other than inventory) and is to receive any payment in a later year, it must use the installment method (unless it elects not to—see below) and file **Form 6252**, Installment Sale Income. Also use Form 6252 if a payment is received this year from a sale made in an earlier year on the installment method.

The corporation may elect out of the installment method by reporting the full amount of the gain on a timely filed return (including extensions).

The installment method may not be used for sales of stock or securities (or certain other property described in the regulations) traded on an established securities market. See section 453(k).

- **Rollover of publicly traded securities gain into specialized small business investment companies (SSBICs).**—A corporation that sells publicly traded securities at a gain may elect under section 1044 to postpone all or part of the gain if the seller buys stock or a partnership interest in an SSBIC during the 60-day period that begins on the date the securities are sold.

An SSBIC is any partnership or corporation licensed by the Small Business Administration under section 301(d) of the Small Business Investment Act of 1958. The corporation must recognize gain on the sale to the extent the proceeds from the sale exceed the cost of the SSBIC stock or partnership interest purchased during the 60-day period that began on the date of the sale (and not previously taken into account). The gain a corporation may postpone each tax year is limited to the lesser of **(a)** $250,000 or **(b)** $1 million, reduced by the gain previously excluded under section 1044. The basis of the SSBIC stock or partnership interest is reduced by any postponed gain.

To make the election to postpone gain, complete line 1 or line 6, whichever applies, showing the entire gain realized in column (f). Directly below the line on which the gain is reported, enter "SSBIC Rollover" in column (a). Enter the amount of the postponed gain (in parentheses) in column (f). Also, attach a schedule showing **(a)** how you figured the postponed gain, **(b)** the name of the SSBIC in which you purchased common stock or a partnership interest, **(c)** the date of that purchase, and **(d)** the new basis in that SSBIC stock or partnership interest.

For more details, see section 1044.

- **Gain or loss on an option to buy or sell property.**—See sections 1032 and 1234 for the rules that apply to a purchaser or grantor of an option.

- **Gain or loss from a short sale of property.**—Report the gain or loss to the extent that the property used to close the short sale is considered a capital asset in the hands of the taxpayer.

- **Gains and losses of foreign corporations from the disposition of investment in U.S. real property.**—Foreign corporations are required to report gains and losses from the disposition of U.S. real property interests. See section 897 for details.

- **Gains on certain insurance property.**—Form 1120-L filers with gains on property held on December 31, 1958, and certain substituted property acquired after 1958 should see section 818(c).

- **Loss from the sale or exchange of capital assets of an insurance company taxable under section 831.**—Under the provisions of section 834(c)(6), capital losses of a casualty insurance company are deductible to the extent that the assets were sold to meet abnormal insurance losses or to provide for the payment of dividend and similar distributions to policyholders.

- **Loss from securities that are capital assets that become worthless during the year.**—Except for securities held by a bank, treat the loss as a capital loss as of the last day of the tax year. (See section 582 for the rules on the treatment of securities held by a bank.)

- **Disposition of market discount bonds.**—See section 1276 for rules on the disposition of market discount bonds.

- **Capital gain distributions.**—Report capital gain distributions paid by regulated investment companies or real estate investment trusts as long-term capital gains on line 6 regardless of how long the corporation owned stock in the fund.

Specific Instructions

Lines 1 and 6, column (d).—Enter either the gross sales price or the net sales price. If the net sales price is entered, do not increase the cost or other basis in column (e) by any expenses reflected in the net sales price.

Lines 1 and 6, column (e).—In determining gain or loss, the basis of property will generally be its cost. See section 1012 and the related regulations. Exceptions to the general rule are provided in sections in subchapters C, K, O, and P of the Code. For example, if the corporation acquired the property by dividend, liquidation of a corporation, transfer from a shareholder, reorganization, bequest, contribution or gift, tax-free exchange, involuntary conversion, certain asset acquisitions, or wash sale of stock, see sections 301 (or 1059), 334, 362 (or 358), 1014, 1015, 1031, 1060, and 1091, respectively. Attach an explanation if the corporation uses a basis other than actual cash cost of the property.

If the gross sales price is reported in column (d), increase the cost or other basis by any expense of sale such as broker's fees, commissions, or option premiums before entering an amount in column (e).

If the corporation is allowed a charitable contribution deduction because it sold property in a bargain sale to a charitable organization, figure the adjusted basis for determining gain from the sale by dividing the amount realized by the fair market value and multiplying that result by the adjusted basis. No loss is allowed in a bargain sale to a charity.

See section 852(f) for the treatment of certain load charges incurred in acquiring stock in a mutual fund with a reinvestment right.

<table>
<tr><td>Form 4626</td><td><h3>Alternative Minimum Tax—Corporations</h3></td><td>OMB No. 1545-0175</td></tr>
<tr><td>Department of the Treasury
Internal Revenue Service</td><td>▶ See separate instructions.
▶ Attach to the corporation's tax return.</td><td>1997</td></tr>
</table>

Name	Employer identification number

1	Taxable income or (loss) before net operating loss deduction	**1**	
2	**Adjustments and preferences:**		
a	Depreciation of post-1986 property	**2a**	
b	Amortization of certified pollution control facilities	**2b**	
c	Amortization of mining exploration and development costs	**2c**	
d	Amortization of circulation expenditures (personal holding companies only) . .	**2d**	
e	Adjusted gain or loss	**2e**	
f	Long-term contracts	**2f**	
g	Installment sales	**2g**	
h	Merchant marine capital construction funds	**2h**	
i	Section 833(b) deduction (Blue Cross, Blue Shield, and similar type organizations only)	**2i**	
j	Tax shelter farm activities (personal service corporations only)	**2j**	
k	Passive activities (closely held corporations and personal service corporations only)	**2k**	
l	Loss limitations	**2l**	
m	Depletion	**2m**	
n	Tax-exempt interest from specified private activity bonds	**2n**	
o	Charitable contributions	**2o**	
p	Intangible drilling costs	**2p**	
q	Accelerated depreciation of real property (pre-1987)	**2q**	
r	Accelerated depreciation of leased personal property (pre-1987) (personal holding companies only)	**2r**	
s	Other adjustments	**2s**	
t	Combine lines 2a through 2s	**2t**	
3	Preadjustment alternative minimum taxable income (AMTI). Combine lines 1 and 2t	**3**	
4	**Adjusted current earnings (ACE) adjustment:**		
a	Enter the corporation's ACE from line 10 of the worksheet on page 8 of the instructions	**4a**	
b	Subtract line 3 from line 4a. If line 3 exceeds line 4a, enter the difference as a negative amount (see examples beginning on page 4 of the instructions) . .	**4b**	
c	Multiply line 4b by 75% (.75). Enter the result as a positive amount	**4c**	
d	Enter the excess, if any, of the corporation's total increases in AMTI from prior year ACE adjustments over its total reductions in AMTI from prior year ACE adjustments (see page 5 of the instructions). **Note:** *You **must** enter an amount on line 4d (even if line 4b is positive).*	**4d**	
e	ACE adjustment: • If you entered a positive number or zero on line 4b, enter the amount from line 4c here as a positive amount. • If you entered a negative number on line 4b, enter the smaller of line 4c or line 4d here as a negative amount.	**4e**	
5	Combine lines 3 and 4e. If zero or less, stop here; the corporation does not owe alternative minimum tax	**5**	
6	Alternative tax net operating loss deduction (see page 5 of the instructions)	**6**	
7	**Alternative minimum taxable income.** Subtract line 6 from line 5. If the corporation held a residual interest in a REMIC, see page 5 of the instructions	**7**	

<table>
<tr><td>For Paperwork Reduction Act Notice, see separate instructions.</td><td>Cat. No. 12955I</td><td>Form 4626 (1997)</td></tr>
</table>

8   Enter the amount from line 7 (alternative minimum taxable income) . . . . | **8**

9 **Exemption phase-out computation** (if line 8 is $310,000 or more, skip lines 9a and 9b and enter -0- on line 9c):

  a Subtract $150,000 from line 8 (if you are completing this line for a member of a controlled group, see page 5 of the instructions). If zero or less, enter -0- . . | **9a**

  b Multiply line 9a by 25% (.25). . . . . | **9b**

  c Exemption. Subtract line 9b from $40,000 (if you are completing this line for a member of a controlled group, see page 5 of the instructions). If zero or less, enter -0- . . . . | **9c**

10 Subtract line 9c from line 8. If zero or less, enter -0- . . . . | **10**

11 Multiply line 10 by 20% (.20). . . . . | **11**

12 Alternative minimum tax foreign tax credit. See page 5 of the instructions . . . . | **12**

13 Tentative minimum tax. Subtract line 12 from line 11. . . . . | **13**

14 Regular tax liability before all credits except the foreign tax credit and possessions tax credit . . . | **14**

15 **Alternative minimum tax.** Subtract line 14 from line 13. Enter the result on the appropriate line of the corporation's income tax return (e.g., Form 1120, Schedule J, line 9). If zero or less, enter -0- . | **15**

S CORPORATION PRACTICE SET

Tech Toys Corp.
Federal Tax Return

FACTS

After graduating from National Institute of Technology (NIT) with a masters degree in engineering, Jordan Harris developed and patented several electronic toys and games. Jordan envisioned a large market for her toys. Jordan set up Tech Toys Corp. to manufacture and sell her products. Tech Toys Corp. is owned by the Harris family. The corporation is a small, closely-held manufacturer (the business code number is 1883, and the employer identification number is 37-6548258). The company is located at 416 Oak Street, Dover, Delaware 21630. The corporation, which uses a calendar year for tax purposes, has been an S corporation since its incorporation on July 1, 1995.

Jordan Harris (social security number 655-27-0412) is president of the corporation. Jordan owned 100% of the stock until September 15, 1997 when she sold 1% to Jeff Harris (Jordan's uncle, social security number 579-54-6828), who serves as vice president for the company. Both officers devote 100 percent of their time to the corporation and live at 490 Pine Hills Road, Dover, Delaware 21630. Annual compensation is $64,800 for Jordan and $32,400 for Jeff. The corporation does not engage in activities to which the at-risk or passive activity loss limitations apply.

The corporation files its tax return on the accrual method. Inventory has been consistently valued at cost under the FIFO method using the full absorption procedure. Inventory capitalization rules of Internal Revenue Code Section 263A do not apply due to the 'small business exception' (average annual gross receipts for the three preceding taxable years do not exceed $10 million). The accounting records are computerized.

The corporation's audited income statement and balance sheet for the current year, prepared by the accounting firm of Bonnie & Clyde, CPAs, follow:

TECH TOYS CORP.
INCOME STATEMENT
For the Year Ending December 31, 1997

Revenue:

Sales (net)	$2,036,719	
Cost of goods sold	(1,508,090)	
Gross profit		$ 528,629

Operating expenses:

Compensation of officers	$ 97,200	
Other salaries and wages	221,036	
Employee benefits	9,904	
Rental expense	23,029	
Interest expense	12,290	
Advertising	6,302	
Key-person life insurance premiums	5,976	
Contributions	756	
Depreciation	29,465	
Taxes (other than income taxes)	20,898	
Repairs and maintenance	11,764	
Miscellaneous expenses	3,565	
Total operating expenses		$(442,185)
Net Income from Operations		$ 86,444

Other income and loss:

Dividend Income	$ 2,562	
Interest Income	405	
Gain on sale of investment in stock	2,184	
Gain on sale of machine	7,830	
Casualty loss on machine	(540)	12,441
Net Income		$ 98,885

TECH TOYS CORP.
STATEMENT OF FINANCIAL POSITION
December 31, 1997

ASSETS	Beginning of Year	End of Year
Current Assets:		
Cash & Marketable Securities	$ 10,101	$ 10,297
Accounts receivable	40,727	25,704
Inventory	173,581	167,223
Total current assets	$224,409	$203,224
Machinery and Equipment (M&E):		
Machinery and Equipment	$257,256	$303,456
Less: Accumulated depreciation	(20,915)	(39,311)
Total machinery and equipment (net)	$236,341	$264,145
Other assets:		
Life insurance cash surrender value	$ 15,533	$ 19,733
Total Assets	$476,283	$487,102

LIABILITIES AND SHAREHOLDERS' EQUITY

	Beginning of Year	End of Year
Current liabilities:		
Accounts payable	$ 15,941	$ 18,703
Notes payable (less than one year)	19,334	20,306
Total current liabilities	$ 35,275	$ 39,009
Notes payable (one year or more)	64,800	54,000
Total Liabilities	$100,075	$ 93,009
Common stock (5,000 shares authorized, issued, and outstanding, $100 par)	$270,000	$270,000
Retained earnings	106,208	124,093
Total Shareholders' Equity	$376,208	$394,093
Total Liabilities and Shareholders' Equity	$476,283	$487,102

STATEMENT OF RETAINED EARNINGS

Beginning Retained Earnings	$106,208
Net income for the year	98,885
Dividends paid in during the year	(81,000)
Ending Retained Earnings	$124,093

19

1. Included in employee benefits expense are $527 and $350 premiums for $50,000 (face) group term life insurance premiums for Jordan and Jeff, respectively. Family members are named beneficiaries in the policies.

2. All notes payable were issued at par and provide market interest rates.

3. Employees account to the company and are reimbursed by the exact amount of travel and entertainment expenses incurred on business. Included in Miscellaneous Expenses are $1,481 for transportation expenses, $270 for meals, and $162 for entertainment.

4. Dividend income is from minor investments in:

Gold Dirt Corp.	$1,804
Traveler's Life Insurance Company (a dividend on the key-person life insurance policy)	758
Total	$2,562

5. Contributions were paid in cash to:

Save The Whales	$ 540
Campaign for Re-election of Al Gore	216
Total Contributions	$ 756

6. The key-person life insurance policy provides $500,000 coverage on Jordan Harris. The company is the owner and beneficiary of the policy.

7. A schedule attached in the prior year's working papers reconciles Retained Earnings and Accumulated Adjustments Account balances at 12/31/96 as follows:

Balance per Schedule L (Balance Sheet)		$106,208
Accumulated depreciation for machinery and equipment (M&E) for tax		
M&E Acquired 07/01/95	$ 8,376	
M&E Acquired 02/01/96	33,677	
	$42,053	
Accumulated depreciation per books	20,915	
Excess of Accumulated Tax over Book Depreciation for M&E		(21,138)
Balance per Schedule M (Analysis of the Accumulated Adjustments Account)		$ 85,070

8. The balance in the "Other Adjustments Account" (Form 1120S, p. 4, Sch. M-2, col. (b)) at the beginning of the year was $-0-.

9. Depreciation information is attached.

10. Machine #23, purchased on 02/01/96 for $54,000, was sold to an unrelated party on 11/01/97 for $55,080.

11. Machine #31, purchased on 07/01/95 for $21,600, was totally destroyed by fire caused by a short in an electrical circuit on 04/01/97. Proceeds of $16,740 were received from the insurance company. On 08/01/97 $16,200 of the proceeds were invested in a replacement machine. Assume there will be no further qualified reinvestment of the proceeds.

12. Interest expense was on loans for the following purposes:

Purchase M&E	$5,818
Invest in stock of Gold Dirt Corp.	972
Invest in Lehigh County, PA water and sewer bonds	108
Cover shortage in working capital	5,392
Total	$12,290

13. On June 5, 1997, 450 shares of Gold Dirt Corp. common stock was sold. The company bought 1,800 shares of the stock on June 2, 1996 for $6,480. The stock was split 3-for-1 on February 21, 1997. (*Clue:* Use the book gain and basis to compute the proceeds.)

14. On May 15, 1997 Tech Toys Corp. purchased at par $10,000 of Lehigh County, PA water and sewer bonds. Interest of $405 was received on the bonds during the year.

REQUIRED

From the above information, prepare Tech Toys Corp.'s 1997 Federal income tax return (Form 1120S), including all supporting statements, schedules, and forms. Unless otherwise noted, assume the corporation makes all available elections to minimize the shareholders' current taxable incomes. Round amounts to the nearest dollar. If additional information is needed, make realistic assumptions and fill in all required data.

Even though the corporation may not be technically required to do so, Jordan has expressed a desire that Schedule L (Balance Sheets), Schedule M-1 (Reconciliation of Income (Loss) per Books With Income (Loss) per Return), and Schedule M-2 (Analysis of Accumulated Adjustments Account, Other Adjustments Account, and Shareholders' Undistributed Taxable Income Previously Taxed) on Form 1120S, p. 4 be completed.

Tech Toys Corp.
Depreciation/Cost Recovery Information

Financial Depreciation Information	Balance 12/31/96	1997 Additions	1997 Retirements	Balance 12/31/97	Balance 12/31/96	1997 Provision	1997 Retirements	Balance 12/31/97
Machinery Acquired on:								
07/01/95	$ 21,600		($21,600)	$ 0	$ 3,240	$ 1,080	($ 4,320)	$ 0
02/01/96	235,656		(54,000)	181,656	17,675	20,866	(6,750)	31,791
05/01/97		$105,600		105,600		6,920		6,920
08/01/97		16,200		16,200		600		600
Total	$257,256	$121,800	($75,600)	$303,456	$20,915	$29,466	($11,070)	$39,311

TAX DEPRECIATION INFORMATION

MACRS (Modified Accelerated Cost Recovery System—For property placed is service after 1986)

Machinery and equipment (7-year statutory life, 200% declining balance switching to straight line, half-year convention). Statutory percentage for assets placed in service during a year are 14.29%, 24.49%, 17.49%, 12.49%, 8.93%, 8.92%, 8.93%, and 4.46% for recovery years 1–8, respectively. One-half of the normal MACRS amount is allowed for the year of disposition.

The corporation has not elected Internal Revenue Code Sec. (IRC Sec.) 179 expense in the past; however, the maximum allowable IRC Sec. 179 expense is to be claimed for machinery and equipment placed in service on 05/01/97.

ALTERNATIVE MINIMUM TAX (Tax Preferences and Adjustments)

For this practice set, ignore effects of the above cost recoveries on the Alternative Minimum Tax (i.e., leave the applicable spaces blank for these items in the 'Adjustments and Tax Preferences Items' section of Schedules K and K-1).

S CORPORATION PRACTICE SET

Tech Toys Corp.

FORMS

<table>
<tr><td>Form 1120S
Department of the Treasury
Internal Revenue Service</td><td><h1>U.S. Income Tax Return for an S Corporation</h1>
▶ Do not file this form unless the corporation has timely filed
Form 2553 to elect to be an S corporation.
▶ See separate instructions.</td><td>OMB No. 1545-0130
1997</td></tr>
</table>

For calendar year 1997, or tax year beginning ______________ **, 1997, and ending** ______________ **, 19** ____

		C Employer identification number
A Date of election as an S corporation	**Use IRS label. Otherwise, please print or type.** Name	
	Number, street, and room or suite no. (If a P.O. box, see page 9 of the instructions.)	**D** Date incorporated
B Business code no. (see Specific Instructions)	City or town, state, and ZIP code	**E** Total assets (see Specific Instructions) $

F Check applicable boxes: (1) ☐ Initial return   (2) ☐ Final return   (3) ☐ Change in address   (4) ☐ Amended return ▶

G Enter number of shareholders in the corporation at end of the tax year . . . . ▶

Caution: *Include **only** trade or business income and expenses on lines 1a through 21. See the instructions for more information.*

Income

1a Gross receipts or sales ________ **b** Less returns and allowances ________ **c** Bal ▶	**1c**	
2 Cost of goods sold (Schedule A, line 8)	**2**	
3 Gross profit. Subtract line 2 from line 1c	**3**	
4 Net gain (loss) from Form 4797, Part II, line 18 *(attach Form 4797)*	**4**	
5 Other income (loss) *(attach schedule)*	**5**	
6 **Total income (loss).** Combine lines 3 through 5 . . . . ▶	**6**	

Deductions (see page 10 of the instructions for limitations)

7 Compensation of officers	**7**	
8 Salaries and wages (less employment credits)	**8**	
9 Repairs and maintenance	**9**	
10 Bad debts	**10**	
11 Rents	**11**	
12 Taxes and licenses	**12**	
13 Interest	**13**	
14a Depreciation *(if required, attach Form 4562)* **14a**		
b Depreciation claimed on Schedule A and elsewhere on return . . **14b**		
c Subtract line 14b from line 14a	**14c**	
15 Depletion **(Do not deduct oil and gas depletion.)**	**15**	
16 Advertising	**16**	
17 Pension, profit-sharing, etc., plans	**17**	
18 Employee benefit programs	**18**	
19 Other deductions *(attach schedule)*	**19**	
20 **Total deductions.** Add the amounts shown in the far right column for lines 7 through 19 . ▶	**20**	
21 Ordinary income (loss) from trade or business activities. Subtract line 20 from line 6	**21**	

Tax and Payments

22 **Tax: a** Excess net passive income tax *(attach schedule)*. . . **22a**		
b Tax from Schedule D (Form 1120S) **22b**		
c Add lines 22a and 22b (see pages 12 and 13 of the instructions for additional taxes) . . .	**22c**	
23 **Payments: a** 1997 estimated tax payments and amount applied from 1996 return **23a**		
b Tax deposited with Form 7004 . . . . **23b**		
c Credit for Federal tax paid on fuels *(attach Form 4136)* . . . **23c**		
d Add lines 23a through 23c	**23d**	
24 Estimated tax penalty. Check if Form 2220 is attached . . . . ▶☐	**24**	
25 **Tax due.** If the total of lines 22c and 24 is larger than line 23d, enter amount owed. See page 4 of the instructions for depository method of payment . . . . ▶	**25**	
26 **Overpayment.** If line 23d is larger than the total of lines 22c and 24, enter amount overpaid ▶	**26**	
27 Enter amount of line 26 you want: **Credited to 1998 estimated tax** ▶ ________ Refunded ▶	**27**	

Please Sign Here

Under penalties of perjury, I declare that I have examined this return, including accompanying schedules and statements, and to the best of my knowledge and belief, it is true, correct, and complete. Declaration of preparer (other than taxpayer) is based on all information of which preparer has any knowledge.

▶ Signature of officer	Date	Title

Paid Preparer's Use Only

Preparer's signature ▶	Date	Check if self-employed ▶ ☐	Preparer's social security number
Firm's name (or yours if self-employed) and address ▶		EIN ▶	
		ZIP code ▶	

For Paperwork Reduction Act Notice, see the separate instructions.   Cat. No. 11510H   Form **1120S** (1997)

Schedule A   Cost of Goods Sold (see page 13 of the instructions)

1	Inventory at beginning of year	**1**	
2	Purchases	**2**	
3	Cost of labor	**3**	
4	Additional section 263A costs *(attach schedule)*	**4**	
5	Other costs *(attach schedule)*	**5**	
6	**Total.** Add lines 1 through 5	**6**	
7	Inventory at end of year	**7**	
8	**Cost of goods sold.** Subtract line 7 from line 6. Enter here and on page 1, line 2	**8**	

9a Check all methods used for valuing closing inventory:

    (i) ☐ Cost as described in Regulations section 1.471-3

    (ii) ☐ Lower of cost or market as described in Regulations section 1.471-4

    (iii) ☐ Other (specify method used and attach explanation) ▶ ....

  b Check if there was a writedown of "subnormal" goods as described in Regulations section 1.471-2(c) . . . . ▶ ☐

  c Check if the LIFO inventory method was adopted this tax year for any goods *(if checked, attach Form 970)*. . . . . . ▶ ☐

  d If the LIFO inventory method was used for this tax year, enter percentage (or amounts) of closing inventory computed under LIFO **9d**

  e Do the rules of section 263A (for property produced or acquired for resale) apply to the corporation?. . . . . ☐ Yes ☐ No

  f Was there any change in determining quantities, cost, or valuations between opening and closing inventory? . . ☐ Yes ☐ No

  If "Yes," attach explanation.

Schedule B   Other Information

		Yes	No

1 Check method of accounting: **(a)** ☐ Cash **(b)** ☐ Accrual **(c)** ☐ Other (specify) ▶ ....

2 Refer to the list on page 23 of the instructions and state the corporation's principal:

  (a) Business activity ▶ .... **(b)** Product or service ▶ ....

3 Did the corporation at the end of the tax year own, directly or indirectly, 50% or more of the voting stock of a domestic corporation? (For rules of attribution, see section 267(c).) If "Yes," attach a schedule showing: **(a)** name, address, and employer identification number and **(b)** percentage owned. . . . .

4 Was the corporation a member of a controlled group subject to the provisions of section 1561? . . . .

5 At any time during calendar year 1997, did the corporation have an interest in or a signature or other authority over a financial account in a foreign country (such as a bank account, securities account, or other financial account)? (See page 14 of the instructions for exceptions and filing requirements for Form TD F 90-22.1.) . . . .

  If "Yes," enter the name of the foreign country ▶ ....

6 During the tax year, did the corporation receive a distribution from, or was it the grantor of, or transferor to, a foreign trust? If "Yes," the corporation may have to file Form 3520 or 926. See page 14 of the instructions . . . . . .

7 Check this box if the corporation has filed or is required to file **Form 8264,** Application for Registration of a Tax Shelter . . . . ▶ ☐

8 Check this box if the corporation issued publicly offered debt instruments with original issue discount . . ▶ ☐

  If so, the corporation may have to file **Form 8281,** Information Return for Publicly Offered Original Issue Discount Instruments.

9 If the corporation: **(a)** filed its election to be an S corporation after 1986, **(b)** was a C corporation before it elected to be an S corporation **or** the corporation acquired an asset with a basis determined by reference to its basis (or the basis of any other property) in the hands of a C corporation, and **(c)** has net unrealized built-in gain (defined in section 1374(d)(1)) in excess of the net recognized built-in gain from prior years, enter the net unrealized built-in gain reduced by net recognized built-in gain from prior years (see page 14 of the instructions) . . . . . ▶ $ ....

10 Check this box if the corporation had accumulated earnings and profits at the close of the tax year (see page 14 of the instructions) . . . . ▶ ☐

Schedule K Shareholders' Shares of Income, Credits, Deductions, etc.

(a) Pro rata share items		(b) Total amount	

Income (Loss)

1	Ordinary income (loss) from trade or business activities (page 1, line 21)	**1**	
2	Net income (loss) from rental real estate activities *(attach Form 8825)*	**2**	
3a	Gross income from other rental activities **3a**		
b	Expenses from other rental activities *(attach schedule)*. **3b**		
c	Net income (loss) from other rental activities. Subtract line 3b from line 3a	**3c**	
4	Portfolio income (loss):		
a	Interest income	**4a**	
b	Dividend income.	**4b**	
c	Royalty income	**4c**	
d	Net short-term capital gain (loss) *(attach Schedule D (Form 1120S))*	**4d**	
e	Net long-term capital gain (loss) *(attach Schedule D (Form 1120S))*:		
	(1) 28% rate gain (loss) ▶ .... **(2)** Total for year ▶	**4e(2)**	
f	Other portfolio income (loss) *(attach schedule)*	**4f**	
5	Net section 1231 gain (loss) (other than due to casualty or theft) *(attach Form 4797)*:		
a	28% rate gain (loss) ▶ .... **b** Total for year ▶	**5b**	
6	Other income (loss) *(attach schedule)*	**6**	

Deductions

7	Charitable contributions *(attach schedule)*.	**7**	
8	Section 179 expense deduction *(attach Form 4562)*.	**8**	
9	Deductions related to portfolio income (loss) (itemize)	**9**	
10	Other deductions *(attach schedule)*.	**10**	

Investment Interest

11a	Interest expense on investment debts	**11a**	
b (1)	Investment income included on lines 4a, 4b, 4c, and 4f above	**11b(1)**	
(2)	Investment expenses included on line 9 above	**11b(2)**	

Credits

12a	Credit for alcohol used as a fuel *(attach Form 6478)*	**12a**	
b	Low-income housing credit:		
(1)	From partnerships to which section 42(j)(5) applies for property placed in service before 1990	**12b(1)**	
(2)	Other than on line 12b(1) for property placed in service before 1990.	**12b(2)**	
(3)	From partnerships to which section 42(j)(5) applies for property placed in service after 1989	**12b(3)**	
(4)	Other than on line 12b(3) for property placed in service after 1989	**12b(4)**	
c	Qualified rehabilitation expenditures related to rental real estate activities *(attach Form 3468)*	**12c**	
d	Credits (other than credits shown on lines 12b and 12c) related to rental real estate activities	**12d**	
e	Credits related to other rental activities	**12e**	
13	Other credits.	**13**	

Adjustments and Tax Preference Items

14a	Depreciation adjustment on property placed in service after 1986	**14a**	
b	Adjusted gain or loss	**14b**	
c	Depletion (other than oil and gas)	**14c**	
d (1)	Gross income from oil, gas, or geothermal properties	**14d(1)**	
(2)	Deductions allocable to oil, gas, or geothermal properties	**14d(2)**	
e	Other adjustments and tax preference items *(attach schedule)*	**14e**	

Foreign Taxes

15a	Type of income ▶		
b	Name of foreign country or U.S. possession		
c	Total gross income from sources outside the United States *(attach schedule)*	**15c**	
d	Total applicable deductions and losses *(attach schedule)*.	**15d**	
e	Total foreign taxes (check one): ▶ ☐ Paid ☐ Accrued	**15e**	
f	Reduction in taxes available for credit *(attach schedule)*	**15f**	
g	Other foreign tax information *(attach schedule)*	**15g**	

Other

16	Section 59(e)(2) expenditures: **a** Type ▶ .... **b** Amount ▶	**16b**	
17	Tax-exempt interest income	**17**	
18	Other tax-exempt income.	**18**	
19	Nondeductible expenses	**19**	
20	Total property distributions (including cash) other than dividends reported on line 22 below	**20**	
21	Other items and amounts required to be reported separately to shareholders *(attach schedule)*		
22	Total dividend distributions paid from accumulated earnings and profits	**22**	
23	**Income (loss).** (Required only if Schedule M-1 must be completed.) Combine lines 1 through 6 in column (b). From the result, subtract the sum of lines 7 through 11a, 15e, and 16b	**23**	

Schedule L	**Balance Sheets per Books**	Beginning of tax year		End of tax year	
	Assets	**(a)**	**(b)**	**(c)**	**(d)**
1	Cash				
2a	Trade notes and accounts receivable				
b	Less allowance for bad debts				
3	Inventories				
4	U.S. Government obligations				
5	Tax-exempt securities				
6	Other current assets (attach schedule)				
7	Loans to shareholders				
8	Mortgage and real estate loans				
9	Other investments (attach schedule)				
10a	Buildings and other depreciable assets				
b	Less accumulated depreciation				
11a	Depletable assets				
b	Less accumulated depletion				
12	Land (net of any amortization)				
13a	Intangible assets (amortizable only)				
b	Less accumulated amortization				
14	Other assets (attach schedule)				
15	Total assets				
	Liabilities and Shareholders' Equity				
16	Accounts payable				
17	Mortgages, notes, bonds payable in less than 1 year				
18	Other current liabilities (attach schedule)				
19	Loans from shareholders				
20	Mortgages, notes, bonds payable in 1 year or more				
21	Other liabilities (attach schedule)				
22	Capital stock				
23	Additional paid-in capital				
24	Retained earnings				
25	Adjustments to shareholders' equity (attach schedule)				
26	Less cost of treasury stock		( )		( )
27	Total liabilities and shareholders' equity				

Schedule M-1   **Reconciliation of Income (Loss) per Books With Income (Loss) per Return** (You are not required to complete this schedule if the total assets on line 15, column (d), of Schedule L are less than $25,000.)

1	Net income (loss) per books		5	Income recorded on books this year not included on Schedule K, lines 1 through 6 (itemize):	
2	Income included on Schedule K, lines 1 through 6, not recorded on books this year (itemize):		a	Tax-exempt interest $	
3	Expenses recorded on books this year not included on Schedule K, lines 1 through 11a, 15e, and 16b (itemize):		6	Deductions included on Schedule K, lines 1 through 11a, 15e, and 16b, not charged against book income this year (itemize):	
a	Depreciation $		a	Depreciation $	
b	Travel and entertainment $		7	Add lines 5 and 6	
4	Add lines 1 through 3		8	Income (loss) (Schedule K, line 23). Line 4 less line 7	

Schedule M-2   **Analysis of Accumulated Adjustments Account, Other Adjustments Account, and Shareholders' Undistributed Taxable Income Previously Taxed** (see page 21 of the instructions)

		(a) Accumulated adjustments account	**(b)** Other adjustments account	**(c)** Shareholders' undistributed taxable income previously taxed
1	Balance at beginning of tax year			
2	Ordinary income from page 1, line 21			
3	Other additions			
4	Loss from page 1, line 21	( )		
5	Other reductions	( )	( )	
6	Combine lines 1 through 5			
7	Distributions other than dividend distributions			
8	Balance at end of tax year. Subtract line 7 from line 6			

<table>
<tr><td>SCHEDULE D
(Form 1120S)

Department of the Treasury
Internal Revenue Service</td><td>Capital Gains and Losses and Built-In Gains

▶ Attach to Form 1120S.

▶ See separate instructions.</td><td>OMB No. 1545-0130

1997</td></tr>
</table>

Name	Employer identification number

Part I — Short-Term Capital Gains and Losses—Assets Held One Year or Less

(a) Description of property (Example, 100 shares of "Z" Co.)	(b) Date acquired (mo., day, yr.)	(c) Date sold (mo., day, yr.)	(d) Sales price	(e) Cost or other basis (see instructions)	(f) Gain or (loss) for entire year ((d) minus (e))	
1						

2 Short-term capital gain from installment sales from Form 6252, line 26 or 37 . .	**2**	
3 Short-term capital gain or (loss) from like-kind exchanges from Form 8824 . . .	**3**	
4 Combine lines 1 through 3 in column (f) and enter here	**4**	
5 Tax on short-term capital gain included on line 32 below	**5** ( )	
6 Net short-term capital gain or (loss). Combine lines 4 and 5. Enter here and on Form 1120S, Schedule K, line 4d or 6	**6**	

Part II — Long-Term Capital Gains and Losses—Assets Held More Than One Year

(a) Description of property (Example, 100 shares of "Z" Co.)	(b) Date acquired (mo., day, yr.)	(c) Date sold (mo., day, yr.)	(d) Sales price	(e) Cost or other basis (see instructions)	(f) Gain or (loss) for entire year ((d) minus (e))	(g) 28% rate gain * or (loss) (see instr. below)
7						

8 Long-term capital gain from installment sales from Form 6252, line 26 or 37 . .	**8**	
9 Long-term capital gain or (loss) from like-kind exchanges from Form 8824 . . .	**9**	
10 Combine lines 7 through 9 in column (f) and enter here	**10**	
11 Tax on long-term capital gain included on lines 24 and 32 below	**11** ( )( )	
12 Combine lines 7 through 11 in column (g). Enter here and on Form 1120S, Schedule K, line 4e(1) or 6	**12**	
13 Net long-term capital gain or (loss). Combine lines 10 and 11 in column (f). Enter here and on Form 1120S, Schedule K, line 4e(2) or 6	**13**	

*** 28% rate gain or (loss)** includes all gains and losses in Part II, column (f) from sales, exchanges, or conversions (including installment payments received) **either:** ● **Before** May 7, 1997, **or**
● **After** July 28, 1997, for assets held more than 1 year but **not** more than 18 months.

It also includes **ALL** "collectibles gains and losses" (as defined in the instructions).

Part III — Capital Gains Tax (See instructions **before** completing this part.)

14 Enter section 1231 gain from Form 4797, line 9, column (g)	**14**	
15 Net long-term capital gain or (loss). Combine lines 10 and 14	**15**	
Note: If the corporation is liable for the excess net passive income tax (Form 1120S, page 1, line 22a) or the built-in gains tax (Part IV below), see the line 16 instructions before completing line 16.		
16 Net capital gain. Enter excess of net long-term capital gain (line 15) over net short-term capital loss (line 4)	**16**	
17 Statutory minimum	**17**	$25,000
18 Subtract line 17 from line 16	**18**	
19 Enter 34% of line 18	**19**	
20 Taxable income (attach computation schedule)	**20**	
21 Enter tax on line 20 amount (attach computation schedule)	**21**	
22 Net capital gain from substituted basis property (attach computation schedule)	**22**	
23 Enter 35% of line 22	**23**	
24 Tax. Enter the smallest of line 19, 21, or 23 here and on Form 1120S, page 1, line 22b	**24**	

Part IV — Built-In Gains Tax (See instructions **before** completing this part.)

25 Excess of recognized built-in gains over recognized built-in losses (attach computation schedule) . .	**25**	
26 Taxable income (attach computation schedule)	**26**	
27 Net recognized built-in gain. Enter the smallest of line 25, line 26, or line 9 of Schedule B	**27**	
28 Section 1374(b)(2) deduction	**28**	
29 Subtract line 28 from line 27. If zero or less, enter -0- here and on line 32	**29**	
30 Enter 35% of line 29	**30**	
31 Business credit and minimum tax credit carryforwards under section 1374(b)(3) from C corporation years	**31**	
32 Tax. Subtract line 31 from line 30 (if zero or less, enter -0-). Enter here and on Form 1120S, page 1, line 22b	**32**	

For Paperwork Reduction Act Notice, see the Instructions for Form 1120S.   Cat. No. 11516V   **Schedule D (Form 1120S) 1997**

<table>
<tr><td>SCHEDULE K-1
(Form 1120S)

Department of the Treasury
Internal Revenue Service</td><td colspan="2">Shareholder's Share of Income, Credits, Deductions, etc.
▶ See separate instructions.
For calendar year 1997 or tax year
beginning   , 1997, and ending   , 19</td><td>OMB No. 1545-0130

1997</td></tr>
</table>

Shareholder's identifying number ▶	**Corporation's identifying number** ▶
Shareholder's name, address, and ZIP code	Corporation's name, address, and ZIP code

A   Shareholder's percentage of stock ownership for tax year (see instructions for Schedule K-1) . . . . ▶ .... %

B   Internal Revenue Service Center where corporation filed its return ▶ ....

C   Tax shelter registration number (see instructions for Schedule K-1) . . . . ▶ ....

D   Check applicable boxes: **(1)** ☐ Final K-1   **(2)** ☐ Amended K-1

	(a) Pro rata share items		**(b)** Amount	**(c)** Form 1040 filers enter the amount in column (b) on:
	1 Ordinary income (loss) from trade or business activities . . .	**1**		See pages 4 and 5 of the Shareholder's Instructions for Schedule K-1 (Form 1120S).
	2 Net income (loss) from rental real estate activities	**2**		
	3 Net income (loss) from other rental activities	**3**		
	4 Portfolio income (loss):			
Income (Loss)	**a** Interest	**4a**		Sch. B, Part I, line 1
	b Dividends	**4b**		Sch. B, Part II, line 5
	c Royalties	**4c**		Sch. E, Part I, line 4
	d Net short-term capital gain (loss).	**4d**		Sch. D, line 5, col. (f)
	e Net long-term capital gain (loss):			
	(1) 28% rate gain (loss)	**e(1)**		Sch. D, line 12, col. (g)
	(2) Total for year.	**e(2)**		Sch. D, line 12, col. (f)
	f Other portfolio income (loss) *(attach schedule)*	**4f**		(Enter on applicable line of your return.)
	5 Net section 1231 gain (loss) (other than due to casualty or theft):			See Shareholder's Instructions for Schedule K-1 (Form 1120S).
	a 28% rate gain (loss).	**5a**		
	b Total for year	**5b**		
	6 Other income (loss) *(attach schedule)*	**6**		(Enter on applicable line of your return.)
Deductions	**7** Charitable contributions *(attach schedule)*	**7**		Sch. A, line 15 or 16
	8 Section 179 expense deduction	**8**		See page 6 of the Shareholder's Instructions for Schedule K-1 (Form 1120S).
	9 Deductions related to portfolio income (loss) *(attach schedule)* .	**9**		
	10 Other deductions *(attach schedule)*	**10**		
Investment Interest	**11a** Interest expense on investment debts	**11a**		Form 4952, line 1
	b **(1)** Investment income included on lines 4a, 4b, 4c, and 4f above	**b(1)**		See Shareholder's Instructions for Schedule K-1 (Form 1120S).
	(2) Investment expenses included on line 9 above	**b(2)**		
Credits	**12a** Credit for alcohol used as fuel	**12a**		Form 6478, line 10
	b Low-income housing credit:			
	(1) From section 42(j)(5) partnerships for property placed in service before 1990.	**b(1)**		Form 8586, line 5
	(2) Other than on line 12b(1) for property placed in service before 1990	**b(2)**		
	(3) From section 42(j)(5) partnerships for property placed in service after 1989	**b(3)**		
	(4) Other than on line 12b(3) for property placed in service after 1989	**b(4)**		
	c Qualified rehabilitation expenditures related to rental real estate activities	**12c**		See pages 6 and 7 of the Shareholder's Instructions for Schedule K-1 (Form 1120S).
	d Credits (other than credits shown on lines 12b and 12c) related to rental real estate activities	**12d**		
	e Credits related to other rental activities.	**12e**		
	13 Other credits	**13**		

For Paperwork Reduction Act Notice, see the Instructions for Form 1120S.   Cat. No. 11520D   **Schedule K-1 (Form 1120S) 1997**

  Page **2**

	(a) Pro rata share items	(b) Amount	(c) Form 1040 filers enter the amount in column (b) on:
Adjustments and Tax Preference Items	**14a** Depreciation adjustment on property placed in service after 1986	**14a**	See page 7 of the Shareholder's Instructions for Schedule K-1 (Form 1120S) and Instructions for Form 6251
	b Adjusted gain or loss	**14b**	
	c Depletion (other than oil and gas)	**14c**	
	d (1) Gross income from oil, gas, or geothermal properties	**d(1)**	
	(2) Deductions allocable to oil, gas, or geothermal properties	**d(2)**	
	e Other adjustments and tax preference items *(attach schedule)*	**14e**	
Foreign Taxes	**15a** Type of income ▶		Form 1116, Check boxes
	b Name of foreign country or U.S. possession ▶		
	c Total gross income from sources outside the United States *(attach schedule)*	**15c**	Form 1116, Part I
	d Total applicable deductions and losses *(attach schedule)*	**15d**	
	e Total foreign taxes (check one): ▶ ☐ Paid ☐ Accrued	**15e**	Form 1116, Part II
	f Reduction in taxes available for credit *(attach schedule)*	**15f**	Form 1116, Part III
	g Other foreign tax information *(attach schedule)*	**15g**	See Instructions for Form 1116
Other	**16** Section 59(e)(2) expenditures: **a** Type ▶		See Shareholder's Instructions for Schedule K-1 (Form 1120S).
	b Amount	**16b**	
	17 Tax-exempt interest income	**17**	Form 1040, line 8b
	18 Other tax-exempt income	**18**	See page 7 of the Shareholder's Instructions for Schedule K-1 (Form 1120S).
	19 Nondeductible expenses	**19**	
	20 Property distributions (including cash) other than dividend distributions reported to you on Form 1099-DIV	**20**	
	21 Amount of loan repayments for "Loans From Shareholders"	**21**	
	22 Recapture of low-income housing credit:		
	a From section 42(j)(5) partnerships	**22a**	Form 8611, line 8
	b Other than on line 22a	**22b**	

23 Supplemental information required to be reported separately to each shareholder *(attach additional schedules if more space is needed)*:

<table>
<tr><td>SCHEDULE K-1
(Form 1120S)</td><td colspan="2">Shareholder's Share of Income, Credits, Deductions, etc.
▶ See separate instructions.
For calendar year 1997 or tax year</td><td>OMB No. 1545-0130</td></tr>
<tr><td>Department of the Treasury
Internal Revenue Service</td><td>beginning</td><td>, 1997, and ending , 19</td><td>1997</td></tr>
</table>

Shareholder's identifying number ▶	**Corporation's identifying number** ▶
Shareholder's name, address, and ZIP code	Corporation's name, address, and ZIP code

A Shareholder's percentage of stock ownership for tax year (see instructions for Schedule K-1) . . . . ▶ .... %

B Internal Revenue Service Center where corporation filed its return ▶ ....

C Tax shelter registration number (see instructions for Schedule K-1) . . . . ▶ ....

D Check applicable boxes: **(1)** ☐ Final K-1   **(2)** ☐ Amended K-1

	(a) Pro rata share items		**(b)** Amount	**(c)** Form 1040 filers enter the amount in column (b) on:
Income (Loss)	**1** Ordinary income (loss) from trade or business activities . . .	**1**		See pages 4 and 5 of the Shareholder's Instructions for Schedule K-1 (Form 1120S).
	2 Net income (loss) from rental real estate activities	**2**		
	3 Net income (loss) from other rental activities	**3**		
	4 Portfolio income (loss):			
	a Interest	**4a**		Sch. B, Part I, line 1
	b Dividends	**4b**		Sch. B, Part II, line 5
	c Royalties	**4c**		Sch. E, Part I, line 4
	d Net short-term capital gain (loss).	**4d**		Sch. D, line 5, col. (f)
	e Net long-term capital gain (loss):			
	(1) 28% rate gain (loss)	**e(1)**		Sch. D, line 12, col. (g)
	(2) Total for year.	**e(2)**		Sch. D, line 12, col. (f)
	f Other portfolio income (loss) *(attach schedule)*	**4f**		*(Enter on applicable line of your return.)*
	5 Net section 1231 gain (loss) (other than due to casualty or theft):			See Shareholder's Instructions for Schedule K-1 (Form 1120S).
	a 28% rate gain (loss).	**5a**		
	b Total for year	**5b**		
	6 Other income (loss) *(attach schedule)*	**6**		*(Enter on applicable line of your return.)*
Deductions	**7** Charitable contributions *(attach schedule)*	**7**		Sch. A, line 15 or 16
	8 Section 179 expense deduction	**8**		See page 6 of the Shareholder's Instructions for Schedule K-1 (Form 1120S).
	9 Deductions related to portfolio income (loss) *(attach schedule)* .	**9**		
	10 Other deductions *(attach schedule)*	**10**		
Investment Interest	**11a** Interest expense on investment debts	**11a**		Form 4952, line 1
	b (1) Investment income included on lines 4a, 4b, 4c, and 4f above	**b(1)**		See Shareholder's Instructions for Schedule K-1 (Form 1120S).
	(2) Investment expenses included on line 9 above	**b(2)**		
Credits	**12a** Credit for alcohol used as fuel	**12a**		Form 6478, line 10
	b Low-income housing credit:			
	(1) From section 42(j)(5) partnerships for property placed in service before 1990.	**b(1)**		Form 8586, line 5
	(2) Other than on line 12b(1) for property placed in service before 1990	**b(2)**		
	(3) From section 42(j)(5) partnerships for property placed in service after 1989	**b(3)**		
	(4) Other than on line 12b(3) for property placed in service after 1989	**b(4)**		
	c Qualified rehabilitation expenditures related to rental real estate activities	**12c**		See pages 6 and 7 of the Shareholder's Instructions for Schedule K-1 (Form 1120S).
	d Credits (other than credits shown on lines 12b and 12c) related to rental real estate activities	**12d**		
	e Credits related to other rental activities.	**12e**		
	13 Other credits	**13**		

For Paperwork Reduction Act Notice, see the Instructions for Form 1120S.   Cat. No. 11520D   **Schedule K-1 (Form 1120S) 1997**

	(a) Pro rata share items		(b) Amount	(c) Form 1040 filers enter the amount in column (b) on:

Adjustments and Tax Preference Items

14a	Depreciation adjustment on property placed in service after 1986	14a		See page 7 of the Shareholder's Instructions for Schedule K-1 (Form 1120S) and Instructions for Form 6251
b	Adjusted gain or loss	14b		
c	Depletion (other than oil and gas)	14c		
d (1)	Gross income from oil, gas, or geothermal properties	d(1)		
(2)	Deductions allocable to oil, gas, or geothermal properties	d(2)		
e	Other adjustments and tax preference items (attach schedule)	14e		

Foreign Taxes

15a	Type of income ▶			Form 1116, Check boxes
b	Name of foreign country or U.S. possession ▶			
c	Total gross income from sources outside the United States (attach schedule)	15c		Form 1116, Part I
d	Total applicable deductions and losses (attach schedule)	15d		
e	Total foreign taxes (check one): ▶ ☐ Paid ☐ Accrued	15e		Form 1116, Part II
f	Reduction in taxes available for credit (attach schedule)	15f		Form 1116, Part III
g	Other foreign tax information (attach schedule)	15g		See Instructions for Form 1116

Other

16	Section 59(e)(2) expenditures: a Type ▶			See Shareholder's Instructions for Schedule K-1 (Form 1120S).
b	Amount	16b		
17	Tax-exempt interest income	17		Form 1040, line 8b
18	Other tax-exempt income	18		See page 7 of the Shareholder's Instructions for Schedule K-1 (Form 1120S).
19	Nondeductible expenses	19		
20	Property distributions (including cash) other than dividend distributions reported to you on Form 1099-DIV	20		
21	Amount of loan repayments for "Loans From Shareholders"	21		
22	Recapture of low-income housing credit:			
a	From section 42(j)(5) partnerships	22a		Form 8611, line 8
b	Other than on line 22a	22b		

Supplemental Information

23 Supplemental information required to be reported separately to each shareholder (attach additional schedules if more space is needed):

Form **4562**

Department of the Treasury
Internal Revenue Service (99)

Depreciation and Amortization
(Including Information on Listed Property)

▶ **See separate instructions.**   ▶ **Attach this form to your return.**

OMB No. 1545-0172

1997

Attachment
Sequence No. **67**

Name(s) shown on return	Business or activity to which this form relates	Identifying number

---

Part I **Election To Expense Certain Tangible Property (Section 179)** (**Note:** *If you have any "listed property," complete Part V before you complete Part I.*)

1	Maximum dollar limitation. If an enterprise zone business, see page 2 of the instructions . .	**1**	$18,000
2	Total cost of section 179 property placed in service. See page 2 of the instructions	**2**	
3	Threshold cost of section 179 property before reduction in limitation	**3**	$200,000
4	Reduction in limitation. Subtract line 3 from line 2. If zero or less, enter -0-	**4**	
5	Dollar limitation for tax year. Subtract line 4 from line 1. If zero or less, enter -0-. If married filing separately, see page 2 of the instructions	**5**	

(a) Description of property	(b) Cost (business use only)	(c) Elected cost
6		

7	Listed property. Enter amount from line 27	**7**	
8	Total elected cost of section 179 property. Add amounts in column (c), lines 6 and 7 . . .	**8**	
9	Tentative deduction. Enter the smaller of line 5 or line 8	**9**	
10	Carryover of disallowed deduction from 1996. See page 3 of the instructions	**10**	
11	Business income limitation. Enter the smaller of business income (not less than zero) or line 5 (see instructions)	**11**	
12	Section 179 expense deduction. Add lines 9 and 10, but do not enter more than line 11 . .	**12**	
13	Carryover of disallowed deduction to 1998. Add lines 9 and 10, less line 12 ▶ **13**		

Note: *Do not use Part II or Part III below for listed property (automobiles, certain other vehicles, cellular telephones, certain computers, or property used for entertainment, recreation, or amusement). Instead, use Part V for listed property.*

Part II **MACRS Depreciation For Assets Placed in Service ONLY During Your 1997 Tax Year (Do Not Include Listed Property.)**

Section A—General Asset Account Election

14   If you are making the election under section 168(i)(4) to group any assets placed in service during the tax year into one or more general asset accounts, check this box. See page 3 of the instructions . . . . ▶ ☐

Section B—General Depreciation System (GDS) (See page 3 of the instructions.)

(a) Classification of property	(b) Month and year placed in service	(c) Basis for depreciation (business/investment use only—see instructions)	(d) Recovery period	(e) Convention	(f) Method	(g) Depreciation deduction
15a 3-year property						
b 5-year property						
c 7-year property						
d 10-year property						
e 15-year property						
f 20-year property						
g 25-year property			25 yrs.		S/L	
h Residential rental property			27.5 yrs.	MM	S/L	
			27.5 yrs.	MM	S/L	
i Nonresidential real property			39 yrs.	MM	S/L	
				MM	S/L	

Section C—Alternative Depreciation System (ADS) (See page 6 of the instructions.)

(a) Classification of property	(b)	(c)	(d) Recovery period	(e) Convention	(f) Method	(g) Depreciation deduction
16a Class life					S/L	
b 12-year			12 yrs.		S/L	
c 40-year			40 yrs.	MM	S/L	

Part III **Other Depreciation (Do Not Include Listed Property.)** (See page 6 of the instructions.)

17	GDS and ADS deductions for assets placed in service in tax years beginning before 1997	**17**	
18	Property subject to section 168(f)(1) election	**18**	
19	ACRS and other depreciation	**19**	

Part IV **Summary** (See page 7 of the instructions.)

20	Listed property. Enter amount from line 26	**20**	
21	**Total.** Add deductions on line 12, lines 15 and 16 in column (g), and lines 17 through 20. Enter here and on the appropriate lines of your return. Partnerships and S corporations—see instructions . .	**21**	
22	For assets shown above and placed in service during the current year, enter the portion of the basis attributable to section 263A costs **22**		

For Paperwork Reduction Act Notice, see the separate instructions.   Cat. No. 12906N   Form **4562** (1997)

Part V — **Listed Property—Automobiles, Certain Other Vehicles, Cellular Telephones, Certain Computers, and Property Used for Entertainment, Recreation, or Amusement**

Note: *For any vehicle for which you are using the standard mileage rate or deducting lease expense, complete **only** 23a, 23b, columns (a) through (c) of Section A, all of Section B, and Section C if applicable.*

Section A—Depreciation and Other Information (Caution: *See page 8 of the instructions for limits for passenger automobiles.***)**

23a Do you have evidence to support the business/investment use claimed? ☐ **Yes** ☐ **No**   **23b** If "Yes," is the evidence written? ☐ **Yes** ☐ **No**

(a) Type of property (list vehicles first)	(b) Date placed in service	(c) Business/ investment use percentage	(d) Cost or other basis	(e) Basis for depreciation (business/investment use only)	(f) Recovery period	(g) Method/ Convention	(h) Depreciation deduction	(i) Elected section 179 cost
24 Property used more than 50% in a qualified business use (See page 7 of the instructions.):								
		%						
		%						
		%						
25 Property used 50% or less in a qualified business use (See page 7 of the instructions.):								
		%				S/L –		
		%				S/L –		
		%				S/L –		

26 Add amounts in column (h). Enter the total here and on line 20, page 1 . . . . . . **26**

27 Add amounts in column (i). Enter the total here and on line 7, page 1 . . . . **27**

Section B—Information on Use of Vehicles

Complete this section for vehicles used by a sole proprietor, partner, or other "more than 5% owner," or related person.

If you provided vehicles to your employees, first answer the questions in Section C to see if you meet an exception to completing this section for those vehicles.

		(a) Vehicle 1	(b) Vehicle 2	(c) Vehicle 3	(d) Vehicle 4	(e) Vehicle 5	(f) Vehicle 6
28	Total business/investment miles driven during the year (DO NOT include commuting miles)						
29	Total commuting miles driven during the year						
30	Total other personal (noncommuting) miles driven						
31	Total miles driven during the year. Add lines 28 through 30.						

		Yes	No	Yes	No	Yes	No	Yes	No	Yes	No	Yes	No
32	Was the vehicle available for personal use during off-duty hours?												
33	Was the vehicle used primarily by a more than 5% owner or related person?												
34	Is another vehicle available for personal use?												

Section C—Questions for Employers Who Provide Vehicles for Use by Their Employees

*Answer these questions to determine if you meet an exception to completing Section B for vehicles used by employees who **are not** more than 5% owners or related persons.*

		Yes	No
35	Do you maintain a written policy statement that prohibits all personal use of vehicles, including commuting, by your employees?		
36	Do you maintain a written policy statement that prohibits personal use of vehicles, except commuting, by your employees? See page 9 of the instructions for vehicles used by corporate officers, directors, or 1% or more owners		
37	Do you treat all use of vehicles by employees as personal use?		
38	Do you provide more than five vehicles to your employees, obtain information from your employees about the use of the vehicles, and retain the information received?		
39	Do you meet the requirements concerning qualified automobile demonstration use? See page 9 of the instructions . .		

Note: *If your answer to 35, 36, 37, 38, or 39 is "Yes," you need not complete Section B for the covered vehicles.*

Part VI **Amortization**

(a) Description of costs	(b) Date amortization begins	(c) Amortizable amount	(d) Code section	(e) Amortization period or percentage	(f) Amortization for this year
40 Amortization of costs that begins during your 1997 tax year:					

41 Amortization of costs that began before 1997 . . . . **41**

42 **Total.** Enter here and on "Other Deductions" or "Other Expenses" line of your return . . . **42**

<table>
<tr><td>Form 4684
Department of the Treasury
Internal Revenue Service</td><td>Casualties and Thefts
► See separate instructions.
► Attach to your tax return.
► Use a separate Form 4684 for each different casualty or theft.</td><td>OMB No. 1545-0177
1997
Attachment
Sequence No. 26</td></tr>
</table>

Name(s) shown on tax return	Identifying number

SECTION A—Personal Use Property (Use this section to report casualties and thefts of property **not** used in a trade or business or for income-producing purposes.)

1 Description of properties (show type, location, and date acquired for each):

Property **A** ....

Property **B** ....

Property **C** ....

Property **D** ....

Properties (Use a separate column for each property lost or damaged from one casualty or theft.)

	A	B	C	D
2 Cost or other basis of each property				
3 Insurance or other reimbursement (whether or not you filed a claim). See instructions **Note:** If line 2 is **more than** line 3, skip line 4.				
4 Gain from casualty or theft. If line 3 is **more than** line 2, enter the difference here and skip lines 5 through 9 for that column. See instructions if line 3 includes insurance or other reimbursement you did not claim, or you received payment for your loss in a later tax year				
5 Fair market value **before** casualty or theft				
6 Fair market value **after** casualty or theft				
7 Subtract line 6 from line 5				
8 Enter the **smaller** of line 2 or line 7				
9 Subtract line 3 from line 8. If zero or less, enter -0-				

10 Casualty or theft loss. Add the amounts on line 9. Enter the total **10**

11 Enter the amount from line 10 or $100, whichever is **smaller** **11**

12 Subtract line 11 from line 10 . . . . **12**

Caution: Use only one Form 4684 for lines 13 through 18.

13 Add the amounts on line 12 of all Forms 4684 . . . . **13**

14 Combine the amounts from line 4 of all Forms 4684 . . . . **14**

15 • If line 14 is **more than** line 13, enter the difference here and on Schedule D. Do not complete the rest of this section (see instructions).

• If line 14 is **less than** line 13, enter -0- here and continue with the form.

• If line 14 is **equal to** line 13, enter -0- here. Do not complete the rest of this section. } **15**

16 If line 14 is **less than** line 13, enter the difference **16**

17 Enter 10% of your adjusted gross income (Form 1040, line 33). Estates and trusts, see instructions **17**

18 Subtract line 17 from line 16. If zero or less, enter -0-. Also enter result on Schedule A (Form 1040), line 19. Estates and trusts, enter on the "Other deductions" line of your tax return **18**

For Paperwork Reduction Act Notice, see page 4 of separate instructions.   Cat. No. 12997O   Form **4684** (1997)

Name(s) shown on tax return. Do not enter name and identifying number if shown on other side. | **Identifying number**

SECTION B—Business and Income-Producing Property (Use this section to report casualties and thefts of property used in a trade or business or for income-producing purposes.)

Part I — Casualty or Theft Gain or Loss (Use a separate Part I for each casualty or theft.)

19 Description of properties (show type, location, and date acquired for each):

Property **A** ....

Property **B** ....

Property **C** ....

Property **D** ....

Properties (Use a separate column for each property lost or damaged from one casualty or theft.)

		A	B	C	D
20	Cost or adjusted basis of each property				
21	Insurance or other reimbursement (whether or not you filed a claim). See the instructions for line 3. **Note:** *If line 20 is **more than** line 21, skip line 22.*				
22	Gain from casualty or theft. If line 21 is **more than** line 20, enter the difference here and on line 29 or line 34, column (c), except as provided in the instructions for line 33. Also, skip lines 23 through 27 for that column. See the instructions for line 4 if line 21 includes insurance or other reimbursement you did not claim, or you received payment for your loss in a later tax year				
23	Fair market value **before** casualty or theft . . .				
24	Fair market value **after** casualty or theft				
25	Subtract line 24 from line 23				
26	Enter the **smaller** of line 20 or line 25				
	Note: *If the property was totally destroyed by casualty or lost from theft, enter on line 26 the amount from line 20.*				
27	Subtract line 21 from line 26. If zero or less, enter -0-				
28	Casualty or theft loss. Add the amounts on line 27. Enter the total here and on line 29 **or** line 34 (see instructions).		**28**		

Part II — Summary of Gains and Losses (from separate Parts I)

(a) Identify casualty or theft	**(b)** Losses from casualties or thefts		**(c)** Gains from casualties or thefts includible in income
	(i) Trade, business, rental or royalty property	*(ii)* Income-producing property	

Casualty or Theft of Property Held One Year or Less

29	_______________________	( )	( )	
	_______________________	( )	( )	
30	Totals. Add the amounts on line 29 . . . . **30**	( )	( )	
31	Combine line 30, columns (b)(i) and (c). Enter the net gain or (loss) here and on Form 4797, line 14. If Form 4797 is not otherwise required, see instructions		**31**	
32	Enter the amount from line 30, column (b)(ii) here and on Schedule A (Form 1040), line 22. Partnerships, S corporations, estates and trusts, see instructions		**32**	

Casualty or Theft of Property Held More Than One Year

33	Casualty or theft gains from Form 4797, line 32		**33**	
34	_______________________	( )	( )	
	_______________________	( )	( )	
35	Total losses. Add amounts on line 34, columns (b)(i) and (b)(ii) . . . **35** ( )	( )		
36	Total gains. Add lines 33 and 34, column (c)		**36**	
37	Add amounts on line 35, columns (b)(i) and (b)(ii)		**37**	
38	If the loss on line 37 is **more than** the gain on line 36:			
a	Combine line 35, column (b)(i) and line 36, and enter the net gain or (loss) here. Partnerships and S corporations see the note below. All others enter this amount on Form 4797, line 14. If Form 4797 is not otherwise required, see instructions		**38a**	
b	Enter the amount from line 35, column (b)(ii) here. Partnerships and S corporations see the note below. Individuals enter this amount on Schedule A (Form 1040), line 22. Estates and trusts, enter on the "Other deductions" line of your tax return		**38b**	
39	If the loss on line 37 is **equal to** or **less than** the gain on line 36, combine these lines and enter here. Partnerships, see the note below. All others, enter this amount on Form 4797, line 3, column (g) and the net 28% rate gain or (loss), if applicable, in column (h)		**39**	

Note: *Partnerships, enter the amount from line 38a, 38b, or line 39 on Form 1065, Schedule K, line 7. S corporations, enter the amount from line 38a or 38b on Form 1120S, Schedule K, line 6.*

38

<table>
<tr>
<td>Form 4797
Department of the Treasury
Internal Revenue Service (99)</td>
<td>Sales of Business Property
(Also Involuntary Conversions and Recapture Amounts
Under Sections 179 and 280F(b)(2))
▶ Attach to your tax return.　　▶ See separate instructions.</td>
<td>OMB No. 1545-0184
1997
Attachment
Sequence No. 27</td>
</tr>
</table>

Name(s) shown on return | Identifying number

1 Enter here the gross proceeds from the sale or exchange of real estate reported to you for 1997 on Form(s) 1099-S (or a substitute statement) that you will be including on line 2, 10, or 20 . . . . | **1**

Part I — Sales or Exchanges of Property Used in a Trade or Business and Involuntary Conversions From Other Than Casualty or Theft—Property Held More Than 1 Year

(a) Description of property	(b) Date acquired (mo., day, yr.)	(c) Date sold (mo., day, yr.)	(d) Gross sales price	(e) Depreciation allowed or allowable since acquisition	(f) Cost or other basis, plus improvements and expense of sale	(g) GAIN or (LOSS) for entire year. Subtract (f) from the sum of (d) and (e)	(h) 28% RATE GAIN or (LOSS) * (see instr. below)
2							

3 Gain, if any, from Form 4684, line 39 . . . . | **3**

4 Section 1231 gain from installment sales from Form 6252, line 26 or 37 . . . . . . | **4**

5 Section 1231 gain or (loss) from like-kind exchanges from Form 8824 . . . . | **5**

6 Gain, if any, from line 32, from other than casualty or theft . . . . | **6**

7 Combine lines 2 through 6 in columns (g) and (h). Enter gain or (loss) here, and on the appropriate line as follows: | **7**

    Partnerships—Enter the gain or (loss) on Form 1065, Schedule K, lines 6a and 6b. Skip lines 8, 9, 11, and 12 below.

    S corporations—Report the gain or (loss) following the instructions for Form 1120S, Schedule K, lines 5 and 6. Skip lines 8, 9, 11, and 12 below, unless line 7, column (g) is a gain and the S corporation is subject to the capital gains tax.

    All others—If line 7, column (g) is zero or a loss, enter that amount on line 11 below and skip lines 8 and 9. If line 7, column (g) is a gain and you did not have any prior year section 1231 losses, or they were recaptured in an earlier year, enter the gain or (loss) in each column as a long-term capital gain or (loss) on Schedule D and skip lines 8, 9, and 12 below.

8 Nonrecaptured net section 1231 losses from prior years (see instructions) . . . . | **8**

9 Subtract line 8 from line 7. If zero or less, enter -0-. Also enter on the appropriate line as follows (see instructions): | **9**

    S corporations—Enter only the gain in column (g) on Schedule D (Form 1120S), line 14, and skip lines 11 and 12 below.

    All others—If line 9, column (g) is zero, enter the gain from line 7, column (g) on line 12 below. If line 9, column (g) is more than zero, enter the amount from line 8, column (g) on line 12 below, and enter the gain or (loss) in each column of line 9 as a long-term capital gain or (loss) on Schedule D.

  ***** Corporations (other than S corporations) should not complete column (h). Partnerships and S corporations must complete column (h). All others must complete column (h) only if line 7, column (g), is a gain. 28% rate gain or loss includes all gains and losses in column (g) from sales, exchanges, or conversions (including installment payments received) **either (a) before** 5/7/97 **or (b) after** 7/28/97 for assets held more than 1 year but not more than 18 months.

Part II — Ordinary Gains and Losses

10 Ordinary gains and losses not included on lines 11 through 17 (include property held 1 year or less):

(a)	(b)	(c)	(d)	(e)	(f)	(g)	(h)

11 Loss, if any, from line 7, column (g) . . . . | **11**

12 Gain, if any, from line 7, column (g) or amount from line 8, column (g) if applicable . . . . | **12**

13 Gain, if any, from line 31 . . . . | **13**

14 Net gain or (loss) from Form 4684, lines 31 and 38a . . . . | **14**

15 Ordinary gain from installment sales from Form 6252, line 25 or 36 . . . . | **15**

16 Ordinary gain or (loss) from like-kind exchanges from Form 8824 . . . . | **16**

17 Recapture of section 179 expense deduction for partners and S corporation shareholders from property dispositions by partnerships and S corporations (see instructions) . . . . . . | **17**

18 Combine lines 10 through 17 in column (g). Enter gain or (loss) here, and on the appropriate line as follows: | **18**

  a For all except individual returns: Enter the gain or (loss) from line 18 on the return being filed.

  b For individual returns:

    (1) If the loss on line 11 includes a loss from Form 4684, line 35, column (b)(ii), enter that part of the loss here and on line 22 of Schedule A (Form 1040). Identify as from "Form 4797, line 18b(1)." See instructions . . . . | **18b(1)**

    (2) Redetermine the gain or (loss) on line 18, excluding the loss, if any, on line 18b(1). Enter here and on Form 1040, line 14 . . . . | **18b(2)**

For Paperwork Reduction Act Notice, see separate instructions. | Cat. No. 13086I | Form **4797** (1997)

Part III Gain From Disposition of Property Under Sections 1245, 1250, 1252, 1254, and 1255

19 **(a)** Description of section 1245, 1250, 1252, 1254, or 1255 property:	**(b)** Date acquired (mo., day, yr.)	**(c)** Date sold (mo., day, yr.)
A		
B		
C		
D		

These columns relate to the properties on lines 19A through 19D. ▶		**Property A**	**Property B**	**Property C**	**Property D**
20 Gross sales price (**Note:** *See line 1 before completing.*)	**20**				
21 Cost or other basis plus expense of sale	**21**				
22 Depreciation (or depletion) allowed or allowable	**22**				
23 Adjusted basis. Subtract line 22 from line 21	**23**				
24 Total gain. Subtract line 23 from line 20	**24**				
25 **If section 1245 property:**					
a Depreciation allowed or allowable from line 22	**25a**				
b Enter the **smaller** of line 24 or 25a	**25b**				
26 **If section 1250 property:** If straight line depreciation was used, enter -0- on line 26g, except for a corporation subject to section 291.					
a Additional depreciation after 1975 (see instructions)	**26a**				
b Applicable percentage multiplied by the **smaller** of line 24 or line 26a (see instructions)	**26b**				
c Subtract line 26a from line 24. If residential rental property or line 24 is not more than line 26a, skip lines 26d and 26e	**26c**				
d Additional depreciation after 1969 and before 1976	**26d**				
e Enter the **smaller** of line 26c or 26d	**26e**				
f Section 291 amount (corporations only)	**26f**				
g Add lines 26b, 26e, and 26f	**26g**				
27 **If section 1252 property:** Skip this section if you did not dispose of farmland or if this form is being completed for a partnership.					
a Soil, water, and land clearing expenses	**27a**				
b Line 27a multiplied by applicable percentage (see instructions)	**27b**				
c Enter the **smaller** of line 24 or 27b	**27c**				
28 **If section 1254 property:**					
a Intangible drilling and development costs, expenditures for development of mines and other natural deposits, and mining exploration costs (see instructions)	**28a**				
b Enter the **smaller** of line 24 or 28a	**28b**				
29 **If section 1255 property:**					
a Applicable percentage of payments excluded from income under section 126 (see instructions)	**29a**				
b Enter the **smaller** of line 24 or 29a (see instructions)	**29b**				

Summary of Part III Gains. Complete property columns A through D through line 29b before going to line 30.

30 Total gains for all properties. Add property columns A through D, line 24	**30**
31 Add property columns A through D, lines 25b, 26g, 27c, 28b, and 29b. Enter here and on line 13	**31**
32 Subtract line 31 from line 30. Enter the portion from casualty or theft on Form 4684, line 33. Enter the portion from other than casualty or theft on Form 4797, line 6, column (g), and if applicable, column (h)	**32**

Part IV Recapture Amounts Under Sections 179 and 280F(b)(2) When Business Use Drops to 50% or Less
See instructions.

		(a) Section 179	**(b) Section 280F(b)(2)**
33 Section 179 expense deduction or depreciation allowable in prior years	**33**		
34 Recomputed depreciation. See instructions	**34**		
35 Recapture amount. Subtract line 34 from line 33. See the instructions for where to report	**35**		

The Extreme Canoe Company
Federal Tax Return

FACTS

The Extreme Canoe Company is a partnership owned and operated by Jake Duncem (social security number 561-10-4442) and Judy Duncem (social security number 322-52-6767). The office is located at 316 River Road, Greenville, North Carolina 27834. The partnership's tax identification number is 26-2623950, and it uses a calendar year for tax purposes. The business was started on March 1, 1987 to manufacture canoes. The partnership has prospered and sells its products throughout the United States on a wholesale basis to retail outlets. Both Jake and Judy are active in the business. The business code number is 1883.

Jake Duncem is a 70 percent general partner, and Judy Duncem is a 30 percent general partner who, among other duties, deals with tax matters for the partnership. Both Jake and Judy devote 100 percent of their time to the business. Jake lives at 3105 Gordon Drive, Greenville, North Carolina 27834, and Judy resides at 622 Walnut Street, Greenville, North Carolina 27834. Both partners and the partnership file Federal income tax returns at the IRS Service Center in Memphis, Tennessee.

The partnership files its tax return on the accrual method. Inventory has been consistently valued at cost under the FIFO method using the full absorption procedure. Inventory capitalization rules of Internal Revenue Code Section 263A do not apply due to the 'small business exception' (average annual gross receipts for the three preceding taxable years do not exceed $10 million). The accounting records are computerized.

The income statement and balance sheet for the current year, prepared by the accounting firm of Wilson and Wilson, CPAs, appear below:

THE EXTREME CANOE COMPANY
INCOME STATEMENT
For the Year Ending December 31, 1997

Revenue:

Sales (net)	$ 680,155	
Cost of goods sold	(279,636)	
Gross profit		$ 400,519

Operating expenses:

Wages to employees	$ 103,544	
Guaranteed payment to Judy Duncem	30,400	
Rental expense	48,310	
Interest expense	18,256	
Advertising	32,102	
Contributions to United Way	3,040	
Depreciation expense	13,718	
Taxes	14,050	
Shipping	18,219	
Repairs and maintenance	4,510	
Total operating expenses		$(286,149)
Net Income from Operations		$ 114,370

Other incomes and expenses:

Dividend income	$ 7,296	
Interest income	2,584	
Interest expense related to investments	(11,636)	
Net loss on sale of investments	(4,713)	
Net loss on sale of business assets	(12,730)	(19,199)
Net Income		$ 95,171

THE EXTREME CANOE COMPANY
STATEMENT OF FINANCIAL POSITION
December 31, 1997

ASSETS	Beginning of Year	End of Year
Current Assets:		
Cash & Marketable Securities	$112,702	$109,693
Accounts Receivable	16,416	23,661
Inventory	46,922	76,130
Total current assets	$176,040	$209,484
Depreciable Assets (Schedule attached)	$205,200	$205,960
Less: Accumulated depreciation	(27,677)	(25,245)
Total depreciable assets (net)	$177,523	$180,715
Other Assets:		
Land (used in the business)	$114,000	$76,000
Total Assets	$467,563	$466,199

LIABILITIES AND CAPITAL

	Beginning of Year	End of Year
Current liabilities:		
Accounts payable	$ 32,592	$ 22,137
Notes payable (less than one year)	144,400	124,820
Total current liabilities	$176,992	$146,957
Capital:		
Jake Duncem	$203,400	$223,470
Judy Duncem	87,171	95,772
Total capital	$290,571	$319,242
Total Liabilities and Capital	$467,563	$466,199

STATEMENT OF PARTNERS' CAPITAL

	Jake Duncem	Judy Duncem	Total
Capital at beginning of year	$203,400	$87,171	$290,571
Net income for the year	66,620	28,551	95,171
Partners' Withdrawals	(46,550)	(19,950)	(66,500)
Capital at end of year	$223,470	$95,772	$319,242

ADDITIONAL INFORMATION ▬▬▬▬▬

1. Dividend income is from the following sources:

Paddle Corporation	$4,104
Intel Corp.	1,500
Gateway Corp.	1,692
Total	$7,296

Paddle Corporation is located in Malaga, Spain. You learn that Spanish law requires an income tax withholding at the rate of 10% on such remittances outside that country.

2. Interest Income includes $1,368 received on City of Greenville, North Carolina General Obligation bonds. The Extreme Canoe Company's employees have been unable to locate a Form 1099 for the interest.

3. Depreciation/Cost Recovery information is attached.

4. On April 8, 1997 a loss of $4,713 was suffered on the sale of 120 shares of common stock of Backpacks, Inc. The stock, purchased on August 12, 1992 for $6,080, had been held for investment. After considering the sale, Jake convinced himself that the sale had been premature because this company's record could only improve. Jake had the partnership repurchase 30 shares of Backpacks, Inc. common stock on May 2, 1997 for $2,113 and purchase 100 shares of Daypacks, Inc. common stock on August 10, 1997 for $4,742.

5. Several business assets were sold during the year. A schedule attached to the partnership's financial statements provides these details:

Asset	Date Sold	Sales Price	Cost	Accumulated Depreciation	Financial Gain (Loss)
Land	* 03/12/97	$30,400	$38,000	$ –0–	$(7,600)
Buildings	* 03/12/97	19,760	22,800	3,610	570
M&E (Acq. 1993)	** 04/20/97	3,800	22,800	9,120	(9,880)
M&E (Acq. 1995)	** 04/20/97	15,960	15,200	3,420	4,180
Totals		$69,920	$98,800	$16,150	$(12,730)

  * The land and buildings were sold to Jake Duncem for independently appraised fair market values. Both assets were acquired on 10/01/92.

  ** All machinery and equipment disposed of during the year was sold to an unrelated third party.

6. The partners wish to claim foreign tax credits for the Spanish income tax withheld on the dividends from the Spanish corporation.

7. Investment interest expense is for:

Loan to buy City of Greenville, North Carolina bonds	$1,900
Loan to buy Intel Corp. stock	3,724
Loan to buy Gateway Corp. stock	6,012
Total	$11,636

8. All liabilities of the partnership are recourse loans, and all notes payable were issued at par and provide market interest rates.

REQUIRED

From the above information, prepare The Extreme Canoe Company's 1997 Federal partnership return of income (Form 1065), including all supporting statements, schedules, and forms. Schedules K-1 for each of the partners should be in the return. Unless otherwise noted, assume the partnership makes all available elections to minimize the partners' current taxable incomes. Round amounts to the nearest dollar. If additional information is needed, make realistic assumptions and fill in all required data.

Even though the partnership may not be technically required to do so, Jake has expressed a desire that Schedule L (Balance Sheets), Schedule M-1 (Reconciliation of Income (Loss) per Books With Income (Loss) per Return), and Schedule M-2 (Analysis of Partners' Capital Accounts) on Form 1065, p. 4 be completed.

The Extreme Canoe Company
Depreciation/Cost Recovery Information
1997

Financial Depreciation Information	Balance 12/31/96	1997 Additions	1997 Retirements	Balance 12/31/97	Balance 12/31/96	1997 Provision	1997 Retirements	Balance 12/31/97
Buildings Acquired on:								
10/01/92	$ 22,800		($22,800)	$ 0	$ 3,230	$ 380	($ 3,610)	$ 0
10/01/93	91,200			91,200	9,880	3,040		12,920
	$114,000	$ 0	($22,800)	$ 91,200	$13,110	$ 3,420	($ 3,610)	$12,920

Continued

Financial Depreciation Information	Balance 12/31/96	1997 Additions	1997 Retirements	Balance 12/31/97	Balance 12/31/96	1997 Provision	1997 Retirements	Balance 12/31/97
Machinery Acquired on:								
06/01/93	$ 22,800		($22,800)	$ 0	$ 7,980	$ 1,140	($ 9,120)	$ 0
03/01/95	30,400		(15,200)	15,200	5,320	2,280	(3,420)	4,180
08/01/96	38,000			38,000	1,267	3,800		5,067
04/01/97		61,560		61,560		3,078		3,078
	$ 91,200	$61,560	($38,000)	$114,760	$14,567	$10,298	($12,540)	$12,325
	$205,200	$61,560	($60,800)	$205,960	$27,677	$13,718	($16,150)	$25,245

TAX DEPRECIATION INFORMATION   (Use 'general' statutory percentages below)

MACRS (Modified Accelerated Cost Recovery System—For property placed is service after 1986)

Nonresidential real property (31.5-year statutory life, straight line, mid-month convention). Statutory percentages for assets placed in service in October are .661% for recovery year 1, 3.175% for years 2–20, 3.174% for years 21–32, and .926% for year 33. (*Note:* The percentages are grouped for ease of presentation; the actual percentage for a year may differ by .001% from the rates shown.)

Machinery and equipment (7-year statutory life, 200% declining balance switching to straight line, half-year convention). Statutory percentage for assets placed in service during a year are 14.29%, 24.49%, 17.49%, 12.49%, 8.93%, 8.92%, 8.93%, and 4.46% for recovery years 1–8, respectively. One-half of the normal MACRS amount is allowed for the year of disposition. The partnership did not claim Internal Revenue Code Sec. (IRC Sec.) 179 expense for assets placed in service prior to 1997. The full allowable IRC Sec. 179 expense of $18,000 is claimed for machinery and equipment placed in service during 1997.

ALTERNATIVE MINIMUM TAX (Tax Preferences and Adjustments)

For this practice set, ignore effects of the above cost recoveries on the Alternative Minimum Tax (i.e., leave the applicable spaces blank for these items in the Adjustments and Tax Preferences Items section of Schedules K and K-1).

PARTNERSHIP PRACTICE SET

The Extreme Canoe Company

FORMS

Form **1065**		**U.S. Partnership Return of Income**	OMB No. 1545-0099
Department of the Treasury Internal Revenue Service		For calendar year 1997, or tax year beginning .... , 1997, and ending .... , 19 .... . ▶ **See separate instructions.**	**1997**

A Principal business activity	**Use the IRS label. Other-wise, please print or type.**	Name of partnership	D Employer identification number
B Principal product or service		Number, street, and room or suite no. If a P.O. box, see page 10 of the instructions.	E Date business started
C Business code number		City or town, state, and ZIP code	F Total assets (see page 10 of the instructions) $

G Check applicable boxes: **(1)** ☐ Initial return **(2)** ☐ Final return **(3)** ☐ Change in address **(4)** ☐ Amended return

H Check accounting method: **(1)** ☐ Cash **(2)** ☐ Accrual **(3)** ☐ Other (specify) ▶ ....

I Number of Schedules K-1. Attach one for each person who was a partner at any time during the tax year ▶ ....

Caution: *Include* **only** *trade or business income and expenses on lines 1a through 22 below. See the instructions for more information.*

Income (see page 11 of the instructions for limitations)

1a Gross receipts or sales	**1a**	
b Less returns and allowances.	**1b**	**1c**
2 Cost of goods sold (Schedule A, line 8)		**2**
3 Gross profit. Subtract line 2 from line 1c		**3**
4 Ordinary income (loss) from other partnerships, estates, and trusts *(attach schedule)*. . .		**4**
5 Net farm profit (loss) *(attach Schedule F (Form 1040))*		**5**
6 Net gain (loss) from Form 4797, Part II, line 18.		**6**
7 Other income (loss) *(attach schedule)*.		**7**
8 **Total income (loss).** Combine lines 3 through 7		**8**

Deductions (see page 11 of the instructions for limitations)

9 Salaries and wages (other than to partners) (less employment credits)		**9**
10 Guaranteed payments to partners		**10**
11 Repairs and maintenance		**11**
12 Bad debts		**12**
13 Rent		**13**
14 Taxes and licenses		**14**
15 Interest		**15**
16a Depreciation (if required, attach Form 4562)	**16a**	
b Less depreciation reported on Schedule A and elsewhere on return	**16b**	**16c**
17 Depletion **(Do not deduct oil and gas depletion.)**		**17**
18 Retirement plans, etc.		**18**
19 Employee benefit programs		**19**
20 Other deductions *(attach schedule)*		**20**
21 **Total deductions.** Add the amounts shown in the far right column for lines 9 through 20 . .		**21**
22 **Ordinary income (loss)** from trade or business activities. Subtract line 21 from line 8 . .		**22**

Please Sign Here

Under penalties of perjury, I declare that I have examined this return, including accompanying schedules and statements, and to the best of my knowledge and belief, it is true, correct, and complete. Declaration of preparer (other than general partner or limited liability company member) is based on all information of which preparer has any knowledge.

▶ _______________________________________   ▶ ______________________
Signature of general partner or limited liability company member   Date

Paid Preparer's Use Only

Preparer's signature ▶	Date	Check if self-employed ▶ ☐	Preparer's social security no.
Firm's name (or yours if self-employed) and address ▶		EIN ▶	
		ZIP code ▶	

For Paperwork Reduction Act Notice, see separate instructions.   Cat. No. 11390Z   Form **1065** (1997)

Schedule A — Cost of Goods Sold (see page 13 of the instructions)

1 Inventory at beginning of year	1
2 Purchases less cost of items withdrawn for personal use	2
3 Cost of labor	3
4 Additional section 263A costs *(attach schedule)*	4
5 Other costs *(attach schedule)*	5
6 **Total.** Add lines 1 through 5	6
7 Inventory at end of year	7
8 **Cost of goods sold.** Subtract line 7 from line 6. Enter here and on page 1, line 2	8

9a Check all methods used for valuing closing inventory:

    (i) ☐ Cost as described in Regulations section 1.471-3

    (ii) ☐ Lower of cost or market as described in Regulations section 1.471-4

    (iii) ☐ Other (specify method used and attach explanation) ▶ ....

  b Check this box if there was a writedown of "subnormal" goods as described in Regulations section 1.471-2(c). ▶ ☐

  c Check this box if the LIFO inventory method was adopted this tax year for any goods *(if checked, attach Form 970)*. ▶ ☐

  d Do the rules of section 263A (for property produced or acquired for resale) apply to the partnership? ☐ **Yes** ☐ **No**

  e Was there any change in determining quantities, cost, or valuations between opening and closing inventory? ☐ **Yes** ☐ **No**

    If "Yes," attach explanation.

Schedule B — Other Information

		Yes	No
1 What type of entity is filing this return? Check the applicable box:			
a ☐ General partnership **b** ☐ Limited partnership **c** ☐ Limited liability company			
d ☐ Other (see page 14 of the instructions) ▶			
2 Are any partners in this partnership also partnerships?			
3 Is this partnership a partner in another partnership?			
4 Is this partnership subject to the consolidated audit procedures of sections 6221 through 6233? If "Yes," see **Designation of Tax Matters Partner** below			
5 Does this partnership meet **ALL THREE** of the following requirements?			
a The partnership's total receipts for the tax year were less than $250,000;			
b The partnership's total assets at the end of the tax year were less than $600,000; **AND**			
c Schedules K-1 are filed with the return and furnished to the partners on or before the due date (including extensions) for the partnership return.			
If "Yes," the partnership is not required to complete Schedules L, M-1, and M-2; Item F on page 1 of Form 1065; or Item J on Schedule K-1			
6 Does this partnership have any foreign partners?			
7 Is this partnership a publicly traded partnership as defined in section 469(k)(2)?			
8 Has this partnership filed, or is it required to file, **Form 8264,** Application for Registration of a Tax Shelter?			
9 At any time during calendar year 1997, did the partnership have an interest in or a signature or other authority over a financial account in a foreign country (such as a bank account, securities account, or other financial account)? See page 14 of the instructions for exceptions and filing requirements for Form TD F 90-22.1. If "Yes," enter the name of the foreign country. ▶			
10 During the tax year, did the partnership receive a distribution from, or was it the grantor of, or transferor to, a foreign trust? If "Yes," the partnership may have to file Form 3520 or 926. See page 14 of the instructions			
11 Was there a distribution of property or a transfer (e.g., by sale or death) of a partnership interest during the tax year? If "Yes," you may elect to adjust the basis of the partnership's assets under section 754 by attaching the statement described under **Elections Made By the Partnership** on page 5 of the instructions			

Designation of Tax Matters Partner (see page 15 of the instructions)

Enter below the general partner designated as the tax matters partner (TMP) for the tax year of this return:

Name of designated TMP ▶	Identifying number of TMP ▶
Address of designated TMP ▶	

Schedule K — Partners' Shares of Income, Credits, Deductions, etc.

(a) Distributive share items		(b) Total amount

Income (Loss)

1 Ordinary income (loss) from trade or business activities (page 1, line 22)	**1**	
2 Net income (loss) from rental real estate activities *(attach Form 8825)*	**2**	
3a Gross income from other rental activities — **3a**		
b Expenses from other rental activities *(attach schedule)* — **3b**		
c Net income (loss) from other rental activities. Subtract line 3b from line 3a	**3c**	
4 Portfolio income (loss):		
a Interest income	**4a**	
b Dividend income	**4b**	
c Royalty income	**4c**	
d Net short-term capital gain (loss) *(attach Schedule D (Form 1065))*	**4d**	
e Net long-term capital gain (loss) *(attach Schedule D (Form 1065))*:		
(1) 28% rate gain (loss) ▶ .... **(2)** Total for year ▶	**4e(2)**	
f Other portfolio income (loss) *(attach schedule)*	**4f**	
5 Guaranteed payments to partners	**5**	
6 Net section 1231 gain (loss) (other than due to casualty or theft) *(attach Form 4797)*:		
a 28% rate gain (loss) ▶ .... **b** Total for year ▶	**6b**	
7 Other income (loss) *(attach schedule)*	**7**	

Deductions

8 Charitable contributions *(attach schedule)*	**8**	
9 Section 179 expense deduction *(attach Form 4562)*	**9**	
10 Deductions related to portfolio income (itemize)	**10**	
11 Other deductions *(attach schedule)*	**11**	

Credits

12a Low-income housing credit:		
(1) From partnerships to which section 42(j)(5) applies for property placed in service before 1990	**12a(1)**	
(2) Other than on line 12a(1) for property placed in service before 1990	**12a(2)**	
(3) From partnerships to which section 42(j)(5) applies for property placed in service after 1989	**12a(3)**	
(4) Other than on line 12a(3) for property placed in service after 1989	**12a(4)**	
b Qualified rehabilitation expenditures related to rental real estate activities *(attach Form 3468)*	**12b**	
c Credits (other than credits shown on lines 12a and 12b) related to rental real estate activities	**12c**	
d Credits related to other rental activities	**12d**	
13 Other credits	**13**	

Investment Interest

14a Interest expense on investment debts	**14a**	
b (1) Investment income included on lines 4a, 4b, 4c, and 4f above	**14b(1)**	
(2) Investment expenses included on line 10 above	**14b(2)**	

Self-Employment

15a Net earnings (loss) from self-employment	**15a**	
b Gross farming or fishing income	**15b**	
c Gross nonfarm income	**15c**	

Adjustments and Tax Preference Items

16a Depreciation adjustment on property placed in service after 1986	**16a**	
b Adjusted gain or loss	**16b**	
c Depletion (other than oil and gas)	**16c**	
d (1) Gross income from oil, gas, and geothermal properties	**16d(1)**	
(2) Deductions allocable to oil, gas, and geothermal properties	**16d(2)**	
e Other adjustments and tax preference items *(attach schedule)*	**16e**	

Foreign Taxes

17a Type of income ▶		
b Name of foreign country or U.S. possession ▶		
c Total gross income from sources outside the United States *(attach schedule)*	**17c**	
d Total applicable deductions and losses *(attach schedule)*	**17d**	
e Total foreign taxes (check one): ▶ ☐ Paid ☐ Accrued	**17e**	
f Reduction in taxes available for credit *(attach schedule)*	**17f**	
g Other foreign tax information *(attach schedule)*	**17g**	

Other

18 Section 59(e)(2) expenditures: **a** Type ▶ .... **b** Amount ▶	**18b**	
19 Tax-exempt interest income	**19**	
20 Other tax-exempt income	**20**	
21 Nondeductible expenses	**21**	
22 Distributions of money (cash and marketable securities)	**22**	
23 Distributions of property other than money	**23**	
24 Other items and amounts required to be reported separately to partners *(attach schedule)*		

Analysis of Net Income (Loss)

1 Net income (loss). Combine Schedule K, lines 1 through 7 in column (b). From the result, subtract the sum of Schedule K, lines 8 through 11, 14a, 17e, and 18b **1**

2 Analysis by partner type:	**(i)** Corporate	**(ii)** Individual (active)	**(iii)** Individual (passive)	**(iv)** Partnership	**(v)** Exempt organization	**(vi)** Nominee/Other
a General partners						
b Limited partners						

Schedule L — Balance Sheets per Books (Not required if Question 5 on Schedule B is answered "Yes.")

Assets	Beginning of tax year (a)	(b)	End of tax year (c)	(d)
1 Cash				
2a Trade notes and accounts receivable				
b Less allowance for bad debts				
3 Inventories				
4 U.S. government obligations				
5 Tax-exempt securities				
6 Other current assets (attach schedule)				
7 Mortgage and real estate loans				
8 Other investments (attach schedule)				
9a Buildings and other depreciable assets				
b Less accumulated depreciation				
10a Depletable assets				
b Less accumulated depletion				
11 Land (net of any amortization)				
12a Intangible assets (amortizable only)				
b Less accumulated amortization				
13 Other assets (attach schedule)				
14 **Total** assets				
Liabilities and Capital				
15 Accounts payable				
16 Mortgages, notes, bonds payable in less than 1 year				
17 Other current liabilities (attach schedule)				
18 All nonrecourse loans				
19 Mortgages, notes, bonds payable in 1 year or more				
20 Other liabilities (attach schedule)				
21 Partners' capital accounts				
22 **Total** liabilities and capital				

Schedule M-1 — Reconciliation of Income (Loss) per Books With Income (Loss) per Return
(Not required if Question 5 on Schedule B is answered "Yes." See page 23 of the instructions.)

1 Net income (loss) per books . . . . .

2 Income included on Schedule K, lines 1 through 4, 6, and 7, not recorded on books this year (itemize): ....

3 Guaranteed payments (other than health insurance) . . . .

4 Expenses recorded on books this year not included on Schedule K, lines 1 through 11, 14a, 17e, and 18b (itemize):

a Depreciation $ ....

b Travel and entertainment $ ....

5 Add lines 1 through 4 . . . .

6 Income recorded on books this year not included on Schedule K, lines 1 through 7 (itemize):

a Tax-exempt interest $ ....

7 Deductions included on Schedule K, lines 1 through 11, 14a, 17e, and 18b, not charged against book income this year (itemize):

a Depreciation $ ....

8 Add lines 6 and 7 . . . .

9 Income (loss) (Analysis of Net Income (Loss), line 1). Subtract line 8 from line 5 . . . . .

Schedule M-2 — Analysis of Partners' Capital Accounts (Not required if Question 5 on Schedule B is answered "Yes.")

1 Balance at beginning of year . . . .

2 Capital contributed during year . . . .

3 Net income (loss) per books . . . . .

4 Other increases (itemize): ....

5 Add lines 1 through 4 . . . .

6 Distributions: **a** Cash . . . .

      b Property . . . . .

7 Other decreases (itemize): ....

8 Add lines 6 and 7 . . . .

9 Balance at end of year. Subtract line 8 from line 5

<table>
<tr><td>

**SCHEDULE D
(Form 1065)**

Department of the Treasury
Internal Revenue Service

</td><td>

Capital Gains and Losses

▶ **Attach to Form 1065.**

</td><td>

OMB No. 1545-0099

1997

</td></tr>
</table>

Name of partnership | Employer identification number

Part I — Short-Term Capital Gains and Losses—Assets Held 1 Year or Less

(a) Description of property (e.g., 100 shares of "Z" Co.)	**(b)** Date acquired (month, day, year)	**(c)** Date sold (month, day, year)	**(d)** Sales price (see instructions)	**(e)** Cost or other basis (see instructions)	**(f)** Gain or (loss) for entire year. ((d) minus (e))	
1						

2 Short-term capital gain from installment sales from Form 6252, line 26 or 37	**2**	
3 Short-term capital gain (loss) from like-kind exchanges from Form 8824	**3**	
4 Partnership's share of net short-term capital gain (loss), including specially allocated short-term capital gains (losses), from other partnerships, estates, and trusts	**4**	
5 **Net short-term capital gain or (loss).** Combine lines 1 through 4 in column (f). Enter here and on Form 1065, Schedule K, line 4d or 7	**5**	

Part II — Long-Term Capital Gains and Losses—Assets Held More Than 1 Year

(a) Description of property (e.g., 100 shares of "Z" Co.)	**(b)** Date acquired (month, day, year)	**(c)** Date sold (month, day, year)	**(d)** Sales price (see instructions)	**(e)** Cost or other basis (see instructions)	**(f)** Gain or (loss) for entire year. ((d) minus (e))	**(g)** 28% rate gain or (loss) *(see instr. below)
6						

7 Long-term capital gain from installment sales from Form 6252, line 26 or 37	**7**	
8 Long-term capital gain (loss) from like-kind exchanges from Form 8824.	**8**	
9 Partnership's share of net long-term capital gain (loss), including specially allocated long-term capital gains (losses), from other partnerships, estates, and trusts	**9**	
10 Capital gain distributions	**10**	
11 Combine lines 6 through 10 in column (g). Enter here and on Form 1065, Schedule K, line 4e(1) or 7	**11**	
12 **Net long-term capital gain or (loss).** Combine lines 6 through 10 in column (f). Enter here and on Form 1065, Schedule K, line 4e(2) or 7	**12**	

***28% rate gain or (loss)** includes all gains and losses in Part II, column (f) from sales, exchanges, or conversions (including installment payments received) **either:**
- **Before** May 7, 1997, **or**
- **After** July 28, 1997, for assets held more than 1 year but **not** more than 18 months.

It also includes **ALL** "collectibles gains and losses" (as defined in the instructions).

General Instructions

Section references are to the Internal Revenue Code.

Purpose of Schedule

Note: *For **Changes to Note,** see the Instructions for Form 1065.*

Use Schedule D (Form 1065) to report sales or exchanges of capital assets, capital gain distributions, and nonbusiness bad debts. Do not report on Schedule D capital gains (losses) specially allocated to any partners.

Enter capital gains (losses) specially allocated to the partnership as a partner in other partnerships and from estates and trusts on Schedule D, line 4 or 9, whichever applies. Enter capital gains (losses) of the partnership that are specially allocated to partners directly on line 4d, 4e(1), 4e(2), or 7 of Schedules K and K-1, whichever applies. See **How Income Is Shared Among Partners** in the Instructions for Form 1065 for more information.

To report sales or exchanges of property other than capital assets, including the sale or exchange of property used in a trade or business and involuntary conversions (other than casualties and thefts), see **Form 4797,** Sales of Business Property, and related instructions. If property is involuntarily converted because of a casualty or theft, use **Form 4684,** Casualties and Thefts.

Gains and losses from section 1256 contracts and straddles are reported on **Form 6781,** Gains and Losses From Section 1256 Contracts and Straddles. If there are limited partners, see section 1256(e)(4) for the limitation on losses from hedging transactions.

An exchange of business or investment property for property of a like kind is reported on **Form 8824,** Like-Kind Exchanges.

For more information, see **Pub. 544,** Sales and Other Dispositions of Assets.

What Are Capital Assets?

Each item of property the partnership held (whether or not connected with its trade or business) is a capital asset **except:**

1. Assets that can be inventoried or property held mainly for sale to customers.

2. Depreciable or real property used in the trade or business.

3. Certain copyrights; literary, musical, or artistic compositions; letters or memoranda; or similar property.

4. Accounts or notes receivable acquired in the ordinary course of trade or business for services rendered or from the sale of property described in **1** above.

5. U.S. Government publications, including the Congressional Record, that the partnership received from the government, other than by purchase at the normal sales price, or that the partnership got from another taxpayer who had received it in a similar way, if the partnership's basis is determined by reference to the previous owner.

Items for Special Treatment and Special Cases

The following items may require special treatment:

- Bonds and other debt instruments. See **Pub. 550,** Investment Income and Expenses.

- Certain real estate subdivided for sale that may be considered a capital asset. See section 1237.

● Gain on the sale of depreciable property to a more than 50%-owned entity, or to a trust in which the partnership is a beneficiary, is treated as ordinary gain.

● Liquidating distributions from a corporation. See Pub. 550 for details.

● Gain on the sale or exchange of stock in certain foreign corporations. See section 1248.

● Gain or loss on options to buy or sell, including closing transactions. See Pub. 550 for details.

● Transfer of property to a foreign corporation as paid-in surplus or as a contribution to capital, or to a foreign estate, trust, or partnership. See **Form 926,** Return by a U.S. Transferor of Property to a Foreign Corporation, Foreign Estate or Trust, or Foreign Partnership.

● Transfer of property to a political organization if the fair market value of the property exceeds the partnership's adjusted basis in such property. See section 84.

● Any loss on the disposition of converted wetland or highly erodible cropland that is first used for farming after March 1, 1986, is reported as a long-term capital loss on Schedule D, but any gain on such a disposition is reported as ordinary income on Form 4797. See section 1257 for details.

● Transfer of partnership assets and liabilities to a newly formed corporation in exchange for all of its stock. See Rev. Rul. 84-111, 1984-2 C.B. 88.

● Disposition of foreign investment in a U.S. real property interest. See section 897.

● Any loss from a sale or exchange of property between the partnership and certain related persons is not allowed, except for distributions in complete liquidation of a corporation. See sections 267 and 707(b) for details.

● Any loss from securities that are capital assets that become worthless during the year is treated as a loss from the sale or exchange of a capital asset on the last day of the tax year.

● Gain from the sale or exchange of stock in a collapsible corporation is not a capital gain. See section 341.

● A nonbusiness bad debt must be treated as a short-term capital loss and can be deducted only in the year the debt becomes totally worthless. For each bad debt, enter the name of the debtor and "schedule attached" in column (a) of line 1 and the amount of the bad debt as a loss in column (f). Also attach a statement of facts to support each bad debt deduction.

● Any loss from a wash sale of stock or securities (including contracts or options to acquire or sell stock or securities) cannot be deducted unless the partnership is a dealer in stock or securities and the loss was sustained in a transaction made in the ordinary course of the partnership's trade or business. A wash sale occurs if the partnership acquires (by purchase or exchange), or has a contract or option to acquire, substantially identical stock or securities within 30 days before or after the date of the sale or exchange. See section 1091 for more information.

● Gains from the sale of property (other than publicly traded stock or securities) for which any payment is to be received in a tax year after the year of sale must be reported using the installment method on **Form 6252,** Installment Sale Income, unless the partnership elects to report the entire gain in the year of sale. The partnership should also use Form 6252 if it received a payment this year from a sale made in an earlier year on the installment method.

If the partnership wants to elect out of the installment method for installment gain that **is not** specially allocated among the partners, it must report the full amount of the gain on a timely filed return (including extensions).

If the partnership wants to elect out of the installment method for installment gain that **is** specially allocated among the partners, it must do the following on a timely filed return (including extensions):

1. For a **short-term capital gain,** report the full amount of the gain on Schedule K, line 4d or 7.

For a **long-term capital gain,** report the full amount of the gain on Schedule K, line 4e(2) or 7. Report the 28% rate gain (defined below) on line 4e(1).

2. Enter each partner's share of the full amount of the gain on Schedule K-1, line 4d, 4e(2), or 7, whichever applies. Report the 28% rate gain, if any, on line 4e(1).

Specific Instructions

Columns (b) and (c)—Date Acquired and Date Sold

Use the trade dates for date acquired and date sold for stocks and bonds traded on an exchange or over-the-counter market.

Column (d)—Sales Price

Enter in this column either the gross sales price or the net sales price from the sale. On sales of stocks and bonds, report the gross amount as reported to the partnership by the partnership's broker on Form 1099-B, Proceeds From Broker and Barter Exchange Transactions, or similar statement. However, if the broker advised the partnership that gross proceeds (gross sales price) less commissions and option premiums were reported to the IRS, enter that net amount in column (d).

Column (e)—Cost or Other Basis

In general, the cost or other basis is the cost of the property plus purchase commissions and improvements and minus depreciation, amortization, and depletion. If the partnership got the property in a tax-free exchange, involuntary conversion, or wash sale of stock, it may not be able to use the actual cash cost as the basis. If the partnership does not use cash cost, attach an explanation of the basis.

When selling stock, adjust the basis by subtracting all the stock-related nontaxable distributions received before the sale. This includes nontaxable distributions from utility company stock and mutual funds. Also adjust the basis for any stock splits or stock dividends.

If a charitable contribution deduction is passed through to a partner because of a sale of property to a charitable organization, the adjusted basis for determining gain from the sale is an amount that has the same ratio to the adjusted basis as the amount realized has to the fair market value.

See section 852(f) for the treatment of certain load charges incurred in acquiring stock in a mutual fund with a reinvestment right.

If the gross sales price is reported in column (d), increase the cost or other basis by any expense of sale, such as broker's fees, commissions, or option premiums, before making an entry in column (e).

For more information, see **Pub. 551,** Basis of Assets.

Column (f)—Gain or (Loss) for Entire Year

Make a separate entry in this column for each transaction reported on lines 1 and 6 and any other line(s) that applies to the partnership. For lines 1 and 6, subtract the amount in column (e) from the amount in column (d). Enter negative amounts in parentheses.

Column (g)—28% Rate Gain or (Loss)

Enter the amount, if any, from Part II, column (f), that is from a sale, exchange, or conversion (or an installment payment received):

● Before May 7, 1997, OR

● After July 28, 1997, for assets held more than 1 year but not more than 18 months.

Also include collectibles gain and losses. A **collectibles gain or loss** is any gain or loss from the sale or exchange of a collectible that is a capital asset but only if that asset was held either:

● More than 18 months, OR

● More than 1 year but not more than 18 months if sold or exchanged after May 6, 1997, but before July 29, 1997.

Collectibles gain also includes gain from the sale of an interest in a partnership or trust attributable to unrealized appreciation of collectibles.

Collectibles include works of art, rugs, antiques, metals (such as gold, silver, and platinum bullion), gems, stamps, coins, alcoholic beverages, and certain other tangible property.

Enter negative amounts in parentheses.

Lines 4 and 9—Capital Gains and Losses From Other Partnerships, Estates, and Trusts

See the Schedule K-1 or other information supplied to you by the other partnership, estate, or trust.

Line 10—Capital Gain Distributions

On line 10, column (f), report as capital gain distributions **(a)** capital gain dividends and **(b)** the partnership's share of undistributed capital gains from a regulated investment company or real estate investment trust (REIT). On line 10, column (g), report the 28% rate gain portion of these amounts. Report the partnership's share of taxes paid on undistributed capital gains by a regulated investment company or REIT on Schedule K, line 24, and Schedule K-1, line 25.

<table>
<tr><td>SCHEDULE K-1
(Form 1065)
Department of the Treasury
Internal Revenue Service</td><td>Partner's Share of Income, Credits, Deductions, etc.
▶ See separate instructions.
For calendar year 1997 or tax year beginning   , 1997, and ending   , 19</td><td>OMB No. 1545-0099
1997</td></tr>
</table>

Partner's identifying number ▶	**Partnership's identifying number** ▶
Partner's name, address, and ZIP code	Partnership's name, address, and ZIP code

A This partner is a ☐ general partner ☐ limited partner ☐ limited liability company member

B What type of entity is this partner? ▶ ....

C Is this partner a ☐ domestic or a ☐ foreign partner?

D Enter partner's percentage of:

	(i) Before change or termination	**(ii)** End of year
Profit sharing	.... %	.... %
Loss sharing	.... %	.... %
Ownership of capital	.... %	.... %

E IRS Center where partnership filed return:

F Partner's share of liabilities (see instructions):

Nonrecourse .... $ ....

Qualified nonrecourse financing . $ ....

Other .... $ ....

G Tax shelter registration number . ▶ ....

H Check here if this partnership is a publicly traded partnership as defined in section 469(k)(2) . . . . ☐

I Check applicable boxes: **(1)** ☐ Final K-1 **(2)** ☐ Amended K-1

J Analysis of partner's capital account:

(a) Capital account at beginning of year	**(b)** Capital contributed during year	**(c)** Partner's share of lines 3, 4, and 7, Form 1065, Schedule M-2	**(d)** Withdrawals and distributions	**(e)** Capital account at end of year (combine columns (a) through (d))
			( )	

	(a) Distributive share item .		**(b)** Amount	**(c)** 1040 filers enter the amount in column (b) on:
Income (Loss)	**1** Ordinary income (loss) from trade or business activities . . .	**1**		See page 6 of Partner's Instructions for Schedule K-1 (Form 1065).
	2 Net income (loss) from rental real estate activities	**2**		
	3 Net income (loss) from other rental activities	**3**		
	4 Portfolio income (loss):			
	a Interest	**4a**		Sch. B, Part I, line 1
	b Dividends	**4b**		Sch. B, Part II, line 5
	c Royalties	**4c**		Sch. E, Part I, line 4
	d Net short-term capital gain (loss)	**4d**		Sch. D, line 5, col. (f)
	e Net long-term capital gain (loss):			
	(1) 28% rate gain (loss)	**e(1)**		Sch. D, line 12, col. (g)
	(2) Total for year.	**e(2)**		Sch. D, line 12, col. (f)
	f Other portfolio income (loss) *(attach schedule)*	**4f**		Enter on applicable line of your return.
	5 Guaranteed payments to partner	**5**		See page 6 of Partner's Instructions for Schedule K-1 (Form 1065).
	6 Net section 1231 gain (loss) (other than due to casualty or theft):			
	a 28% rate gain (loss).	**6a**		
	b Total for year.	**6b**		
	7 Other income (loss) *(attach schedule)*	**7**		Enter on applicable line of your return.
Deduc-tions	**8** Charitable contributions (see instructions) *(attach schedule)* . .	**8**		Sch. A, line 15 or 16
	9 Section 179 expense deduction.	**9**		See page 7 of Partner's Instructions for Schedule K-1 (Form 1065).
	10 Deductions related to portfolio income *(attach schedule)* . . .	**10**		
	11 Other deductions *(attach schedule)*.	**11**		
Credits	**12a** Low-income housing credit:			
	(1) From section 42(j)(5) partnerships for property placed in service before 1990	**a(1)**		Form 8586, line 5
	(2) Other than on line 12a(1) for property placed in service before 1990	**a(2)**		
	(3) From section 42(j)(5) partnerships for property placed in service after 1989	**a(3)**		
	(4) Other than on line 12a(3) for property placed in service after 1989	**a(4)**		
	b Qualified rehabilitation expenditures related to rental real estate activities	**12b**		
	c Credits (other than credits shown on lines 12a and 12b) related to rental real estate activities.	**12c**		See page 8 of Partner's Instructions for Schedule K-1 (Form 1065).
	d Credits related to other rental activities	**12d**		
	13 Other credits	**13**		

For Paperwork Reduction Act Notice, see Instructions for Form 1065.   Cat. No. 11394R   **Schedule K-1 (Form 1065) 1997**

	(a) Distributive share item		(b) Amount	(c) 1040 filers enter the amount in column (b) on:
Investment Interest	**14a** Interest expense on investment debts	**14a**		Form 4952, line 1
	b (1) Investment income included on lines 4a, 4b, 4c, and 4f	**b(1)**		See page 8 of Partner's Instructions for Schedule K-1 (Form 1065).
	(2) Investment expenses included on line 10	**b(2)**		
Self-employment	**15a** Net earnings (loss) from self-employment	**15a**		Sch. SE, Section A or B
	b Gross farming or fishing income	**15b**		See page 9 of Partner's Instructions for Schedule K-1 (Form 1065).
	c Gross nonfarm income	**15c**		
Adjustments and Tax Preference Items	**16a** Depreciation adjustment on property placed in service after 1986	**16a**		See page 9 of Partner's Instructions for Schedule K-1 (Form 1065) and Instructions for Form 6251.
	b Adjusted gain or loss	**16b**		
	c Depletion (other than oil and gas)	**16c**		
	d (1) Gross income from oil, gas, and geothermal properties	**d(1)**		
	(2) Deductions allocable to oil, gas, and geothermal properties	**d(2)**		
	e Other adjustments and tax preference items (attach schedule)	**16e**		
Foreign Taxes	**17a** Type of income ▶			Form 1116, check boxes
	b Name of foreign country or possession ▶			
	c Total gross income from sources outside the United States (attach schedule)	**17c**		Form 1116, Part I
	d Total applicable deductions and losses (attach schedule)	**17d**		
	e Total foreign taxes (check one): ▶ ☐ Paid ☐ Accrued	**17e**		Form 1116, Part II
	f Reduction in taxes available for credit (attach schedule)	**17f**		Form 1116, Part III
	g Other foreign tax information (attach schedule)	**17g**		See Instructions for Form 1116.
Other	**18** Section 59(e)(2) expenditures: **a** Type ▶			See page 9 of Partner's Instructions for Schedule K-1 (Form 1065).
	b Amount	**18b**		
	19 Tax-exempt interest income	**19**		Form 1040, line 8b
	20 Other tax-exempt income	**20**		See page 9 of Partner's Instructions for Schedule K-1 (Form 1065).
	21 Nondeductible expenses	**21**		
	22 Distributions of money (cash and marketable securities)	**22**		
	23 Distributions of property other than money	**23**		
	24 Recapture of low-income housing credit:			
	a From section 42(j)(5) partnerships	**24a**		Form 8611, line 8
	b Other than on line 24a	**24b**		

Supplemental Information	**25** Supplemental information required to be reported separately to each partner (attach additional schedules if more space is needed):

Partner's Share of Income, Credits, Deductions, etc.

► **See separate instructions.**

For calendar year 1997 or tax year beginning ____________ , 1997, and ending ____________ , 19____

OMB No. 1545-0099

1997

Partner's identifying number ► ____________

Partnership's identifying number ► ____________

Partner's name, address, and ZIP code

Partnership's name, address, and ZIP code

A This partner is a ☐ general partner ☐ limited partner
☐ limited liability company member

B What type of entity is this partner? ► ____________

C Is this partner a ☐ domestic or a ☐ foreign partner?

D Enter partner's percentage of:

	(i) Before change or termination	(ii) End of year
Profit sharing	____ %	____ %
Loss sharing	____ %	____ %
Ownership of capital	____ %	____ %

E IRS Center where partnership filed return: ____________

F Partner's share of liabilities (see instructions):

Nonrecourse . . . . $ ____________

Qualified nonrecourse financing . $ ____________

Other . . . . $ ____________

G Tax shelter registration number . ► ____________

H Check here if this partnership is a publicly traded partnership as defined in section 469(k)(2) . . . . ☐

I Check applicable boxes: **(1)** ☐ Final K-1 **(2)** ☐ Amended K-1

J Analysis of partner's capital account:

(a) Capital account at beginning of year	(b) Capital contributed during year	(c) Partner's share of lines 3, 4, and 7, Form 1065, Schedule M-2	(d) Withdrawals and distributions	(e) Capital account at end of year (combine columns (a) through (d))
			( )	

	(a) Distributive share item	(b) Amount	(c) 1040 filers enter the amount in column (b) on:
Income (Loss)	**1** Ordinary income (loss) from trade or business activities . . .	**1**	See page 6 of Partner's Instructions for Schedule K-1 (Form 1065).
	2 Net income (loss) from rental real estate activities	**2**	
	3 Net income (loss) from other rental activities	**3**	
	4 Portfolio income (loss):		
	a Interest	**4a**	Sch. B, Part I, line 1
	b Dividends	**4b**	Sch. B, Part II, line 5
	c Royalties	**4c**	Sch. E, Part I, line 4
	d Net short-term capital gain (loss)	**4d**	Sch. D, line 5, col. (f)
	e Net long-term capital gain (loss):		
	(1) 28% rate gain (loss)	**e(1)**	Sch. D, line 12, col. (g)
	(2) Total for year	**e(2)**	Sch. D, line 12, col. (f)
	f Other portfolio income (loss) *(attach schedule)*	**4f**	Enter on applicable line of your return.
	5 Guaranteed payments to partner	**5**	See page 6 of Partner's Instructions for Schedule K-1 (Form 1065).
	6 Net section 1231 gain (loss) (other than due to casualty or theft):		
	a 28% rate gain (loss)	**6a**	
	b Total for year	**6b**	
	7 Other income (loss) *(attach schedule)*	**7**	Enter on applicable line of your return.
Deductions	**8** Charitable contributions (see instructions) *(attach schedule)* . .	**8**	Sch. A, line 15 or 16
	9 Section 179 expense deduction	**9**	See page 7 of Partner's Instructions for Schedule K-1 (Form 1065).
	10 Deductions related to portfolio income *(attach schedule)* . . .	**10**	
	11 Other deductions *(attach schedule)*	**11**	
Credits	**12a** Low-income housing credit:		
	(1) From section 42(j)(5) partnerships for property placed in service before 1990	**a(1)**	Form 8586, line 5
	(2) Other than on line 12a(1) for property placed in service before 1990	**a(2)**	
	(3) From section 42(j)(5) partnerships for property placed in service after 1989	**a(3)**	
	(4) Other than on line 12a(3) for property placed in service after 1989	**a(4)**	
	b Qualified rehabilitation expenditures related to rental real estate activities	**12b**	
	c Credits (other than credits shown on lines 12a and 12b) related to rental real estate activities	**12c**	See page 8 of Partner's Instructions for Schedule K-1 (Form 1065).
	d Credits related to other rental activities	**12d**	
	13 Other credits	**13**	

For Paperwork Reduction Act Notice, see Instructions for Form 1065.

Cat. No. 11394R

Schedule K-1 (Form 1065) 1997

(a) Distributive share item		(b) Amount	(c) 1040 filers enter the amount in column (b) on:
Investment Interest	**14a** Interest expense on investment debts	14a	Form 4952, line 1
	b (1) Investment income included on lines 4a, 4b, 4c, and 4f . .	b(1)	} See page 8 of Partner's Instructions for Schedule K-1 (Form 1065).
	(2) Investment expenses included on line 10.	b(2)	
Self-employment	**15a** Net earnings (loss) from self-employment	15a	Sch. SE, Section A or B
	b Gross farming or fishing income.	15b	} See page 9 of Partner's Instructions for Schedule K-1 (Form 1065).
	c Gross nonfarm income.	15c	
Adjustments and Tax Preference Items	**16a** Depreciation adjustment on property placed in service after 1986	16a	} See page 9 of Partner's Instructions for Schedule K-1 (Form 1065) and Instructions for Form 6251.
	b Adjusted gain or loss	16b	
	c Depletion (other than oil and gas)	16c	
	d (1) Gross income from oil, gas, and geothermal properties . .	d(1)	
	(2) Deductions allocable to oil, gas, and geothermal properties	d(2)	
	e Other adjustments and tax preference items *(attach schedule)*	16e	
Foreign Taxes	**17a** Type of income ▶ --------------------		Form 1116, check boxes
	b Name of foreign country or possession ▶ --------------------		
	c Total gross income from sources outside the United States *(attach schedule)*	17c	} Form 1116, Part I
	d Total applicable deductions and losses *(attach schedule)*.	17d	
	e Total foreign taxes (check one): ▶ ☐ Paid ☐ Accrued . . .	17e	Form 1116, Part II
	f Reduction in taxes available for credit *(attach schedule)* . . .	17f	Form 1116, Part III
	g Other foreign tax information *(attach schedule)*	17g	See Instructions for Form 1116.
Other	**18** Section 59(e)(2) expenditures: **a** Type ▶ --------------------		} See page 9 of Partner's Instructions for Schedule K-1 (Form 1065).
	b Amount	18b	
	19 Tax-exempt interest income	19	Form 1040, line 8b
	20 Other tax-exempt income.	20	} See page 9 of Partner's Instructions for Schedule K-1 (Form 1065).
	21 Nondeductible expenses	21	
	22 Distributions of money (cash and marketable securities) . . .	22	
	23 Distributions of property other than money	23	
	24 Recapture of low-income housing credit:		
	a From section 42(j)(5) partnerships	24a	} Form 8611, line 8
	b Other than on line 24a.	24b	

25 Supplemental information required to be reported separately to each partner *(attach additional schedules if more space is needed):*

<table>
<tr><td>Form 4562
Department of the Treasury
Internal Revenue Service (99)</td><td>Depreciation and Amortization
(Including Information on Listed Property)
▶ See separate instructions. ▶ Attach this form to your return.</td><td>OMB No. 1545-0172
1997
Attachment
Sequence No. 67</td></tr>
<tr><td colspan="2">Name(s) shown on return</td><td>Business or activity to which this form relates</td><td>Identifying number</td></tr>
</table>

Part I **Election To Expense Certain Tangible Property (Section 179)** (**Note:** *If you have any "listed property," complete Part V before you complete Part I.*)

1	Maximum dollar limitation. If an enterprise zone business, see page 2 of the instructions . .	**1** $18,000
2	Total cost of section 179 property placed in service. See page 2 of the instructions	**2**
3	Threshold cost of section 179 property before reduction in limitation	**3** $200,000
4	Reduction in limitation. Subtract line 3 from line 2. If zero or less, enter -0-	**4**
5	Dollar limitation for tax year. Subtract line 4 from line 1. If zero or less, enter -0-. If married filing separately, see page 2 of the instructions	**5**

(a) Description of property	(b) Cost (business use only)	(c) Elected cost
6		

7	Listed property. Enter amount from line 27.	**7**
8	Total elected cost of section 179 property. Add amounts in column (c), lines 6 and 7 . . .	**8**
9	Tentative deduction. Enter the smaller of line 5 or line 8	**9**
10	Carryover of disallowed deduction from 1996. See page 3 of the instructions	**10**
11	Business income limitation. Enter the smaller of business income (not less than zero) or line 5 (see instructions)	**11**
12	Section 179 expense deduction. Add lines 9 and 10, but do not enter more than line 11 . .	**12**
13	Carryover of disallowed deduction to 1998. Add lines 9 and 10, less line 12 ▶	**13**

Note: *Do not use Part II or Part III below for listed property (automobiles, certain other vehicles, cellular telephones, certain computers, or property used for entertainment, recreation, or amusement). Instead, use Part V for listed property.*

Part II **MACRS Depreciation For Assets Placed in Service ONLY During Your 1997 Tax Year (Do Not Include Listed Property.)**

Section A—General Asset Account Election

14   If you are making the election under section 168(i)(4) to group any assets placed in service during the tax year into one or more general asset accounts, check this box. See page 3 of the instructions . . . . ▶ ☐

Section B—General Depreciation System (GDS) (See page 3 of the instructions.)

(a) Classification of property	(b) Month and year placed in service	(c) Basis for depreciation (business/investment use only—see instructions)	(d) Recovery period	(e) Convention	(f) Method	(g) Depreciation deduction
15a 3-year property						
b 5-year property						
c 7-year property						
d 10-year property						
e 15-year property						
f 20-year property						
g 25-year property			25 yrs.		S/L	
h Residential rental property			27.5 yrs.	MM	S/L	
			27.5 yrs.	MM	S/L	
i Nonresidential real property			39 yrs.	MM	S/L	
				MM	S/L	

Section C—Alternative Depreciation System (ADS) (See page 6 of the instructions.)

(a) Classification of property	(b) Month and year placed in service	(c) Basis	(d) Recovery period	(e) Convention	(f) Method	(g) Depreciation deduction
16a Class life					S/L	
b 12-year			12 yrs.		S/L	
c 40-year			40 yrs.	MM	S/L	

Part III **Other Depreciation (Do Not Include Listed Property.)** (See page 6 of the instructions.)

17	GDS and ADS deductions for assets placed in service in tax years beginning before 1997	**17**
18	Property subject to section 168(f)(1) election	**18**
19	ACRS and other depreciation	**19**

Part IV **Summary** (See page 7 of the instructions.)

20	Listed property. Enter amount from line 26.	**20**
21	**Total.** Add deductions on line 12, lines 15 and 16 in column (g), and lines 17 through 20. Enter here and on the appropriate lines of your return. Partnerships and S corporations—see instructions . .	**21**
22	For assets shown above and placed in service during the current year, enter the portion of the basis attributable to section 263A costs	**22**

For Paperwork Reduction Act Notice, see the separate instructions.   Cat. No. 12906N   Form **4562** (1997)

Part V **Listed Property—Automobiles, Certain Other Vehicles, Cellular Telephones, Certain Computers, and Property Used for Entertainment, Recreation, or Amusement**

Note: *For any vehicle for which you are using the standard mileage rate or deducting lease expense, complete **only** 23a, 23b, columns (a) through (c) of Section A, all of Section B, and Section C if applicable.*

Section A—Depreciation and Other Information (Caution: *See page 8 of the instructions for limits for passenger automobiles.*)

23a Do you have evidence to support the business/investment use claimed? ☐ **Yes** ☐ **No**   **23b** If "Yes," is the evidence written? ☐ **Yes** ☐ **No**

(a) Type of property (list vehicles first)	(b) Date placed in service	(c) Business/ investment use percentage	(d) Cost or other basis	(e) Basis for depreciation (business/investment use only)	(f) Recovery period	(g) Method/ Convention	(h) Depreciation deduction	(i) Elected section 179 cost
24 Property used more than 50% in a qualified business use (See page 7 of the instructions.):								
		%						
		%						
		%						
25 Property used 50% or less in a qualified business use (See page 7 of the instructions.):								
		%				S/L –		
		%				S/L –		
		%				S/L –		

26 Add amounts in column (h). Enter the total here and on line 20, page 1 . . . .   **26**

27 Add amounts in column (i). Enter the total here and on line 7, page 1 . . . .   **27**

Section B—Information on Use of Vehicles

Complete this section for vehicles used by a sole proprietor, partner, or other "more than 5% owner," or related person.

If you provided vehicles to your employees, first answer the questions in Section C to see if you meet an exception to completing this section for those vehicles.

	(a) Vehicle 1	(b) Vehicle 2	(c) Vehicle 3	(d) Vehicle 4	(e) Vehicle 5	(f) Vehicle 6
28 Total business/investment miles driven during the year (DO NOT include commuting miles)						
29 Total commuting miles driven during the year						
30 Total other personal (noncommuting) miles driven						
31 Total miles driven during the year. Add lines 28 through 30.						

	Yes	No	Yes	No	Yes	No	Yes	No	Yes	No	Yes	No
32 Was the vehicle available for personal use during off-duty hours?												
33 Was the vehicle used primarily by a more than 5% owner or related person?												
34 Is another vehicle available for personal use?												

Section C—Questions for Employers Who Provide Vehicles for Use by Their Employees

Answer these questions to determine if you meet an exception to completing Section B for vehicles used by employees who ***are not*** *more than 5% owners or related persons.*

	Yes	No
35 Do you maintain a written policy statement that prohibits all personal use of vehicles, including commuting, by your employees?		
36 Do you maintain a written policy statement that prohibits personal use of vehicles, except commuting, by your employees? See page 9 of the instructions for vehicles used by corporate officers, directors, or 1% or more owners		
37 Do you treat all use of vehicles by employees as personal use?		
38 Do you provide more than five vehicles to your employees, obtain information from your employees about the use of the vehicles, and retain the information received?		
39 Do you meet the requirements concerning qualified automobile demonstration use? See page 9 of the instructions . .		

Note: *If your answer to 35, 36, 37, 38, or 39 is "Yes," you need not complete Section B for the covered vehicles.*

Part VI **Amortization**

(a) Description of costs	(b) Date amortization begins	(c) Amortizable amount	(d) Code section	(e) Amortization period or percentage	(f) Amortization for this year
40 Amortization of costs that begins during your 1997 tax year:					

41 Amortization of costs that began before 1997 . . . .   **41**

42 **Total.** Enter here and on "Other Deductions" or "Other Expenses" line of your return . . .   **42**

<table>
<tr><td>Form 4797</td><td colspan="2">Sales of Business Property
(Also Involuntary Conversions and Recapture Amounts
Under Sections 179 and 280F(b)(2))</td><td>OMB No. 1545-0184
1997</td></tr>
<tr><td>Department of the Treasury
Internal Revenue Service (99)</td><td colspan="2">► Attach to your tax return. ► See separate instructions.</td><td>Attachment
Sequence No. 27</td></tr>
</table>

Name(s) shown on return	Identifying number

1   Enter here the gross proceeds from the sale or exchange of real estate reported to you for 1997 on Form(s) 1099-S (or a substitute statement) that you will be including on line 2, 10, or 20 . . . .   **1**

Part I   Sales or Exchanges of Property Used in a Trade or Business and Involuntary Conversions From Other Than Casualty or Theft—Property Held More Than 1 Year

(a) Description of property	**(b)** Date acquired (mo., day, yr.)	**(c)** Date sold (mo., day, yr.)	**(d)** Gross sales price	**(e)** Depreciation allowed or allowable since acquisition	**(f)** Cost or other basis, plus improvements and expense of sale	**(g)** GAIN or (LOSS) for entire year. Subtract (f) from the sum of (d) and (e)	**(h)** 28% RATE GAIN or (LOSS) * (see instr. below)
2							

3   Gain, if any, from Form 4684, line 39 . . . .   **3**

4   Section 1231 gain from installment sales from Form 6252, line 26 or 37 . . . . . .   **4**

5   Section 1231 gain or (loss) from like-kind exchanges from Form 8824 . . . .   **5**

6   Gain, if any, from line 32, from other than casualty or theft **6**

7   Combine lines 2 through 6 in columns (g) and (h). Enter gain or (loss) here, and on the appropriate line as follows: **7**

    Partnerships—Enter the gain or (loss) on Form 1065, Schedule K, lines 6a and 6b. Skip lines 8, 9, 11, and 12 below.

    S corporations—Report the gain or (loss) following the instructions for Form 1120S, Schedule K, lines 5 and 6. Skip lines 8, 9, 11, and 12 below, unless line 7, column (g) is a gain and the S corporation is subject to the capital gains tax.

    All others—If line 7, column (g) is zero or a loss, enter that amount on line 11 below and skip lines 8 and 9. If line 7, column (g) is a gain and you did not have any prior year section 1231 losses, or they were recaptured in an earlier year, enter the gain or (loss) in each column as a long-term capital gain or (loss) on Schedule D and skip lines 8, 9, and 12 below.

8   Nonrecaptured net section 1231 losses from prior years (see instructions) **8**

9   Subtract line 8 from line 7. If zero or less, enter -0-. Also enter on the appropriate line as follows (see instructions):   **9**

    S corporations—Enter only the gain in column (g) on Schedule D (Form 1120S), line 14, and skip lines 11 and 12 below.

    All others—If line 9, column (g) is zero, enter the gain from line 7, column (g) on line 12 below. If line 9, column (g) is more than zero, enter the amount from line 8, column (g) on line 12 below, and enter the gain or (loss) in each column of line 9 as a long-term capital gain or (loss) on Schedule D.

    * Corporations (other than S corporations) should not complete column (h). Partnerships and S corporations must complete column (h). All others must complete column (h) only if line 7, column (g), is a gain. 28% rate gain or loss includes all gains and losses in column (g) from sales, exchanges, or conversions (including installment payments received) **either (a) before 5/7/97 or (b) after 7/28/97** for assets held more than 1 year but not more than 18 months.

Part II   Ordinary Gains and Losses

10   Ordinary gains and losses not included on lines 11 through 17 (include property held 1 year or less):

11   Loss, if any, from line 7, column (g) **11**

12   Gain, if any, from line 7, column (g) or amount from line 8, column (g) if applicable **12**

13   Gain, if any, from line 31 . . . .   **13**

14   Net gain or (loss) from Form 4684, lines 31 and 38a **14**

15   Ordinary gain from installment sales from Form 6252, line 25 or 36 . . . .   **15**

16   Ordinary gain or (loss) from like-kind exchanges from Form 8824 . . . .   **16**

17   Recapture of section 179 expense deduction for partners and S corporation shareholders from property dispositions by partnerships and S corporations (see instructions) **17**

18   Combine lines 10 through 17 in column (g). Enter gain or (loss) here, and on the appropriate line as follows: **18**

   a   For all except individual returns: Enter the gain or (loss) from line 18 on the return being filed.

   b   For individual returns:

     (1)   If the loss on line 11 includes a loss from Form 4684, line 35, column (b)(ii), enter that part of the loss here and on line 22 of Schedule A (Form 1040). Identify as from "Form 4797, line 18b(1)." See instructions . . . .   **18b(1)**

     (2)   Redetermine the gain or (loss) on line 18, excluding the loss, if any, on line 18b(1). Enter here and on Form 1040, line 14 . . . .   **18b(2)**

For Paperwork Reduction Act Notice, see separate instructions.   Cat. No. 13086I   Form **4797** (1997)

Part III Gain From Disposition of Property Under Sections 1245, 1250, 1252, 1254, and 1255

19	(a) Description of section 1245, 1250, 1252, 1254, or 1255 property:	(b) Date acquired (mo., day, yr.)	(c) Date sold (mo., day, yr.)
A			
B			
C			
D			

	These columns relate to the properties on lines 19A through 19D. ▶		Property A	Property B	Property C	Property D
20	Gross sales price (**Note:** *See line 1 before completing.*)	20				
21	Cost or other basis plus expense of sale	21				
22	Depreciation (or depletion) allowed or allowable	22				
23	Adjusted basis. Subtract line 22 from line 21	23				
24	Total gain. Subtract line 23 from line 20	24				
25	**If section 1245 property:**					
a	Depreciation allowed or allowable from line 22	25a				
b	Enter the **smaller** of line 24 or 25a	25b				
26	**If section 1250 property:** If straight line depreciation was used, enter -0- on line 26g, except for a corporation subject to section 291.					
a	Additional depreciation after 1975 (see instructions)	26a				
b	Applicable percentage multiplied by the **smaller** of line 24 or line 26a (see instructions)	26b				
c	Subtract line 26a from line 24. If residential rental property or line 24 is not more than line 26a, skip lines 26d and 26e	26c				
d	Additional depreciation after 1969 and before 1976	26d				
e	Enter the **smaller** of line 26c or 26d	26e				
f	Section 291 amount (corporations only)	26f				
g	Add lines 26b, 26e, and 26f	26g				
27	**If section 1252 property:** Skip this section if you did not dispose of farmland or if this form is being completed for a partnership.					
a	Soil, water, and land clearing expenses	27a				
b	Line 27a multiplied by applicable percentage (see instructions)	27b				
c	Enter the **smaller** of line 24 or 27b	27c				
28	**If section 1254 property:**					
a	Intangible drilling and development costs, expenditures for development of mines and other natural deposits, and mining exploration costs (see instructions)	28a				
b	Enter the **smaller** of line 24 or 28a	28b				
29	**If section 1255 property:**					
a	Applicable percentage of payments excluded from income under section 126 (see instructions)	29a				
b	Enter the **smaller** of line 24 or 29a (see instructions)	29b				

Summary of Part III Gains. Complete property columns A through D through line 29b before going to line 30.

30	Total gains for all properties. Add property columns A through D, line 24	30	
31	Add property columns A through D, lines 25b, 26g, 27c, 28b, and 29b. Enter here and on line 13	31	
32	Subtract line 31 from line 30. Enter the portion from casualty or theft on Form 4684, line 33. Enter the portion from other than casualty or theft on Form 4797, line 6, column (g), and if applicable, column (h)	32	

Part IV Recapture Amounts Under Sections 179 and 280F(b)(2) When Business Use Drops to 50% or Less
See instructions.

			(a) Section 179	(b) Section 280F(b)(2)
33	Section 179 expense deduction or depreciation allowable in prior years	33		
34	Recomputed depreciation. See instructions	34		
35	Recapture amount. Subtract line 34 from line 33. See the instructions for where to report	35		

INSTRUCTIONS FOR FORM 1065

U.S. Partnership Return of Income

1997

Department of the Treasury
Internal Revenue Service

Instructions for Form 1065

U.S. Partnership Return of Income

Section references are to the Internal Revenue Code unless otherwise noted.

Paperwork Reduction Act Notice. We ask for the information on this form to carry out the Internal Revenue laws of the United States. You are required to give us the information. We need it to ensure that you are complying with these laws and to allow us to figure and collect the right amount of tax.

You are not required to provide the information requested on a form that is subject to the Paperwork Reduction Act unless the form displays a valid OMB control number. Books or records relating to a form or its instructions must be retained as long as their contents may become material in the administration of any Internal Revenue law. Generally, tax returns and return information are confidential, as required by section 6103.

The time needed to complete and file this form and related schedules will vary depending on individual circumstances. The estimated average times are:

Form	Recordkeeping	Learning about the law or the form	Preparing the form	Copying, assembling, and sending the form to the IRS
1065	39 hr., 50 min.	21 hr., 40 min.	37 hr., 23 min.	4 hr., 1 min.
Schedule D (Form 1065)	6 hr., 56 min.	1 hr., 29 min.	1 hr., 40 min.	
Schedule K-1 (Form 1065)	25 hr., 21 min.	9 hr., 20 min.	10 hr., 10 min.	
Schedule L (Form 1065)	15 hr., 32 min.	6 min.	22 min.	
Schedule M-1 (Form 1065)	3 hr., 21 min.	12 min.	16 min.	
Schedule M-2 (Form 1065)	2 hr., 52 min.	6 min.	9 min.	

If you have comments concerning the accuracy of these time estimates or suggestions for making these forms simpler, we would be happy to hear from you. You can write to the Tax Forms Committee, Western Area Distribution Center, Rancho Cordova, CA 95743-0001. **DO NOT** send the tax form to this address. Instead, see **Where To File** on page 3.

Contents

Changes To Note

The Taxpayer Relief Act of 1997 (the Act) made several changes that affect partnerships and partners. Some of the changes are highlighted below.

- The Act generally reduced the tax rates for individuals, estates, and trusts that apply to net capital gain for sales, exchanges, and conversions of assets (including installment payments received) after May 6, 1997. Schedule D and Schedules K and K-1 have been revised to reflect the reporting of capital gains to partners under the new law.

- The partnership may have to recognize gain if it enters into a constructive sale after June 8, 1997, of property in which it held an appreciated position (such as a "short sale against the box"). See section 1259 for more details.

- For tax years ending after August 5, 1997, the Act expanded the small partnership exemption from the consolidated audit procedures to include partnerships that specially allocate partnership items or that have C corporations as partners. For more details, see the instructions for Question 4 on page 14.

- Under the Act, the amount received by a partner in exchange for his or her partnership interest that is attributable to inventory (whether or not substantially appreciated) is considered to give rise to ordinary income. This provision generally applies to sales or exchanges after August 5, 1997.

- The Act extends to 7 years the period in which a partner may be required to recognize precontribution gain for contributions of property after June 8, 1997, to a partnership.

- Employers that pay wages to long-term family assistance recipients may qualify for the welfare-to-work credit. This new credit is based on wages paid to qualified individuals who begin work after December 31, 1997, and is figured on **Form 8861,** Welfare-to-Work Credit.

• The Act imposed additional limits on the deduction of premiums and interest on debt related to life insurance, annuity, or endowment contracts issued after June 8, 1997. The Act also reduces interest deductions that are allocable under proration rules described in new section 264(f) to the unborrowed policy cash values of certain life insurance, endowment, or annuity contracts issued after June 8, 1997. For more details, see section 264.

Unresolved Tax Problems

The Problem Resolution Program is for taxpayers that have been unable to resolve their problems with the IRS. If the partnership has a tax problem it cannot clear up through normal channels, write to the partnership's local IRS District Director or call the partnership's local IRS office and ask for Problem Resolution assistance. Persons who have access to TTY/TDD equipment may call 1-800-829-4059 to ask for help from Problem Resolution. This office cannot change the tax law or technical decisions. But it can help the partnership clear up problems that resulted from previous contacts.

How To Get Forms and Publications

Personal Computer

Visit the IRS's Internet Web Site at **www.irs.ustreas.gov** to get:
• Forms and instructions
• Publications
• IRS press releases and fact sheets
  You can also reach us using:
• Telnet at **iris.irs.ustreas.gov**
• File Transfer Protocol at **ftp.irs.ustreas.gov**
• Direct Dial (by modem). Dial direct to the Internal Revenue Information Services (IRIS) by calling **703-321-8020** using your modem. IRIS is an on-line information service on FedWorld.

CD-ROM

A CD-ROM containing over 2,000 tax products (including many prior year forms) can be purchased from the Government Printing Office (GPO). To order the CD-ROM, call the Superintendent of Documents at **202-512-1800** or go through GPO's Internet Web Site **(www.access.gpo.gov/su_docs).**

By Phone and In Person

To order forms and publications, call **1-800-TAX-FORM (1-800-829-3676)** between 7:30 a.m. and 5:30 p.m. on weekdays. You can also get most forms and publications at your local IRS office.

General Instructions

Purpose of Form

Form 1065 is an information return used to report the income, deductions, gains, losses, etc., from the operation of a partnership. A partnership does not pay tax on its income but "passes through" any profits or losses to its partners. Partners must include partnership items on their tax returns.

Definitions

Partnership

A partnership is the relationship between two or more persons who join to carry on a trade or business, with each person contributing money, property, labor, or skill and each expecting to share in the profits and losses of the business whether or not a formal partnership agreement is made.

The term "partnership" includes a limited partnership, syndicate, group, pool, joint venture, or other unincorporated organization, through or by which any business, financial operation, or venture is carried on, that is not, within the meaning of the regulations under section 7701, a corporation, trust, estate, or sole proprietorship.

A joint undertaking merely to share expenses is not a partnership. Mere co-ownership of property that is maintained and leased or rented is not a partnership. However, if the co-owners provide services to the tenants, a partnership exists.

General Partner

A general partner is a partner who is personally liable for partnership debts.

General Partnership

A general partnership is composed only of general partners.

Limited Partner

A limited partner is a partner in a partnership formed under a state limited partnership law, whose personal liability for partnership debts is limited to the amount of money or other property that the partner contributed or is required to contribute to the partnership. Some members of other entities, such as domestic or foreign business trusts or limited liability companies that are classified as partnerships, may be treated as limited partners for certain purposes. See, for example, Temporary Regulations section 1.469-5T(e)(3), which treats all members with limited liability as limited partners for purposes of section 469(h)(2).

Limited Partnership

A limited partnership is formed under a state limited partnership law and composed of at least one general partner and one or more limited partners.

Limited Liability Company

A limited liability company (LLC) is an entity formed under state law by filing articles of organization as an LLC. Unlike a partnership, none of the members of an LLC are personally liable for its debts. An LLC may be classified for Federal income tax purposes either as a partnership, a corporation, or an entity disregarded as an entity separate from its owner by applying the rules in Regulations section 301.7701-3. See **Form 8832,** Entity Classification Election, for more details.

Nonrecourse Loans

Nonrecourse loans are those liabilities of the partnership for which no partner bears the economic risk of loss.

Who Must File

Every partnership that engages in a trade or business or has gross income derived from sources in the United States must file Form 1065. A partnership must file even if its principal place of business is outside the United States or all its members are nonresident aliens.

A partnership is not considered to engage in a trade or business, and is therefore not required to file, for any tax year in which it neither receives income nor incurs any expenditures treated as deductions or credits for Federal income tax purposes.

Entities formed as limited liability companies and treated as partnerships for Federal income tax purposes must file Form 1065.

A religious or apostolic organization exempt from income tax under section 501(d) must file Form 1065 to report its taxable income, which must be allocated to its members as a dividend, whether distributed or not. Such an organization must figure its taxable income on an attachment to Form 1065 in the same manner as a corporation. **Form 1120,** U.S. Corporation Income Tax Return, may be used for this purpose. Enter the organization's taxable income, if any, on line 4b of Schedule K and each member's pro rata share on line 4b of Schedule K-1. Net operating losses are not deductible by the members but may be carried back or forward by the organization under the rules of section 172.

A qualifying syndicate, pool, joint venture, or similar organization may elect under section 761(a) not to be treated as a partnership for Federal income tax purposes and will not be required to file Form 1065 except for the year of election. See section 761(a) and Regulations section 1.761-2 for more information.

Real estate mortgage investment conduits (REMICs) must file Form 1066.

Certain publicly traded partnerships treated as corporations under section 7704 must file Form 1120.

Termination of the Partnership

A partnership terminates when:

1. All its operations are discontinued and no part of any business, financial operation, or venture is continued by any of its partners in a partnership, **or**

2. At least 50% of the total interest in partnership capital and profits is sold or exchanged within a 12-month period, including a sale or exchange to another partner. See Regulations section 1.708-1(b)(1) for more details.

The partnership's tax year ends on the date of termination. For purposes of **1** above, the date of termination is the date the partnership completes the winding up of its affairs. For purposes of **2** above, the date of termination is the date the partnership interest is sold or exchanged that, of itself or together with other sales or exchanges in the preceding 12 months, transfers an interest of 50% or more in both partnership capital and profits.

Special rules apply in the case of a merger, consolidation, or division of a partnership. See Regulations section 1.708-1(b)(2) for details.

Electronic and Magnetic Media Filing

Qualified partnerships or transmitters can file Form 1065 and related schedules electronically or on magnetic media. Tax return data may be filed electronically using a dial-up MITRON communications device or remote bulletin board system or on magnetic media using magnetic tape or floppy diskette.

If the partnership wishes to do this, **Form 9041,** Application for Electronic/Magnetic Media Filing of Business and Employee Benefit Plan Returns, must be filed. If the partnership return is filed electronically or on magnetic media, **Form 8453-P,** U.S. Partnership Declaration and Signature for Electronic and Magnetic Media Filing, must also be filed. For more details, see **Pub. 1524,** Procedures for Electronic and Magnetic Media Filing of Form 1065, U.S. Partnership Return of Income (Including the "Paper-Parent Option") for Tax Year 1997, and **Pub. 1525,** File Specifications, Validation Criteria, and Record Layouts for Electronic and Magnetic Media Filing of Form 1065, U.S. Partnership Return of Income (Including the "Paper-Parent Option"). To order these forms and publications, or for more information on electronic and magnetic media filing of Form 1065, call the Electronic Filing Section at the Andover Service Center at 978-474-9486 (not a toll-free number), or write to:

Internal Revenue Service Center
Electronic Filing Section, Stop 983
P.O. Box 4050
Woburn, MA 01889-4050

When To File

Generally, a domestic partnership must file Form 1065 by the 15th day of the 4th month following the date its tax year ended as shown at the top of Form 1065. A partnership whose partners are all nonresident aliens must file its return by the 15th day of the 6th month following the date its tax year ended. If the due date falls on a Saturday, Sunday, or legal holiday, file on the next business day. A business day is any day that is not a Saturday, Sunday, or legal holiday.

Private Delivery Services

You can use certain private delivery services designated by the IRS to meet the "timely mailing as timely filing/paying" rule for Form 1065. The IRS publishes a list of the designated private delivery services in September of each year. The list published in September 1997 includes only the following:

- Airborne Express (Airborne): Overnight Air Express Service, Next Afternoon Service, Second Day Service.
- DHL Worldwide Express (DHL): DHL "Same Day" Service, DHL USA Overnight.
- Federal Express (FedEx): FedEx Priority Overnight, FedEx Standard Overnight, FedEx 2Day.
- United Parcel Service (UPS): UPS Next Day Air, UPS Next Day Air Saver, UPS 2nd Day Air, UPS 2nd Day Air A.M.

The private delivery service can tell you how to get written proof of the mailing date.

Extension

If you need more time to file a partnership return, file **Form 8736,** Application for Automatic Extension of Time To File U.S. Return for a Partnership, REMIC, or for Certain Trusts, for an automatic 3-month extension. File Form 8736 by the regular due date of the partnership return.

If, after you have filed Form 8736, you still need more time to file the partnership return, file **Form 8800,** Application for Additional Extension of Time To File U.S. Return for a Partnership, REMIC, or for Certain Trusts, for an additional extension of up to 3 months. The partnership must show reasonable cause to get this additional extension. Form 8800 must be filed by the extended due date of the partnership return.

Period Covered

Form 1065 is an information return for calendar year 1997 and fiscal years beginning in 1997 and ending in 1998. If the return is for a fiscal year or a short tax year, fill in the tax year space at the top of the form.

The 1997 Form 1065 may also be used if:

1. The partnership has a tax year of less than 12 months that begins and ends in 1998; and

2. The 1998 Form 1065 is not available by the time the partnership is required to file its return.

However, the partnership must show its 1998 tax year on the 1997 Form 1065 and incorporate any tax law changes that are effective for tax years beginning after 1997.

Where To File

File Form 1065 at the applicable IRS address listed below.

If the partnership's principal business, office, or agency is located in	Use the following Internal Revenue Service Center address

New Jersey, New York (New York City and counties of Nassau, Rockland, Suffolk, and Westchester)	Holtsville, NY 00501-0011
New York (all other counties), Connecticut, Maine, Massachusetts, New Hampshire, Rhode Island, Vermont	Andover, MA 05501-0011
Florida, Georgia, South Carolina	Atlanta, GA 39901-0011
Indiana, Kentucky, Michigan, Ohio, West Virginia	Cincinnati, OH 45999-0011
Kansas, New Mexico, Oklahoma, Texas	Austin, TX 73301-0011
Alaska, Arizona, California (counties of Alpine, Amador, Butte, Calaveras, Colusa, Contra Costa, Del Norte, El Dorado, Glenn, Humboldt, Lake, Lassen, Marin, Mendocino, Modoc, Napa, Nevada, Placer, Plumas, Sacramento, San Joaquin, Shasta, Sierra, Siskiyou, Solano, Sonoma, Sutter, Tehama, Trinity, Yolo, and Yuba), Colorado, Idaho, Montana, Nebraska, Nevada, North Dakota, Oregon, South Dakota, Utah, Washington, Wyoming	Ogden, UT 84201-0011
California (all other counties), Hawaii	Fresno, CA 93888-0011
Illinois, Iowa, Minnesota, Missouri, Wisconsin	Kansas City, MO 64999-0011
Alabama, Arkansas, Louisiana, Mississippi, North Carolina, Tennessee	Memphis, TN 37501-0011
Delaware, District of Columbia, Maryland, Pennsylvania, Virginia	Philadelphia, PA 19255-0011

A partnership without a principal office or agency or principal place of business in the United States must file its return with the Internal Revenue Service Center, Philadelphia, PA 19255-0011.

Who Must Sign

General Partner or Limited Liability Company Member

Form 1065 is not considered to be a return unless it is signed. One general partner or limited liability company member must sign the return. If a receiver, trustee in bankruptcy, or assignee controls the organization's property or business, that person must sign the return.

Paid Preparer's Information

If someone prepares the return and does not charge the partnership, that person should not sign the partnership return.

Generally, anyone who is paid to prepare the partnership return must sign the return and fill in the other blanks in the **Paid Preparer's Use Only** area of the return.

The preparer required to sign the partnership return **must** complete the required preparer information and:

- Sign it, by hand, in the space provided for the preparer's signature. Signature stamps or labels are not acceptable.
- Give the partnership a copy of the return in addition to the copy to be filed with the IRS.

Penalties

Late Filing of Return

A penalty is assessed against the partnership if it is required to file a partnership return and it **(a)** fails to file the return by the due date, including extensions, or **(b)** files a return that fails to show all the information required, unless such failure is due to reasonable cause. If the failure is due to reasonable cause, attach an explanation to the partnership return. The penalty is $50 for each month or part of a month (for a maximum of 5 months) the failure continues, multiplied by the total number of persons who were partners in the partnership during any part of the partnership's tax year for which the return is due. This penalty will not be imposed on partnerships for which the answer to Question 4 on Schedule B of Form 1065 is **No,** provided all partners have timely filed income tax returns fully reporting their shares of the income, deductions, and credits of the partnership. See page 14 of the instructions for further information.

Failure To Furnish Information Timely

For each failure to furnish Schedule K-1 to a partner when due and each failure to include on Schedule K-1 all the information required to be shown (or the inclusion of incorrect information), a $50 penalty may be imposed with respect to each Schedule K-1 for which a failure occurs. The maximum penalty is

Page 3

$100,000 for all such failures during a calendar year. If the requirement to report correct information is intentionally disregarded, each $50 penalty is increased to $100 or, if greater, 10% of the aggregate amount of items required to be reported, and the $100,000 maximum does not apply.

Trust Fund Recovery Penalty

This penalty may apply if certain excise, income, social security, and Medicare taxes that must be collected or withheld are not collected or withheld, or these taxes are not paid to the IRS. These taxes are generally reported on Forms 720, 941, 943, or 945. The trust fund recovery penalty may be imposed on all persons who are determined by the IRS to have been **responsible** for collecting, accounting for, and paying over these taxes, and who acted willfully in not doing so. The penalty is equal to the unpaid trust fund tax. See the instructions for Form 720, **Pub. 15 (Circular E),** Employer's Tax Guide, or **Pub. 51 (Circular A),** Agricultural Employer's Tax Guide, for more details, including the definition of a responsible person.

Accounting Methods

Figure ordinary income using the method of accounting regularly used in keeping the partnership's books and records. Generally, permissible methods include the cash method, the accrual method, or any other method authorized by the Internal Revenue Code. In all cases, the method used must clearly reflect income.

Generally, a partnership may not use the cash method of accounting if **(a)** it has at least one corporate partner, average annual gross receipts of more than $5 million, and it is not a farming business or **(b)** it is a tax shelter (as defined in section 448(d)(3)). See section 448 for details.

Under the accrual method, an amount is includible in income when all the events have occurred that fix the right to receive the income and the amount can be determined with reasonable accuracy.

Generally, an accrual basis taxpayer can deduct accrued expenses in the tax year in which:

- All events that determine liability have occurred,
- The amount of the liability can be figured with reasonable accuracy, and
- Economic performance takes place with respect to the expense. There are exceptions for certain items, including recurring expenses.

Except for certain home construction contracts and other real property small construction contracts, long-term contracts must generally be accounted for using the percentage of completion method described in section 460.

Generally, the partnership may change its method of accounting used to report income (for income as a whole or for any material item) only by getting consent on **Form 3115,** Application for Change in Accounting Method. For more information, see **Pub. 538,** Accounting Periods and Methods.

Accounting Periods

A partnership is generally required to have one of the following tax years:

1. The tax year of a majority of its partners (majority tax year).

2. If there is no majority tax year, then the tax year common to all of the partnership's principal partners (partners with an interest of 5% or more in the partnership profits or capital).

3. If there is neither a majority tax year nor a tax year common to all principal partners, then the tax year that results in the least aggregate deferral of income.

4. Some other tax year, if:

- The partnership can establish that there is a business purpose for the tax year (see Rev. Proc. 87-32, 1987-2 C.B. 396); or
- The tax year is a "grandfathered" year (see Rev. Proc. 87-32); or
- The partnership elects under section 444 to have a tax year other than a required tax year by filing **Form 8716,** Election to Have a Tax Year Other Than a Required Tax Year. For a partnership to have this election in effect, it must make the payments required by section 7519 and file **Form 8752,** Required Payment or Refund Under Section 7519.

A section 444 election ends if a partnership changes its accounting period to its required tax year or some other permitted year or it is penalized for willfully failing to comply with the requirements of section 7519. If the termination results in a short tax year, type or legibly print at the top of the first page of Form 1065 for the short tax year, "SECTION 444 ELECTION TERMINATED."

To change an accounting period, see Pub. 538 and **Form 1128,** Application To Adopt, Change, or Retain a Tax Year (unless the partnership is making an election under section 444).

Note: *Under the provisions of section 584(h), the tax year of a common trust fund must be the calendar year.*

Rounding Off to Whole Dollars

You may round off cents to whole dollars on your return and accompanying schedules. To do so, drop amounts under 50 cents and increase amounts from 50 to 99 cents to the next higher dollar.

Recordkeeping

The partnership must keep its records as long as they may be needed for the administration of any provision of the Internal Revenue Code. If the consolidated audit procedures of sections 6221 through 6233 apply, the partnership usually must keep records that support an item of income, deduction, or credit on the partnership return for 3 years from the date the return is due or is filed, whichever is later. If the consolidated audit procedures do not apply, these records usually must be kept for 3 years from the date each partner's return is due or is filed, whichever is later. Keep records that verify the partnership's basis in property for as long as they are needed to figure the basis of the original or replacement property.

The partnership should also keep copies of all returns it has filed. They help in preparing future returns and in making computations when filing an amended return.

Amended Return

To correct an error on a Form 1065 already filed, file an amended Form 1065 and check box G(4) on page 1. If the income, deductions, credits, or other information provided to any partner on Schedule K-1 are incorrect, file an amended Schedule K-1 (Form 1065) for that partner with the amended Form 1065. Also give a copy of the amended Schedule K-1 to that partner. Be sure to check box I(2) on the Schedule K-1 to indicate that it is an amended Schedule K-1.

Exception: *If you are filing an amended partnership return and you answered* **Yes** *to Question 4 in Schedule B, the tax matters partner must file* **Form 8082,** *Notice of Inconsistent Treatment or Administrative Adjustment Request (AAR).*

A change to the partnership's Federal return may affect its state return. This includes changes made as a result of an examination of the partnership return by the IRS. For more information, contact the state tax agency for the state in which the partnership return is filed.

Other Forms That May Be Required

- **Forms W-2** and **W-3,** Wage and Tax Statement; and Transmittal of Wage and Tax Statements.

- **Form 720,** Quarterly Federal Excise Tax Return. Use Form 720 to report environmental excise taxes, communications and air transportation taxes, fuel taxes, luxury tax on passenger vehicles, manufacturers' taxes, ship passenger tax, and certain other excise taxes.

Caution: *See* **Trust Fund Recovery Penalty** *above.*

- **Form 940** or **Form 940-EZ,** Employer's Annual Federal Unemployment (FUTA) Tax Return. The partnership may be liable for FUTA tax and may have to file Form 940 or 940-EZ if it paid wages of $1,500 or more in any calendar quarter during the calendar year (or the preceding calendar year) or one or more employees worked for the partnership for some part of a day in any 20 different weeks during the calendar year (or the preceding calendar year).

- **Form 941,** Employer's Quarterly Federal Tax Return. Employers must file this form quarterly to report income tax withheld on wages and employer and employee social security and Medicare taxes. Agricultural employers must file **Form 943,** Employer's Annual Tax Return for Agricultural Employees, instead of Form 941, to report income tax withheld and employer and employee social security and Medicare taxes on farmworkers.

Caution: *See* **Trust Fund Recovery Penalty** *above.*

- **Form 945,** Annual Return of Withheld Federal Income Tax. Use this form to report income tax withheld from nonpayroll payments, including pensions, annuities, IRAs, gambling winnings, and backup withholding.

Caution: *See* **Trust Fund Recovery Penalty** *above.*

- **Forms 1042** and **1042-S,** Annual Withholding Tax Return for U.S. Source Income of Foreign Persons; and Foreign Person's U.S. Source Income Subject to Withholding. Use these forms to report and send withheld tax on payments or distributions made to nonresident alien individuals, foreign partnerships, or foreign corporations to the extent such payments or distributions constitute gross income from sources within the United States that is not effectively connected with a U.S. trade or business. A domestic partnership must also withhold tax on a foreign partner's distributive share of such income, including amounts that are not actually

Page 4

distributed. Withholding on amounts not previously distributed to a foreign partner must be made and paid over by the earlier of **(a)** the date on which Schedule K-1 is sent to that partner or **(b)** the 15th day of the 3rd month after the end of the partnership's tax year. For more information, see sections 1441 and 1442 and **Pub. 515**, Withholding of Tax on Nonresident Aliens and Foreign Corporations.

● **Form 1096,** Annual Summary and Transmittal of U.S. Information Returns.

● **Form 1098,** Mortgage Interest Statement. Use this form to report the receipt from any individual of $600 or more of mortgage interest and points in the course of the partnership's trade or business for any calendar year.

● **Forms 1099-A, B, INT, LTC, MISC, MSA, OID, R,** and **S.** You may have to file these information returns to report acquisitions or abandonments of secured property; proceeds from broker and barter exchange transactions; interest payments; payments of long-term care and accelerated death benefits; miscellaneous income payments; distributions from a medical savings account; original issue discount; distributions from pensions, annuities, retirement or profit-sharing plans, IRAs, insurance contracts, etc.; and proceeds from real estate transactions. Also, use certain of these returns to report amounts that were received as a nominee on behalf of another person.

For more information, see the Instructions for Forms 1099, 1098, 5498, and W-2G.

Important: *Every partnership must file Forms 1099-MISC if, in the course of its trade or business, it makes payments of rents, commissions, or other fixed or determinable income (see section 6041) totaling $600 or more to any one person during the calendar year.*

● **Form 5471,** Information Return of U.S. Persons With Respect to Certain Foreign Corporations. A partnership may have to file Form 5471 if it **(a)** controls a foreign corporation; or **(b)** acquires, disposes of, or owns 5% or more in value of the outstanding stock of a foreign corporation; or **(c)** owns stock in a corporation that is a controlled foreign corporation for an uninterrupted period of 30 days or more during any tax year of the foreign corporation, and it owned that stock on the last day of that year.

● **Form 5713,** International Boycott Report, is used by persons having operations in, or related to, a "boycotting" country, company, or national of a country, to report those operations and figure the loss of certain tax benefits. The partnership must give each partner a copy of the Form 5713 filed by the partnership if there has been participation in, or cooperation with, an international boycott.

● **Form 8264,** Application for Registration of a Tax Shelter. Tax shelter organizers must file Form 8264 to get a tax shelter registration number from the IRS.

● **Form 8271,** Investor Reporting of Tax Shelter Registration Number. Partnerships that have acquired an interest in a tax shelter that is required to be registered use Form 8271 to report the tax shelter's registration number. Attach Form 8271 to any return on which a deduction, credit, loss, or other tax benefit attributable to a tax shelter is taken or any income attributable to a tax shelter is reported.

● **Form 8275,** Disclosure Statement. File Form 8275 to disclose items or positions, except those contrary to a regulation, that are not otherwise adequately disclosed on a tax return. The disclosure is made to avoid the parts of the accuracy-related penalty imposed for disregard of rules or substantial understatement of tax. Form 8275 is also used for disclosures relating to preparer penalties for understatements due to unrealistic positions or disregard of rules.

● **Form 8275-R,** Regulation Disclosure Statement, is used to disclose any item on a tax return for which a position has been taken that is contrary to Treasury regulations.

● **Forms 8288** and **8288-A,** U.S. Withholding Tax Return for Dispositions by Foreign Persons of U.S. Real Property Interests; and Statement of Withholding on Dispositions by Foreign Persons of U.S. Real Property Interests. Use these forms to report and send withheld tax on the sale of U.S. real property by a foreign person. See section 1445 and the related regulations for additional information.

● **Form 8300,** Report of Cash Payments Over $10,000 Received in a Trade or Business. File this form to report the receipt of more than $10,000 in cash or foreign currency in one transaction or a series of related transactions.

● **Form 8594,** Asset Acquisition Statement. Both the purchaser and seller of a group of assets constituting a trade or business must file this form if section 197 intangibles attach, or could attach, to such assets and if the purchaser's basis in the assets is determined only by the amount paid for the assets.

● **Form 8697,** Interest Computation Under the Look-Back Method for Completed Long-Term Contracts. Partnerships that are not closely held use this form to figure the interest due or to be refunded under the look-back method of section 460(b)(2) on certain long-term contracts that are accounted for under either the percentage of completion-capitalized cost method or the percentage of completion method. Closely held partnerships should see the instructions on page 22 for line 25, item 10, of Schedule K-1 for details on the Form 8697 information they must provide to their partners.

● **Forms 8804, 8805,** and **8813,** Annual Return for Partnership Withholding Tax (Section 1446); Foreign Partner's Information Statement of Section 1446 Withholding Tax; and Partnership Withholding Tax Payment (Section 1446). File Forms 8804 and 8805 if the partnership had effectively connected gross income and foreign partners for the tax year. Use Form 8813 to send installment payments of withheld tax based on effectively connected taxable income allocable to foreign partners.

Exception: *Publicly traded partnerships that do not elect to pay tax based on effectively connected taxable income do not file these forms. They must instead withhold tax on distributions to foreign partners and report and send payments using Forms 1042 and 1042-S. See section 1446 for more information.*

● **Form 8832,** Entity Classification Election. Except for a business entity automatically classified as a corporation, a business entity with at least two members may choose to be classified either as a partnership or an association taxable as a corporation. A domestic eligible entity with at least two members that does not file Form 8832 is classified under the default rules as a partnership. However, a foreign eligible entity with at least two members is classified under the default rules as a partnership only if at least one member does not have limited liability. File Form 8832 **only** if the entity does not want to be classified under these default rules or if it wants to change its classification.

Attachments

Attach schedules in alphabetical order and other forms in numerical order after Form 1065.

To assist us in processing the return, complete every applicable entry space on Form 1065 and Schedule K-1. **If you attach statements, do not write "See attached" instead of completing the entry spaces on the forms. Penalties may be assessed if the partnership files an incomplete return.**

If you need more space on the forms or schedules, attach separate sheets. Use the same size and format as on the printed forms. **But show your totals on the printed forms.** Be sure to put the partnership's name and employer identification number (EIN) on each sheet.

Separately Stated Items

Partners are required to take into account separately (under section 702(a)) their distributive shares of the following items (whether or not they are actually distributed):

1. Ordinary income or loss from trade or business activities.

2. Net income or loss from rental real estate activities.

3. Net income or loss from other rental activities.

4. Gains and losses from sales or exchanges of capital assets.

5. Gains and losses from sales or exchanges of property described in section 1231.

6. Charitable contributions.

7. Dividends (passed through to corporate partners) that qualify for the dividends-received deduction.

8. Taxes described in section 901 paid or accrued to foreign countries and to possessions of the United States.

9. Other items of income, gain, loss, deduction, or credit, to the extent provided by regulations. Examples of such items include nonbusiness expenses, intangible drilling and development costs, and soil and water conservation expenditures.

Elections Made by the Partnership

Generally, the partnership decides how to figure taxable income from its operations. For example, it chooses the accounting method and depreciation methods it will use. The partnership also makes elections under the following sections:

1. Section 179 (election to expense certain tangible property).

2. Section 614 (definition of property— mines, wells, and other natural deposits). This election must be made before the partners figure their individual depletion allowances under section 613A(c)(7)(D).

3. Section 1033 (involuntary conversions).

4. Section 754 (manner of electing optional adjustment to basis of partnership property).

Under section 754, a partnership may elect to adjust the basis of partnership property when property is distributed or when a partnership interest is transferred. If the election is made with respect to a transfer of a partnership interest (section 743(b)) and the assets of the partnership constitute a trade or business for purposes of section 1060(c), then the value of any goodwill transferred must be determined in the manner provided in Temporary Regulations section 1.1060-1T. Once an election is made under section 754, it applies both to all distributions and to all transfers made during the tax year and in all subsequent tax years unless the election is revoked. See Regulations section 1.754-1(c).

This election must be made in a statement that is filed with the partnership's timely filed return (including any extension) for the tax year during which the distribution or transfer occurs. The statement must include:

• The name and address of the partnership.

• A declaration that the partnership elects under section 754 to apply the provisions of section 734(b) and section 743(b).

• The signature of the general partner authorized to sign the partnership return.

The partnership can get an automatic 12-month extension to make the section 754 election provided corrective action is taken within 12 months of the original deadline for making the election. For details, see Temporary Regulations section 301.9100-2T.

See section 754 and the related regulations for more information.

If there is a distribution of property consisting of an interest in another partnership, see section 734(b).

Elections Made by Each Partner

Elections under the following sections are made by each partner separately on the partner's tax return:

1. Section 59(e) (election to deduct ratably certain qualified expenditures such as intangible drilling costs, mining exploration expenses, or research and experimental expenditures).

2. Section 108 (income from discharge of indebtedness).

3. Section 617 (deduction and recapture of certain mining exploration expenditures paid or incurred).

4. Section 901 (foreign tax credit).

Partner's Dealings With Partnership

If a partner engages in a transaction with his or her partnership, other than in his or her capacity as a partner, the partner is treated as not being a member of the partnership for that transaction. Special rules apply to sales or exchanges of property between partnerships and certain persons, as explained in Pub. 541.

Contributions to the Partnership

Generally, no gain (loss) is recognized to the partnership or any of the partners when property is contributed to the partnership in exchange for an interest in the partnership. This rule does not apply to any gain realized on a transfer of property to a partnership that would be treated as an investment company (within the meaning of section 351) if the partnership were incorporated. If, as a result of a transfer of property to a partnership, there is a direct or indirect transfer of money or other property to the transferring partner, the partner may have to recognize gain on the exchange.

The basis to the partnership of property contributed by a partner is the adjusted basis in the hands of the partner at the time it was contributed, plus any gain recognized (under section 721(b)) by the partner at that time. See section 723 for more information.

Dispositions of Contributed Property

If the partnership disposes of property contributed to the partnership by a partner, income, gain, loss, and deductions from that property must be allocated among the partners to take into account the difference between the property's basis and its fair market value at the time of the contribution.

For property contributed to the partnership, the contributing partner must recognize gain or loss on a distribution of the property to another partner within 5 years of being contributed. For property contributed after June 8, 1997, the 5-year period is generally extended to 7 years. The gain or loss is equal to the amount that the contributing partner should have recognized if the property had been sold for its fair market value when distributed, because of the difference between the property's basis and its fair market value at the time of contribution.

See section 704(c) for details and other rules on dispositions of contributed property. See section 724 for the character of any gain or loss recognized on the disposition of unrealized receivables, inventory items, or capital loss property contributed to the partnership by a partner.

Recognition of Precontribution Gain on Certain Partnership Distributions

A partner who contributes appreciated property to the partnership must include in income any precontribution gain to the extent the fair market value of other property (other than money) distributed to the partner by the partnership exceeds the adjusted basis of his or her partnership interest just before the distribution. Precontribution gain is the net gain, if any, that would have been recognized under section 704(c)(1)(B) if the partnership had distributed to another partner all the property that had been contributed to the partnership by the distributee partner within 5 years of the distribution and that was held by the partnership just before the distribution. For property contributed after June 8, 1997, the 5-year period is generally extended to 7 years.

Appropriate basis adjustments are to be made to the adjusted basis of the distributee partner's interest in the partnership and the partnership's basis in the contributed property to reflect the gain recognized by the partner.

For more details and exceptions, see section 737.

Unrealized Receivables and Inventory Items

Generally, if a partner sells or exchanges a partnership interest where unrealized receivables or inventory items are involved, the transferor partner must notify the partnership, in writing, within 30 days of the exchange. The partnership must then file **Form 8308,** Report of a Sale or Exchange of Certain Partnership Interests. For sales or exchanges before August 6, 1997 (or those made under a written binding contract in effect on June 8, 1997, and at all times thereafter), the inventory items also must have been substantially appreciated.

If a partnership distributes unrealized receivables or substantially appreciated inventory items in exchange for all or part of a partner's interest in other partnership property (including money), treat the transaction as a sale or exchange between the partner and the partnership. Treat the partnership gain (loss) as ordinary income (loss). The income (loss) is specially allocated only to partners other than the distributee partner.

If a partnership gives other property (including money) for all or part of that partner's interest in the partnership's unrealized receivables or substantially appreciated inventory items, treat the transaction as a sale or exchange of the property.

See Rev. Rul. 84-102, 1984-2 C.B. 119, for information on the tax consequences that result when a new partner joins a partnership that has liabilities and unrealized receivables. Also, see Pub. 541 for more information on unrealized receivables and inventory items.

Passive Activity Limitations

In general, section 469 limits the amount of losses, deductions, and credits that partners may claim from "passive activities." The passive activity limitations do not apply to the partnership. Instead, they apply to each partner's share of any income or loss and credit attributable to a passive activity. Because the treatment of each partner's share of partnership income or loss and credit depends on the nature of the activity that generated it, the partnership must report income or loss and credits separately for each activity.

The instructions below (pages 6-9) and the instructions for Schedules K and K-1 (pages 15-22) explain the applicable passive activity limitation rules and specify the type of information the partnership must provide to its partners for each activity. If the partnership has more than one activity, it must report information for each activity on an attachment to Schedules K and K-1.

Generally, passive activities include **(a)** activities that involve the conduct of a trade or business if the partner does not materially participate in the activity; and **(b)** all rental activities (defined on page 7), regardless of the partner's participation. For exceptions, see **Activities That Are Not Passive Activities** on page 7. The level of each partner's participation in an activity must be determined by the partner.

The passive activity rules provide that losses and credits from passive activities can generally be applied only against income and tax from passive activities. Thus, passive losses and credits cannot be applied against income from salaries, wages, professional fees, or a business in which the taxpayer materially participates; against "portfolio income" (defined on page 8); or against the tax related to any of these types of income.

Special provisions apply to certain activities. First, the passive activity limitations must be applied separately with respect to a net loss from passive activities held through a publicly traded partnership. Second, special rules require that net income from certain activities that would otherwise be treated as passive income must be recharacterized as nonpassive income for purposes of the passive activity limitations.

To allow each partner to correctly apply the passive activity limitations, the partnership must report income or loss and credits separately for each of the following types of activities and income: trade or business activities, rental real estate activities, rental activities other than rental real estate, and portfolio income.

Activities That Are Not Passive Activities

Passive activities **do not** include:

1. Trade or business activities in which the partner materially participated for the tax year.

2. Any rental real estate activity in which the partner materially participated and met both of the following conditions for the tax year:

a. More than half of the personal services the partner performed in trades or businesses were performed in real property trades or businesses in which he or she materially participated, and

b. The partner performed more than 750 hours of services in real property trades or businesses in which he or she materially participated.

Note: *For a partner that is a closely held C corporation (defined in section 465(a)(1)(B)), the above conditions are treated as met if more than 50% of the corporation's gross receipts are from real property trades or businesses in which the corporation materially participated.*

For purposes of this rule, each interest in rental real estate is a separate activity, unless the partner elects to treat all interests in rental real estate as one activity.

If the partner is married filing jointly, either the partner or his or her spouse must separately meet both of the above conditions, without taking into account services performed by the other spouse.

A real property trade or business is any real property development, redevelopment, construction, reconstruction, acquisition, conversion, rental, operation, management, leasing, or brokerage trade or business. Services the partner performed as an employee are not treated as performed in a real property trade or business unless he or she owned more than 5% of the stock (or more than 5% of the capital or profits interest) in the employer.

3. An interest in an oil or gas well drilled or operated under a working interest if at any time during the tax year the partner held the working interest directly or through an entity that did not limit the partner's liability (e.g., an interest as a general partner). This exception applies regardless of whether the partner materially participated for the tax year.

4. The rental of a dwelling unit used by a partner for personal purposes during the year for more than the greater of 14 days or 10% of the number of days that the residence was rented at fair rental value.

5. An activity of trading personal property for the account of owners of interests in the activity. See Temporary Regulations section 1.469-1T(e)(6).

Trade or Business Activities

A trade or business activity is an activity (other than a rental activity or an activity treated as incidental to an activity of holding property for investment) that:

1. Involves the conduct of a trade or business (within the meaning of section 162),

2. Is conducted in anticipation of starting a trade or business, or

3. Involves research or experimental expenditures deductible under section 174 (or that would be if you chose to deduct rather than capitalize them).

If the partner does not materially participate in the activity, a trade or business activity held through a partnership is generally a passive activity of the partner.

Each partner must determine if he or she materially participated in an activity. As a result, while the partnership's overall trade or business income (loss) is reported on page 1 of Form 1065, the specific income and deductions from each separate trade or business activity must be reported on attachments to Form 1065. Similarly, while each partner's allocable share of the partnership's overall trade or business income (loss) is reported on line 1 of Schedule K-1, each partner's allocable share of the income and deductions from each trade or business activity must be reported on attachments to each Schedule K-1. See **Passive Activity Reporting Requirements** on page 9 for more information.

Rental Activities

Generally, except as noted below, if the gross income from an activity consists of amounts paid principally for the use of real or personal tangible property held by the partnership, the activity is a rental activity.

There are several exceptions to this general rule. Under these exceptions, an activity involving the use of real or personal tangible property is not a rental activity if any of the following apply:

• The average period of customer use (defined below) for such property is 7 days or less.

• The average period of customer use for such property is 30 days or less and significant personal services (defined below) are provided by or on behalf of the partnership.

• Extraordinary personal services (defined below) are provided by or on behalf of the partnership.

• The rental of such property is treated as incidental to a nonrental activity of the partnership under Temporary Regulations section 1.469-1T(e)(3)(vi) and Regulations section 1.469-1(e)(3)(vi).

• The partnership customarily makes the property available during defined business hours for nonexclusive use by various customers.

• The partnership provides property for use in a nonrental activity of a partnership or joint venture in its capacity as an owner of an interest in such partnership or joint venture. Whether the partnership provides property used in an activity of another partnership or of a joint venture in the partnership's capacity as an owner of an interest in the partnership or joint venture is determined on the basis of all the facts and circumstances.

In addition, a guaranteed payment described in section 707(c) is not income from a rental activity under any circumstances.

Average period of customer use. Figure the average period of customer use for a class of property by dividing the total number of days in all rental periods by the number of rentals during the tax year. If the activity involves renting more than one class of property, multiply the average period of customer use of each class by the ratio of the gross rental income from that class to the activity's total gross rental income. The activity's average period of customer use equals the sum of these class-by-class average periods weighted by gross income. See Regulations section 1.469-1(e)(3)(iii).

Significant personal services. Personal services include only services performed by individuals. In determining whether personal services are significant personal services, consider all the relevant facts and circumstances. Relevant facts and circumstances include how often the services are provided, the type and amount of labor required to perform the services, and the value of the services in relation to the amount charged for use of the property.

The following services are not considered in determining whether personal services are significant:

• Services necessary to permit the lawful use of the rental property.

• Services performed in connection with improvements or repairs to the rental property that extend the useful life of the property substantially beyond the average rental period.

• Services provided in connection with the use of any improved real property that are similar to those commonly provided in connection with long-term rentals of high-grade commercial or residential property. Examples include cleaning and maintenance of common areas, routine repairs, trash collection, elevator service, and security at entrances.

Extraordinary personal services. Services provided in connection with making rental property available for customer use are extraordinary personal services only if the services are performed by individuals and the customers' use of the rental property is incidental to their receipt of the services.

For example, a patient's use of a hospital room generally is incidental to the care received from the hospital's medical staff. Similarly, a student's use of a dormitory room in a boarding school is incidental to the personal services provided by the school's teaching staff.

Rental activity incidental to a nonrental activity. An activity is not a rental activity if the rental of the property is incidental to a nonrental activity, such as the activity of holding property for investment, a trade or business activity, or the activity of dealing in property.

Rental of property is incidental to an activity of holding property for investment if both of the following apply:

• The main purpose for holding the property is to realize a gain from the appreciation of the property.

• The gross rental income from such property for the tax year is less than 2% of the smaller of the property's unadjusted basis or its fair market value.

Rental of property is incidental to a trade or business activity if all of the following apply:

• The partnership owns an interest in the trade or business at all times during the year.

• The rental property was mainly used in the trade or business activity during the tax year or during at least 2 of the 5 preceding tax years

• The gross rental income from the property for the tax year is less than 2% of the smaller of the property's unadjusted basis or its fair market value.

The sale or exchange of property that is both rented and sold or exchanged during the tax year (where the gain or loss is recognized) is treated as incidental to the activity of dealing in property if, at the time of the sale or exchange, the property was held primarily for sale to customers in the ordinary course of the partnership's trade or business.

See Temporary Regulations section 1.469-1T(e)(3) and Regulations section 1.469-1(e)(3) for more information on the definition of rental activities for purposes of the passive activity limitations.

Reporting of rental activities. In reporting the partnership's income or losses and credits from rental activities, the partnership must separately report rental real estate activities and rental activities other than rental real estate activities.

Partners who actively participate in a rental real estate activity may be able to deduct part or all of their rental real estate losses (and the deduction equivalent of rental real estate credits) against income (or tax) from nonpassive activities. The combined amount of rental real estate losses and the deduction equivalent of rental real estate credits from all sources (including rental real estate activities not held through the partnership) that may be claimed is limited to $25,000. This $25,000 amount is generally reduced for high-income partners.

Report rental real estate activity income (loss) on **Form 8825,** Rental Real Estate Income and Expenses of a Partnership or an S Corporation, and line 2 of Schedules K and K-1 rather than on page 1 of Form 1065. Report credits related to rental real estate activities on lines 12b and 12c and low-income housing credits on line 12a of Schedules K and K-1.

Report income (loss) from rental activities other than rental real estate on line 3 and credits related to rental activities other than rental real estate on line 12d of Schedules K and K-1.

Portfolio Income

Generally, portfolio income includes all gross income, other than income derived in the ordinary course of a trade or business, that is attributable to interest; dividends; royalties; income from a real estate investment trust, a regulated investment company, a real estate mortgage investment conduit, a common trust fund, a controlled foreign corporation, a qualified electing fund, or a cooperative; income from the disposition of property that produces income of a type defined as portfolio income; and income from the disposition of property held for investment.

Solely for purposes of the preceding paragraph, gross income derived in the ordinary course of a trade or business includes (and portfolio income, therefore, does not include) only the following types of income:

● Interest income on loans and investments made in the ordinary course of a trade or business of lending money.

● Interest on accounts receivable arising from the performance of services or the sale of property in the ordinary course of a trade or business of performing such services or selling such property, but only if credit is customarily offered to customers of the business.

● Income from investments made in the ordinary course of a trade or business of furnishing insurance or annuity contracts or reinsuring risks underwritten by insurance companies.

● Income or gain derived in the ordinary course of an activity of trading or dealing in any property if such activity constitutes a trade or business (unless the dealer held the property for investment at any time before such income or gain is recognized).

● Royalties derived by the taxpayer in the ordinary course of a trade or business of licensing intangible property.

● Amounts included in the gross income of a patron of a cooperative by reason of any payment or allocation to the patron based on patronage occurring with respect to a trade or business of the patron.

● Other income identified by the IRS as income derived by the taxpayer in the ordinary course of a trade or business.

See Temporary Regulations section 1.469-2T(c)(3) for more information on portfolio income.

Report portfolio income on line 4 of Schedules K and K-1, rather than on page 1 of Form 1065. Report deductions related to portfolio income on line 10 of Schedules K and K-1.

Grouping Activities

Generally, one or more trade or business activities or rental activities may be treated as a single activity if the activities make up an appropriate economic unit for the measurement of gain or loss under the passive activity rules. Whether activities make up an appropriate economic unit depends on all the relevant facts and circumstances. The factors given the greatest weight in determining whether activities make up an appropriate economic unit are:

● Similarities and differences in types of trades or businesses.

● The extent of common control.

● The extent of common ownership.

● Geographical location.

● Reliance between or among the activities.

Example: The partnership has a significant ownership interest in a bakery and a movie theater in Baltimore and a bakery and a movie theater in Philadelphia. Depending on the relevant facts and circumstances, there may be more than one reasonable method for grouping the partnership's activities. For instance, the following groupings may or may not be permissible: a single activity, a movie theater activity and a bakery activity, a Baltimore activity and a Philadelphia activity, or four separate activities.

Once the partnership chooses a grouping under these rules, it must continue using that grouping in later tax years unless a material change in the facts and circumstances makes it clearly inappropriate.

The IRS may regroup the partnership's activities if the partnership's grouping fails to reflect one or more appropriate economic units and one of the primary purposes of the grouping is to avoid the passive activity limitations.

Limitation on grouping certain activities. The following activities may not be grouped together:

1. A rental activity with a trade or business activity unless the activities being grouped together make up an appropriate economic unit, and

a. The rental activity is insubstantial relative to the trade or business activity or vice versa, or

b. Each owner of the trade or business activity has the same proportionate ownership interest in the rental activity. If so, the portion of the rental activity involving the rental of property to be used in the trade or business activity may be grouped with the trade or business activity.

2. An activity involving the rental of real property with an activity involving the rental of personal property (except for personal property provided in connection with the real property or vice versa).

3. Any activity with another activity in a different type of business and in which the partnership holds an interest as a limited partner or as a limited entrepreneur (as defined in section 464(e)(2)) if that other activity engages in holding, producing, or distributing motion picture films or videotapes; farming; leasing section 1245 property; or exploring for (or exploiting) oil and gas resources or geothermal deposits.

Activities conducted through other partnerships. Once a partnership determines its activities under these rules, the partnership as a partner may use these rules to group those activities with each other, with activities conducted directly by the partnership, and with activities conducted through other partnerships. A partner may not treat as separate activities those activities grouped together by a partnership.

Recharacterization of Passive Income

Under Temporary Regulations section 1.469-2T(f) and Regulations section 1.469-2(f), net passive income from certain passive activities must be treated as nonpassive income. Net passive income is the excess of an activity's passive activity gross income over its passive activity deductions (current year deductions and prior year unallowed losses).

Income from the following six sources is subject to recharacterization. Note that any net passive income recharacterized as nonpassive income is treated as investment income for purposes of figuring investment interest expense limitations if it is from **(a)** an activity of renting substantially nondepreciable property from an equity-financed lending activity or **(b)** an activity related to an interest in a pass-through entity that licenses intangible property.

1. Significant participation passive activities. A significant participation passive activity is any trade or business activity in which the partner both participates for more than 100 hours during the tax year and does not materially participate. Because each partner must determine the partner's level of participation, the partnership will not be able to identify significant participation passive activities.

2. Certain nondepreciable rental property activities. Net passive income from a rental activity is nonpassive income if less than 30% of the unadjusted basis of the property used or held for use by customers in the activity is subject to depreciation under section 167.

3. Passive equity-financed lending activities. If the partnership has net income from a passive equity-financed lending activity, the smaller of the net passive income or the

Page 8

equity-financed interest income from the activity is nonpassive income.

Note: *The amount of income from the activities in paragraphs 1 through 3 that any partner will be required to recharacterize as nonpassive income may be limited under Temporary Regulations section 1.469-2T(f)(8). Because the partnership will not have information regarding all of a partner's activities, it must identify all partnership activities meeting the definitions in paragraphs 2 and 3 as activities that may be subject to recharacterization.*

4. Rental of property incidental to a development activity. Net rental activity income is nonpassive income for a partner if all of the following apply: **(a)** the partnership recognizes gain from the sale, exchange, or other disposition of the rental property during the tax year; **(b)** the use of the item of property in the rental activity started less than 12 months before the date of disposition (the use of an item of rental property begins on the first day that (i) the partnership owns an interest in the property; (ii) substantially all of the property is either rented or held out for rent and ready to be rented; and (iii) no significant value-enhancing services remain to be performed); and **(c)** the partner materially participated or significantly participated for any tax year in an activity that involved the performance of services for the purpose of enhancing the value of the property (or any other item of property, if the basis of the property disposed of is determined in whole or in part by reference to the basis of that item of property). "Net rental activity income" means the excess of passive activity gross income from renting or disposing of property over passive activity deductions (current year deductions and prior year unallowed losses) that are reasonably allocable to the rented property.

Because the partnership cannot determine a partner's level of participation, the partnership must identify net income from property described in items **(a)** and **(b)** of paragraph **4** as income that may be subject to recharacterization.

5. Rental of property to a nonpassive activity. If a taxpayer rents property to a trade or business activity in which the taxpayer materially participates, the taxpayer's net rental activity income from the property is nonpassive income.

6. Acquisition of an interest in a pass-through entity that licenses intangible property. Generally, net royalty income from intangible property is nonpassive income if the taxpayer acquired an interest in the pass-through entity after the pass-through entity created the intangible property or performed substantial services, or incurred substantial costs in developing or marketing the intangible property. "Net royalty income" means the excess of passive activity gross income from licensing or transferring any right in intangible property over passive activity deductions (current year deductions and prior year unallowed losses) that are reasonably allocable to the intangible property.

See Temporary Regulations section 1.469-2T(f)(7)(iii) for exceptions to this rule.

Passive Activity Reporting Requirements

To allow partners to correctly apply the passive activity loss and credit rules, any partnership that carries on more than one activity must:

1. Provide an attachment for each activity conducted through the partnership that identifies the type of activity conducted (trade or business, rental real estate, rental activity other than rental real estate, or investment).

2. On the attachment for each activity, provide a schedule, using the same line numbers as shown on Schedule K-1, detailing the net income (loss), credits, and all items required to be separately stated under section 702(a) from each trade or business activity, from each rental real estate activity, from each rental activity other than a rental real estate activity, and from investments.

3. Identify the net income (loss) and credits from each oil or gas well drilled or operated under a working interest that any partner (other than a partner whose only interest in the partnership during the year is as a limited partner) holds through the partnership. Further, if any partner had an interest as a general partner in the partnership during less than the entire year, the partnership must identify both the disqualified deductions from each well that the partner must treat as passive activity deductions, and the ratable portion of the gross income from each well that the partner must treat as passive activity gross income.

4. Identify the net income (loss) and the partner's share of partnership interest expense from each activity of renting a dwelling unit that any partner uses for personal purposes during the year for more than the greater of 14 days or 10% of the number of days that the residence is rented at fair rental value.

5. Identify the net income (loss) and the partner's share of partnership interest expense from each activity of trading personal property conducted through the partnership.

6. For any gain (loss) from the disposition of an interest in an activity or of an interest in property used in an activity (including dispositions before 1987 from which gain is being recognized after 1986):

a. Identify the activity in which the property was used at the time of disposition.

b. If the property was used in more than one activity during the 12 months preceding the disposition, identify the activities in which the property was used and the adjusted basis allocated to each activity.

c. For gains only, if the property was substantially appreciated at the time of the disposition and the applicable holding period specified in Regulations section 1.469-2(c)(2)(iii)(A) was not satisfied, identify the amount of the nonpassive gain and indicate whether the gain is investment income under the provisions of Regulations section 1.469-2(c)(2)(iii)(F).

7. Specify the amount of gross portfolio income, the interest expense properly allocable to portfolio income, and expenses other than interest expense that are clearly and directly allocable to portfolio income.

8. Identify separately any of the following types of payments to partners:

a. Payments to a partner for services other than in the partner's capacity as a partner under section 707(a).

b. Guaranteed payments to a partner for services under section 707(c).

c. Guaranteed payments for use of capital.

d. If section 736(a)(2) payments are made for unrealized receivables or for goodwill, the amount of the payments and the activities to which the payments are attributable.

e. If section 736(b) payments are made, the amount of the payments and the activities to which the payments are attributable.

9. Identify the ratable portion of any section 481 adjustment (whether a net positive or a net negative adjustment) allocable to each partnership activity.

10. Identify the amount of gross income from each oil or gas property of the partnership.

11. Identify any gross income from sources that are specifically excluded from passive activity gross income, including:

a. Income from intangible property if the partner is an individual and the partner's personal efforts significantly contributed to the creation of the property.

b. Income from state, local, or foreign income tax refunds.

c. Income from a covenant not to compete (in the case of a partner who is an individual and who contributed the covenant to the partnership).

12. Identify any deductions that are not passive activity deductions.

13. If the partnership makes a full or partial disposition of its interest in another entity, identify the gain (loss) allocable to each activity conducted through the entity, and the gain allocable to a passive activity that would have been recharacterized as nonpassive gain had the partnership disposed of its interest in property used in the activity (because the property was substantially appreciated at the time of the disposition, and the gain represented more than 10% of the partner's total gain from the disposition).

14. Identify the following items from activities that may be subject to the recharacterization rules under Temporary Regulations section 1.469-2T(f) and Regulations section 1.469-2(f):

a. Net income from an activity of renting substantially nondepreciable property.

b. The smaller of equity-financed interest income or net passive income from an equity-financed lending activity.

c. Net rental activity income from property that was developed (by the partner or the partnership), rented, and sold within 12 months after the rental of the property commenced.

d. Net rental activity income from the rental of property by the partnership to a trade or business activity in which the partner had an interest (either directly or indirectly).

e. Net royalty income from intangible property if the partner acquired the partner's interest in the partnership after the partnership created the intangible property or performed substantial services, or incurred substantial costs in developing or marketing the intangible property.

15. Identify separately the credits from each activity conducted by or through the partnership.

Specific Instructions

These instructions follow the line numbers on the first page of Form 1065 and on the schedules that accompany it. Specific instructions for most of the lines are provided on the following pages. Lines that are not discussed in the instructions are self-explanatory.

Fill in all applicable lines and schedules.

Enter any items specially allocated to the partners on the appropriate line of the applicable partner's Schedule K-1. Enter the total amount on the appropriate line of Schedule K. **Do not** enter separately stated amounts on the numbered lines on Form 1065, page 1, or on Schedule A or D.

Be sure to file all four pages of Form 1065. However, if the answer to Question 5 of Schedule B is **Yes**, the completion of page 4 is optional. Also attach a Schedule K-1 to Form 1065 for each partner.

File only one Form 1065 for each partnership. Mark "duplicate copy" on any copy you give to a partner.

If a syndicate, pool, joint venture, or similar group files Form 1065, it must attach a copy of the agreement and all amendments to the return, unless a copy has previously been filed.

General Information

Name, Address, and Employer Identification Number

Use the label that was mailed to the partnership. Cross out any errors and print the correct information on the label.

Name. If the partnership did not receive a label, print or type the legal name of the partnership as it appears in the partnership agreement.

Address. Include the suite, room, or other unit number after the street address. If a preaddressed label is used, include this information on the label.

If the Post Office does not deliver mail to the street address and the partnership has a P.O. box, show the box number instead of the street address.

If the partnership has had a change of address, check box G(3).

If the partnership's address is outside the United States or its possessions or territories, enter the information on the line for "City or town, state, and ZIP code" in the following order: city, province or state, and the name of the foreign country. Follow the foreign country's practice in placing the postal code in the address. **Do not** abbreviate the country name.

If the partnership changes its mailing address after filing its return, it can notify the IRS by filing **Form 8822,** Change of Address.

Employer identification number (EIN). Show the correct EIN in item D on page 1 of Form 1065. If the partnership does not have an EIN, it must apply for one on **Form SS-4,** Application for Employer Identification Number. Form SS-4 has information on how to apply for an EIN by mail or by telephone. If the partnership has not received its EIN by the time the return is due, write "Applied for" in the space for the EIN. See **Pub. 583,** Starting a Business and Keeping Records, for more information.

Do not request a new EIN for a partnership that terminated because of a sale or exchange of at least 50% of the total interests in partnership capital and profits.

Items A and C

Enter the applicable activity name and code number from the list on page 24.

For example, if, as its principal business activity, the partnership **(a)** purchases raw materials, **(b)** subcontracts out for labor to make a finished product from the raw materials, and **(c)** retains title to the goods, the partnership is considered to be a manufacturer and must enter "Manufacturer" in item A and enter in item C one of the codes (2000 through 3970) listed under "Manufacturing" on page 24.

You are not required to complete item C if the business code on the label is correct.

Item F—Total Assets

You are not required to complete item F if the answer to Question 5 of Schedule B is **Yes.**

If you are required to complete this item, enter the partnership's total assets at the end of the tax year, as determined by the accounting method regularly used in keeping the partnership's books and records. If there were no assets at the end of the tax year, enter the total assets as of the beginning of the tax year.

Item G

Do not check "Final return" (box G(2)) for a partnership that terminated because of a sale or exchange of at least 50% of the total interests in partnership capital and profits.

Income

Caution: *Report only trade or business activity income on lines 1a through 8. **Do not report rental activity income or portfolio income on these lines.** See the instructions on **Passive Activity Limitations** beginning on page 6 for definitions of rental income and portfolio income. Rental activity income and portfolio income are reported on Schedules K and K-1. Rental real estate activities are also reported on Form 8825.*

Do not include any tax-exempt income on lines 1a through 8. A partnership that receives any tax-exempt income other than interest, or holds any property or engages in any activity that produces tax-exempt income reports the amount of this income on line 20 of Schedules K and K-1.

Report tax-exempt interest income, including exempt-interest dividends received as a shareholder in a mutual fund or other regulated investment company, on line 19 of Schedules K and K-1.

See **Deductions** on page 11 for information on how to report expenses related to tax-exempt income.

If the partnership has had debt discharged resulting from a title 11 bankruptcy proceeding or while insolvent, see **Form 982,** Reduction of Tax Attributes Due to Discharge of Indebtedness, and **Pub. 908,** Bankruptcy Tax Guide.

Line 1a—Gross Receipts or Sales

Enter the gross receipts or sales from all trade or business operations except those that must be reported on lines 4 through 7. For example, do not include gross receipts from farming on this line. Instead, show the net profit (loss) from farming on line 5. Also, do not include on line 1a rental activity income or portfolio income. See section 460 for special rules that apply to long-term contracts.

Installment sales. Generally, the installment method cannot be used for dealer dispositions of property. A "dealer disposition" is any disposition of personal property by a person who regularly sells or otherwise disposes of personal property of the same type on the installment plan or any disposition of real property held for sale to customers in the ordinary course of the taxpayer's trade or business. The disposition of property used or produced in a farming business is not included as a dealer disposition. See section 453(l) for details and exceptions.

Enter on line 1a the gross profit on collections from installment sales for any of the following:

- Dealer dispositions of property before March 1, 1986.
- Dispositions of property used or produced in the trade or business of farming.
- Certain dispositions of timeshares and residential lots reported under the installment method.

Attach a schedule showing the following information for the current year and the 3 preceding years:
- Gross sales.
- Cost of goods sold.
- Gross profits.
- Percentage of gross profits to gross sales.
- Amount collected.
- Gross profit on amount collected.

Line 2—Cost of Goods Sold

See the instructions for Schedule A on page 13.

Line 4—Ordinary Income (Loss) From Other Partnerships, Estates, and Trusts

Enter the amount shown on Schedule K-1 (Form 1065) or Schedule K-1 (Form 1041). Be sure to show the partnership's, estate's, or trust's name, address, and EIN on a separate statement attached to this return. If the amount entered is from more than one source, identify the amount from each source.

Do not include portfolio income or rental activity income (loss) from other partnerships, estates, or trusts on this line. Instead, report these amounts on the applicable lines of Schedules K and K-1, or on line 20a of Form 8825 if the amount is from a rental real estate activity.

Ordinary income or loss from another partnership that is a publicly traded partnership is not reported on this line. Instead, report the amount separately on line 7 of Schedules K and K-1.

Treat shares of other items separately reported on Schedule K-1 issued by the other entity as if the items were realized or incurred by this partnership.

If there is a loss from another partnership, the amount of the loss that may be claimed is subject to the at-risk and basis limitations as appropriate.

If the tax year of your partnership does not coincide with the tax year of the other partnership, estate, or trust, include the ordinary income (loss) from the other entity in the tax year in which the other entity's tax year ends.

Line 5—Net Farm Profit (Loss)

Enter the partnership's net farm profit (loss) from **Schedule F (Form 1040),** Profit or Loss From Farming. Attach Schedule F (Form 1040) to Form 1065. **Do not** include on this line any farm profit (loss) from other partnerships. Report those amounts on line 4. In figuring the partnership's net farm profit (loss), do not include any section 179 expense deduction; this amount must be separately stated.

Also report the partnership's fishing income on this line.

Page 10

For a special rule concerning the method of accounting for a farming partnership with a corporate partner and for other tax information on farms, see **Pub. 225,** Farmer's Tax Guide.

Note: *Because the election to deduct the expenses of raising any plant with a preproductive period of more than 2 years is made by the partner and not the partnership, farm partnerships that are not required to use an accrual method should not capitalize such expenses. Instead, state them separately on an attachment to Schedule K, line 24, and on Schedule K-1, line 25, Supplemental Information. See Temporary Regulations section 1.263A-4T for more information.*

Line 6—Net Gain (Loss) From Form 4797

Caution: *Include only ordinary gains or losses from the sale, exchange, or involuntary conversion of assets used in a trade or business activity. Ordinary gains or losses from the sale, exchange, or involuntary conversion of rental activity assets are reported separately on line 19 of Form 8825 or line 3 of Schedules K and K-1, generally as a part of the net income (loss) from the rental activity.*

A partnership that is a partner in another partnership must include on **Form 4797,** Sales of Business Property, its share of ordinary gains (losses) from sales, exchanges, or involuntary conversions (other than casualties or thefts) of the other partnership's trade or business assets.

Do not include any recapture of section 179 expense deduction. See the instructions for Schedule K-1, line 25, Supplemental Information, item 4, and the Instructions for Form 4797 for more information.

Line 7—Other Income (Loss)

Enter on line 7 trade or business income (loss) that is not included on lines 1a through 6. Examples of such income include:

1. Interest income derived in the ordinary course of the partnership's trade or business, such as interest charged on receivable balances.

2. Recoveries of bad debts deducted in earlier years under the specific charge-off method.

3. Taxable income from insurance proceeds.

4. The amount of credit figured on **Form 6478,** Credit for Alcohol Used as Fuel.

5. All section 481 income adjustments resulting from changes in accounting methods. Show the computation of the section 481 adjustments on an attached schedule.

6. The amount of any deduction previously taken under section 179A that is subject to recapture. See Pub. 535 for details, including how to figure the recapture.

7. The recapture amount for section 280F if the business use of listed property drops to 50% or less. To figure the recapture amount, the partnership must complete Part IV of Form 4797.

Do not include items requiring separate computations that must be reported on Schedules K and K-1. See the instructions for Schedules K and K-1 later in these instructions.

Do not report portfolio or rental activity income (loss) on this line.

Deductions

Caution: *Report **only** trade or business activity deductions on lines 9 through 21.*

Do not report the following expenses on lines 9 through 21:

• Rental activity expenses. Report these expenses on Form 8825 or line 3b of Schedule K.

• Deductions allocable to portfolio income. Report these deductions on line 10 of Schedules K and K-1.

• Nondeductible expenses (e.g., expenses connected with the production of tax-exempt income). Report nondeductible expenses on line 21 of Schedules K and K-1.

• Qualified expenditures to which an election under section 59(e) may apply. The instructions for lines 18a and 18b of Schedules K and K-1 explain how to report these amounts.

• Items the partnership must state separately that require separate computations by the partners. Examples include expenses incurred for the production of income instead of in a trade or business, charitable contributions, foreign taxes paid, intangible drilling and development costs, soil and water conservation expenditures, and exploration expenditures. The distributive shares of these expenses are reported separately to each partner on Schedule K-1.

Limitations on Deductions

Section 263A uniform capitalization rules. The uniform capitalization rules of section 263A require partnerships to capitalize or include in inventory certain costs incurred in connection with:

• The production of real and tangible personal property held in inventory or held for sale in the ordinary course of business.

• Personal property (tangible and intangible) acquired for resale.

• The production of property constructed or improved by a partnership for use in its trade or business or in an activity engaged in for profit.

The costs required to be capitalized under section 263A are not deductible until the property to which the costs relate is sold, used, or otherwise disposed of by the partnership.

Exceptions: Section 263A **does not** apply to:

• Personal property acquired for resale if the partnership's average annual gross receipts for the 3 prior tax years were $10 million or less.

• Timber.

• Most property produced under a long-term contract.

• Certain property produced in a farming business. See the note at the end of the instructions for line 5.

The partnership must report the following costs separately to the partners for purposes of determinations under section 59(e):

• Research and experimental costs under section 174.

• Intangible drilling costs for oil, gas, and geothermal property.

• Mining exploration and development costs.

Tangible personal property produced by a partnership includes a film, sound recording, video tape, book, or similar property.

Partnerships subject to the rules are required to capitalize not only direct costs but an allocable part of most indirect costs (including taxes) that benefit the assets produced or acquired for resale.

For inventory, some of the **indirect costs** that must be capitalized are:

• Administration expenses.

• Taxes.

• Depreciation.

• Insurance.

• Compensation paid to officers attributable to services.

• Rework labor.

• Contributions to pension, stock bonus, and certain profit-sharing, annuity, or deferred compensation plans.

Regulations section 1.263A-1(e)(3) specifies other indirect costs that relate to production or resale activities that must be capitalized and those that may be currently deductible.

Interest expense paid or incurred during the production period of certain property must be capitalized and is governed by special rules. For more details, see Regulations sections 1.263A-8 through 1.263A-15.

For more details on the uniform capitalization rules, see Regulations sections 1.236A-1 through 1.263A-3.

Transactions between related taxpayers. Generally, an accrual basis partnership may deduct business expenses and interest owed to a related party (including any partner) only in the tax year of the partnership that includes the day on which the payment is includible in the income of the related party. See section 267 for details.

Business start-up expenses. Business start-up expenses must be capitalized. An election may be made to amortize them over a period of not less than 60 months. See Pub. 535.

Organization costs. Amounts paid or incurred to organize a partnership are capital expenditures. They are not deductible as a current expense.

The partnership may elect to amortize organization expenses over a period of 60 or more months, beginning with the month in which the partnership begins business. Include the amortization expense on line 20. On the balance sheet (Schedule L) show the unamortized balance of organization costs. See the instructions for line 10 for the treatment of organization expenses paid to a partner. See Pub. 535 for more information.

Syndication costs. Costs for issuing and marketing interests in the partnership, such as commissions, professional fees, and printing costs, must be capitalized. They cannot be depreciated or amortized. See the instructions for line 10 for the treatment of syndication fees paid to a partner.

Reducing certain expenses for which credits are allowable. For each of the following credits, the partnership must reduce the otherwise allowable deductions for expenses used to figure the credit by the amount of the current year credit:

1. The work opportunity credit.

2. The welfare-to-work credit.

3. The credit for increasing research activities.

4. The enhanced oil recovery credit.

5. The disabled access credit.

6. The empowerment zone employment credit.

7. The Indian employment credit.

Page 11

8. The credit for employer social security and Medicare taxes paid on certain employee tips.

9. The orphan drug credit.

If the partnership has any of these credits, be sure to figure each current year credit before figuring the deductions for expenses on which the credit is based.

Line 9—Salaries and Wages

Enter on line 9 the salaries and wages paid or incurred for the tax year, reduced by any applicable employment credits from **Form 5884,** Work Opportunity Credit, **Form 8861,** Welfare-to-Work Credit, **Form 8844,** Empowerment Zone Employment Credit, and **Form 8845,** Indian Employment Credit. See the instructions for these forms for more information.

Do not include salaries and wages reported elsewhere on the return, such as amounts included in cost of goods sold, elective contributions to a section 401(k) cash or deferred arrangement, or amounts contributed under a salary reduction SEP agreement.

Line 10—Guaranteed Payments to Partners

Deduct payments or credits to a partner for services or for the use of capital if the payments or credits are determined without regard to partnership income and are allocable to a trade or business activity. Also include on line 10 amounts paid during the tax year for insurance that constitutes medical care for a partner, a partner's spouse, or a partner's dependents.

Do not include any payments and credits that should be capitalized. For example, although payments or credits to a partner for services rendered in organizing or syndicating a partnership may be guaranteed payments, they are not deductible on line 10. They are capital expenditures. However, they should be separately reported on Schedules K and K-1, line 5.

Do not include distributive shares of partnership profits.

Report the guaranteed payments to the appropriate partners on Schedule K-1, line 5.

Line 11—Repairs and Maintenance

Enter the costs of incidental repairs and maintenance that do not add to the value of the property or appreciably prolong its life, but only to the extent that such costs relate to a trade or business activity and are not claimed elsewhere on the return.

New buildings, machinery, or permanent improvements that increase the value of the property are not deductible. They are chargeable to capital accounts and may be depreciated or amortized.

Line 12—Bad Debts

Enter the total debts that became worthless in whole or in part during the year, but only to the extent such debts relate to a trade or business activity. Report deductible nonbusiness bad debts as a short-term capital loss on Schedule D (Form 1065).

Caution: *Cash method partnerships cannot take a bad debt deduction unless the amount was previously included in income.*

Line 13—Rent

Enter rent paid on business property used in a trade or business activity. Do not deduct rent for a dwelling unit occupied by any partner for personal use.

If the partnership rented or leased a vehicle, enter the total annual rent or lease expense paid or incurred in the trade or business activities of the partnership. Also complete Part V of **Form 4562,** Depreciation and Amortization. If the partnership leased a vehicle for a term of 30 days or more, the deduction for vehicle lease expense may have to be reduced by an amount called the **inclusion amount.** You may have an inclusion amount if:

The lease term began:	And the vehicle's fair market value on the first day of the lease exceeded:
After 12/31/96	$15,800
After 12/31/94 but before 1/1/97	$15,500
After 12/31/93 but before 1/1/95	$14,600
After 12/31/92 but before 1/1/94	$14,300
After 12/31/91 but before 1/1/93	$13,700

If the lease term began before January 1, 1992, see **Pub. 463,** Travel, Entertainment, Gift, and Car Expenses, to find out if the partnership has an inclusion amount.

See Pub. 463 for instructions on figuring the inclusion amount.

Line 14—Taxes and Licenses

Enter taxes and licenses paid or incurred in the trade or business activities of the partnership if not reflected in cost of goods sold. Federal import duties and Federal excise and stamp taxes are deductible only if paid or incurred in carrying on the trade or business of the partnership.

Do not deduct the following taxes on line 14:
- State and local sales taxes paid or incurred in connection with the acquisition or disposition of business property. These taxes must be added to the cost of the property, or, in the case of a disposition, subtracted from the amount realized.
- Taxes assessed against local benefits to the extent that they increase the value of the property assessed, such as for paving, etc.
- Federal income taxes or taxes reported elsewhere on the return.
- Section 901 foreign taxes. Report these taxes separately on Schedules K and K-1, line 17e.
- Taxes allocable to a rental activity. Taxes allocable to a rental real estate activity are reported on Form 8825. Taxes allocable to a rental activity other than a rental real estate activity are reported on line 3b of Schedule K.
- Taxes allocable to portfolio income. These taxes are reported on line 10 of Schedules K and K-1.
- Taxes paid or incurred for the production or collection of income, or for the management, conservation, or maintenance of property held to produce income. Report these taxes separately on line 11 of Schedules K and K-1.

See section 263A(a) for rules on capitalization of allocable costs (including taxes) for any property.

Line 15—Interest

Include only interest incurred in the trade or business activities of the partnership that is not claimed elsewhere on the return.

Do not include interest expense on debt required to be allocated to the production of designated property. Designated property includes real property, personal property that has a class life of 20 years or more, and other tangible property requiring more than 2 years (1 year in the case of property with a cost of more than $1 million) to produce or construct. Interest that is allocable to designated property produced by a partnership for its own use or for sale must be capitalized.

In addition, a partnership must also capitalize any interest on debt that is allocable to an asset used to produce designated property. A partner may have to capitalize interest that the partner incurs during the tax year with respect to the production expenditures of the partnership. Similarly, interest incurred by a partnership may have to be capitalized by a partner with respect to the partner's own production expenditures. The information required by the partner to properly capitalize interest for this purpose must be provided by the partnership in an attachment to Schedule K-1. See section 263A(f) and Regulations sections 1.263A-8 through 1.263A-15.

Do not include interest expense on debt used to purchase rental property or debt used in a rental activity. Interest allocable to a rental real estate activity is reported on Form 8825 and is used in arriving at net income (loss) from rental real estate activities on line 2 of Schedules K and K-1. Interest allocable to a rental activity other than a rental real estate activity is included on line 3b of Schedule K and is used in arriving at net income (loss) from a rental activity (other than a rental real estate activity). This net amount is reported on line 3c of Schedule K and line 3 of Schedule K-1.

Do not include interest expense on debt used to buy property held for investment. Do not include interest expense that is clearly and directly allocable to interest, dividend, royalty, or annuity income not derived in the ordinary course of a trade or business. Interest paid or incurred on debt used to purchase or carry investment property is reported on line 14a of Schedules K and K-1. See the instructions for line 14a of Schedules K and K-1 and **Form 4952,** Investment Interest Expense Deduction, for more information on investment property.

Do not include interest on debt proceeds allocated to distributions made to partners during the tax year. Instead, report such interest on line 11 of Schedules K and K-1. To determine the amount to allocate to distributions to partners, see Notice 89-35, 1989-1 C.B. 675.

Temporary Regulations section 1.163-8T gives rules for allocating interest expense among activities so that the limitations on passive activity losses, investment interest, and personal interest can be properly figured. Generally, interest expense is allocated in the same manner that debt is allocated. Debt is allocated by tracing disbursements of the debt proceeds to specific expenditures, as provided in the regulations.

Interest paid by a partnership to a partner for the use of capital should be entered on line 10 as guaranteed payments.

Prepaid interest can only be deducted over the period to which the prepayment applies.

Note: *Additional limitations on interest deductions apply when the partnership is a policyholder or beneficiary with respect to a life insurance, endowment, or annuity contract issued after June 8, 1997. For details, see* *section 264. Attach a statement showing the computation of the deduction disallowed under section 264.*

Line 16—Depreciation

On line 16a, enter **only** the depreciation claimed on assets used in a trade or business activity. Enter on line 16b the depreciation reported elsewhere on the return (e.g., on Schedule A) that is attributable to assets used in trade or business activities. See the Instructions for Form 4562 or **Pub. 946,** How To Depreciate Property, to figure the amount of depreciation to enter on this line.

For depreciation, you must complete and attach Form 4562 only if the partnership placed property in service during 1997 or claims depreciation on any car or other listed property.

Do not include any section 179 expense deduction on this line. This amount is not deducted by the partnership. Instead, it is passed through to the partners on line 9 of Schedule K-1.

Line 17—Depletion

If the partnership claims a deduction for timber depletion, complete and attach **Form T,** Forest Activities Schedules.

Caution: *Do not deduct depletion for oil and gas properties. Each partner figures depletion on oil and gas properties. See the instructions for Schedule K-1, line 25, item 3, for the information on oil and gas depletion that must be supplied to the partners by the partnership.*

Line 18—Retirement Plans, etc.

Do not deduct payments for partners to retirement or deferred compensation plans including IRAs, Keoghs, and simplified employee pension (SEP) and SIMPLE plans on this line. These amounts are reported on Schedule K-1, line 11, and are deducted by the partners on their own returns.

Enter the deductible contributions not claimed elsewhere on the return made by the partnership for its common-law employees under a qualified pension, profit-sharing, annuity, or SEP or SIMPLE plan, and under any other deferred compensation plan.

If the partnership contributes to an individual retirement arrangement (IRA) for employees, include the contribution in salaries and wages on page 1, line 9, or Schedule A, line 3, and not on line 18.

Employers who maintain a pension, profit-sharing, or other funded deferred compensation plan (other than a SEP), whether or not the plan is qualified under the Internal Revenue Code and whether or not a deduction is claimed for the current year, generally must file one of the following forms:

● **Form 5500,** Annual Return/Report of Employee Benefit Plan, for each plan with 100 or more participants.

● **Form 5500-C/R,** Return/Report of Employee Benefit Plan, for each plan with fewer than 100 participants.

● **Form 5500-EZ,** Annual Return of One-Participant (Owners and Their Spouses) Retirement Plan, for each plan that covers only partners or partners and their spouses.

There are penalties for not filing these forms on time.

Line 19—Employee Benefit Programs

Enter the partnership's contributions to employee benefit programs not claimed elsewhere on the return (e.g., insurance, health, and welfare programs) that are not part of a pension, profit-sharing, etc., plan included on line 18.

Do not include amounts paid during the tax year for insurance that constitutes medical care for a partner, a partner's spouse, or a partner's dependents. Instead, include these amounts on line 10 as guaranteed payments and on Schedule K, line 5, and Schedule K-1, line 5, of each partner on whose behalf the amounts were paid. Also report these amounts on Schedule K, line 11, and Schedule K-1, line 11, of each partner on whose behalf the amounts were paid.

Line 20—Other Deductions

Attach your own schedule, listing by type and amount, all allowable deductions related to a trade or business activity for which there is no separate line on page 1 of Form 1065. Enter the total on this line. Do not include items that must be reported separately on Schedules K and K-1.

A partnership is not allowed the deduction for net operating losses.

Do not include qualified expenditures to which an election under section 59(e) may apply.

Include on line 20 the deduction taken for amortization. You must complete and attach Form 4562 if the partnership is claiming amortization of costs that begins during its 1997 tax year. The instructions for Form 4562 provide code section references for specific amortizable property. See Pub. 535 for more information on amortization.

Do not deduct amounts paid or incurred to participate or intervene in any political campaign on behalf of a candidate for public office, or to influence the general public regarding legislative matters, elections, or referendums. In addition, partnerships generally cannot deduct expenses paid or incurred to influence Federal or state legislation, or to influence the actions or positions of certain Federal executive branch officials. However, certain in-house lobbying expenditures that do not exceed $2,000 are deductible. See section 162(e) for more details.

Do not deduct fines or penalties paid to a government for violating any law.

A deduction is allowed for part of the cost of qualified clean-fuel vehicle property and qualified clean-fuel vehicle refueling property. For more details, see section 179A.

Travel, meals, and entertainment. Subject to limitations and restrictions discussed below, a partnership can deduct ordinary and necessary travel, meals, and entertainment expenses paid or incurred in its trade or business. Special rules apply to deductions for gifts, skybox rentals, luxury water travel, convention expenses, and entertainment tickets. See section 274 and Pub. 463 for more details.

Travel. The partnership cannot deduct travel expenses of any individual accompanying a partner or partnership employee, including a spouse or dependent of the partner or employee, unless:

● That individual is an employee of the partnership, and

● His or her travel is for a bona fide business purpose and would otherwise be deductible by that individual.

Meals and entertainment. Generally, the partnership can deduct only 50% of the amount otherwise allowable for meals and entertainment expenses. In adddition (subject to exceptions under section 274(k)(2)):

● Meals must not be lavish or extravagant,

● A bona fide business discussion must occur during, immediately before, or immediately after the meal, and

● A partner or employee of the partnership must be present at the meal.

Membership dues. The partnership may deduct amounts paid or incurred for membership dues in civic or public service organizations, professional organizations (such as bar and medical associations), business leagues, trade associations, chambers of commerce, boards of trade, and real estate boards. However, no deduction is allowed if a principal purpose of the organization is to entertain, or provide entertainment facilities for, members or their guests. In addition, the partnership may not deduct membership dues in any club organized for business, pleasure, recreation, or other social purpose. This includes country clubs, golf and athletic clubs, airline and hotel clubs, and clubs operated to provide meals under conditions favorable to business discussion.

Entertainment facilities. The partnership cannot deduct an expense paid or incurred for a facility (such as a yacht or hunting lodge) used for an activity usually considered entertainment, amusement, or recreation.

Note: *The partnership may be able to deduct otherwise nondeductible meals, travel, and entertainment expenses if the amounts are treated as compensation and reported on Form W-2 for an employee or on Form 1099-MISC for an independent contractor.*

Schedule A—Cost of Goods Sold

Inventories are required at the beginning and end of each tax year if the production, purchase, or sale of merchandise is an income-producing factor. See Regulations section 1.471-1.

Section 263A Uniform Capitalization Rules

The uniform capitalization rules of section 263A are discussed under **Limitations on Deductions** on page 11. See those instructions before completing Schedule A.

Line 1—Inventory at Beginning of Year

This figure should match the ending inventory reported on the partnership's 1996 Form 1065, Schedule A, line 7. If it is different, attach an explanation.

Line 2—Purchases

Reduce purchases by items withdrawn for personal use. The cost of these items should be shown on line 23 of Schedules K and K-1 as distributions to partners.

Line 4—Additional Section 263A Costs

An entry is required on this line only for partnerships that have elected a simplified method.

For partnerships that have elected the simplified production method, additional section 263A costs are generally those costs, other than interest, that were not capitalized under the partnership's method of accounting immediately prior to the effective date of section 263A that are required to be capitalized under section 263A. Interest is to be accounted

Page 13

for separately. For new partnerships, additional section 263A costs are the costs, other than interest, that must be capitalized under section 263A, but which the partnership would not have been required to capitalize if it had existed before the effective date of section 263A. For more details, see Regulations section 1.263A-2(b).

For partnerships that have elected the simplified resale method, additional section 263A costs are generally those costs incurred with respect to the following categories:

- Off-site storage or warehousing.
- Purchasing.
- Handling, processing, assembly, and repackaging.
- General and administrative costs (mixed service costs).

For more details, see Regulations section 1.263A-3(d).

Enter on line 4 the balance of section 263A costs paid or incurred during the tax year not included on lines 2, 3, and 5. Attach a schedule listing these costs.

Line 5—Other Costs

Enter on line 5 any other inventoriable costs paid or incurred during the tax year not entered on lines 2 through 4. Attach a schedule.

Line 7—Inventory at End of Year

See Regulations sections 1.263A-1 through 1.263A-3 for details on figuring the costs to be included in ending inventory.

Lines 9a through 9c—Inventory Valuation Methods

Inventories can be valued at:
- Cost,
- Cost or market value (whichever is lower), or
- Any other method approved by the IRS that conforms to the requirements of the applicable regulations.

The average cost (rolling average) method of valuing inventories generally does not conform to the requirements of the regulations. See Rev. Rul. 71-234, 1971-1 C.B. 148.

Partnerships that use erroneous valuation methods must change to a method permitted for Federal tax purposes. To make this change, use Form 3115.

On line 9a, check the methods used for valuing inventories. Under lower of cost or market, the term "market" (for normal goods) means the current bid price prevailing on the inventory valuation date for the particular merchandise in the volume usually purchased by the taxpayer. For a manufacturer, market applies to the basic elements of cost—raw materials, labor, and burden. If section 263A applies to the taxpayer, the basic elements of cost must reflect the current bid price of all direct costs and all indirect costs properly allocable to goods on hand at the inventory date.

Inventory may be valued below cost when the merchandise is unsalable at normal prices or unusable in the normal way because the goods are subnormal due to damage, imperfections, shop wear, etc., within the meaning of Regulations section 1.471-2(c). These goods may be valued at the current bona fide selling price minus the direct cost of disposition (but not less than scrap value) if such a price can be established.

If this is the first year the last-in first-out (LIFO) inventory method was either adopted or extended to inventory goods not previously valued under the LIFO method, attach **Form 970,** Application To Use LIFO Inventory Method, or a statement with the information required by Form 970. Also check the box on line 9c.

If the partnership has changed or extended its inventory method to LIFO and has had to write up its opening inventory to cost in the year of election, report the effect of this write-up as income (line 7, page 1, Form 1065) proportionately over a 3-year period that begins in the tax year of the LIFO election.

For more information on inventory valuation methods, see Pub. 538.

Schedule B—Other Information

Question 1

Check box 1(d) for any other type of entity and state the type (e.g., limited liability partnership).

Question 4—Consolidated Audit Procedures

Generally, the tax treatment of partnership items is determined at the partnership level in a consolidated audit proceeding, rather than in separate proceedings with individual partners.

Answer **Yes** to Question 4 if **ANY** of the following apply:

- The partnership had more than 10 partners at any one time during the tax year. For purposes of this question, a husband and wife, and their estates, count as one person.
- Any partner was a nonresident alien or was other than an individual, an estate, or a C corporation.
- The partnership is a "small partnership" that has elected to be subject to the rules for consolidated audit proceedings. "Small partnerships" as defined in section 6231(a)(1)(B)(i) are not subject to the rules for consolidated audit proceedings, but may make an irrevocable election under Temporary Regulations section 301.6231(a)(1)-1T(b)(2) to be covered by them.

Caution: *The partnership does not make this election when it answers* **Yes** *to Question 4. The election must be made separately.*

Note: *Answer* **Yes** *to Question 4 if the partnership had:*

- *A short tax year that ended* **before** *August 6, 1997,* **and**
- *Any partner was a C corporation* **or** *the partnership made a special allocation of any partnership item.*

If a partnership return is filed by an entity for a tax year, but it is determined that the entity is not a partnership for that tax year, the consolidated partnership audit procedures will generally apply to that entity and to persons holding an interest in that entity. See Temporary Regulations section 301.6233-1T for details and exceptions.

Question 6—Foreign Partners

Answer **Yes** to Question 6 if the partnership had any foreign partners (for purposes of section 1446) at any time during the tax year. Otherwise, answer **No.**

If the partnership had gross income effectively connected with a trade or business in the United States **and** foreign partners, it may be required to withhold tax under section

1446 on income allocable to foreign partners (without regard to distributions) and file Forms 8804, 8805, and 8813.

Question 7

Answer **Yes** to Question 7 if interests in the partnership are traded on an established securities market or are readily tradable on a secondary market (or its substantial equivalent).

Question 8

Organizers of certain tax shelters are required to register the tax shelters by filing Form 8264 no later than the day on which an interest in the shelter is first offered for sale. Organizers filing a properly completed Form 8264 will receive a tax shelter registration number that they must furnish to their investors. See the Instructions for Form 8264 for the definition of a tax shelter and the investments exempted from tax shelter registration.

Question 9—Foreign Accounts

Answer **Yes** to Question 9 if either **1** or **2** below applies to the partnership. Otherwise, check the **No** box.

1. At any time during calendar year 1997, the partnership had an interest in or signature or other authority over a bank account, securities account, or other financial account in a foreign country; **AND**

- The combined value of the accounts was more than $10,000 at any time during the calendar year; **AND**
- The accounts were NOT with a U.S. military banking facility operated by a U.S. financial institution.

2. The partnership owns more than 50% of the stock in any corporation that would answer the question **Yes** based on item **1** above.

Get **Form TD F 90-22.1,** Report of Foreign Bank and Financial Accounts, to see if the partnership is considered to have an interest in or signature or other authority over a bank account, securities account, or other financial account in a foreign country.

If you answered **Yes** to Question 9, file Form TD F 90-22.1 by June 30, 1998, with the Department of the Treasury at the address shown on the form. Because Form TD F 90-22.1 is not a tax return, **do not** file it with Form 1065. You may order Form TD F 90-22.1 by calling 1-800-829-3676.

Question 10

The partnership may be required to file **Form 3520,** Annual Return To Report Transactions With Foreign Trusts and Receipt of Certain Foreign Gifts, if:

- It directly or indirectly transferred property or money to a foreign trust. For this purpose, any U.S. person who created a foreign trust is considered a transferor.
- It is treated as the owner of any part of the assets of a foreign trust under the grantor trust rules.
- It received a distribution from a foreign trust.

For more information, see the Instructions for Form 3520.

Note: *An owner of a foreign trust must ensure that the trust files an annual information return on Form 3520-A, as well as U.S. owner and beneficiary statements. For details, see Notice 97-34, 1997-25 I.R.B. 22.*

The partnership may be required to file **Form 926,** Return by a U.S. Transferor of

Property to a Foreign Corporation, Foreign Estate or Trust, or Foreign Partnership, to:

• Pay any excise tax due under section 1491.

• Report information required under section 6038B.

• Report transfers of property to a foreign corporation, estate, trust, or partnership, and make elections under section 1492 with respect to those transfers.

For more information, see the Instructions for Form 926.

Designation of Tax Matters Partner (TMP)

If the partnership is subject to the rules for consolidated audit proceedings in sections 6221 through 6233, the partnership may designate a partner as the TMP for the tax year for which the return is filed by completing the **Designation of Tax Matters Partner** section on page 2 of Form 1065. See the instructions for Question 4, consolidated audit procedures, to determine if the partnership is subject to these rules. The designated TMP must be a general partner and, in most cases, must also be a U.S. person. For details, see Regulations section 301.6231(a)(7)-1.

For an LLC, only a member-manager of the LLC is treated as a general partner. A member-manager is any owner of an interest in the LLC who, alone or together with others, has the continuing exclusive authority to make the management decisions necessary to conduct the business for which the LLC was formed. If there are no elected or designated member-managers, each owner is treated as a member-manager. For details, see Regulations section 301.6231(a)(7)-2.

General Instructions for Schedules K and K-1— Partners' Shares of Income, Credits, Deductions, etc.

Purpose of Schedules

Although the partnership is not subject to income tax, the partners are liable for tax on their shares of the partnership income, whether or not distributed, and must include their shares on their tax returns.

Schedule K (page 3 of Form 1065) is a summary schedule of all the partners' shares of the partnership's income, credits, deductions, etc.

Schedule K-1 (Form 1065) shows each partner's separate share. Attach a copy of each Schedule K-1 to the Form 1065 filed with the IRS; keep a copy with a copy of the partnership return as a part of the partnership's records; and furnish a copy to each partner. If a partnership interest is held by a nominee on behalf of another person, the partnership may be required to furnish Schedule K-1 to the nominee. See Temporary Regulations sections 1.6031(b)-1T and 1.6031(c)-1T for more information.

Be sure to give each partner a copy of either the Partner's Instructions for Schedule K-1 (Form 1065) or specific instructions for each item reported on the partner's Schedule K-1 (Form 1065).

Substitute Forms

The partnership does not need IRS approval to use a substitute Schedule K-1 if it is an exact copy of the IRS schedule, or if it contains only those lines the taxpayer is required to use. The lines must use the same numbers and titles and must be in the same order and format as on the comparable IRS Schedule K-1. The substitute schedule must include the OMB number. The partnership must provide each partner with the Partner's Instructions for Schedule K-1 (Form 1065) or other prepared specific instructions.

The partnership must request IRS approval to use other substitute Schedules K-1. To request approval, write to Internal Revenue Service, Attention: Substitute Forms Program Coordinator, T:FP:S, 1111 Constitution Avenue, N.W., Washington, DC 20224.

Each partner's information must be on a separate sheet of paper. Therefore, separate all continuously printed substitutes before you file them with the IRS.

The partnership may be subject to a penalty if it files Schedules K-1 that do not conform to the specifications of Rev. Proc. 96-48, 1996-2 C.B. 339.

How Income Is Shared Among Partners

Allocate shares of income, gain, loss, deduction, or credit among the partners according to the partnership agreement for sharing income or loss generally. Partners may agree to allocate specific items in a ratio different from the ratio for sharing income or loss. For instance, if the net income exclusive of specially allocated items is divided evenly among three partners but some special items are allocated 50% to one, 30% to another, and 20% to the third partner, report the specially allocated items on the appropriate line of the applicable partner's Schedule K-1 and the total on the appropriate line of Schedule K, instead of on the numbered lines on page 1 of Form 1065 or Schedules A or D.

If a partner's interest changed during the year, see section 706(d) before determining each partner's distributive share of any item of income, gain, loss, deduction, etc. Income (loss) is allocated to a partner only for the part of the year in which that person is a member of the partnership. The partnership will either allocate on a daily basis or divide the partnership year into segments and allocate income, loss, or special items in each segment among the persons who were partners during that segment. Partnerships that report their income on the cash basis must allocate interest expense, taxes, and any payment for services or for the use of property on a daily basis if there is any change in any partner's interest during the year. See Pub. 541 for more details.

Special rules on the allocation of income, gain, loss, and deductions generally apply if a partner contributes property to the partnership and the fair market value of that property at the time of contribution differs from the contributing partner's adjusted tax basis. Under these rules, the partnership must use a reasonable method of making allocations of income, gain, loss, and deductions from the property so that the contributing partner receives the tax burdens and benefits of any built-in gain or loss (i.e., precontribution appreciation or diminution of value of the contributed property). See Regulations section 1.704-3 for details on how

to make these allocations, including a description of specific allocation methods that are generally reasonable.

See **Dispositions of Contributed Property** on page 6 for special rules on the allocation of income, gain, loss, and deductions on the disposition of property contributed to the partnership by a partner.

If the partnership agreement does not provide for the partner's share of income, gain, loss, deduction, or credit, or if the allocation under the agreement does not have substantial economic effect, the partner's share is determined according to the partner's interest in the partnership. See Regulations section 1.704-1 for more information.

Specific Instructions (Schedule K Only)

All partnerships must complete Schedule K. Rental activity income (loss) and portfolio income are not reported on page 1 of Form 1065. These amounts are not combined with trade or business activity income (loss). Schedule K is used to report the totals of these and other amounts.

Specific Instructions (Schedule K-1 Only)

General Information

Prepare and give a Schedule K-1 to each person who was a partner in the partnership at any time during the year. **Schedule K-1 must be provided to each partner on or before the day on which the partnership return is required to be filed.**

Generally, any person who holds an interest in a partnership as a nominee for another person must furnish to the partnership the name, address, etc., of the other person.

On each Schedule K-1, enter the names, addresses, and identifying numbers of the partner and partnership and the partner's distributive share of each item.

For an individual partner, enter the partner's social security number. For all other partners, enter the partner's EIN. However, if a partner is an individual retirement arrangement (IRA), enter the identifying number of the custodian of the IRA. Do not enter the social security number of the person for whom the IRA is maintained.

If a husband and wife each had an interest in the partnership, prepare a separate Schedule K-1 for each of them. If a husband and wife held an interest together, prepare one Schedule K-1 if the two of them are considered to be one partner.

There is space on line 25 of Schedule K-1 for you to provide information to the partners. This space may be used instead of attachments.

Specific Items and Questions

Question A

Answer Question A on all Schedules K-1. If a partner holds interests as both a general and limited partner, check the first two boxes and attach a schedule for each activity that shows the amounts allocable to the partner's interest as a limited partner.

Question B—What Type of Entity Is This Partner?

State on this line whether the partner is an individual, a corporation, an estate, a trust, a partnership, an exempt organization, or a nominee (custodian). If the partner is a nominee, use one of the following codes to indicate the type of entity the nominee represents: I—Individual; C—Corporation; F—Estate or Trust; P—Partnership; E—Exempt Organization; or IRA—Individual Retirement Arrangement.

Question C—Domestic/Foreign Partner

Check the foreign partner box if the partner is a nonresident alien individual, foreign partnership, foreign corporation, or a foreign estate or trust. Otherwise, check the domestic partner box.

Item D—Partner's Profit, Loss, and Capital Sharing Percentages

Enter in Item D, column (ii), the appropriate percentages as of the end of the year. However, if a partner's interest terminated during the year, enter in column (i) the percentages that existed immediately before the termination. When the profit or loss sharing percentage has changed during the year, show the percentage before the change in column (i) and the end-of-year percentage in column (ii). If there are multiple changes in the profit and loss sharing percentage during the year, attach a statement giving the date and percentage before each change.

"Ownership of capital" means the portion of the capital that the partner would receive if the partnership was liquidated at the end of the year by the distribution of undivided interests in partnership assets and liabilities.

Item F—Partner's Share of Liabilities

Enter each partner's share of nonrecourse liabilities, partnership-level qualified nonrecourse financing, and other liabilities.

"Nonrecourse liabilities" are those liabilities of the partnership for which no partner bears the economic risk of loss. The extent to which a partner bears the economic risk of loss is determined under the rules of Regulations section 1.752-2. Do not include partnership-level qualified nonrecourse financing (defined below) on the line for nonrecourse liabilities.

If the partner terminated his or her interest in the partnership during the year, enter the share that existed immediately before the total disposition. In all other cases, enter it as of the end of the year.

If the partnership is engaged in two or more different types of at-risk activities, or a combination of at-risk activities and any other activity, attach a statement showing the partner's share of nonrecourse liabilities, partnership-level qualified nonrecourse financing, and other liabilities for **each** activity. See Pub. 925 to determine if the partnership is engaged in more than one at-risk activity.

The at-risk rules of section 465 generally apply to any activity carried on by the partnership as a trade or business or for the production of income. These rules generally limit the amount of loss and other deductions a partner can claim from any partnership activity to the amount for which that partner is considered at risk. However, for partners who acquired their partnership interests before

1987, the at-risk rules do not apply to losses from an activity of holding real property the partnership placed in service before 1987. The activity of holding mineral property does not qualify for this exception. Identify on an attachment to Schedule K-1 the amount of any losses that are not subject to the at-risk rules.

If a partnership is engaged in an activity subject to the limitations of section 465(c)(1) (i.e., films or videotapes, leasing section 1245 property, farming, or oil and gas property), give each partner his or her share of the total pre-1976 losses from that activity for which there existed a corresponding amount of nonrecourse liability at the end of each year in which the losses occurred. See **Form 6198,** At-Risk Limitations, and related instructions for more information.

Qualified nonrecourse financing secured by real property used in an activity of holding real property that is subject to the at-risk rules is treated as an amount at risk. "Qualified nonrecourse financing" generally includes financing for which no one is personally liable for repayment that is borrowed for use in an activity of holding real property and that is loaned or guaranteed by a Federal, state, or local government or that is borrowed from a "qualified" person. Qualified persons include any person actively and regularly engaged in the business of lending money, such as a bank or savings and loan association. Qualified persons generally do not include related parties (unless the nonrecourse financing is commercially reasonable and on substantially the same terms as loans involving unrelated persons), the seller of the property, or a person who receives a fee for the partnership's investment in the real property. See section 465 for more information on qualified nonrecourse financing.

The partner as well as the partnership must meet the qualified nonrecourse rules. Therefore, the partnership must enter on an attached statement any other information the partner needs to determine if the qualified nonrecourse rules are also met at the partner level.

Item G—Tax Shelter Registration Number

If the partnership is a registration-required tax shelter or has invested in a registration-required tax shelter, it must enter the tax shelter registration number in Item G. Also, a partnership that has invested in a registration-required tax shelter must furnish a copy of its Form 8271 to its partners. See Form 8271 for more details.

Item J—Analysis of Partner's Capital Account

You are not required to complete Item J if the answer to Question 5 of Schedule B is **Yes**. If you are required to complete this item, see the instructions for Schedule M-2 on page 23.

Specific Instructions (Schedules K and K-1, Except as Noted)

Schedules K and K-1 have the same line numbers for lines 1 through 23.

Special Allocations

An item is specially allocated if it is allocated to a partner in a ratio different from the ratio for sharing income or loss generally.

Report specially allocated ordinary gain (loss) on Schedules K and K-1, line 7. Report other specially allocated items on the applicable lines of the partner's Schedule K-1, with the total amount on the applicable line of Schedule K. For example, specially allocated long-term capital gain is entered on line 4e(2) of the partner's Schedule K-1, and the total is entered on line 4e(2) of Schedule K, along with any net long-term capital gain (or loss) from line 12(f) of Schedule D (Form 1065).

Income (Loss)

Line 1—Ordinary Income (Loss) From Trade or Business Activities

Enter the amount from page 1, line 22. Enter the income or loss without reference to (a) the basis of the partners' interests in the partnership, (b) the partners' at-risk limitations, or (c) the passive activity limitations. These limitations, if applicable, are determined at the partner level.

If the partnership has more than one trade or business activity, identify on an attachment to Schedule K-1 the amount from each separate activity. See **Passive Activity Reporting Requirements** on page 9.

Line 1 should not include rental activity income (loss) or portfolio income (loss).

Line 2—Net Income (Loss) From Rental Real Estate Activities

Enter the net income or loss from rental real estate activities of the partnership from Form 8825. Attach this form to Form 1065. If the partnership has more than one rental real estate activity, identify on an attachment to Schedule K-1 the amount attributable to each activity.

Line 3—Net Income (Loss) From Other Rental Activities

On Schedule K, line 3a, enter gross income from rental activities other than rental real estate activities. See page 7 of these instructions and Pub. 925 for the definition of rental activities. Include on line 3a, the gain (loss) from line 18 of Form 4797 that is attributable to the sale, exchange, or involuntary conversion of an asset used in a rental activity other than a rental real estate activity.

On line 3b of Schedule K, enter the deductible expenses of the activity. Attach a schedule of these expenses to Form 1065.

Enter the net income (loss) on line 3c of Schedule K. Enter each partner's share on line 3 of Schedule K-1.

If the partnership has more than one rental activity reported on line 3, identify on an attachment to Schedule K-1 the amount from each activity.

Lines 4a Through 4f—Portfolio Income (Loss)

Enter portfolio income (loss) on lines 4a through 4f.

See page 8 of these instructions for a definition of portfolio income. Do not reduce portfolio income by deductions allocable to it. Report such deductions (other than interest expense) on line 10 of Schedules K and K-1. Interest expense allocable to portfolio income is generally investment interest expense and is reported on line 14a of Schedules K and K-1.

Lines 4a and 4b. Enter only taxable interest and dividends on these lines. Taxable interest is interest from all sources except interest exempt from tax and interest on tax-free covenant bonds.

Lines 4d, 4e(1), and 4e(2). Enter on line 4d of Schedule K the gain or loss from line 5 of Schedule D (Form 1065) plus any short-term capital gain (loss) that is specially allocated to partners. Report each partner's share on line 4d of Schedule K-1.

Enter on line 4e(1) the gain or loss from line 11 of Schedule D (Form 1065) plus any 28% rate gain (loss) that is specially allocated to partners. Enter on line 4e(2) the gain or loss from line 12 of Schedule D (Form 1065) plus any long-term capital gain (loss) that is specially allocated to partners. Report each partner's share on lines 4e(1) and 4e(2) of Schedule K-1, respectively.

Caution: *If any capital gain or loss is from the disposition of nondepreciable personal property used in a trade or business, it may not be treated as portfolio income. Report such gain or loss on line 7 of Schedules K and K-1.*

Line 4f. Report and identify other portfolio income or loss on an attachment for line 4f.

For example, income reported to the partnership from a real estate mortgage investment conduit (REMIC), in which the partnership is a residual interest holder, would be reported on an attachment for line 4f. If the partnership holds a residual interest in a REMIC, report on the attachment for line 4f the partner's share of the following:

• Taxable income (net loss) from the REMIC (line 1b of Schedules Q (Form 1066)).

• "Excess inclusion" (line 2c of Schedules Q (Form 1066)).

• Section 212 expenses (line 3b of Schedules Q (Form 1066)). Do not report these section 212 expenses on line 10 of Schedules K and K-1.

Because Schedule Q (Form 1066) is a quarterly statement, the partnership must follow the Schedule Q instructions to figure the amounts to report to the partner for the partnership's tax year.

Line 5—Guaranteed Payments to Partners

Guaranteed payments to partners include:
• Payments for salaries, health insurance, and interest deducted by the partnership and reported on Form 1065, page 1, line 10; Form 8825; or on Schedule K, line 3b; and
• Payments the partnership must capitalize. See the Instructions for Form 1065, line 10.

Generally, amounts reported on line 5 are not considered to be related to a passive activity. For example, guaranteed payments for personal services paid to a partner would not be passive activity income. Likewise, interest paid to any partner is not passive activity income.

Lines 6a and 6b—Net Section 1231 Gain (Loss) (Other Than Due to Casualty or Theft)

Enter on line 6a the 28% rate gain or loss from Form 4797, line 7, column (h). Enter on line 6b the total net section 1231 gain or loss from Form 4797, line 7, column (g). Do not include specially allocated ordinary gains and losses on this line. Instead, report them on line 7. If the partnership has more than one activity, attach a statement to Schedule K-1 that identifies the activity to which the section 1231 gain (loss) relates.

Line 7—Other Income (Loss)

Use line 7 to report other items of income, gain, or loss not included on lines 1 through 6. If the partnership has more than one activity, identify on an attachment the amount and the activity to which each amount relates.

Items to report on line 7 include:

• Gains from the disposition of farm recapture property (see Form 4797) and other items to which section 1252 applies.

• Gains from the disposition of an interest in oil, gas, geothermal, or other mineral properties (section 1254).

• Any net gain or loss from section 1256 contracts from **Form 6781,** Gains and Losses From Section 1256 Contracts and Straddles.

• Recoveries of tax benefit items (section 111).

• Gambling gains and losses subject to the limitations in section 165(d).

• Any income, gain, or loss to the partnership under section 751(b).

• Specially allocated ordinary gain (loss).

• Net gain (loss) from involuntary conversions due to casualty or theft. The amount for this line is shown on **Form 4684,** Casualties and Thefts, line 38a, 38b, or 39. Also, separately report the 28% rate gain (loss), if any, from involuntary conversions due to casualty or theft.

• Eligible gain from the sale or exchange of qualified small business stock (as defined in section 1202(c)). Also report on an attachment to Schedules K and K-1 the name of the corporation that issued the stock and the adjusted basis of that stock.

Each partner's share must be entered on Schedule K-1. Give each partner a schedule that shows the amounts to be reported on the partner's Form 4684, line 34, columns (b)(i), (b)(ii), and (c).

If there was a gain (loss) from a casualty or theft to property not used in a trade or business or for income-producing purposes, notify the partner. The partnership should not complete Form 4684 for this type of casualty or theft. Instead, each partner will complete his or her own Form 4684.

Deductions

Line 8—Charitable Contributions

Enter the total amount of charitable contributions made by the partnership during its tax year on Schedule K. Enter each partner's distributive share on Schedule K-1. On an attachment to Schedules K and K-1, show separately the dollar amount of contributions subject to each of the 50%, 30%, and 20% of adjusted gross income limits. For additional information, see **Pub. 526,** Charitable Contributions.

Generally, no deduction is allowed for any contribution of $250 or more unless the partnership obtains a written acknowledgment from the charitable organization that shows the amount of cash contributed, describes any property contributed, and gives an estimate of the value of any goods or services provided in return for the contribution. The acknowledgment must be obtained by the due date (including extensions) of the partnership return, or if earlier, the date the partnership files its return. Do not attach the acknowledgment to the tax return, but keep it with the partnership's records. These rules apply in addition to the filing requirements for Form 8283 described below.

Certain contributions made to an organization conducting lobbying activities are not deductible. See section 170(f)(9) for more details.

Form 8283, Noncash Charitable Contributions, must be completed and attached to Form 1065 if the deduction claimed for noncash contributions exceeds $500. The partnership must give a copy of its Form 8283 to every partner if the deduction for an item or group of similar items of contributed property exceeds $5,000. Each partner must be furnished a copy even if the amount allocated to any partner is $5,000 or less.

If the deduction for an item or group of similar items of contributed property is $5,000 or less, the partnership should pass through each partner's share of the amount of noncash contributions so the partners will be able to complete their own Forms 8283. See the Instructions for Form 8283 for additional information.

If the partnership made a qualified conservation contribution, include the fair market value of the underlying property before and after the donation and describe the conservation purpose furthered by the donation. Give a copy of this information to each partner.

Line 9—Section 179 Expense Deduction

A partnership may elect to expense part of the cost of certain tangible property the partnership purchased this year for use in its trade or business or certain rental activities. See Pub. 946 for a definition of what kind of property qualifies for the section 179 expense deduction and the Instructions for Form 4562 for limitations on the amount of the section 179 expense deduction.

Complete Part I of Form 4562 to figure the partnership's section 179 expense deduction. The partnership does not claim the deduction itself but instead passes it through to the partners. Attach Form 4562 to Form 1065 and show the total section 179 expense deduction on Schedule K, line 9. Report each partner's allocable share on Schedule K-1, line 9. Do not complete line 9 of Schedule K-1 for any partner that is an estate or trust.

If the partnership is an enterprise zone business, also report on an attachment to Schedules K and K-1 the cost of section 179 property placed in service during the year that is qualified zone property.

See the instructions for line 25 of Schedule K-1, item 4, for any recapture of a section 179 amount.

Line 10—Deductions Related to Portfolio Income

Enter on line 10 and attach an itemized list of the deductions clearly and directly allocable to portfolio income (other than interest expense and section 212 expenses from a REMIC). Interest expense related to portfolio income is investment interest expense and is reported on line 14a of Schedules K and K-1. Section 212 expenses from the partnership's interest in a REMIC are reported on an attachment for line 4f of Schedules K and K-1.

No deduction is allowable under section 212 for expenses allocable to a convention, seminar, or similar meeting.

Line 11—Other Deductions

Use line 11 to report deductions not included on lines 8, 9, 10, 17e, and 18b. On an attachment, identify the deduction and amount, and if the partnership has more than one activity, the activity to which the deduction relates.

Examples of items to be reported on an attachment to line 11 include:

• Amounts paid by the partnership that would be allowed as itemized deductions on any of the partners' income tax returns if they were paid directly by a partner for the same purpose. However, do not enter expenses related to portfolio income or investment interest expense on this line.

If there was a loss from an involuntary conversion due to casualty or theft of income-producing property, include in the total amount for this line the relevant amount from Form 4684, line 32.

• Any penalty on early withdrawal of savings.

• Soil and water conservation expenditures (section 175).

• Expenditures for the removal of architectural and transportation barriers to the elderly and handicapped and which the partnership has elected to treat as a current expense (section 190).

• Contributions to a capital construction fund.

• Any amounts paid during the tax year for health insurance coverage for a partner (including that partner's spouse and dependents). For 1997, a partner may be allowed to deduct up to 40% of such amounts on Form 1040, line 27.

• Payments for a partner to an IRA, Keogh, SEP, or SIMPLE plan. If there is a defined benefit plan (Keogh), attach to the Schedule K-1 for each partner a statement showing the amount of benefit accrued for the tax year.

• Interest expense allocated to debt-financed distributions. See Notice 89-35 for more information.

• Interest paid or accrued on debt properly allocable to each general partner's share of a working interest in any oil or gas property (if the partner's liability is not limited). General partners that did not materially participate in the oil or gas activity treat this interest as investment interest; for other general partners, it is trade or business interest.

Credits

Line 12a—Low-Income Housing Credit

Section 42 provides a credit that may be claimed by owners of low-income residential rental buildings. If the partners are eligible to take the low-income housing credit, complete and attach **Form 8586,** Low-Income Housing Credit; **Form 8609,** Low-Income Housing Credit Allocation Certification; and **Schedule A (Form 8609),** Annual Statement, to Form 1065.

Report on line 12a(1) the total low-income housing credit for property placed in service before 1990 with respect to which a partnership is to be treated under section 42(j)(5) as the taxpayer to which the low-income housing credit was allowed. Report any other low-income housing credit for property placed in service before 1990 on line 12a(2). On lines 12a(3) and (4), report the low-income housing credit for property placed in service after 1989.

Line 12b—Qualified Rehabilitation Expenditures Related to Rental Real Estate Activities

Enter total qualified rehabilitation expenditures related to rental real estate activities of the partnership. Also complete the applicable lines of **Form 3468,** Investment Credit, that apply to qualified rehabilitation expenditures for property related to rental real estate activities of the partnership for which income or loss is reported on line 2 of Schedule K. See Form 3468 for details on qualified rehabilitation expenditures. Attach Form 3468 to Form 1065.

For line 12b of Schedule K-1, enter each partner's distributive share of the expenditures. On the dotted line to the left of the entry space for line 12b, enter the line number of Form 3468 on which the partner should report the expenditures. If there is more than one type of expenditure, or the expenditures are from more than one rental real estate activity, report this information separately for each expenditure or activity on an attachment to Schedules K and K-1.

Caution: *Qualified rehabilitation expenditures for property not related to rental real estate activities must be listed separately on line 25 of Schedule K-1.*

Line 12c—Credits (Other Than Credits Shown on Lines 12a and 12b) Related to Rental Real Estate Activities

Report any information that the partners need to figure credits related to a rental real estate activity, other than the low-income housing credit and qualified rehabilitation expenditures. On the dotted line to the left of the entry space for line 12c (or in the margin), identify the type of credit. If there is more than one type of credit or the credit is from more than one activity, report this information separately for each credit or activity on an attachment to Schedules K and K-1.

Line 12d—Credits Related to Other Rental Activities

Use this line to report information that the partners need to figure credits related to a rental activity other than a rental real estate activity. On the dotted line to the left of the entry space for line 12d, identify the type of credit. If there is more than one type of credit or the credit is from more than one activity, report this information separately for each credit or activity on an attachment to Schedules K and K-1.

Line 13—Other Credits

Enter on line 13 any other credit, except credits or expenditures shown or listed for lines 12a through 12d of Schedules K and K-1. On the dotted line to the left of the entry space for line 13, identify the type of credit. If there is more than one type of credit or the credit is from more than one activity, report this information separately for each credit or activity on an attachment to Schedules K and K-1. The credits to be reported on line 13 and other required attachments are as follows:

• Credit for backup withholding on dividends, interest, or patronage dividends.

• Nonconventional source fuel credit. The credit is figured at the partnership level and then is apportioned to the partners based on their distributive shares of partnership income attributable to sales of qualified fuels. Attach a separate schedule to the return to show the computation of the credit. See section 29 for more information.

• Qualified electric vehicle credit (Form 8834).

• Unused credits from cooperatives. The unused credits are apportioned to persons who were partners in the partnership on the last day of the partnership's tax year.

• Work opportunity credit (Form 5884). This credit is apportioned among the partners according to their interest in the partnership at the time the wages on which the credit is figured were paid or accrued.

• Welfare-to-work credit (Form 8861). This credit is apportioned in the same manner as the work opportunity credit.

• Credit for alcohol used as fuel (Form 6478). This credit is apportioned to persons who were partners on the last day of the partnership's tax year. The credit must be included in income on page 1, line 7, of Form 1065. See section 40(f) for an election the partnership can make to not have the credit apply.

If this credit includes the small ethanol producer credit, identify on a statement attached to each Schedule K-1 **(a)** the amount of the small producer credit included in the total credit allocated to the partner, **(b)** the number of gallons of qualified ethanol fuel production allocated to the partner, and **(c)** the partner's share in gallons of the partnership's productive capacity for alcohol.

• Credit for increasing research activities (Form 6765).

• Enhanced oil recovery credit (Form 8830).

• Disabled access credit (Form 8826).

• Renewable electricity production credit (Form 8835).

• Empowerment zone employment credit (Form 8844).

• Indian employment credit (Form 8845).

• Credit for employer social security and Medicare taxes paid on certain employee tips (Form 8846).

• Orphan drug credit (Form 8820).

• Credit for contributions to selected community development corporations (Form 8847).

See the instructions for line 25, item 13 of Schedule K-1 to report expenditures qualifying for the **(a)** rehabilitation credit not related to rental real estate activities, **(b)** energy credit, or **(c)** reforestation credit.

Investment Interest

Lines 14a through 14b(2) must be completed for all partners.

Line 14a—Interest Expense on Investment Debts

Include on this line interest paid or accrued on debt properly allocable to property held for investment. Property held for investment includes property that produces income (unless derived in the ordinary course of a trade or business) from interest, dividends, annuities, or royalties; and gains from the disposition of property that produces those types of income or is held for investment.

Property held for investment also includes each general partner's share of a working interest in any oil or gas property for which the partner's liability is not limited and in which the partner did not materially participate. However, the level of each partner's participation in an activity is determined by the partner and not by the partnership. As a result, interest

Page 18

allocable to a general partner's share of a working interest in any oil or gas property (if the partner's liability is not limited) should not be reported on line 14a. Instead, report this interest on line 11.

Investment interest does not include interest expense allocable to a passive activity.

The amount on line 14a will be deducted (after applying the investment interest expense limitations of section 163(d)) by individual partners on Schedule A (Form 1040), line 13.

For more information, see **Form 4952,** Investment Interest Expense Deduction.

Lines 14b(1) and 14b(2)—Investment Income and Expenses

Enter on line 14b(1) only the investment income included on lines 4a, 4b, 4c, and 4f of Schedules K and K-1. Do not include other portfolio gains or losses on this line.

Enter on line 14b(2) only the investment expense included on line 10 of Schedules K and K-1.

If there are other items of investment income or expense included in the amounts that are required to be passed through separately to the partner on Schedule K-1, such as net short-term capital gain or loss, net long-term capital gain or loss, and other portfolio gains or losses, give each partner a schedule identifying these amounts.

Investment income includes gross income from property held for investment, the excess of net gain from the disposition of property held for investment over net capital gain from the disposition of property held for investment, and any net capital gain from the disposition of property held for investment that each partner elects to include in investment income under section 163(d)(4)(B)(iii). Generally, investment income and investment expenses do not include any income or expenses from a passive activity.

Property subject to a net lease is not treated as investment property because it is subject to the passive loss rules. Do not reduce investment income by losses from passive activities.

Investment expenses are deductible expenses (other than interest) directly connected with the production of investment income. See the Form 4952 instructions for more information on investment income and expenses.

Self-Employment

Note: *If the partnership is an options dealer or a commodities dealer, see section 1402(i) before completing lines 15a, 15b, and 15c, to determine the amount of any adjustment that may have to be made to the amounts shown on the **Worksheet for Figuring Net Earnings (Loss) From Self-Employment** below. If the partnership is engaged solely in the operation of a group investment program, earnings from the operation are not self-employment earnings for either general or limited partners.*

General partners. General partners' net earnings (loss) from self-employment do not include:

• Dividends on any shares of stock and interest on any bonds, debentures, notes, etc., unless the dividends or interest are received in the course of a trade or business, such as a dealer in stocks or securities or interest on notes or accounts receivable.

• Rentals from real estate, except rentals of real estate held for sale to customers in the course of a trade or business as a real estate dealer or payments for rooms or space when significant services are provided.

• Royalty income, except royalty income received in the course of a trade or business.

See the instructions for **Schedule SE (Form 1040),** Self-Employment Tax, for more information.

Limited partners. Generally, a limited partner's share of partnership income (loss) is not included in net earnings (loss) from self-employment. Limited partners treat as self-employment earnings only guaranteed payments for services they actually rendered to, or on behalf of, the partnership to the extent that those payments are payment for those services.

Worksheet Instructions

Line 1b. Include on line 1b any part of the net income (loss) from rental real estate activities from Schedule K, line 2. that is from:

1. Rentals of real estate held for sale to customers in the course of a trade or business as a real estate dealer. or

2. Rentals for which services were rendered to the occupants (other than services usually or customarily rendered for the rental of space for occupancy only). The supplying of maid service is such a service: but the furnishing of heat and light, the cleaning of public entrances, exits. stairways and lobbies, trash collection. etc., are not considered services rendered to the occupants.

Lines 3b and 4b. Allocate the amounts on these lines in the same way Form 1065, page 1, line 22, is allocated to these particular partners.

Line 4a. Include in the amount on line 4a any guaranteed payments to partners reported on Schedules K and K-1, line 5, and derived from a trade or business as defined in section 1402(c). Also include other ordinary income and expense items (other than expense items subject to separate limitations at the partner level, such as the section 179 expense deduction) reported on Schedules K and K-1 that are used to figure self-employment earnings under section 1402.

Line 15a—Net Earnings (Loss) From Self-Employment

Schedule K. Enter on line 15a the amount from line 5 of the worksheet.

Schedule K-1. Do not complete this line for any partner that is an estate, trust, corporation, exempt organization, or individual retirement arrangement (IRA).

Enter on line 15a of Schedule K-1 each individual general partner's share of the amount shown on line 5 of the worksheet and each individual limited partner's share of the amount shown on line 4c of the worksheet.

Worksheet for Figuring Net Earnings (Loss) From Self-Employment

1a Ordinary income (loss) (Schedule K, line 1)	**1a**		
b Net income (loss) from **CERTAIN** rental real estate activities (see instructions) . . .	**1b**		
c Net income (loss) from other rental activities (Schedule K, line 3c)	**1c**		
d Net loss from Form 4797, Part II, line 18, included on line 1a above. Enter as a positive amount	**1d**		
e Combine lines 1a through 1d	**1e**		
2 Net gain from Form 4797, Part II, line 18, included on line 1a above	**2**		
3a Subtract line 2 from line 1e. If line 1e is a loss, increase the loss on line 1e by the amount on line 2	**3a**		
b Part of line 3a allocated to limited partners, estates, trusts, corporations, exempt organizations, and IRAs	**3b**		
c Subtract line 3b from line 3a. If line 3a is a loss, reduce the loss on line 3a by the amount on line 3b. Include each individual general partner's share on line 15a of Schedule K-1		**3c**	
4a Guaranteed payments to partners (Schedule K, line 5) derived from a trade or business as defined in section 1402(c) (see instructions)	**4a**		
b Part of line 4a allocated to individual limited partners for **other than** services and to estates, trusts, corporations, exempt organizations, and IRAs	**4b**		
c Subtract line 4b from line 4a. Include each individual general partner's share and each individual limited partner's share on line 15a of Schedule K-1		**4c**	
5 Net earnings (loss) from self-employment. Combine lines 3c and 4c. Enter here and on Schedule K, line 15a	**5**		

Line 15b—Gross Farming or Fishing Income

Enter the partnership's gross farming or fishing income from self-employment. Individual partners need this amount to figure net earnings from self-employment under the farm optional method in Section B, Part II of Schedule SE (Form 1040).

Line 15c—Gross Nonfarm Income

Enter the partnership's gross nonfarm income from self-employment. Individual partners need this amount to figure net earnings from self-employment under the nonfarm optional method in Section B, Part II of Schedule SE (Form 1040).

Adjustments and Tax Preference Items

Lines 16a through 16e must be completed for all partners.

Enter items of income and deductions that are adjustments or tax preference items. See **Form 6251,** Alternative Minimum Tax—Individuals; **Form 4626,** Alternative Minimum Tax—Corporations; or Schedule I of **Form 1041,** U.S. Income Tax Return for Estates and Trusts, to determine the amounts to enter and for other information.

Do not include as a tax preference item any qualified expenditures to which an election under section 59(e) may apply. Instead, report these expenditures on lines 18a and 18b. Because these expenditures are subject to an election by each partner, the partnership cannot figure the amount of any tax preference related to them.

Line 16a—Depreciation Adjustment on Property Placed in Service After 1986

Figure the adjustment for line 16a based only on tangible property placed in service after 1986 (and tangible property placed in service after July 31, 1986, and before 1987 for which the partnership elected to use the General Depreciation System). **Do not** make an adjustment for motion picture films, videotapes, sound recordings, certain public utility property (as defined in section 168(f)(2)), or property depreciated under the unit-of-production method (or any other method not expressed in a term of years).

Using the same convention you used for regular tax purposes, refigure depreciation as follows:

• For property that is neither real property nor property depreciated using the straight line method, use the 150% declining balance method over the property's class life (instead of the recovery period), switching to straight line for the first tax year that method gives a better result. See Pub. 946 for a table of class lives. For property having no class life, use 12 years.

• For property depreciated using the straight line method (other than real property), use the straight line method over the property's class life (instead of the recovery period). For property having no class life, use 12 years.

• For residential rental and nonresidential real property, use the straight line method over 40 years.

Determine the depreciation adjustment by subtracting the refigured depreciation from the depreciation claimed on Form 4562. If the refigured depreciation exceeds the depreciation claimed on Form 4562, enter the difference as a negative amount. See the instructions for Form 4562 and Form 6251 for more information.

Line 16b—Adjusted Gain or Loss

If the partnership disposed of any tangible property placed in service after 1986 (or after July 31, 1986, if an election was made to use the General Depreciation System), or if it disposed of a certified pollution control facility placed in service after 1986, refigure the gain or loss from the disposition using the adjusted basis for the alternative minimum tax (AMT). The property's adjusted basis for the AMT is its cost or other basis minus all depreciation or amortization deductions allowed or allowable for the AMT during the current tax year and previous tax years. Enter on this line the difference between the regular tax gain (or loss) and the AMT gain (or loss). If the AMT gain is less than the regular tax gain, **or** the AMT loss is more than the regular tax loss, **or** there is an AMT loss and a regular tax gain, enter the difference as a negative amount.

If any part of the adjustment is allocable to net short-term capital gain (loss), net long-term capital gain (loss), or net section 1231 gain (loss), attach a schedule that identifies the amount of the adjustment allocable to each type of gain or loss. For a net long-term capital gain (loss) or net section 1231 gain (loss), also identify the amount of adjustment that is 28% rate gain (loss) and unrecaptured section 1250 gain. No schedule is required if the adjustment is allocable solely to ordinary gain (loss).

Line 16c—Depletion (Other Than Oil and Gas)

Do not include any depletion on oil and gas wells. The partners must figure their depletion deductions and preference items separately.

Refigure the depletion deduction under section 611 for mines, wells (other than oil and gas wells), and other natural deposits for the AMT. Percentage depletion is limited to 50% of the taxable income from the property as figured under section 613(a), using only income and deductions allowed for the AMT. Also, the deduction is limited to the property's adjusted basis at the end of the year, as refigured for the AMT. Figure this limit separately for each property. When refiguring the property's adjusted basis, take into account any AMT adjustments made this year or in previous years that affect basis (other than the current year's depletion).

Enter the difference between the regular tax and AMT deduction. If the AMT deduction is greater, enter the difference as a negative amount.

Lines 16d(1) and 16d(2)

Enter only the income and deductions for oil, gas, and geothermal properties that are used to figure the partnership's ordinary income or loss (line 22 of Form 1065). If there are items of income or deduction for oil, gas, and geothermal properties included in the amounts required to be passed through separately to the partners on Schedule K-1 (items not reported on line 1 of Schedule K-1), give each partner a schedule identifying these amounts.

Figure the amount for lines 16d(1) and (2) separately for oil and gas properties that are not geothermal deposits and for all properties that are geothermal deposits.

Give each partner a schedule that shows the separate amounts that are included in the computation of the amounts on lines 16d(1) and (2).

Line 16d(1)—Gross income from oil, gas, and geothermal properties. Enter the aggregate amount of gross income (within the meaning of section 613(a)) from all oil, gas, and geothermal properties that was received or accrued during the tax year and included on page 1, Form 1065.

Line 16d(2)—Deductions allocable to oil, gas, and geothermal properties. Enter the amount of any deductions allowed for the AMT that are allocable to oil, gas, and geothermal properties.

Line 16e—Other Adjustments and Tax Preference Items

Attach a schedule that shows each partner's share of other items not shown on lines 16a through 16d(2) that are adjustments or tax preference items or that the partner needs to complete Form 6251, Form 4626, or Schedule I of Form 1041. See these forms and their instructions to determine the amount to enter.

Other adjustments or tax preference items include the following:

• Accelerated depreciation of real property under pre-1987 rules.

• Accelerated depreciation of leased personal property under pre-1987 rules.

• Long-term contracts entered into after February 28, 1986. Except for certain home construction contracts, the taxable income from these contracts must be figured using the percentage of completion method of accounting for the AMT.

• Losses from tax shelter farm activities. No loss from any tax shelter farm activity is allowed for the AMT.

Foreign Taxes

Lines 17a through 17g must be completed whether or not a partner is eligible for the foreign tax credit if the partnership has foreign income, deductions, or losses or has paid or accrued foreign taxes.

In addition to the instructions below, see the following for more information:

• **Form 1116,** Foreign Tax Credit (Individual, Estate, Trust, or Nonresident Alien Individual), and the related instructions.

• **Form 1118,** Foreign Tax Credit—Corporations, and the related instructions.

• **Pub. 514,** Foreign Tax Credit for Individuals.

Line 17a—Type of Income

Enter the type of income from outside the United States as follows:

• Passive income.

• High withholding tax interest.

• Financial services income.

• Shipping income.

• Dividends from a DISC or former DISC.

• Distributions from a foreign sales corporation (FSC) or former FSC.

• Dividends from each noncontrolled section 902 corporation.

• Taxable income attributable to foreign trade income (within the meaning of section 923(b)).

• General limitation income—all other income from sources outside the United States (including income from sources within U.S. possessions).

If, for the country or U.S. possession shown on line 17b, the partnership had **more than one** type of income, enter **"See attached"** and attach a schedule for each type of income for lines 17c through 17g.

Line 17b—Foreign Country or U.S. Possession

Enter the name of the foreign country or U.S. possession. If, for the type of income shown on line 17a, the partnership had income from, or paid taxes to, **more than one** foreign country or U.S. possession, enter **"See attached"** and attach a schedule for each country for lines 17a and 17c through 17g.

Line 17c—Total Gross Income From Sources Outside the United States

Enter in U.S. dollars the total gross income from sources outside the United States. Attach a schedule that shows each type of income listed in the instructions for line 17a.

See section 904(d) for types of income that must be reported to partners for figuring their foreign tax credit.

Line 17d—Total Applicable Deductions and Losses

Enter in U.S. dollars the total applicable deductions and losses attributable to income on line 17c. Attach a schedule that shows each type of deduction or loss as follows:

- Expenses directly allocable to each type of income listed above.
- Pro rata share of all other deductions not directly allocable to specific items of income.
- Pro rata share of losses from other separate limitation categories.

Line 17e—Total Foreign Taxes

Enter in U.S. dollars the total foreign taxes (described in section 901) that were paid or accrued by the partnership to foreign countries or U.S. possessions. Attach a schedule that shows the dates the taxes were paid or accrued, and the amount in both foreign currency and in U.S. dollars, as follows:

- Taxes withheld at source on dividends.
- Taxes withheld at source on rents and royalties.
- Other foreign taxes paid or accrued.

Line 17f—Reduction in Taxes Available for Credit

Enter in U.S. dollars the total reduction in taxes available for credit. Attach a schedule that shows separately the:

- Reduction for foreign mineral income (section 901(e)).
- Reduction for failure to furnish returns required under section 6038.
- Reduction for taxes attributable to boycott operations (section 908).
- Reduction for foreign oil and gas extraction income (section 907(a)).
- Reduction for any other items (specify).

Line 17g—Other Foreign Tax Information

Enter in U.S. dollars any items not covered on lines 17c through 17f. For noncorporate partners, enter gross income from all sources. Noncorporate partners need this information to complete Form 1116. For corporate partners, enter gross income and definitely allocable deductions from sources outside the United States and for foreign branches. Corporations need this information to complete Form 1118, Schedule F.

Other

Lines 18a and 18b

Generally, section 59(e) allows each partner to make an election to deduct the partner's distributive share of the partnership's otherwise deductible qualified expenditures ratably over 10 years (3 years for circulation expenditures), beginning with the tax year in which the expenditures were made (or for intangible drilling and development costs, over the 60-month period beginning with the month in which such costs were paid or incurred). The term "qualified expenditures" includes only the following types of expenditures paid or incurred during the tax year:

- Circulation expenditures.
- Research and experimental expenditures.
- Intangible drilling and development costs.
- Mining exploration and development costs.

If a partner makes this election, these items are not treated as tax preference items.

Because the partners are generally allowed to make this election, the partnership cannot deduct these amounts or include them as adjustments or tax preference items on Schedule K-1. Instead, on lines 18a and 18b of Schedule K-1, the partnership passes through the information the partners need to figure their separate deductions.

On line 18a, enter the type of expenditures claimed on line 18b. Enter on line 18b the qualified expenditures paid or incurred during the tax year to which an election under section 59(e) may apply. Enter this amount for all partners whether or not any partner makes an election under section 59(e). If the expenditures are for intangible drilling and development costs, enter the month in which the expenditures were paid or incurred (after the type of expenditure on line 18a). If there is more than one type of expenditure included in the total shown on line 18b (or intangible drilling and development costs were paid or incurred for more than 1 month), report this information separately for each type of expenditure (or month) on an attachment to Schedules K and K-1.

Line 19—Tax-Exempt Interest Income

Enter on line 19 tax-exempt interest income, including any exempt-interest dividends received from a mutual fund or other regulated investment company. This information must be reported by individuals on line 8b of Form 1040. The adjusted basis of the partner's interest is increased by the amount shown on this line under section 705(a)(1)(B).

Line 20—Other Tax-Exempt Income

Enter on line 20 all income of the partnership exempt from tax other than tax-exempt interest (e.g., life insurance proceeds). The adjusted basis of the partner's interest is increased by the amount shown on this line under section 705(a)(1)(B).

Line 21—Nondeductible Expenses

Enter on line 21 nondeductible expenses paid or incurred by the partnership. Do not include separately stated deductions shown elsewhere on Schedules K and K-1, capital expenditures, or items the deduction for which is deferred to a later tax year. The adjusted basis of the partner's interest is decreased by the amount shown on this line under section 705(a)(2)(B).

Line 22—Distributions of Money (Cash and Marketable Securities)

Enter on line 22 the total distributions to each partner of cash and marketable securities that are treated as money under section 731(c)(1). Generally, marketable securities are valued at fair market value on the date of distribution. However, the value of marketable securities does not include the distributee partner's share of the gain on the securities distributed to that partner. See section 731(c)(3)(B) for details.

If the amount on line 22 includes marketable securities treated as money, state separately on an attachment to Schedules K and K-1 **(a)** the partnership's adjusted basis of those securities immediately before the distribution and **(b)** the fair market value of those securities on the date of distribution (excluding the distributee partner's share of the gain on the securities distributed to that partner).

Line 23—Distributions of Property Other Than Money

Enter on line 23 the total distributions to each partner of property not included on line 22. The property is valued at its adjusted basis to the partnership immediately before the distribution.

Line 24 (Schedule K Only)

Attach a statement to report the partnership's total income, expenditures, or other information for the items listed under **Supplemental Information (Schedule K-1 Only)** below.

Lines 24a and 24b (Schedule K-1 Only)—Recapture of Low-Income Housing Credit

If recapture of part or all of the low-income housing credit is required because: **(a)** prior year qualified basis of a building decreased, or **(b)** the partnership disposed of a building or part of its interest in a building, see **Form 8611**, Recapture of Low-Income Housing Credit. The instructions for Form 8611 indicate when the form is completed by the partnership and what information is provided to partners when recapture is required.

If a partner's ownership interest in a building decreased because of a transaction at the partner level, the partnership must provide the necessary information to the partner to enable the partner to figure the recapture.

Report on line 24a the total low-income housing credit recapture with respect to a partnership treated under section 42(j)(5) as the taxpayer to which the low-income housing credit was allowed. Report any other low-income housing credit recapture on line 24b.

If the partnership filed **Form 8693**, Low-Income Housing Credit Disposition Bond, to avoid recapture of the low-income housing credit, no entry should be made on line 24 of Schedule K-1.

See Form 8586, Form 8611, and section 42 for more information.

Supplemental Information (Schedule K-1 Only)

Line 25

Enter in the line 25 Supplemental Information space of Schedule K-1, or on an attached schedule if more space is needed, each partner's share of any information asked for on lines 1 through 24b that must be reported in detail, and items **1** through **19** on page 22. Identify the applicable line number next to the information entered in the Supplemental Information space. Show income or gains as a positive number. Show losses in parentheses.

1. Taxes paid on undistributed capital gains by a regulated investment company or a real estate investment trust (REIT). As a shareholder of a regulated investment company or a REIT, the partnership will receive notice on **Form 2439,** Notice to Shareholder of Undistributed Long-Term Capital Gains, of the amount of tax paid on undistributed capital gains.

2. The number of gallons of each fuel used during the tax year in a use qualifying for the credit for taxes paid on fuels and the applicable credit per gallon. See **Form 4136,** Credit for Federal Tax Paid on Fuels, for details.

3. The partner's share of gross income from each property, share of production for the tax year, etc., needed to figure the partner's depletion deduction for oil and gas wells. The partnership should also allocate to each partner a proportionate share of the adjusted basis of each partnership oil or gas property. The allocation of the basis of each property is made as specified in section 613A(c)(7)(D).

The partnership cannot deduct depletion on oil and gas wells. The partner must determine the allowable amount to report on his or her return. See Pub. 535 for more information.

4. Recapture of section 179 expense deduction. For property placed in service after 1986, the section 179 expense deduction is recaptured at any time the business use of the property drops to 50% or less. Enter the amount that was originally passed through to the partners and the partnership's tax year in which the amount was passed through. Inform the partner if the recapture amount was caused by the disposition of the section 179 property. Do not include this amount in the partnership's income.

5. Recapture of certain mining exploration expenditures (section 617).

6. Any information or statements a partner needs to comply with section 6111 (registration of tax shelters) or section 6662(d)(2)(B)(ii) (regarding adequate disclosure of items that may cause an understatement of income tax).

7. The partner's share of preproductive period farm expenses, if the partnership is not required to use the accrual method of accounting. See Temporary Regulations section 1.263A-4T.

8. Any information needed by a partner to figure the interest due under section 453(l)(3). If the partnership elected to report the disposition of certain timeshares and residential lots on the installment method, each partner's tax liability must be increased by the partner's allocable share of the interest on tax attributable to the installment payments received during the tax year.

9. Any information needed by a partner to figure interest due under section 453A(c). If an obligation arising from the disposition of property to which section 453A applies is outstanding at the close of the year, report each partner's allocable share of the outstanding installment obligation to which section 453A(b) applies.

10. For closely held partnerships (as defined in section 460(b)(4)), provide the information needed by a partner to figure the partner's allocable share of any interest due or to be refunded under the look-back method of section 460(b)(2) on certain long-term contracts that are accounted for under either the percentage of completion-capitalized cost method or the percentage of completion method. Also attach to Form 1065 the information specified in the instructions for Form 8697, Part II, lines 1 and 3, for each tax year in which such a long-term contract is completed.

11. Any information needed by a partner relating to interest expense that the partner is required to capitalize. Under section 263A, a partner may be required to capitalize interest expense incurred by the partner during the tax year with respect to the production expenditures of the partnership. Similarly, interest incurred by a partnership may have to be capitalized by a partner with respect to the partner's own production expenditures. The information required by the partner to properly capitalize interest for this purpose must be provided on an attachment to Schedule K-1. See Regulations sections 1.263A-8 through 1.263A-15 for more information.

12. Any information a partner that is a tax-exempt organization may need to figure that partner's share of unrelated business taxable income under section 512(a)(1) (but excluding any modifications required by paragraphs (8) through (15) of section 512(b)). Partners are required to notify the partnership of their tax-exempt status.

13. Expenditures qualifying for the **(a)** rehabilitation credit not related to rental real estate activities, **(b)** energy credit, or **(c)** reforestation credit. Complete and attach Form 3468 to Form 1065. See Form 3468 and the related instructions for information on eligible property and the lines on Form 3468 to complete. Do not include that part of the cost of the property the partnership has elected to expense under section 179. Attach to each Schedule K-1 a separate schedule in a format similar to that shown on Form 3468 detailing each partner's share of qualified expenditures. Also indicate the lines of Form 3468 on which the partners should report these amounts.

14. Recapture of investment credit. Complete and attach **Form 4255,** Recapture of Investment Credit, when investment credit property is disposed of, or it no longer qualifies for the credit, before the end of the recapture period or the useful life applicable to the property. State the type of property at the top of Form 4255 and complete lines 2, 4, and 5, whether or not any partner is subject to recapture of the credit. Attach to each Schedule K-1 a separate schedule providing the information the partnership is required to show on Form 4255, but list only the partner's distributive share of the cost of the property subject to recapture. Also indicate the lines of Form 4255 on which the partners should report these amounts.

15. Any information a partner may need to figure the recapture of the qualified electric vehicle credit. See Pub. 535 for more information.

16. Any information a partner may need to figure recapture of the Indian employment credit. Generally, if a partnership terminates a qualified employee less than 1 year after the date of initial employment, any Indian employment credit allowed for a prior tax year by reason of wages paid or incurred to that employee must be recaptured. For details, see section 45A(d).

17. Nonqualified withdrawals by the partnership from a capital construction fund.

18. Unrecaptured section 1250 gain. Figure this amount for each section 1250 property in Part III of Form 4797 for which you had an entry in column (g), but not in column (h), of Part I of Form 4797 by subtracting line 26g of Form 4797 from the **smaller** of line 22 or line 24 of Form 4797. Figure the total of these amounts for all section 1250 properties. Report each partner's distributive share of the total amount as "Unrecaptured section 1250 gain."

If the partnership also received a Schedule K-1 or Form 1099-DIV from an estate, a trust, a REIT, or a mutual fund reporting "unrecaptured section 1250 gain," **do not** add it to the partnership's own unrecaptured section 1250 gain. Instead, report it as a separate amount. For example, if the partnership received a Form 1099-DIV from a REIT with unrecaptured section 1250 gain, report it as "Unrecaptured section 1250 gain from a REIT."

19. Any other information a partner may need to file his or her return that is not shown anywhere else on Schedule K-1. For example, if one of the partners is a pension plan, that partner may need special information to properly file its tax return.

Specific Instructions

Analysis of Net Income (Loss)

For each type of partner shown, enter the portion of the amount shown on line 1 that was allocated to that type of partner. Report all amounts for limited liability company members on the line for limited partners. The sum of the amounts shown on line 2 must equal the amount shown on line 1. In addition, the amount on line 1 must equal the amount on line 9, Schedule M-1 (if the partnership is required to complete Schedule M-1).

In classifying partners who are individuals as "active" or "passive," the partnership should apply the rules below. In applying these rules, a partnership should classify each partner to the best of its knowledge and belief. It is assumed that in most cases the level of a particular partner's participation in an activity will be apparent:

1. If the partnership's principal activity is a trade or business, classify a general partner as "active" if the partner materially participated in all partnership trade or business activities; otherwise, classify a general partner as "passive."

2. If the partnership's principal activity consists of a working interest in an oil or gas well, classify a general partner as "active."

3. If the partnership's principal activity is a rental real estate activity, classify a general partner as "active" if the partner actively participated in all of the partnership's rental real estate activities; otherwise, classify a general partner as "passive."

4. Classify as "passive" all partners in a partnership whose principal activity is a rental activity other than a rental real estate activity.

5. If the partnership's principal activity is a portfolio activity, classify all partners as "active."

6. Classify as "passive" all limited partners and limited liability company members in a partnership whose principal activity is a trade or business or rental activity.

7. If the partnership cannot make a reasonable determination whether a partner's participation in a trade or business activity is material or whether a partner's participation in a rental real estate activity is active, classify the partner as "passive."

Schedule L—Balance Sheets per Books

Note: *Schedules L, M-1, and M-2 are not required to be completed if the partnership answered* **Yes** *to Question 5 of Schedule B.*

The balance sheets should agree with the partnership's books and records. Attach a statement explaining any differences.

Partnerships reporting to the Interstate Commerce Commission or to any national, state, municipal, or other public officer may send copies of their balance sheets prescribed by the Commission or state or municipal authorities, as of the beginning and end of the tax year, instead of completing Schedule L. However, statements filed under this procedure must contain sufficient information to enable the IRS to reconstruct a balance sheet similar to that contained on Form 1065 without contacting the partnership during processing.

Line 5—Tax-Exempt Securities

Include on this line:

1. State and local government obligations, the interest on which is excludable from gross income under section 103(a), and

2. Stock in a mutual fund or other regulated investment company that distributed exempt-interest dividends during the tax year of the partnership.

Line 18—All Nonrecourse Loans

Nonrecourse loans are those liabilities of the partnership for which no partner bears the economic risk of loss.

Schedule M-1—Reconciliation of Income (Loss) per Books With Income (Loss) per Return

Line 3—Guaranteed Payments

Include on this line guaranteed payments shown on Schedule K, line 5 (other than amounts paid for insurance that constitutes medical care for a partner, a partner's spouse, and a partner's dependents).

Line 4b—Travel and Entertainment

Include on this line:

- 50% of meals and entertainment not allowed under section 274(n).
- Expenses for the use of an entertainment facility.
- The part of business gifts over $25.
- Expenses of an individual allocable to conventions on cruise ships over $2,000.
- Employee achievement awards over $400.
- The part of the cost of entertainment tickets that exceeds face value (also subject to 50% disallowance).
- The part of the cost of skyboxes that exceeds the face value of nonluxury box seat tickets.
- The part of the cost of luxury water travel not allowed under section 274(m).
- Expenses for travel as a form of education.
- Nondeductible club dues.
- Other travel and entertainment expenses not allowed as a deduction.

Schedule M-2—Analysis of Partners' Capital Accounts

Show what caused the changes during the tax year in the partners' capital accounts as reflected on the partnership's books and records. The amounts on Schedule M-2 should equal the total of the amounts reported in Item J of all the partners' Schedules K-1.

The partnership may, but is not required to, use the rules in Regulations section 1.704-1(b)(2)(iv) to determine the partners' capital accounts in Schedule M-2 and Item J of the partners' Schedules K-1. If the beginning and ending capital accounts reported under these rules differ from the amounts reported on Schedule L, attach a statement reconciling any differences.

Line 2—Capital Contributed During Year

Include on line 2 the amount of money and property contributed by each partner to the partnership as reflected on the partnership's books and records.

Line 3—Net Income per Books

Enter on line 3 the net income shown on the partnership books from Schedule M-1, line 1.

Line 6—Distributions

1. On line 6a, enter the amount of money distributed to each partner by the partnership.

2. On line 6b, enter the amount of property distributed to each partner by the partnership as reflected on the partnership's books and records. Include withdrawals from inventory for the personal use of a partner.

Codes for Principal Business Activity and Principal Product or Service

These codes for the Principal Business Activity are designed to classify an enterprise by the type of activity in which it is engaged to facilitate the administration of the Internal Revenue Code. Though similar in format and structure to the Standard Industrial Classification Codes (SIC), they should not be used as SIC codes.

Using the list below, enter on page 1, Item C, the code for the specific industry group for which the largest percentage of "total assets (Schedule L, line 14, column (d))" is used.

In Item A, state the principal business activity. In Item B, state the principal product or service that accounts for the largest percentage of total assets. For example, if the principal business activity is "Retail food store," the principal product or service may be "dairy products."

Agriculture, Forestry, and Fishing

Code

Farms:
- 0120 Field crop.
- 0160 Vegetable and melon farms.
- 0170 Fruit and nut tree farms.
- 0180 Horticultural specialty.
- 0211 Beef cattle feedlots.
- 0212 Beef cattle, except feedlots.
- 0215 Hogs, sheep, and goats.
- 0240 Dairy farms.
- 0250 Poultry and eggs.
- 0260 General livestock (except animal specialty).
- 0270 Animal specialty.

Agricultural services and forestry:
- 0740 Veterinary services.
- 0753 Livestock breeding.
- 0754 Animal services, except livestock breeding and veterinary.
- 0780 Landscape and horticultural services.
- 0790 Other agricultural services.
- 0800 Forestry, except logging.
- 2400 Logging.

Fishing, hunting, and trapping:
- 0930 Commercial fishing, hatcheries, and preserves.
- 0970 Hunting, trapping, and game propagation.

Mining
- 1000 Metal mining.
- 1200 Coal mining.
- 1300 Oil and gas extraction.
- 1400 Nonmetallic minerals except fuel.

Construction

General building contractors and operative builders:
- 1510 General building contractors.
- 1531 Operative builders.

Heavy construction contractors:
- 1611 Highway and street construction.
- 1620 Heavy construction, except highway.

Special trade contractors:
- 1711 Plumbing, heating, and air conditioning.
- 1721 Painting, paperhanging, and decorating.
- 1731 Electrical work.
- 1740 Masonry, drywall, stone, tile.
- 1750 Carpentering and flooring.
- 1761 Roofing, siding, and sheet metal.
- 1771 Concrete work.
- 1781 Water well drilling.
- 1790 Other building trade contractors (excavation, glazing, etc.)

Manufacturing
- 2000 Food and kindred products.
- 2200 Textile mill products.
- 2300 Apparel and other textile products.
- 2400 Lumber and wood products, except furniture.
- 2500 Furniture and fixtures.
- 2700 Printing, publishing, and allied industries.
- 2800 Chemicals and allied products.
- 3000 Rubber and plastic products.
- 3100 Leather and leather products.
- 3200 Stone, clay, and glass products.
- 3300 Primary metal industries.
- 3400 Fabricated metal products.
- 3500 Machinery, except electrical.
- 3600 Electrical and electronic equipment.
- 3700 Transportation equipment.
- 3970 Other manufacturing industries.

Transportation, Communication, Electric, Gas, and Sanitary Services

Code

Local and interurban passenger transit:
- 4121 Taxicabs.
- 4189 Other passenger transportation.

Trucking and warehousing:
- 4210 Trucking (local and long distance), except trash collection.
- 4216 Trash collection without own dump.
- 4220 Public warehousing.

Other transportation including transportation services:
- 4400 Water transportation.
- 4540 Transportation by air.
- 4722 Passenger transportation arrangement.
- 4799 Other transportation services.
- **4800 Communication.**
- **4900 Utilities, including dumps, snowplowing, etc.**

Wholesale Trade—Selling Goods to Other Businesses, Government, or Institutions, etc.

Durable goods, including machinery, equipment, wood, metals, etc.:
- 5001 Selling for your own account.
- 5002 Agent or broker for other firms–more than 50% of gross sales on commission.

Nondurable goods, including food, fiber, chemicals, etc.:
- 5101 Selling for your own account.
- 5102 Agent or broker for other firms–more than 50% of gross sales on commission.

Retail Trade

Building materials, hardware, garden supply, and mobile home dealers:
- 5211 Lumber and other building materials dealers.
- 5231 Paint, glass, and wallpaper stores.
- 5251 Hardware stores.
- 5261 Retail nurseries and garden stores.
- 5271 Mobile home dealers.

General merchandise:
- 5331 Variety stores.
- 5398 Other general merchandise stores.

Food stores:
- 5411 Grocery stores.
- 5420 Meat and fish markets freezer provisioners.
- 5431 Fruit stores and vegetable markets.
- 5441 Candy, nut, and confectionery stores.
- 5451 Dairy products stores.
- 5460 Retail bakeries.
- 5490 Other food stores.

Automotive dealers and service stations:
- 5511 New car dealers (franchised).
- 5521 Used car dealers.
- 5531 Auto and home supply stores.
- 5541 Gasoline service stations.
- 5551 Boat dealers.
- 5561 Recreational vehicle dealers.
- 5571 Motorcycle dealers.
- 5599 Aircraft and other automotive dealers.

Apparel and accessory stores:
- 5611 Men's and boys' clothing and furnishings.
- 5621 Women's ready-to-wear stores.
- 5631 Women's accessory and specialty stores.
- 5641 Children's and infants' wear stores.
- 5651 Family clothing stores.
- 5661 Shoe stores.
- 5681 Furriers and fur shops.
- 5699 Other apparel and accessory stores.

Furniture, home furnishings, and equipment stores:
- 5712 Furniture stores.
- 5713 Floor covering stores.
- 5714 Drapery, curtain, and upholstery stores.
- 5719 Home furnishings, except appliances.
- 5722 Household appliance stores.
- 5732 Radio and television stores.
- 5733 Music stores.
- 5734 Computer and software stores.

Eating and drinking places:
- 5812 Eating places.
- 5813 Drinking places.

Miscellaneous retail stores:
- 5912 Drug stores and proprietary stores.
- 5921 Liquor stores.
- 5932 Used merchandise and antique stores (except motor vehicle parts).
- 5941 Sporting goods stores and bicycle shops.
- 5942 Book stores.
- 5943 Stationery stores.
- 5944 Jewelry stores.
- 5945 Hobby, toy, and game shops.
- 5946 Camera and photographic supply stores.
- 5947 Gift, novelty, and souvenir shops.
- 5948 Luggage and leather goods stores.
- 5949 Sewing, needlework, and piece goods stores.
- 5961 Mail order houses.
- 5962 Merchandising machine operators.
- 5963 Direct selling organizations.
- 5983 Fuel oil dealers.
- 5984 Liquefied petroleum gas (bottled gas) dealers.
- 5989 Other fuel dealers (except gasoline)
- 5992 Florists.
- 5996 Other miscellaneous retail stores.

Finance, Insurance, and Real Estate
- **6000 Banking.**
- **6100 Credit agencies other than banks.**

Security and commodity brokers, dealers, exchanges, and services:
- 6212 Security underwriting syndicates.
- 6218 Security brokers and dealers, except underwriting syndicates.
- 6299 Commodity contracts brokers and dealers; security and commodity exchanges; and allied services.
- **6411 Insurance agents, brokers, and services.**

Real estate:
- 6511 Real estate operators (except developers) and lessors of buildings.
- 6520 Lessors of real property other than buildings.
- 6531 Real estate agents, brokers, and managers.
- 6541 Title abstract offices.
- 6552 Subdividers and developers, except cemeteries.
- 6553 Cemetery subdividers and developers.

Holding and other investment companies:
- 6746 Investment clubs.
- 6747 Common trust funds.
- 6748 Other holding and investment companies.

Services

Hotels and other lodging places:
- 7012 Hotels.
- 7013 Motels, motor hotels, and tourist courts.
- 7021 Rooming and boarding houses.
- 7032 Sporting and recreational camps.
- 7033 Trailer parks and camp sites.

Personal services:
- 7215 Coin-operated laundries and dry cleaning.
- 7219 Other laundry, cleaning, and garment services.
- 7221 Photographic studios and portrait studios.
- 7231 Beauty shops.
- 7241 Barber shops.
- 7251 Shoe repair and hat cleaning shops.
- 7261 Funeral services and crematories.
- 7291 Income tax preparation.
- 7299 Miscellaneous personal services.

Business services:
- 7310 Advertising.
- 7340 Janitorial and window cleaning.
- 7350 Equipment rental and leasing.
- 7370 Computer and data processing services.
- 7398 Other business services.

Automotive repair and services:
- 7510 Automotive rentals and leasing, without drivers.
- 7520 Automobile parking.
- 7538 General automobile repair shops.
- 7539 Other automotive repair shops.
- 7540 Automotive services, except repair.

Miscellaneous repair services:
- 7622 Radio and TV repair shops.
- 7628 Electrical repair shops, except radio and TV.
- 7641 Reupholstery and furniture repair.
- 7680 Other miscellaneous repair shops.

Motion picture:
- 7812 Other motion picture and TV film and tape activities.
- 7830 Motion picture theaters.
- 7840 Video tape rental stores.

Amusement and recreation services:
- 7920 Producers, orchestras, and entertainers.
- 7933 Bowling alleys.
- 7941 Professional sports clubs and promoters.
- 7948 Racing, including track operation.
- 7980 Other amusement and recreation services.
- 7991 Physical fitness facilities.

Medical and health services:
- 8011 Offices and clinics of medical doctors (MDs).
- 8021 Offices and clinics of dentists.
- 8031 Offices of osteopathic physicians.
- 8041 Offices of chiropractors.
- 8042 Offices of optometrists.
- 8047 Other licensed health practitioners.
- 8048 Registered and practical nurses.
- 8050 Nursing and personal care facilities.
- 8060 Hospitals.
- 8072 Dental laboratories.
- 8098 Other medical and health services.

Other services:
- 8111 Legal services.
- 8200 Educational services.
- 8351 Child day care.
- 8722 Certified public accountants.
- 8723 Other accounting, auditing, and bookkeeping services.
- 8740 Management, consulting, and public relations services.
- 8911 Engineering and architectural services.
- 8999 Other services not classified elsewhere.

Instructions for Form 1120

U.S. Corporation Income Tax Return

1997

Instructions for Forms 1120 and 1120-A

Department of the Treasury
Internal Revenue Service

Section references are to the Internal Revenue Code unless otherwise noted.

Paperwork Reduction Act Notice.— We ask for the information on these forms to carry out the Internal Revenue laws of the United States. You are required to give us the information. We need it to ensure that you are complying with these laws and to allow us to figure and collect the right amount of tax.

You are not required to provide the information requested on a form that is subject to the Paperwork Reduction Act unless the form displays a valid OMB control number. Books or records relating to a form or its instructions must be retained as long as their contents may become material in the administration of any Internal Revenue law. Generally, tax returns and return information are confidential, as required by section 6103.

The time needed to complete and file the following forms will vary depending on individual circumstances. The estimated average times are:

Form	Recordkeeping	Learning about the law or the form	Preparing the form	Copying, assembling, and sending the form to the IRS
1120	71 hr., 31 min.	41 hr., 46 min.	71 hr., 2 min.	7 hr., 47 min.
1120-A	44 hr., 14min.	23 hr., 33 min.	41 hr., 7 min.	4 hr., 34 min.
Sch. D (1120)	6 hr., 56 min.	3 hr., 31 min.	5 hr., 39 min.	32 min.
Sch. H (1120)	5 hr., 59 min.	35 min.	43 min.	0 min.
Sch. PH (1120)	15 hr.; 19 min.	6 hr., 12 min.	8 hr., 35 min.	32 min.

If you have comments concerning the accuracy of these time estimates or suggestions for making this form and related schedules simpler, we would be happy to hear from you. You can write to the Tax Forms Committee, Western Area Distribution Center, Rancho Cordova, CA 95743-0001. **DO NOT** send the tax form to this address. Instead, see **Where To File** on page 3.

Changes To Note

The Taxpayer Relief Act of 1997 ("The Act") made changes to the tax law for corporations. Some of the changes are discussed below.

● The holding period for the dividends-received deduction has been changed. Generally, for dividends received or accrued after September 4, 1997, a corporation is not entitled to a dividends-received deduction if the dividend paying stock is held less than 46 days during the 90–day period beginning 45 days before the stock becomes ex-dividend with respect to the dividend. For more information, including transitional rules and special rules for dividends on preferred stock, see the instructions for Schedule C, line 17, and Act section 1015.

● The carryback and carryforward period for net operating losses (NOLs) has changed. Generally, NOLs that occur in tax years beginning after August 5, 1997, are carried back two years and then forward to each of the 20 taxable years following the year of the loss. Certain corporations that qualify as "small businesses" or that are engaged in the trade or business of farming may use a 3–year carryback period for losses attributable to Presidentially declared disasters. For more information, see Act section 1082.

Special rules apply to specified liability losses. excess interest losses, and capital losses. See section 172(b)(1) and section 1212(a).

● For tax years ending after August 5, 1997, commodities dealers and traders in commodities and securities may make an election to use the mark-to-market accounting method. For more information, see Act section 1001.

● The Act imposed additional limitations on the deduction of premiums and interest on debt with respect to life insurance, annuity, or endowment contracts. The Act also reduces interest deductions that are allocable, under proration rules described in new section 264(f), to the unborrowed policy cash values of certain life insurance, endowment, or annuity contracts issued after June 8, 1997. These proration rules generally apply to life insurance, endowment, or annuity contracts with a direct or indirect business beneficiary, regardless of whether the business is listed as a policy holder or beneficiary on the policy. For more information, see section 264 and the instructions for Interest on page 7.

● The penalty for failure to make electronic deposits of depository taxes using the Electronic Federal Tax Payment System (EFTPS), has been temporarily waived for filers who were first required to use EFTPS on or after July 1, 1997. For more information, see **Electronic Deposit Requirement** on page 4.

● Employers that pay wages to qualified long-term family assistance (AFDC or its successor program) recipients who began work after December 31, 1997, may qualify to claim the welfare-to-work credit under new section 51A. The credit is figured on **Form 8861,** Welfare-to-Work Credit.

● The research credit has been extended for amounts paid or incurred through June 30, 1998. For details, get **Form 6765,** Credit for Increasing Researching Activities.

● The orphan drug credit has been permanently extended. For details, get **Form 8820,** Orphan Drug Credit.

● The work opportunity credit has been extended for wages paid to qualified individuals who begin work for the employer before July 1, 1998. For details, get **Form 5884,** Work Opportunity Credit.

Unresolved Tax Problems

The Problem Resolution Program is for corporations that have been unable to resolve their problems with the IRS. If the corporation has a tax problem it cannot clear up through

Cat. No. 11455T

normal channels, write to the corporation's local IRS District Director or call the corporation's local IRS office and ask for Problem Resolution assistance. Persons who have access to TTY/TDD equipment may call 1–800–829–4059 to ask for help from Problem Resolution. This office cannot change the law or technical decisions. But it can help the corporation clear up problems that resulted from previous contacts.

How To Make a Contribution To Reduce the Public Debt

To help reduce the public debt, send a check made payable to "Bureau of the Public Debt" to Bureau of the Public Debt, Department G, Washington, DC 20239–0601. Or, enclose a check with the income tax return. Contributions to reduce the public debt are deductible subject to the rules and limitations for charitable contributions.

How To Get Forms and Publications

Personal computer.— Visit the IRS's Internet Web Site at **www.irs.ustreas.gov** to get:
- Forms and instructions
- Publications
- IRS press releases and fact sheets
  You can also reach us using:
- Telnet at **iris.irs.ustreas.gov**
- File Transfer Protocol at **ftp.irs.ustreas.gov**
- Direct Dial (by modem) — Dial direct to the Internal Revenue Information Services (IRIS) by calling **703–321–8020** using your modem. IRIS is an on-line information service on FedWorld.

CD-ROM.— A CD-ROM containing over 2,000 tax products (including many prior year forms) can be purchased from the Government Printing Office (GPO). To order the CD-ROM, call the Superintendent of Documents at **202–512–1800,** or go through GPO's Internet Web Site (**www.access.gpo.gov/su_docs**).

By phone and in person.— To order forms and publications, call **1–800–TAX–FORM (1–800–829–3676)** between 7:30 a.m. and 5:30 p.m. on weekdays. You can also get most forms and publications at your local IRS office.

General Instructions

Purpose of Form

Use **Form 1120,** U.S. Corporation Income Tax Return, and **Form 1120-A,** U.S. Corporation Short-Form Income Tax Return, to report the income, gains, losses, deductions, credits, and to figure the income tax liability of a corporation. Also see **Pub. 542,** Corporations, for more information.

Who Must File

Unless exempt under section 501, all domestic corporations (including corporations in bankruptcy) must file whether or not they have taxable income. Domestic corporations must file Form 1120, or, if they qualify, Form 1120-A, unless they are required to file a special return (see **Special Returns for Certain Organizations** below).

Note: *If an organization resembles a corporation more than it resembles a partnership or trust, it will be considered an association taxed as a corporation.*

Limited liability companies.— If an entity was formed as a limited liability company under state law and is treated as a partnership for Federal income tax purposes, it should not file

Form 1120 or 1120-A. Instead, it should file **Form 1065,** U.S. Partnership Return of Income. For the definition of a limited liability company, see the Instructions for Form 1065.

Ownership Interest in a FASIT

If a corporation holds an ownership interest in a financial asset securitization investment trust (FASIT), it must report all items of income, gain, deductions, losses, and credits on the corporation's income tax return (except as provided in section 860H). Show a breakdown of the items on an attached schedule. For more information, see sections 860H and 860L.

Special Returns for Certain Organizations

Certain organizations, as shown below, have to file special returns.

If the organization is a	File Form
Farmers' cooperative (sec. 1381)	990-C
Exempt organization with unrelated trade or business income	990-T
Entity formed as a limited liability company under state law and treated as a partnership for Federal income tax purposes	1065
Religious or apostolic organization exempt under section 501(d)	1065
Entity that elects to be treated as a real estate mortgage investment conduit (REMIC) under sec. 860D	1066
Settlement fund (sec. 468B)	1120-SF

Who May File Form 1120-A

A corporation may file Form 1120-A if it meets all of the following requirements:

▶ All of the following amounts are **under** $500,000:
  - Gross receipts (line 1a)
  - Total income (line 11)
  - Total assets (Form 1120, Schedule L, line 15)

▶ Its only dividend income is from domestic corporations, and the dividends:
  - Qualify for the 70% deduction
  - Are not from debt-financed securities.

▶ It does not have any of the "write-in" additions to tax listed on pages 13 and 14 in the instructions for:
  - Form 1120, Schedule J, line 3
  - Form 1120, Schedule J, line 10.

▶ It has no nonrefundable tax credits (other than the general business credit or the credit for prior year minimum tax).

▶ It is not:
  - A member of a controlled group
  - A personal holding company
  - Filing a consolidated return
  - Filing its final return
  - Dissolving or liquidating
  - Electing to forego the carryback period of an NOL
  - Required to file one of the returns listed under **Special Returns for Certain Organizations,** below.

▶ It does not have:
  - Any ownership in a foreign corporation
  - Foreign shareholders that directly or indirectly own 25% or more of its stock.

	File Form
Interest charge domestic international sales corporation (sec. 992)	1120-IC-DISC
Foreign corporation (other than life and property and casualty insurance company filing Form 1120-L or Form 1120-PC)	1120-F
Foreign sales corporation (sec. 922)	1120-FSC
Condominium management association or residential real estate management association that elects to be treated as a homeowners association under sec. 528	1120-H
Life insurance company (sec. 801)	1120-L
Fund set up to pay for nuclear decommissioning costs (sec. 468A)	1120-ND
Property and casualty insurance company (sec. 831)	1120-PC
Political organization (sec. 527)	1120-POL
Real estate investment trust (sec. 856)	1120-REIT
Regulated investment company (sec. 851)	1120-RIC
S corporation (sec. 1361)	1120S

When To File

Generally, a corporation must file its income tax return by the 15th day of the 3rd month after the end of the tax year. A new corporation filing a short-period return must generally file by the 15th day of the 3rd month after the short period ends. A corporation that has dissolved must generally file by the 15th day of the 3rd month after the date it dissolved.

If the due date falls on a Saturday, Sunday, or legal holiday, the corporation may file on the next business day.

Private delivery services.— You can use certain private delivery services designated by the IRS to meet the "timely mailing as timely filing/paying" rule for tax returns and payments. The IRS publishes a list of the designated private delivery services in September of each year. The list published in September 1997 includes only the following:
- Airborne Express (Airborne): Overnight Air Express Service, Next Afternoon Service, Second Day Service.
- DHL Worldwide Express (DHL): DHL "Same Day" Service, DHL USA Overnight.
- Federal Express (FedEx): FedEx Priority Overnight, FedEx Standard Overnight, FedEx 2 Day.
- United Parcel Service (UPS): UPS Next Day Air, UPS Next Day Air Saver, UPS 2nd Day Air, UPS 2nd Day Air A.M.

The private delivery service can tell you how to get written proof of the mailing date.

Extension.— File **Form 7004,** Application for Automatic Extension of Time To File Corporation Income Tax Return, to request a 6-month extension of time to file.

Who Must Sign

The return must be signed and dated by:
- The president, vice president, treasurer, assistant treasurer, chief accounting officer, or
- Any other corporate officer (such as tax officer) authorized to sign.

Receivers, trustees, or assignees must also sign and date any return filed on behalf of a corporation.

If a corporate officer completes Form 1120 or Form 1120-A, the Paid Preparer's space should remain blank. Anyone who prepares Form 1120 or Form 1120-A but does not charge the corporation should not sign the return. Generally, anyone who is paid to prepare the return must sign it and fill in the Paid Preparer's Use Only area.

The paid preparer must complete the required preparer information and—
- Sign the return, by hand, in the space provided for the preparer's signature (signature stamps and labels are not acceptable).
- Give a copy of the return to the taxpayer.

Where To File

File your return at the applicable IRS address listed below.

If the corporation's principal business, office, or agency is located in ▼	Use the following Internal Revenue Service Center address ▼
New Jersey, New York (New York City and counties of Nassau, Rockland, Suffolk, and Westchester)	Holtsville, NY 00501–0012
New York (all other counties), Connecticut, Maine, Massachusetts, New Hampshire, Rhode Island, Vermont	Andover, MA 05501–0012
Florida, Georgia, South Carolina	Atlanta, GA 39901–0012
Indiana, Kentucky, Michigan, Ohio, West Virginia	Cincinnati, OH 45999–0012
Kansas, New Mexico, Oklahoma, Texas	Austin, TX 73301–0012
Illinois, Iowa, Minnesota, Missouri, Wisconsin	Kansas City, MO 64999–0012
Alabama, Arkansas, Louisiana, Mississippi, North Carolina, Tennessee	Memphis, TN 37501–0012
Delaware, District of Columbia, Maryland, Pennsylvania, Virginia	Philadelphia, PA 19255–0012
Alaska, Arizona, California (counties of Alpine, Amador, Butte, Calaveras, Colusa, Contra Costa, Del Norte, El Dorado, Glenn, Humboldt, Lake, Lassen, Marin, Mendocino, Modoc, Napa, Nevada, Placer, Plumas, Sacramento, San Joaquin, Shasta, Sierra, Siskiyou, Solano, Sonoma, Sutter, Tehama, Trinity, Yolo, and Yuba), Colorado, Idaho, Montana, Nebraska, Nevada, North Dakota, Oregon, South Dakota, Utah, Washington, Wyoming	Ogden, UT 84201–0012
California (all other counties), Hawaii	Fresno, CA 93888–0012

Corporations with their principal place of business outside the United States or claiming a possessions tax credit (sections 936 and 30A) must file with the Internal Revenue Service Center, Philadelphia, PA 19255–0012.

A group of corporations located in several service center regions will often keep all the books and records at the principal office of the managing corporation. In this case, the income tax returns of the corporations may be filed with the service center for the region in which the principal office is located.

Other Forms, Returns, and Statements That May Be Required

Forms

To find out what other forms the corporation may have to file, see **Other Forms That May Be Required** on page 17

Consolidated Return

The parent corporation of an affiliated group of corporations must attach **Form 851,** Affiliations Schedule, to the consolidated return. For the first year a consolidated return is filed, each subsidiary must attach **Form 1122,** Authorization and Consent of Subsidiary Corporation to be Included in a Consolidated Income Tax Return.

File supporting statements for each corporation included in the consolidated return. Do not use Form 1120 as a supporting statement. On the supporting statement, use columns to show the following, both before and after adjustments:
- Items of gross income and deductions.
- A computation of taxable income.
- Balance sheets as of the beginning and end of the tax year.
- A reconciliation of income per books with income per return.
- A reconciliation of retained earnings.

Enter the totals for the consolidated group on Form 1120. Attach consolidated balance sheets and a reconciliation of consolidated retained earnings. For more information on consolidated returns, see the regulations under section 1502.

Farm Return

Do not file **Schedule F (Form 1040),** Profit or Loss From Farming. Instead, enter income on lines 1a through 10, and read the related instructions. Forms 1120 and 1120-A have entry lines for many of the expenses deducted by farming corporations. Expenses not listed on the form should be entered on the line for "Other deductions." Attach a schedule, listing by type and amount, all deductions shown on this line. Also, see the instructions for lines 12 through 26, Form 1120 (lines 12 through 22, Form 1120-A).

Amended Return

Use **Form 1120X,** Amended U.S. Corporation Income Tax Return, to correct any error in a previously filed Form 1120 or Form 1120-A.

Statements

Stock ownership in foreign corporations.— Attach the statement required by section 551(c) if:
- The corporation owned 5% or more in value of the outstanding stock of a foreign personal holding company, and
- The corporation was required to include in its gross income any undistributed foreign personal holding company income from a foreign personal holding company.

Transfers to a corporation controlled by the transferor.— If a person receives stock of a corporation in exchange for property, and no gain or loss is recognized under section 351, the person (transferor) and the transferee must each attach to their tax returns the information required by Regulations section 1.351-3.

Dual consolidated losses.— If a domestic corporation incurs a dual consolidated loss (as defined in Regulations section 1.1503-2(c)(5)), the corporation (or consolidated group) may need to attach an elective relief agreement and/or an annual certification as provided in Regulations section 1.1503-2(g)(2).

Attachments

Attach **Form 4136,** Credit for Federal Tax Paid on Fuels, after page 4, Form 1120, or page 2, Form 1120-A. Attach schedules in alphabetical order and other forms in numerical order after Form 4136.

Complete every applicable entry space on Form 1120 or Form 1120-A. Do not write "See attached" instead of completing the entry spaces. If you need more space on the forms or schedules, attach separate sheets, using the same size and format as the printed forms. Show the totals on the printed forms. Attach these separate sheets after all the schedules and forms. Be sure to put the corporation's name and EIN on each sheet.

Accounting Methods

An accounting method is a set of rules used to determine when and how income and expenses are reported.

Figure taxable income using the method of accounting regularly used in keeping the corporation's books and records. Generally, permissible methods include:
- Cash,
- Accrual, or
- Any other method authorized by the Internal Revenue Code.

In all cases, the method used must clearly show taxable income.

Generally, a corporation (other than a qualified personal service corporation) must use the accrual method of accounting if its average annual gross receipts exceed $5 million. See section 448(c). A corporation engaged in farming operations must also use the accrual method. For exceptions, see section 447.

Page 3

Under the accrual method, an amount is includible in income when:

• All the events have occurred that fix the right to receive the income, and

• The amount can be determined with reasonable accuracy.

See Regulations section 1.451-1(a) for details.

Generally, an accrual basis taxpayer can deduct accrued expenses in the tax year when:

• All events that determine the liability have occurred,

• The amount of the liability can be figured with reasonable accuracy, and

• Economic performance takes place with respect to the expense.

There are exceptions to the economic performance rule for certain items, including recurring expenses. See section 461(h) and the related regulations for the rules for determining when economic performance takes place.

Long-term contracts (except for certain real property construction contracts) must generally be accounted for using the percentage of completion method described in section 460. See section 460 for general rules on long-term contracts.

Mark-to-market accounting method for dealers in securities.— Dealers in securities must use the mark-to-market accounting method described in section 475. Under this method, any security that is inventory to the dealer must be included in inventory at its fair market value. Any security held by a dealer that is not inventory and is held at the close of the tax year is treated as sold at its fair market value on the last business day of the tax year. Any gain or loss must be taken into account in determining gross income. The gain or loss taken into account is generally treated as ordinary gain or loss. For details, including exceptions, see section 475, the related regulations, and Rev. Rul. 94-7, 1994-1 C.B. 151.

Note: *For tax years ending after August 5, 1997, dealers in commodities and traders in securities and commodities may make the election to use the mark-to-market accounting method. For detaiils, see sections 475(e) and (f).*

Change in accounting method.— Generally, the corporation may change the method of accounting used to report taxable income (for income as a whole or for any material item) only by getting consent on **Form 3115,** Application for Change in Accounting Method. For more information, get **Pub. 538,** Accounting Periods and Methods.

Accounting Periods

A corporation must figure its taxable income on the basis of a tax year. The tax year is the annual accounting period the corporation uses to keep its records and report its income and expenses. Generally, corporations can use a calendar year or a fiscal year. Personal service corporations, however, must use a calendar year unless they meet one of the exceptions discussed in **Accounting Period** under **Item A** on page 5.

For more information about accounting periods, see Temporary Regulations sections 1.441–1T, 1.441–2T, and Pub. 538.

Calendar year.— If the calendar year is adopted as the annual accounting period, the corporation must maintain its books and records and report its income and expenses for the period from January 1 through December 31 of each year.

Fiscal year.— A fiscal year is 12 consecutive months ending on the last day of any month except December. A 52–53 week year is a fiscal year that varies from 52 to 53 weeks.

Adoption of tax year.— A corporation adopts a tax year when it files its first income tax return. It must adopt a tax year by the due date (not including extensions) of its first income tax return.

Change of tax year.— Generally, a corporation must get the consent of the IRS before changing its tax year by filing **Form 1128,** Application To Adopt, Change, or Retain a Tax Year. However, under certain conditions, a corporation (other than a personal service corporation) may change its tax year without getting the consent. See Regulations section 1.442-1 and Pub. 538.

Rounding Off to Whole Dollars

The corporation may show amounts on the return and accompanying schedules as whole dollars. To do so, drop amounts less than 50 cents and increase amounts from 50 cents through 99 cents to the next higher dollar.

Recordkeeping

Keep the corporation's records for as long as they may be needed for the administration of any provision of the Internal Revenue Code. Usually, records that support an item of income, deduction, or credit on the return must be kept for 3 years from the date the return is due or filed, whichever is later. Keep records that verify the corporation's basis in property for as long as they are needed to figure the basis of the original or replacement property.

The corporation should keep copies of all filed returns. They help in preparing future returns and amended returns.

Depository Method of Tax Payment

The corporation must pay the tax due in full no later than the 15th day of the 3rd month after the end of the tax year. Some corporations (described below), are required to electronically deposit all depository taxes, including corporation income tax payments.

Electronic Deposit Requirement

The corporation must make electronic deposits of all depository tax liabilities that occur after 1997 if:

• It was required to electronically deposit taxes in prior years,

• It deposited more than $50,000 in social security, Medicare, Railroad Retirement, and withheld income taxes in 1996, or

• It **did not** deposit social security, Medicare, or withheld income taxes in 1995 or 1996, but deposited more than $50,000 in other taxes under section 6302 (such as the corporate income tax) in either year.

For details, see Regulations section 31.6302–1(h).

The Electronic Federal Tax Payment System (EFTPS) must be used to make electronic deposits. If the corporation is required to make electronic deposits and fails to do so, it may be subject to a 10% penalty.

Note: *A penalty will not be imposed prior to July 1, 1998, if the corporation was first required to use EFTPS on or after July 1, 1997.*

Corporations that are not required to make electronic deposits may voluntarily participate in EFTPS. To enroll in EFTPS, call 1–800–945–8400 or 1–800–555–4477. For general information about EFTPS, call 1–800–829–1040.

Deposits With Form 8109

If the corporation does not use EFTPS, deposit corporation income tax payments (and estimated tax payments) with Form 8109. Do not send deposits directly to an IRS office. Mail or deliver the completed Form 8109 with the payment to a qualified depositary for Federal taxes or to the Federal Reserve bank (FRB) servicing the corporation's geographic area. Make checks or money orders payable to that depositary or FRB. To help ensure proper crediting, write the corporation's EIN, the tax period to which the deposit applies, and "Form 1120" on the check or money order. Be sure to darken the "1120" box on the coupon. Records of these deposits will be sent to the IRS.

A penalty may be imposed if the deposits are mailed or delivered to an IRS office rather than to an authorized depositary or FRB. For more information on deposits, see the instructions in the coupon booklet (Form 8109) and **Pub. 583,** Starting a Business and Keeping Records.

Caution: *If the corporation owes tax when it files Form 1120 or Form 1120-A, do not include the payment with the tax return. Instead, mail or deliver the payment with Form 8109 to a qualified depositary or FRB, or use EFTPS, if applicable.*

Estimated Tax Payments

Generally, the following rules apply to the corporation's payments of estimated tax.

• The corporation must make installment payments of estimated tax if it expects its estimated tax (income tax minus credits) to be $500 or more.

• The installments are due by the 15th day of the 4th, 6th, 9th, and 12th months of the tax year. If any date falls on a Saturday, Sunday, or legal holiday, the installment is due on the next regular business day.

• Use **Form 1120-W,** Estimated Tax for Corporations, as a worksheet to compute estimated tax.

• If the corporation does not use EFTPS, use the deposit coupons (Forms 8109) to make deposits of estimated tax.

For more information on estimated tax payments, including penalties that apply if the corporation fails to make required payments, see the instructions for line 33 on page 10.

Overpaid estimated tax.— If the corporation overpaid estimated tax, it may be able to get a quick refund by filing **Form 4466,** Corporation Application for Quick Refund of Overpayment of Estimated Tax. The overpayment must be at least 10% of the corporation's expected income tax liability and at least $500. File Form 4466 before the 16th day of the 3rd month after the end of the tax year, but before the corporation files its income tax return. Do not file Form 4466 before the end of the corporation's tax year.

Interest and Penalties

Interest.— Interest is charged on taxes paid late even if an extension of time to file is granted. Interest is also charged on penalties imposed for failure to file, negligence, fraud, gross valuation overstatements, and substantial understatements of tax from the due date (including extensions) to the date of payment. The interest charge is figured at a rate determined under section 6621.

Penalty for late filing of return.— A corporation that does not file its tax return by the due date, including extensions, may be penalized 5% of the unpaid tax for each month or part of a month the return is late, up to a

Page 4

maximum of 25% of the unpaid tax. The minimum penalty for a return that is over 60 days late is the smaller of the tax due or $100. The penalty will not be imposed if the corporation can show that the failure to file on time was due to reasonable cause. Corporations that file late must attach a statement explaining the reasonable cause.

Penalty for late payment of tax.— A corporation that does not pay the tax when due may be penalized ½ of 1% of the unpaid tax for each month or part of a month the tax is not paid, up to a maximum of 25% of the unpaid tax. The penalty will not be imposed if the corporation can show that the failure to pay on time was due to reasonable cause.

Trust fund recovery penalty.— This penalty may apply if certain excise, income, social security, and Medicare taxes that must be collected or withheld are not collected or withheld, or these taxes are not paid to the IRS. These taxes are generally reported on Forms 720, 941, 943, or 945 (see **Other Forms That May Be Required,** on page 17). The trust fund recovery penalty may be imposed on all persons who are determined by the IRS to have been responsible for collecting, accounting for, and paying over these taxes, and who acted willfully in not doing so. The penalty is equal to the unpaid trust fund tax. See the instructions for Form 720, **Pub. 15** (Circular E), Employer's Tax Guide, or **Pub. 51** (Circular A), Agricultural Employer's Tax Guide, for details, including the definition of responsible persons.

Other penalties.— Other penalties can be imposed for negligence, substantial understatement of tax, and fraud. See sections 6662 and 6663.

Specific Instructions

Period Covered

File the 1997 return for calendar year 1997 and fiscal years that begin in 1997 and end in 1998. For a fiscal year, fill in the tax year space at the top of the form.

Note: *The 1997 Form 1120 may also be used if:*

- *The corporation has a tax year of less than 12 months that begins and ends in 1998, and*
- *The 1998 Form 1120 is not available at the time the corporation is required to file its return. The corporation must show its 1998 tax year on the 1997 Form 1120 and incorporate any tax law changes that are effective for tax years beginning after December 31, 1997.*

Name, Address, and Employer Identification Number (EIN)

Use the label on the postcard or package that was mailed to the corporation. Cross out any errors and print the correct information on the label. If the corporation doesn't have a label, print or type the corporation's true name (as set forth in the charter or other legal document creating it), address, and EIN on the appropriate lines.

Address.— Include the suite, room, or other unit number after the street address. If a preaddressed label is used, include this information on the label.

If the Post Office does not deliver mail to the street address and the corporation has a P.O. box, show the box number instead of the street address.

Note: *If a change in address occurs after the return is filed, use* **Form 8822,** *Change of Address, to notify the IRS of the new address.*

Employer identification number (EIN).— Show the correct EIN in item B on page 1 of Form 1120 or Form 1120-A. If the corporation does not have an EIN, it should apply for one on **Form SS-4,** Application for Employer Identification Number. Form SS-4 can be obtained at Social Security Administration (SSA) offices, or by calling 1–800–TAX–FORM. If the corporation has not received its EIN by the time the return is due, write "Applied for" in the space for the EIN. See Pub. 583 for details.

Item A—Personal Service Corporation

A personal service corporation is a corporation whose principal activity for the testing period (defined below) for the tax year is the performance of personal services. The services must be substantially performed by employee-owners. Employee-owners must own more than 10% of the fair market value of the corporation's outstanding stock on the last day of the testing period.

Testing period.— Generally, the testing period for a tax year is the prior tax year. The testing period for a new corporation starts with the first day of its first tax year and ends on the **earlier** of:

- The last day of its first tax year, or
- The last day of the calendar year in which the first tax year began.

Principal activity.— The principal activity of a corporation is considered to be the performance of personal services if, during the testing period, the corporation's compensation costs for the performance of personal services (defined below) are more than 50% of its total compensation costs.

Performance of personal services.— Personal services are those performed in the health, law, engineering, architecture, accounting, actuarial science, performing arts, or consulting fields (as defined in Temporary Regulations section 1.448-1T(e)). The term "performance of personal services" includes any activity involving the performance of personal services in these fields.

Substantial performance by employee-owners.— Personal services are substantially performed by employee-owners if, for the testing period, more than 20% of the corporation's compensation costs for the performance of personal services are for services performed by employee-owners.

Employee-owner.— A person is considered to be an employee-owner if the person:

- Is an employee of the corporation on any day of the testing period, and
- Owns any outstanding stock of the corporation on any day of the testing period. Stock ownership is determined under the attribution rules of section 318, except that "any" is substituted for "50%" in section 318(a)(2)(C).

Accounting period.— A personal service corporation must use a calendar tax year unless:

- It can establish a business purpose for a different tax year (see Rev. Proc. 87-32, 1987-2 C.B. 396, and Rev. Rul. 87-57, 1987-2 C.B. 117), or
- It elects under section 444 to have a tax year other than a calendar year. To make the election, get **Form 8716,** Election To Have a Tax Year Other Than a Required Tax Year.

Personal service corporations that want to change their tax year must also file Form 1128.

If a corporation makes the section 444 election, its deduction for certain amounts paid to employee-owners may be limited. Get

Schedule H (Form 1120), Section 280H Limitations for a Personal Service Corporation (PSC), to figure the maximum deduction.

If a section 444 election is terminated and the termination results in a short tax year, type or print at the top of the first page of Form 1120 or 1120-A for the short tax year "SECTION 444 ELECTION TERMINATED." See Temporary Regulations section 1.444-1T(a)(5) for more information.

For more information about personal service corporations, see Temporary Regulations section 1.441-4T.

Other rules.— For other rules that apply to personal service corporations, see **Passive activity limitations** on page 6 and **Contributions of property other than cash** on page 8.

Item D—Total Assets

Enter the corporation's total assets (as determined by the accounting method regularly used in keeping the corporation's books and records) at the end of the tax year. If there are no assets at the end of the tax year, enter the total assets as of the beginning of the tax year.

Item E—Initial Return, Final Return, or Change of Address

If this is the corporation's first return, check the "Initial return" box. If the corporation ceases to exist, file Form 1120 and check the "Final return" box. Do not file Form 1120-A.

If the corporation has changed its address since it last filed a return, check the box for "Change of address."

Income

Note: *Generally, income from all sources, whether U.S. or foreign, must be included.*

Line 1

Gross Receipts

Enter gross receipts or sales from all business operations except those that must be reported on lines 4 through 10. For reporting advance payments, see Regulations section 1.451-5. To report income from long-term contracts, see section 460.

Installment sales.— Generally, the installment method cannot be used for dealer dispositions of property. A "dealer disposition" means any disposition of personal property by a person who regularly sells or otherwise disposes of property of the same type on the installment plan. The disposition of property used or produced in the farming business is not included as a dealer disposition. See section 453(l) for details and exceptions.

Enter on line 1 (and carry to line 3), the gross profit on collections from installment sales for any of the following:

- Dealer dispositions of property before March 1, 1986.
- Dispositions of property used or produced in the trade or business of farming.
- Certain dispositions of timeshares and residential lots reported under the installment method.

Attach a schedule showing the following information for the current and the 3 preceding years: **(a)** gross sales, **(b)** cost of goods sold, **(c)** gross profits, **(d)** percentage of gross profits to gross sales, **(e)** amount collected, and **(f)** gross profit on the amount collected.

For sales of timeshares and residential lots reported under the installment method, the corporation's income tax is increased by the interest payable under section 453(l)(3). To report this addition to the tax, see the instructions for line 10, Schedule J, Form 1120.

Nonaccrual experience method.— Accrual method taxpayers need not accrue certain amounts to be received from the performance of services that, on the basis of their experience, will not be collected (section 448(d)(5)). This provision does not apply to any amount if interest is required to be paid on the amount or if there is any penalty for failure to timely pay the amount. Corporations that fall under this provision should attach a schedule showing total gross receipts, the amount not accrued as a result of the application of section 448(d)(5), and the net amount accrued. Enter the net amount on line 1a. For more information and guidelines on this "nonaccrual experience method," see Temporary Regulations section 1.448-2T.

Line 2

Cost of Goods Sold

Enter the cost of goods sold on line 2, page 1. Before making this entry, a Form 1120 filer must complete Schedule A on page 2 of Form 1120. Form 1120-A filers may use the worksheet on page 10 to figure the amount to enter on line 2. All filers should see the instructions for Schedule A and the worksheet.

Line 4

Dividends

Form 1120 filers.— See the instructions for Schedule C. Then, complete Schedule C and enter on line 4 the amount from Schedule C, line 19.

Form 1120-A filers.— Enter the total dividends received (that are not from debt-financed stock) from domestic corporations that qualify for the 70% dividends-received deduction.

Line 5

Interest

Enter taxable interest on U.S. obligations and on loans, notes, mortgages, bonds, bank deposits, corporate bonds, tax refunds, etc.

Do not offset interest expense against interest income.

Special rules apply to interest income from certain below-market-rate loans. See section 7872 for more information.

Line 6

Gross Rents

Enter the gross amount received for the rent of property. Deduct expenses such as repairs, interest, taxes, and depreciation on the proper lines for deductions. A rental activity held by a closely held corporation or a personal service corporation may be subject to the passive activity loss rules. See Form 8810 and its instructions.

Line 8

Capital Gain Net Income

Every sale or exchange of a capital asset must be reported in detail on **Schedule D (Form 1120),** Capital Gains and Losses, even though no gain or loss is indicated.

Line 9

Net Gain or (Loss)

Enter the net gain or (loss) from line 18, Part II, **Form 4797,** Sales of Business Property.

Line 10

Other Income

Enter any other taxable income not reported on lines 1 through 9. List the type and amount of income on an attached schedule. If the corporation has only one item of other income, describe it in parentheses on line 10. Examples of other income to report on line 10 are:

● Any adjustment under section 481(a) required to be included in income during the current tax year due to a change in a method of accounting.

● Recoveries of bad debts deducted in prior years under the specific charge-off method.

● The amount of credit for alcohol used as fuel (determined without regard to the limitation based on tax) entered on **Form 6478,** Credit for Alcohol Used as Fuel.

● Refunds of taxes deducted in prior years to the extent they reduced income subject to tax in the year deducted (see section 111). Do not offset current year taxes against tax refunds.

● The amount of any deduction previously taken under section 179A that is subject to recapture. The corporation must recapture the benefit of any allowable deduction for clean-fuel vehicle property (or clean-fuel vehicle refueling property), if the property later ceases to qualify. See Regulations section 1.179A-1 for details.

● Ordinary income from trade or business activities of a partnership (from Schedule K-1 (Form 1065), line 1).

● Any LIFO recapture amount under section 1363(d). The corporation may have to include a LIFO recapture amount in income if it:

1. Used the LIFO inventory method for its last tax year before the first tax year for which it elected to become an S corporation, or

2. Transferred LIFO inventory assets to an S corporation in a nonrecognition transaction in which those assets were transferred basis property.

The LIFO recapture amount is the amount by which the C corporation's inventory under the FIFO method exceeds the inventory amount under the LIFO method at the close of the corporation's last tax year as a C corporation (or for the year of the transfer, if **2** above applies). For more information, see Regulations section 1.1363-2 and Rev. Proc. 94-61, 1994-2 C.B. 775. Also see the instructions for Schedule J, line 10.

Deductions

Limitations on Deductions

Section 263A uniform capitalization rules.— The uniform capitalization rules of section 263A require corporations to capitalize or include in inventory certain costs incurred in connection with:

● The production of real property and tangible personal property held in inventory or held for sale in the ordinary course of business.

● Personal property (tangible and intangible) acquired for resale.

● The production of property constructed or improved by a corporation for use in its trade or business or in an activity engaged in for profit.

Tangible personal property produced by a corporation includes a film, sound recording, videotape, book, or similar property.

Corporations subject to the rules are required to capitalize not only direct costs but an allocable part of most indirect costs (including taxes) that benefit the assets produced or acquired for resale.

For inventory, some of the **indirect expenses** that must be capitalized are:

● Administration expenses.

● Taxes.

● Depreciation.

● Insurance.

● Compensation paid to officers attributable to services.

● Rework labor.

● Contributions to pension, stock bonus, and certain profit-sharing, annuity, or deferred compensation plans.

Regulations section 1.263A-1(e)(3) specifies other indirect costs that relate to production or resale activities that must be capitalized and those that may be currently deductible.

Interest expense paid or incurred during the production period of certain property must be capitalized and is governed by special rules. For more details, see Regulations sections 1.263A-8 through 1.263A-15.

The costs required to be capitalized under section 263A are not deductible until the property to which the costs relate is sold, used, or otherwise disposed of by the corporation.

Exceptions.— Section 263A **does not** apply to:

● Personal property acquired for resale if the corporation's average annual gross receipts for the 3 prior tax years were $10 million or less.

● Timber.

● Most property produced under long-term contract.

● Certain property produced in a farming business.

● Research and experimental costs under section 174.

● Intangible drilling costs for oil, gas, and geothermal property.

● Mining exploration and development costs.

For more details on the uniform capitalization rules, see Regulations sections 1.263A-1 through 1.263A-3.

Transactions between related taxpayers.— Generally, an accrual basis taxpayer may only deduct business expenses and interest owed to a related party in the year the payment is included in the income of the related party. See sections 163(e)(3), 163(j), and 267 for limitations on deductions for unpaid interest and expenses.

Section 291 limitations.— Corporations may be required to adjust deductions for depletion of iron ore and coal, intangible drilling and exploration and development costs, certain deductions for financial institutions, and the amortizable basis of pollution control facilities. See section 291 to determine the amount of adjustment. Also see section 43.

Golden parachute payments.— A portion of the payments made by a corporation to key personnel that exceeds their usual compensation may not be deductible. This occurs when the corporation has an agreement (golden parachute) with these key employees to pay them these excessive amounts if control of the corporation changes. See section 280G.

Business startup expenses.— Business startup expenses must be capitalized unless an election is made to amortize them over a period of 60 months. See section 195.

Passive activity limitations.— Limitations on passive activity losses and credits under section 469 apply to personal service corporations as defined in Temporary Regulations section 1.441-4T (see **Item A—Personal Service Corporation** on page 5) and closely held corporations (see below).

Generally, the two kinds of passive activities are:

- Trade or business activities in which the corporation did not materially participate for the tax year (see Temporary Regulations section 1.469-1T(g)(3)), and
- Rental activities regardless of its participation.

For exceptions, see Form 8810.

An activity is a trade or business activity if it is not a rental activity, and
- The activity involves the conduct of a trade or business (i.e., deductions from the activity would be allowable under section 162 if other limitations, such as the passive loss rules, did not apply), or
- The activity involves research and experimental costs that are deductible under section 174 (or would be deductible if the corporation chose to deduct rather than capitalize them).

Corporations subject to the passive activity limitations must complete Form 8810 to compute their allowable passive activity loss and credit. Before completing Form 8810, see Temporary Regulations section 1.163-8T, which provides rules for allocating interest expense among activities. If a passive activity is also subject to the earnings stripping rules of section 163(j) or the at-risk rules of section 465, those rules apply before the passive loss rules. For more information, see section 469, the related regulations, and **Pub. 925**, Passive Activity and At-Risk Rules.

Closely held corporations.— For this purpose, a corporation is a closely held corporation if:
- At any time during the last half of the tax year more than 50% in value of its outstanding stock is owned, directly or indirectly, by or for not more than five individuals, and
- The corporation is not a personal service corporation.

Certain organizations are treated as individuals for purposes of this test. (See section 542(a)(2).) For rules of determining stock ownership, see section 544 (as modified by section 465(a)(3)).

Reducing certain expenses for which credits are allowable.— For each credit listed below, the corporation must reduce the otherwise allowable deductions for expenses used to figure the credit by the amount of the current year credit:
- Work opportunity credit.
- Research credit.
- Enhanced oil recovery credit.
- Disabled access credit.
- Empowerment zone employment credit.
- Indian employment credit.
- Employer credit for social security and Medicare taxes paid on certain employee tips.
- Orphan drug credit.
- Welfare-to-work credit.

If the corporation has any of these credits, be sure to figure each current year credit before figuring the deduction for expenses on which the credit is based.

Line 12

Compensation of Officers

Enter deductible officers' compensation on line 12. Form 1120 filers must complete Schedule E if their total receipts (line 1a, plus lines 4 through 10) are $500,000 or more. Do not include compensation deductible elsewhere on the return, such as amounts included in cost of goods sold, elective contributions to a section 401(k) cash or deferred arrangement, or amounts contributed under a salary reduction SEP agreement or a SIMPLE retirement plan (savings incentive match plan).

Include only the deductible part of officers' compensation on Schedule E. (See **Disallowance of deduction for employee compensation in excess of $1 million,** below.) Complete Schedule E, line 1, columns (a) through (f), for all officers. The corporation determines who is an officer under the laws of the state where incorporated.

If a consolidated return is filed, each member of an affiliated group must furnish this information.

Disallowance of deduction for employee compensation in excess of $1 million.— Publicly held corporations may not deduct compensation to a "covered employee" to the extent that the compensation exceeds $1 million. Generally, a covered employee is:
- The chief executive officer of the corporation (or an individual acting in that capacity) as of the end of the tax year, or
- An employee whose total compensation must be reported to shareholders under the Securities Exchange Act of 1934 because the employee is among the four highest compensated officers for that tax year (other than the chief executive officer).

For this purpose, compensation does not include the following:
- Income from certain employee trusts, annuity plans, or pensions;
- Any benefit paid to an employee that is excluded from the employee's income.

The deduction limit does not apply to:
- Commissions based on individual performance;
- Qualified performance-based compensation; and
- Income payable under a written, binding contract in effect on February 17, 1993.

The $1 million limit is reduced by amounts disallowed as excess parachute payments under section 280G.

For details, see section 162(m) and Regulations section 1.162-27.

Line 13

Salaries and Wages

Enter the amount of salaries and wages paid for the tax year, reduced by:
- Any work opportunity credit from Form 5884,
- Any empowerment zone employment credit from Form 8844,
- Any Indian employment credit from Form 8845, and
- Any welfare-to-work credit from Form 8861.

See the instructions for these forms for more information. Do not include salaries and wages deductible elsewhere on the return, such as amounts included in cost of goods sold, elective contributions to a section 401(k) cash or deferred arrangement, or amounts contributed under a salary reduction SEP agreement or a SIMPLE retirement plan (savings incentive match plan).

Caution: *If the corporation provided taxable fringe benefits to its employees, such as personal use of a car, do not deduct as wages the amount allocated for depreciation and other expenses claimed on lines 20 and 26, Form 1120, or lines 20 and 22, Form 1120-A.*

Line 14

Repairs and Maintenance

Enter the cost of incidental repairs and maintenance not claimed elsewhere on the return, such as labor and supplies, that do not add to the value of the property or appreciably prolong its life. New buildings, machinery, or permanent improvements that increase the value of the property are not deductible. They must be depreciated or amortized.

Line 15

Bad Debts

Enter the total debts that became worthless in whole or in part during the tax year. A small bank or thrift institution using the reserve method of section 585 should attach a schedule showing how it arrived at the current year's provision.

Caution: *A cash basis taxpayer may not claim a bad debt deduction unless the amount was previously included in income.*

Line 16

Rents

If the corporation rented or leased a vehicle, enter the total annual rent or lease expense paid or incurred during the year. Also complete Part V of **Form 4562**, Depreciation and Amortization. If the corporation leased a vehicle for a term of 30 days or more, the deduction for vehicle lease expense may have to be reduced by an amount called the **inclusion amount.** The corporation may have an inclusion amount if:

The lease term began:	And the vehicle's fair market value on the first day of the lease exceeded:
After 12/31/96	$15,800
After 12/31/94 but before 1/1/97	$15,500
After 12/31/93 but before 1/1/95	$14,600
After 12/31/92 but before 1/1/94	$14,300

If the lease term began before January 1, 1993, get **Pub. 463**, Travel, Entertainment, Gift, and Car Expenses, to find out if the corporation has an inclusion amount. Also see Pub. 463 for instructions on figuring the inclusion amount.

Line 17

Taxes and Licenses

Enter taxes paid or accrued during the tax year, but do not include the following:
- Federal income taxes.
- Foreign or U.S. possession income taxes if a tax credit is claimed (however, see the Instructions for Form 5735 for special rules for possession income taxes).
- Taxes not imposed on the corporation.
- Taxes, including state or local sales taxes, that are paid or incurred in connection with an acquisition or disposition of property (these taxes must be treated as a part of the cost of the acquired property or, in the case of a disposition, as a reduction in the amount realized on the disposition).
- Taxes assessed against local benefits that increase the value of the property assessed (such as for paving, etc.).
- Taxes deducted elsewhere on the return, such as those reflected in cost of goods sold.

See section 164(d) for apportionment of taxes on real property between seller and purchaser.

Line 18

Interest

The corporation must make an interest allocation if the proceeds of a loan were used for more than one purpose (e.g., to purchase a portfolio investment and to acquire an interest in a passive activity). See Temporary Regulations section 1.163-8T for the interest allocation rules.

Mutual savings banks, building and loan associations, and cooperative banks can deduct the amounts paid or credited to the

Page 7

accounts of depositors as dividends, interest, or earnings. See section 591.

Do not include the following interest:

- Interest on indebtedness incurred or continued to purchase or carry obligations if the interest is wholly exempt from income tax. For exceptions, see section 265(b).
- For cash basis taxpayers, prepaid interest allocable to years following the current tax year. (For example, a cash basis calendar year taxpayer who in 1997 prepaid interest allocable to any period after 1997 can deduct only the amount allocable to 1997.)
- Interest and carrying charges on straddles. Generally, these amounts must be capitalized. See section 263(g).
- Interest on debt allocable to the production of qualified property or to property produced by a corporation for its own use or for sale. This interest must be capitalized. A corporation must also capitalize any interest on debt allocable to an asset used to produce the above property. See section 263A and Regulations section 1.263A-8 through 1.263A-15 for definitions and more information.

Special rules apply to:

- Interest on which no tax is imposed (see section 163(j)).
- Foregone interest on certain below-market-rate loans (see section 7872).
- Original issue discount on certain high-yield discount obligations (See section 163(e) to figure the disqualified portion.)

Note: *The Taxpayer Relief Act of 1997 imposed additional limitations on interest deductions when the corporation is a policyholder or beneficiary with respect to a life insurance, endowment, or annuity contract issued after June 8, 1997. For details, see Act section 1084 and section 264(f). Attach a statement showing the computation of the deduction disallowed under section 264(f).*

Line 19

Charitable Contributions

Enter contributions or gifts actually paid within the tax year to or for the use of charitable and governmental organizations described in section 170(c) and any unused contributions carried over from prior years.

Corporations on the accrual basis may elect to deduct contributions paid by the 15th day of the 3rd month after the end of the tax year if the contributions are authorized by the board of directors during the tax year. Attach a declaration to the return, signed by an officer, stating that the resolution authorizing the contributions was adopted by the board of directors during the tax year. Also attach a copy of the resolution.

Limitation on deduction.— The total amount claimed may not be more than 10% of taxable income (line 30, Form 1120, or line 26, Form 1120-A) computed without regard to the following:

- Any deduction for contributions,
- The special deductions on line 29b, Form 1120 (line 25b, Form 1120-A),
- The deduction allowed under section 249,
- Any net operating loss (NOL) carryback to the tax year under section 172, and
- Any capital loss carryback to the tax year under section 1212(a)(1).

Charitable contributions over the 10% limitation may not be deducted for the tax year but may be carried over to the next 5 tax years.

Special rules apply if the corporation has an NOL carryover to the tax year. In figuring the charitable contributions deduction for the tax year, the 10% limit is applied using the taxable income after taking into account any deduction for the NOL.

To figure the amount of any remaining NOL carryover to later years, taxable income must be modified (see section 172(b)). To the extent that contributions are used to reduce taxable income for this purpose and increase an NOL carryover, a contributions carryover is not allowed. See section 170(d)(2)(B).

Substantiation requirements.— Generally, no deduction is allowed for any contribution of $250 or more unless the corporation gets a written acknowledgment from the donee organization that shows the amount of cash contributed, describes any property contributed, and gives an estimate of the value of any goods or services provided in return for the contribution. The acknowledgment must be obtained by the due date (including extensions) of the corporation's return, or, if earlier, the date the return is filed. Do not attach the acknowledgment to the tax return, but keep it with the corporation's records. These rules apply in addition to the filing requirements for Form 8283 described below.

For more information on substantiation and recordkeeping requirements, see the regulations under section 170 and **Pub. 526,** Charitable Contributions.

Contributions to organizations conducting lobbying activities.— Contributions made to an organization that conducts lobbying activities are not deductible if:

- The lobbying activities relate to matters of direct financial interest to the donor's trade or business, and
- The principal purpose of the contribution was to avoid Federal income tax by obtaining a deduction for activities that would have been nondeductible under the lobbying expense rules if conducted directly by the donor.

Contributions of property other than cash.— If a corporation (other than a closely held or personal service corporation) contributes property other than cash and claims over a $500 deduction for the property, it must attach a schedule to the return describing the kind of property contributed and the method used to determine its fair market value. Closely held corporations and personal service corporations must complete **Form 8283,** Noncash Charitable Contributions, and attach it to their returns. All other corporations generally must complete and attach Form 8283 to their returns for contributions of property other than money if the total claimed deduction for all property contributed was more than $5,000.

If the corporation made a "qualified conservation contribution" under section 170(h), also include the fair market value of the underlying property before and after the donation, as well as the type of legal interest contributed, and describe the conservation purpose benefited by the donation. If a contribution carryover is included, show the amount and how it was determined.

Special rule for contributions of certain property.— For a charitable contribution of property, the corporation must reduce the contribution by the sum of:

- The ordinary income, short-term capital gain that would have resulted if the property were sold at its fair market value, and
- For certain contributions, all of the long-term capital gain that would have resulted if the property were sold at its fair market value.

The reduction for the long-term capital gain applies to:

- Contributions of tangible personal property for use by an exempt organization for a purpose or function unrelated to the basis for its exemption, and

- Contributions of any property to or for the use of certain private foundations, except for stock contributed before July 1, 1998, for which market quotations are readily available (section 170(e)(5)).

For more information, including special rules for contributions of inventory and other property to certain organizations, see section 170(e)(3) and Regulations section 1.170A-4.

Charitable contributions of scientific equipment used for research.— A corporation (other than a personal holding company or a service organization) can receive a larger deduction for contributing scientific equipment used for research to an institution of higher education. For more details, see section 170(e).

Line 20

Depreciation

Besides depreciation, include on line 20 the part of the cost that the corporation elected to expense under section 179 for certain tangible property placed in service during tax year 1997 or carried over from 1996. See **Form 4562,** Depreciation and Amortization, and its instructions.

Line 22 (Form 1120 Only)

Depletion

See sections 613 and 613A for percentage depletion rates applicable to natural deposits. Also, see section 291 for the limitation on the depletion deduction for iron ore and coal (including lignite).

Attach **Form T (Timber),** Forest Activities Schedules, if a deduction for depletion of timber is taken.

Foreign intangible drilling costs and foreign exploration and development costs must either be added to the corporation's basis for cost depletion purposes or be deducted ratably over a 10-year period. See sections 263(i), 616, and 617 for details.

Line 24 (Form 1120 Only)

Pension, Profit-Sharing, etc., Plans

Enter the deduction for contributions to qualified pension, profit-sharing, or other funded deferred compensation plans. Employers who maintain such a plan generally must file one of the forms listed below, even if the plan is not a qualified plan under the Internal Revenue Code. The filing requirement applies even if the corporation does not claim a deduction for the current tax year. There are penalties for failure to file these forms on time and for overstating the pension plan deduction. See sections 6652(e) and 6662(f).

Form 5500.— File this form for each plan with 100 or more participants.

Form 5500-C/R.— File this form for each plan with fewer than 100 participants.

Form 5500-EZ.— File this form for a one-participant plan. The term "one-participant plan" also means a plan that covers the owner and his or her spouse, or a plan that covers partners in a business partnership (or the partners and their spouses).

Line 25 (Form 1120 Only)

Employee Benefit Programs

Enter contributions to employee benefit programs not claimed elsewhere on the return (e.g., insurance, health and welfare programs, etc.) that are not an incidental part of a pension, profit-sharing, etc., plan included on line 24.

Line 26, Form 1120 (Line 22, Form 1120-A)

Other Deductions

Note: *Do not deduct fines or penalties paid to a government for violating any law.*

Attach a schedule, listing by type and amount, all allowable deductions that are not deductible elsewhere on Form 1120 or Form 1120-A. Form 1120-A filers should include amounts described in the instructions above for lines 22, 24, and 25 of Form 1120. Enter the total of other deductions on line 26, Form 1120 (line 22, Form 1120-A).

Generally, a deduction may not be taken for any amount that is allocable to a class of exempt income. See section 265(b) for exceptions.

Examples of amounts to include are:

- The deduction for amortization of pollution control facilities, organization expenses, etc. (see Form 4562).
- Ordinary losses from trade or business activities of a partnership (from Schedule K-1 (Form 1065), line 1).
- Dividends paid in cash on stock held by an employee stock ownership plan. However, a deduction may only be taken if, according to the plan, the dividends are:

1. Paid in cash directly to the plan participants or beneficiaries;

2. Paid to the plan, which distributes them in cash to the plan participants or their beneficiaries no later than 90 days after the end of the plan year in which the dividends are paid; or

3. Used to make payments on a loan described in section 404(a)(9).

See section 404(k) for more details and the limitation on certain dividends.

Travel, meals, and entertainment.— Subject to limitations and restrictions discussed below, a corporation can deduct ordinary and necessary travel, meals, and entertainment expenses paid or incurred in its trade or business. Also, special rules apply to deductions for gifts, skybox rentals, luxury water travel, convention expenses, and entertainment tickets. See section 274 and Pub. 463 for more details.

Travel.— The corporation cannot deduct travel expenses of any individual accompanying a corporate officer or employee, including a spouse or dependent of the officer or employee, unless:

- That individual is an employee of the corporation, and
- His or her travel is for a bona fide business purpose and would otherwise be deductible by that individual.

Meals and entertainment.— Generally, the corporation can deduct only 50% of the amount otherwise allowable for meals and entertainment expenses paid or incurred in its trade or business. In addition (subject to exceptions under section 274(k)(2)):

- Meals must not be lavish or extravagant;
- A bona fide business discussion must occur during, immediately before, or immediately after the meal; and
- An employee of the corporation must be present at the meal.

Membership dues.— The corporation may deduct amounts paid or incurred for membership dues in civic or public service organizations, professional organizations (such as bar and medical associations), business leagues, trade associations, chambers of commerce, boards of trade, and real estate boards. However, no deduction is allowed if a principal purpose of the organization is to entertain, or provide entertainment facilities for, members or their guests. In addition, corporations may not deduct membership dues in any club organized for business, pleasure, recreation, or other social purpose. This includes country clubs, golf and athletic clubs, airline and hotel clubs, and clubs operated to provide meals under conditions favorable to business discussion.

Entertainment facilities.— The corporation cannot deduct an expense paid or incurred for a facility (such as a yacht or hunting lodge) used for an activity usually considered entertainment, amusement, or recreation.

Note: *The corporation may be able to deduct otherwise nondeductible meals, travel, and entertainment expenses if the amounts are treated as compensation and reported on Form W-2 for an employee or on Form 1099-MISC for an independent contractor.*

Deduction for clean-fuel vehicles and certain refueling property.— Section 179A allows a deduction for part of the cost of qualified clean-fuel vehicle property and qualified clean-fuel vehicle refueling property placed in service during the tax year. For more information, see Pub. 535.

Lobbying expenses.— Generally, lobbying expenses are not deductible. These expenses include:

- Amounts paid or incurred in connection with influencing Federal or state legislation (but not local legislation), or
- Amounts paid or incurred in connection with any communication with certain Federal executive branch officials in an attempt to influence the official actions or positions of the officials. See Regulations section 1.162-29 for the definition of "influencing legislation."

Dues and other similar amounts paid to certain tax-exempt organizations may not be deductible. See section 162(e)(3). If certain in-house lobbying expenditures do not exceed $2,000, they are deductible. For information on contributions to charitable organizations that conduct lobbying activities, see the instructions for line 19. For more information on lobbying expenses, see section 162(e).

Line 28, Form 1120 (Line 24, Form 1120-A)

Taxable Income Before NOL Deduction and Special Deductions

At-risk rules.— Generally, special at-risk rules under section 465 apply to closely held corporations (see **Passive activity limitations** on page 6) engaged in any activity as a trade or business or for the production of income. These corporations may have to adjust the amount on line 28, Form 1120, or line 24, Form 1120-A. (See below.)

But the at-risk rules do not apply to:

- Holding real property placed in service by the taxpayer before 1987;
- Equipment leasing under sections 465(c)(4), (5), and (6); or
- Any qualifying business of a qualified corporation under section 465(c)(7).

However, the at-risk rules do apply to the holding of mineral property.

If the at-risk rules apply, adjust the amount on this line for any section 465(d) losses. These losses are limited to the amount for which the corporation is at risk for each separate activity at the close of the tax year. If the corporation is involved in one or more activities, any of which incurs a loss for the year, report the losses for each activity separately. Attach **Form 6198,** At-Risk Limitations, showing the amount at risk and gross income and deductions for the activities with the losses.

If the corporation sells or otherwise disposes of an asset or its interest (either total or partial) in an activity to which the at-risk rules apply, determine the net profit or loss from the activity by combining the gain or loss on the sale or disposition with the profit or loss from the activity. If the corporation has a net loss, it may be limited because of the at-risk rules.

Treat any loss from an activity not allowed for the tax year as a deduction allocable to the activity in the next tax year.

Line 29a, Form 1120 (Line 25a, Form 1120-A)

Net Operating Loss Deduction

A corporation may use the net operating loss (NOL) incurred in one tax year to reduce its taxable income in another year. Generally, a corporation may carry an NOL back to each of the 3 years (2 years for NOLs incurred in tax years beginning after August 5, 1997), preceding the year of the loss and then carry any remaining amount over to each of the 15 years (20 years for NOLs incurred in tax years beginning after August 5, 1997), following the year of the loss (but Form 1120 filers see **Exceptions to carryback rules** below). Enter on line 29a (line 25a, Form 1120-A), the total NOL carryovers from prior tax years, but do not enter more than the corporation's taxable income (after special deductions). An NOL deduction cannot be taken in a year in which the corporation has a negative taxable income. Attach a schedule showing the computation of the NOL deduction. Form 1120 filers must also complete question 15 on Schedule K.

For details on the NOL deduction, get **Pub. 536,** Net Operating Losses.

Carryback and carryover rules.— Generally, an NOL must first be carried back to the third tax year (second tax year for NOLs incurred in tax years beginning after August 5, 1997), preceding the year of the loss. To carry back the loss and obtain a quick refund of taxes, use **Form 1139,** Corporation Application for Tentative Refund. Form 1139 must be filed within 12 months after the close of the tax year of the loss. See section 6411 for details. For carryback claims filed later than 12 months after the close of the tax year of the loss, file **Form 1120X,** Amended U.S. Corporation Income Tax Return, instead of Form 1139.

After the corporation applies the NOL to the first tax year to which it may be carried, the taxable income of that year is modified (as described in section 172(b)) to determine how much of the remaining loss may be carried to other years. See section 172(b) and the related regulations for details.

Special rules apply when an ownership change occurs (i.e., the amount of the taxable income of a loss corporation that can be offset by pre-change NOL carryovers is limited). See section 382 and the related regulations. Also see Temporary Regulations section 1.382-2T(a)(2)(ii), which requires that a loss corporation file an information statement with its income tax return for each tax year that it is a loss corporation and certain shifts in ownership occurred. See Regulations section 1.382-6(b) for details on how to make the closing-of-the-books election.

See section 384 for the limitation on the use of preacquistion losses of one corporation to offset recognized built-in gains of another corporation.

Note: *See section 383 and the related regulations for limits that apply to net capital losses and credits when an ownership change occurs.*

Page 9

Exceptions to carryback rules (Form 1120 filers only).— A corporation may make an irrevocable election to forego the carryback period and instead carry the NOL forward to years following the year of the loss. To make this election, check the box in question 14 on Schedule K. The return must be timely filed (including extensions).

Different carryback periods apply for certain losses. The part of an NOL that is attributable to a specified liability loss, including a product liability loss, may be carried back 10 years (section 172(b)(1)(C)). See Regulations section 1.172-13(c) for the statement that must be attached to Form 1120 if the corporation is claiming the 10-year carryback period for a product liability loss.

Special rules apply to the carryback of losses that are attributable to interest paid in connection with corporate equity reduction transactions. See section 172(b)(1)(E).

Personal service corporations may not carry back an NOL to or from any tax year to which a section 444 election applies.

Line 29b, Form 1120
(Line 25b, Form 1120-A)

Special Deductions

Form 1120 filers.— See the Instructions for Schedule C.

Form 1120-A filers.— Generally, enter 70% of line 4, page 1, on line 25b. However, this deduction may not be more than 70% of line 24, page 1. Compute line 24 without regard to any adjustment under section 1059 and without regard to any capital loss carryback to the tax year under section 1212(a)(1).

In a year in which an NOL occurs, this 70% limitation does not apply even if the loss is created by the dividends-received deduction. See sections 172(d) and 246(b).

Line 30, Form 1120
(Line 26, Form 1120-A)

Taxable Income

Capital construction fund.— To take a deduction for amounts contributed to a capital construction fund, reduce the amount that would otherwise be entered on line 30 (line 26, Form 1120-A) by the amount of the deduction. On the dotted line next to the entry space, write "CCF" and the amount of the deduction. For more information, get **Pub. 595,** Tax Highlights for Commercial Fishermen.

Line 32b, Form 1120
(Line 28b, Form 1120-A)

Estimated Tax Payments

Enter any estimated tax payments the corporation made for the tax year.

Beneficiaries of trusts.— If the corporation is the beneficiary of a trust, and the trust makes a section 643(g) election to credit its estimated tax payments to its beneficiaries, include the corporation's share of the payment in the total for line 32b, Form 1120 (line 28b, Form 1120-A). Write "T" and the amount on the dotted line next to the entry space.

Special estimated tax payments for certain life insurance companies.— If the corporation is required to make or apply special estimated tax payments (SETP) under section 847 in addition to its regular estimated tax payments, enter on line 32b (line 28b, Form 1120-A), the corporation's total estimated tax payments. On the dotted line next to the entry space, write "SETP" and the amount. Attach a schedule showing your computation of estimated tax payments. See section 847(2) and **Form 8816,** Special Loss Discount Account and Special

---

Cost of Goods Sold Worksheet

Form 1120-A
(Keep for your records.)

1. Inventory at start of year. Enter here and in Part III, line 3, column (a), Form 1120-A . . . . **1.** ________
2. Purchases. Enter here and in Part II, line 5a(1), Form 1120-A . . **2.** ________
3. Cost of labor. Enter here and include in total in Part II, line 5a(3), Form 1120-A . . . . **3.** ________
4. Additional section 263A costs. Enter here and in Part II, line 5a(2), Form 1120-A (see instructions for line 4) . . . . **4.** ________
5. Other costs. Enter here and include in Part II, line 5a(3), Form 1120-A . . . . **5.** ________
6. Total. Add lines 1 through 5 . . . . **6.** ________
7. Inventory at end of year. Enter here and in Part III, line 3, column (b), Form 1120-A . . . . **7.** ________
8. Cost of goods sold. Subtract line 7 from line 6. Enter the result here and on page 1, line 2, Form 1120-A . . . . **8.** ________

Estimated Tax Payments for Insurance Companies, for more information.

Line 32f, Form 1120
(Line 28f, Form 1120-A)

Enter the credit (from **Form 2439,** Notice to Shareholder of Undistributed Long-Term Capital Gains), for the corporation's share of the tax paid by a regulated investment company or a real estate investment trust on undistributed long-term capital gains included in the corporation's income. Attach Form 2439 to Form 1120 or 1120-A.

Line 32g, Form 1120
(Line 28g, Form 1120-A)

Credit for Federal Tax on Fuels

Complete **Form 4136,** Credit for Federal Tax Paid on Fuels, if the corporation qualifies to take this credit.

Credit for tax on ozone-depleting chemicals.— Include on line 32g (line 28g, Form 1120-A) any credit the corporation is claiming under section 4682(g)(4) for tax on ozone-depleting chemicals. Write "ODC" to the left of the entry space.

Line 32h, Form 1120
(Line 28h, Form 1120-A)

Total Payments

On Form 1120, add the amounts on lines 32d through 32g and enter the total on line 32h. On Form 1120-A, add the amounts on lines 28d through 28g and enter the total on line 28h.

Backup withholding.— If the corporation had income tax withheld from any payments it received, because, for example, it failed to give the payer its correct EIN, include the amount withheld in the total for line 32h, Form 1120 (line 28h, Form 1120-A). This type of withholding is called backup withholding. On Form 1120, show the amount withheld in the blank space in the right-hand column between lines 31 and 32h, and write "backup withholding". On Form 1120-A, show the amount withheld on the dotted line to the left of line 28h, and write "backup withholding".

Line 33, Form 1120
(Line 29, Form 1120-A)

Estimated Tax Penalty

A corporation that does not make estimated tax payments when due may be subject to an underpayment penalty for the period of underpayment. Generally, a corporation is subject to the penalty if its tax liability is $500 or more, and it did not timely pay the smaller of:

- 100% of its tax liability for 1997, or

- 100% of its prior year's tax.
  See section 6655 for details and exceptions, including special rules for large corporations.

Use **Form 2220,** Underpayment of Estimated Tax by Corporations, to see if the corporation owes a penalty and to figure the amount of the penalty. Generally, the corporation does not have to file this form because the IRS can figure the amount of any penalty and bill the corporation for it. However, even if the corporation does not owe the penalty, you must complete and attach Form 2220 if:

- The annualized income or adjusted seasonal installment method is used, or

- The corporation is a large corporation computing its first required installment based on the prior year's tax. (See the Form 2220 instructions for the definition of a large corporation.)

If you attach Form 2220, check the box on line 33, Form 1120 (line 29, Form 1120-A), and enter the amount of any penalty on this line.

Schedule A, Form 1120
(Worksheet, Form 1120-A)

Cost of Goods Sold

Inventories are required at the beginning and end of each tax year if the production, purchase, or sale of merchandise is an income-producing factor. See Regulations section 1.471-1. If inventories are not used, enter zero on lines 1 and 7 of Schedule A, Form 1120, or the worksheet.

All filers should see **Section 263A uniform capitalization rules** on page 6 before completing Schedule A or the worksheet above. The instructions for lines 4 through 7 below apply to Schedule A and the worksheet.

Line 4

Additional Section 263A Costs

An entry is required on this line only for corporations that have elected a simplified method of accounting.

For corporations that have elected the **simplified production method,** additional section 263A costs are generally those costs, other than interest, that were not capitalized under the corporation's method of accounting immediately prior to the effective date of section 263A that are now required to be capitalized under section 263A. For details, see Regulations section 1.263A-2(b).

For corporations that have elected the **simplified resale method,** additional section 263A costs are generally those costs incurred with respect to the following categories:

1. Refigure line 28, page 1, Form 1120, without any adjustment under section 1059 and without any capital loss carryback to the tax year under section 1212(a)(1) . . . . 1. __________
2. Complete lines 10, 11, and 12, column (c), and enter the total here 2. __________
3. Subtract line 2 from line 1 . . . . 3. __________
4. Multiply line 3 by 80% . . . . 4. __________
5. Add lines 2, 5, 7, and 8, column (c), and the part of the deduction on line 3, column (c), that is attributable to dividends from 20%-or-more-owned corporations . . . . 5. __________
6. Enter the smaller of line 4 or 5. If line 5 is greater than line 4, stop here; enter the amount from line 6 on line 9, column (c), and do not complete the rest of this worksheet . . . . 6. __________
7. Enter the total amount of dividends from 20%-or-more-owned corporations that are included on lines 2, 3, 5, 7, and 8, column (a) 7. __________
8. Subtract line 7 from line 3 . . . . 8. __________
9. Multiply line 8 by 70% . . . . 9. __________
10. Subtract line 5 above from line 9, column (c). . . . . . 10. __________
11. Enter the smaller of line 9 or line 10 . . . . 11. __________
12. Dividends-received deduction after limitation (sec. 246(b)). Add lines 6 and 11. Enter the result here and on line 9, column (c) . . . 12. __________

- Off-site storage or warehousing;
- Purchasing;
- Handling, processing, assembly, and repackaging; and
- General and administrative costs (mixed service costs).

For details, see Regulations section 1.263A-3(d).

Enter on line 4 the balance of section 263A costs paid or incurred during the tax year not included on lines 2, 3, and 5.

Line 5

Other Costs

Enter on line 5 any costs paid or incurred during the tax year not entered on lines 2 through 4.

Line 7

Inventory at End of Year

See Regulations section 1.263A-1 through 1.263A-3 for details on figuring the amount of additional section 263A costs to be included in ending inventory.

Lines 9a Through 9f (Schedule A)

Inventory Valuation Methods

Inventories can be valued at:
- Cost;
- Cost or market value (whichever is lower); or
- Any other method approved by the IRS that conforms to the requirements of the applicable regulations cited below.

The average cost (rolling average) method of valuing inventories generally does not conform to the requirements of the regulations. See Rev. Rul. 71-234, 1971-1 C.B. 148.

Corporations that use erroneous valuation methods must change to a method permitted for Federal income tax purposes. To make this change, use Form 3115.

On line 9a, check the method(s) used for valuing inventories. Under lower of cost or market, the term "market" (for normal goods) means the current bid price prevailing on the inventory valuation date for the particular merchandise in the volume usually purchased by the taxpayer. For a manufacturer, market applies to the basic elements of cost—raw materials, labor, and burden. If section 263A applies to the taxpayer, the basic elements of cost must reflect the current bid price of all

direct costs and all indirect costs properly allocable to goods on hand at the inventory date.

Inventory may be valued below cost when the merchandise is unsaleable at normal prices or unusable in the normal way because the goods are subnormal due to damage, imperfections, shopwear, etc., within the meaning of Regulations section 1.471-2(c). The goods may be valued at the current bona fide selling price, minus direct cost of disposition (but not less than scrap value) if such a price can be established.

If this is the first year the Last-in, First-out (LIFO) inventory method was either adopted or extended to inventory goods not previously valued under the LIFO method provided in section 472, attach **Form 970,** Application To Use LIFO Inventory Method, or a statement with the information required by Form 970. Also check the LIFO box on line 9c. On line 9d, enter the amount or the percent of total closing inventories covered under section 472. Estimates are acceptable.

If the corporation changed or extended its inventory method to LIFO and had to write up the opening inventory to cost in the year of election, report the effect of the writeup as other income (line 10, page 1), proportionately over a 3-year period that begins with the year of the LIFO election (section 472(d)).

Note: *Corporations using the LIFO method that make an S corporation election or transfer LIFO inventory to an S corporation in a nonrecognition transaction may be subject to an additional tax attributable to the LIFO recapture amount. See the instructions for line 10, Schedule J.*

For more information on inventory valuation methods, get **Pub. 538,** Accounting Periods and Methods.

Schedule C
(Form 1120 Only)

Dividends and Special Deductions

For purposes of the 20% ownership test on lines 1 through 7, the percentage of stock owned by the corporation is based on voting power and value of the stock. Preferred stock described in section 1504(a)(4) is not taken into account. Corporations filing a consolidated return should see Regulations sections 1.1502-13, 1.1502-26, and 1.1502-27 before completing Schedule C.

Line 1, Column (a)

Enter dividends (except those received on debt-financed stock acquired after July 18, 1984—see section 246A) that:

- Are received from less-than-20%-owned domestic corporations subject to income tax; and
- Qualify for the 70% deduction under section 243(a)(1).

Include taxable distributions from an IC-DISC or former DISC that are designated as eligible for the 70% deduction and certain dividends of Federal Home Loan Banks. See section 246(a)(2).

Also include on line 1 dividends (except those received on debt-financed stock acquired after July 18, 1984) from a regulated investment company (RIC). The amount of dividends eligible for the dividends-received deduction under section 243 is limited by section 854(b). The corporation should receive a notice from the RIC specifying the amount of dividends that qualify for the deduction.

Report so-called dividends or earnings received from mutual savings banks, etc., as interest. Do not treat them as dividends.

Line 2, Column (a)

Enter dividends (except those received on debt-financed stock acquired after July 18, 1984) that are received from 20%-or-more-owned domestic corporations subject to income tax and that are subject to the 80% deduction under section 243(c). Include on this line taxable distributions from an IC-DISC or former DISC that are considered eligible for the 80% deduction.

Line 3, Column (a)

Enter dividends received on debt-financed stock acquired after July 18, 1984, from domestic and foreign corporations subject to income tax that would otherwise be subject to the dividends-received deduction under section 243(a)(1), 243(c), or 245(a). Generally, debt-financed stock is stock that the corporation acquired by incurring a debt (e.g., it borrowed money to buy the stock).

Include on line 3 dividends received from a regulated investment company (RIC) on debt-financed stock. The amount of dividends eligible for the dividends-received deduction is limited by section 854(b). The corporation should receive a notice from the RIC specifying the amount of dividends that qualify for the deduction.

Line 3, Columns (b) and (c)

Dividends received on debt-financed stock acquired after July 18, 1984, are not entitled to the full 70% or 80% dividends-received deduction. The 70% or 80% deduction is reduced by a percentage that is related to the amount of debt incurred to acquire the stock. See section 246A. Also see section 245(a) before making this computation for an additional limitation that applies to dividends received from foreign corporations. Attach a schedule to Form 1120 showing how the amount on line 3, column (c), was figured.

Line 4, Column (a)

Enter dividends received on the preferred stock of a less-than-20%-owned public utility that is subject to income tax and is allowed the deduction provided in section 247 for dividends paid.

Line 5, Column (a)

Enter dividends received on preferred stock of a 20%-or-more-owned public utility that is subject to income tax and is allowed the

Page 11

deduction provided in section 247 for dividends paid.

Line 6, Column (a)

Enter the U.S.-source portion of dividends that:
- Are received from less-than-20%-owned foreign corporations, and
- Qualify for the 70% deduction under section 245(a). To qualify for the 70% deduction, the corporation must own at least 10% of the stock of the foreign corporation by vote and value.

Also include dividends received from a less-than-20%-owned FSC that are:
- Attributable to income treated as effectively connected with the conduct of a trade or business within the United States (excluding foreign trade income), and
- Qualify for the 70% deduction provided in section 245(c)(1)(B).

Line 7, Column (a)

Enter the U.S.-source portion of dividends that are received from 20%-or-more-owned foreign corporations that qualify for the 80% deduction under section 245(a). Also include dividends received from a 20%-or-more-owned FSC that:
- Are attributable to income treated as effectively connected with the conduct of a trade or business within the United States (excluding foreign trade income), and
- Qualify for the 80% deduction provided in section 245(c)(1)(B).

Line 8, Column (a)

Enter dividends received from wholly owned foreign subsidiaries that are eligible for the 100% deduction provided in section 245(b).

In general, the deduction under section 245(b) applies to dividends paid out of the earnings and profits of a foreign corporation for a tax year during which:
- All of its outstanding stock is owned (directly or indirectly) by the domestic corporation receiving the dividends, and
- All of its gross income from all sources is effectively connected with the conduct of a trade or business within the United States.

Line 9, Column (c)

Limitation on Dividends-Received Deduction

Generally, line 9, column (c) may not exceed the amount from the worksheet on page 11. However, in a year in which an NOL occurs, this limitation does not apply even if the loss is created by the dividends-received deduction. See sections 172(d) and 246(b).

Line 10, Columns (a) and (c)

Small business investment companies operating under the Small Business Investment Act of 1958 (15 U.S.C. 661 and following) must enter dividends that are received from domestic corporations subject to income tax even though a deduction is allowed for the entire amount of those dividends. To claim the 100% deduction on line 10, column (c), the company must file with its return a statement that it was a Federal licensee under the Small Business Investment Act of 1958 at the time it received the dividends.

Line 11, Column (a)

Enter dividends from FSCs that are attributable to foreign trade income and that are eligible for the 100% deduction provided in section 245(c)(1)(A).

Line 12, Columns (a) and (c)

Enter only those dividends that qualify under section 243(b) for the 100% dividends-received

Page 12

Tax Computation Worksheet for Members of a Controlled Group
(Keep for your records.)

Note: *Each member of a controlled group (except a qualified personal service corporation) must compute the tax using this worksheet.*

1. Enter taxable income (line 30, page 1, Form 1120) . . . . . **1.** ________
2. Enter line 1 or the corporation's share of the $50,000 taxable income bracket, whichever is less . . . . **2.** ________
3. Subtract line 2 from line 1 . . . . **3.** ________
4. Enter line 3 or the corporation's share of the $25,000 taxable income bracket, whichever is less . . . . **4.** ________
5. Subtract line 4 from line 3 . . . . **5.** ________
6. Enter line 5 or the corporation's share of the $9,925,000 taxable income bracket, whichever is less . . . . **6.** ________
7. Subtract line 6 from line 5 . . . . **7.** ________
8. Multiply line 2 by 15% . . . . **8.** ________
9. Multiply line 4 by 25% . . . . **9.** ________
10. Multiply line 6 by 34% . . . . **10.** ________
11. Multiply line 7 by 35% . . . . **11.** ________
12. If the taxable income of the controlled group exceeds $100,000, enter this member's share of: 5% of the taxable income in excess of $100,000, or $11,750 (See the instructions for Schedule J, line 2b.) . . . . **12.** ________
13. If the taxable income of the controlled group exceeds $15 million, enter this member's share of the smaller of: 3% of the taxable income in excess of $15 million, or $100,000 (See the instructions for Schedule J, line 2b.) . . . . **13.** ________
14. Add lines 8 through 13. Enter here and on line 3, Schedule J, Form 1120. . . . . **14.** ________

---

deduction described in section 243(a)(3). Corporations taking this deduction are subject to the provisions of section 1561.

Note: *The 100% deduction does not apply to affiliated group members that are joining in the filing of a consolidated return.*

Line 13, Column (a)

Enter foreign dividends not reportable on lines 3, 6, 7, 8, or 11 of column (a). Include on line 13 the corporation's share of the ordinary earnings of a qualified electing fund from Form 8621, line 6c. Exclude distributions of amounts constructively taxed in the current year or in prior years under subpart F (sections 951 through 964).

Line 14, Column (a)

Include income constructively received from controlled foreign corporations under subpart F. This amount should equal the total subpart F income reported on Schedule I, Form 5471.

Line 15, Column (a)

Include gross-up for taxes deemed paid under sections 902 and 960.

Line 16, Column (a)

Enter taxable distributions from an IC-DISC or former DISC that are designated as not eligible for a dividends-received deduction.

No deduction is allowed under section 243 for a dividend from an IC-DISC or former DISC (as defined in section 992(a)) to the extent the dividend:
- Is paid out of the corporation's accumulated IC-DISC income or previously taxed income, or
- Is a deemed distribution under section 995(b)(1).

Line 17, Column (a)

Include the following:
1. Dividends (other than capital gain dividends and exempt-interest dividends) that are received from regulated investment companies and that are not subject to the 70% deduction.
2. Dividends from tax-exempt organizations.
3. Dividends (other than capital gain dividends) received from a real estate investment trust that, for the tax year of the trust in which the dividends are paid, qualifies under sections 856 through 860.

4. Dividends not eligible for a dividends-received deduction because of the holding period of the stock or an obligation to make corresponding payments with respect to similar stock.

Two situations in which the dividends-received deduction will not be allowed on any share of stock are:
- If the corporation held it 45 days or less (see **Note** below and section 246(c)(1)(A)), or
- To the extent the corporation is under an obligation to make related payments for substantially similar or related property.

5. Any other taxable dividend income not properly reported above (including distributions under section 936(h)(4)).

Note: *For dividends received or accrued after September 4, 1997, the corporation is not entitled to a dividends-received deduction if it held the stock less than 46 days during the 90-day period beginning 45 days before the stock became ex-dividend with respect to the dividend. See the transition rules in Act section 1015(c)(2) of the Taxpayer Relief Act of 1997.*

If patronage dividends or per-unit retain allocations are included on line 17, identify the total of these amounts in a schedule attached to Form 1120.

Line 18, Column (c)

Section 247 allows public utilities a deduction of 40% of the smaller of:
- Dividends paid on their preferred stock during the tax year, or
- Taxable income computed without regard to this deduction.

In a year in which an NOL occurs, compute the deduction without regard to section 247(a)(1)(B). See section 172(d).

Schedule J, Form 1120 (Part I, Form 1120–A)

Tax Computation

Note: *Members of a controlled group must attach a statement showing the computation of the tax entered on line 3.*

Lines 1 and 2, Form 1120

Members of a controlled group (Form 1120 only).— A member of a controlled group, as defined in section 1563, must check the box on line 1 and complete lines 2a and 2b of Schedule J, Form 1120.

Line 2a.— Members of a controlled group are entitled to one $50,000, one $25,000, and one $9,925,000 taxable income bracket amount (in that order) on line 2a.

When a controlled group adopts or later amends an apportionment plan, each member must attach to its tax return a copy of its consent to this plan. The copy (or an attached statement) must show the part of the amount in each taxable income bracket apportioned to that member. See Regulations section 1.1561-3(b) for other requirements and for the time and manner of making the consent.

Unequal apportionment plan.— Members of a controlled group may elect an unequal apportionment plan and divide the taxable income brackets as they want. There is no need for consistency among taxable income brackets. Any member may be entitled to all, some, or none of the taxable income bracket. However, the total amount for all members cannot be more than the total amount in each taxable income bracket.

Equal apportionment plan.— If no apportionment plan is adopted, members of a controlled group must divide the amount in each taxable income bracket equally among themselves. For example, Controlled Group AB consists of Corporation A and Corporation B. They do not elect an apportionment plan. Therefore, each corporation is entitled to:

- $25,000 (one-half of $50,000) on line 2a(1),
- $12,500 (one-half of $25,000) on line 2a(2), and
- $4,962,500 (one-half of $9,925,000) on line 2a(3).

Line 2b.— Members of a controlled group are treated as one group to figure the applicability of the additional 5% tax and the additional 3% tax. If an additional tax applies, each member will pay that tax based on the part of the amount used in each taxable income bracket to reduce that member's tax. See section 1561(a). If an additional tax applies, attach a schedule showing the taxable income of the entire group and how the corporation figured its share of the additional tax.

Line 2b(1).— Enter the corporation's share of the additional 5% tax on line 2b(1).

Line 2b(2).— Enter the corporation's share of the additional 3% tax on line 2b(2).

Line 3, Form 1120
(Line 1, Form 1120-A)

Most corporations figure their tax by using the Tax Rate Schedule below. Exceptions apply to members of a controlled group (see worksheet on page 12) and qualified personal service corporations (see below).

Tax Rate Schedule

If taxable income (line 30, Form 1120, or line 26, Form 1120-A) on page 1 is:

Over—	But not over—	Tax is:	Of the amount over—
$0	$50,000	15%	$0
50,000	75,000	$ 7,500 + 25%	50,000
75,000	100,000	13,750 + 34%	75,000
100,000	335,000	22,250 + 39%	100,000
335,000	10,000,000	113,900 + 34%	335,000
10,000,000	15,000,000	3,400,000 + 35%	10,000,000
15,000,000	18,333,333	5,150,000 +38%	15,000,000
18,333,333	- - - - -	35%	0

Qualified personal service corporation.— A qualified personal service corporation is taxed at a flat rate of 35% on taxable income. A corporation is a qualified personal service corporation if it meets **BOTH** of the following tests:

- Substantially all of the corporation's activities involve the performance of services in the fields of health, law, engineering, architecture, accounting, actuarial science, performing arts, or consulting, and
- At least 95% of the corporation's stock, by value, is owned, directly or indirectly, by **(1)** employees performing the services, **(2)** retired employees who had performed the services listed above, **(3)** any estate of the employee or retiree described above, or **(4)** any person who acquired the stock of the corporation as a result of the death of an employee or retiree (but only for the 2-year period beginning on the date of the employee's or retiree's death). See Temporary Regulations section 1.448-1T(e) for details.

Note: *If the corporation meets these tests, check the box on line 3, Schedule J, Form 1120 (line 1, Part I, Form 1120-A).*

Mutual savings bank conducting life insurance business.— The tax under section 594 consists of the sum of **(a)** a partial tax computed on Form 1120 on the taxable income of the bank determined without regard to income or deductions allocable to the life insurance department, and **(b)** a partial tax on the taxable income computed on Form 1120-L of the life insurance department. Enter the combined tax on line 3 of Schedule J, Form 1120. Attach Form 1120-L as a schedule and identify it as such.

Deferred tax under section 1291.— If the corporation was a shareholder in a passive foreign investment company (PFIC) and received an excess distribution or disposed of its investment in the PFIC during the year, it must include the increase in taxes due under section 1291(c)(2) in the total for line 3, Schedule J, Form 1120. On the dotted line next to line 3, write "Section 1291" and the amount.

Do not include on line 3 any interest due under section 1291(c)(3). Instead, show the amount of interest owed in the bottom margin of page 1, Form 1120, and write "Section 1291 interest". For details, see **Form 8621,** Return by a Shareholder of a Passive Foreign Investment Company or Qualified Electing Fund.

Additional tax under section 197(f).— A corporation that elects to pay tax on the gain from the sale of an intangible under the related person exception to the anti-churning rules, should include any additional tax due under section 197(f)(9)(B) in the total for line 3. On the dotted line next to line 3, write "Section 197" and the amount. For more information, see **Pub. 535,** Business Expenses.

Line 4a
(Form 1120 Only)

Foreign Tax Credit

To find out when a corporation can take the credit for payment of income tax to a foreign country or U.S. possession, see **Form 1118,** Foreign Tax Credit—Corporations.

Line 4b
(Form 1120 Only)

Possessions Tax Credit

The Small Business Job Protection Act of 1996 repealed the possessions credit. However, existing credit claimants may qualify for a credit under the transitional rules. Get **Form 5735,** Possessions Corporation Tax Credit (Under Sections 936 and 30A).

Line 4c
(Form 1120 Only)

Complete line 4c if the corporation can take either of the following credits. Be sure to check the appropriate box.

Nonconventional source fuel credit.— A credit is allowed for the sale of qualified fuels produced from a nonconventional source. Section 29 contains a definition of qualified fuels, provisions for figuring the credit, and other special rules. Attach a separate schedule to the return showing the computation of the credit.

Qualified electric vehicle (QEV) credit.— Include on line 4c any credit from **Form 8834,** Qualified Electric Vehicle Credit. Vehicles that qualify for this credit are not eligible for the deduction for clean-fuel vehicles under section 179A.

Line 4d, Form 1120
(Line 2a, Form 1120-A)

General Business Credit

Complete this line if the corporation can take any of the following credits. Complete **Form 3800,** General Business Credit, if the corporation has two or more of these credits, a credit carryforward or carryback (including an ESOP credit), a trans-Alaska pipeline liability fund credit, or a passive activity credit. Enter the amount of the general business credit on line 4d (line 2a, Form 1120-A), and check the box for Form 3800.

If the corporation has only one credit, enter on line 4d (line 2a, Form 1120-A), the amount of the credit from the form. Also be sure to check the appropriate box for that form.

Form 3468, Investment Credit.

Form 5884, Work Opportunity Credit.

Form 6478, Credit for Alcohol Used as Fuel.

Form 6765, Credit for Increasing Research Activities.

Form 8586, Low-Income Housing Credit.

Form 8820, Orphan Drug Credit.

Form 8826, Disabled Access Credit.

Form 8830, Enhanced Oil Recovery Credit.

Form 8835, Renewable Electricity Production Credit.

Form 8844, Empowerment Zone Employment Credit.

Note: *While the empowerment zone employment credit is a component of the general business credit, it is figured separately and is not carried to Form 3800.*

Form 8845, Indian Employment Credit.

Form 8846, Credit for Employer Social Security and Medicare Taxes Paid on Certain Employee Tips.

Form 8847, Credit for Contributions to Selected Community Development Corporations.

Form 8861, Welfare-to-Work Credit.

Line 4e, Form 1120
(Line 2b, Form 1120-A)

Credit for Prior Year Minimum Tax

To figure the minimum tax credit and any carryforward of that credit, use **Form 8827,** Credit for Prior Year Minimum Tax—Corporations. Also see Form 8827 if any of the corporation's 1996 nonconventional source fuel credit or qualified electric vehicle credit was disallowed solely because of the tentative minimum tax limitation. See section 53(d).

Line 7
(Form 1120 Only)

Personal Holding Company Tax

A corporation is taxed as a personal holding company under section 542 if:
- At least 60% of its adjusted ordinary gross income for the tax year is personal holding company income, and
- At any time during the last half of the tax year more than 50% in value of its outstanding stock is owned, directly or indirectly, by five or fewer individuals.

See **Schedule PH (Form 1120),** U.S. Personal Holding Company Tax, for definitions and details on how to figure the tax.

Line 8, Form 1120
(Line 5, Form 1120-A)

Recapture Taxes

Recapture of investment credit. If the corporation disposed of investment credit property or changed its use before the end of its useful life or recovery period, it may owe a tax. See **Form 4255,** Recapture of Investment Credit, for details.

Recapture of low-income housing credit. If the corporation disposed of property (or there was a reduction in the qualified basis of the property) for which it took the low-income housing credit, it may owe a tax. See **Form 8611,** Recapture of Low-Income Housing Credit.

Recapture of qualified electric vehicle (QEV) credit. The corporation must recapture part of the QEV credit it claimed in a prior year, if, within 3 years of the date the vehicle was placed in service, it ceases to qualify for the credit. See Regulations section 1.30-1 for details on how to figure the recapture. Include the amount of the recapture in the total for line 8, Schedule J, Form 1120 (line 5, Part I, Form 1120-A). On the dotted line next to the entry space, write "QEV recapture" and the amount.

Recapture of Indian employment credit. Generally, if an employer terminates the employment of a qualified employee less than 1 year after the date of initial employment, any Indian employment credit allowed for a prior tax year because of wages paid or incurred to that employee must be recaptured. For details, see Form 8845 and section 45A. Include the amount of the recapture in the total for line 8, Schedule J, Form 1120 (line 5, Part I, Form 1120-A). On the dotted line next to the entry space, write "45" and the amount.

Line 9, Form 1120
(Line 6, Form 1120-A)

Alternative Minimum Tax

The corporation may owe the alternative minimum tax if it has any of the adjustments and tax preference items listed on **Form 4626,** Alternative Minimum Tax—Corporations. The corporation must file Form 4626 if its taxable income (loss) combined with these adjustments and tax preference items is more than the smaller of $40,000, or the corporation's allowable exemption amount (from Form 4626).

For this purpose, taxable income does not include the NOL deduction. Get Form 4626 for details.

Reduce alternative minimum tax by any amounts from Form 3800, Schedule A, line 36 and Form 8844, line 23. On the dotted line next to line 9a (line 6, Form 1120-A), write "Section 38(c)(2)" ("EZE" if from Form 8844) and the amounts.

Line 10 (Form 1120 Only)

Other Tax and Interest Amounts

Other tax and interest amounts may be included in or subtracted from the total tax reported on line 10.

Amounts to include in the total for line 10 are:
- Tax and interest on a nonqualified withdrawal from a capital construction fund (section 7518).
- Interest on deferred tax attributable to:
    1. Installment sales of certain timeshares and residential lots (section 453(l)(3)), and
    2. Certain nondealer installment obligations (section 453A(c)).
- Interest due under the look-back method (see Form 8697).
- For shareholders in qualified electing funds, deferred tax due upon the termination of a section 1294 election (see Form 8621, Part IV).

Amounts to subtract from the total for line 10 are:
- Deferred tax on the corporation's share of the undistributed earnings of a qualified electing fund (see Form 8621, Part II).
- Deferred LIFO recapture tax (section 1363(d)). See **Deferred LIFO recapture tax,** below, and the instructions for "LIFO recapture amount" under **Line 10, Other Income,** on page 6.

How to report.— Attach a schedule showing your computation of each item included in or subtracted from the total for line 10. On the dotted line next to line 10, enter the amount of tax or interest and:
- Identify it as tax or interest
- Specify the Code section that applies.

Example. To show $50 of interest due on deferred tax from the installment sale of a timeshare, write "Sec. 453(l)(3) interest – $50."

If you figured the tax or interest using another form (e.g., Form 8621 or Form 8697), see the instructions for that form to find out how to report the amount.

Deferred LIFO recapture tax.— The deferred LIFO recapture tax is the part of the LIFO recapture tax that will be deferred and paid with Form 1120S in the future. To figure the deferred tax you must first figure the total LIFO recapture tax. Follow the steps below to figure the total LIFO recapture tax and the deferred amount.

Step 1. Figure the tax on the corporation's income **including** the LIFO recapture amount. (Complete Schedule J through line 9, but do not enter a total on line 10 yet.)

Step 2. On a separate worksheet using the Schedule J format, figure the tax again, but this time **do not** include the LIFO recapture amount in taxable income.

Step 3. Compare the tax in *Step 2* to the tax in *Step 1.* The difference between the two is the **LIFO recapture tax.**

Step 4. Multiply the amount from *Step 3* above by 75%. The result is the **deferred LIFO recapture tax.** Subtract this amount from the total for line 10, Schedule J, and enter the amount on the dotted line next to line 10. Label it "Sec. 1363 deferred tax."

Schedule K, Form 1120
(Part II, Form 1120-A)

Other Information

The following instructions apply to questions 1 through 15 on Form 1120, page 3, Schedule K, or questions 1 through 6 on Form 1120-A,

page 2, Part II. Be sure to answer all the questions that apply to the corporation.

Question 4
(Form 1120 Only)

Check the "Yes" box for question 4 if:
- The corporation is a subsidiary in an affiliated group (defined below), but is not filing a consolidated return for the tax year with that group, or
- The corporation is a subsidiary in a parent-subsidiary controlled group (defined below).

Any corporation that meets either of the requirements above should check the "Yes" box. This applies even if the corporation is a subsidiary member of one group and the parent corporation of another.

Note: *If the corporation is an "excluded member" of a controlled group (see section 1563(b)(2)), it is still considered a member of a controlled group for this purpose.*

Affiliated group.— The term "affiliated group" means one or more chains of includible corporations (section 1504(a)) connected through stock ownership with a common parent corporation. The common parent must be an includible corporation and the following requirements must be met:

1. The common parent must own directly stock that represents at least 80% of the total voting power and at least 80% of the total value of the stock of at least one of the other includible corporations.

2. Stock that represents at least 80% of the total voting power, and at least 80% of the total value of the stock of each of the other corporations (except for the common parent) must be owned directly by at least one of the other includible corporations.

For this purpose, the term "stock" generally does not include any stock that **(a)** is nonvoting, **(b)** is nonconvertible, **(c)** is limited and preferred as to dividends and does not participate significantly in corporate growth, and **(d)** has redemption and liquidation rights that do not exceed the issue price of the stock (except for a reasonable redemption or liquidation premium). See section 1504(a)(4).

Parent-subsidiary controlled group.— The term "parent-subsidiary controlled group" means one or more chains of corporations connected through stock ownership (section 1563(a)(1)). Both of the following requirements must be met:

1. 80% of the total combined voting power of all classes of stock entitled to vote or at least 80% of the total value of all classes of stock of each corporation in the group (except the parent) must be owned by one or more of the other corporations in the group.

2. The common parent must own at least 80% of the total combined voting power of all classes of stock entitled to vote or at least 80% of the total value of all classes of stock of at least one of the other corporations in the group. Stock owned directly by other members of the group is not counted when computing the voting power or value.

See section 1563(d)(1) for the definition of "stock" for purposes of determining stock ownership above.

Question 8, Form 1120
(Question 6, Form 1120-A)

Foreign financial accounts.— Check the "Yes" box if either **1** or **2** below applies to the corporation. Otherwise, check the "No" box:

1. At any time during the 1997 calendar year the corporation had an interest in or signature or other authority over a bank, securities, or other financial account in a foreign country; and

• The combined value of the accounts was more than $10,000 at any time during the calendar year, and

• The account was NOT with a U.S. military banking facility operated by a U.S. financial institution.

2. The corporation owns more than 50% of the stock in any corporation that would answer "Yes" to item **1** above.

Get **Form TD F 90-22.1,** Report of Foreign Bank and Financial Accounts, to see if the corporation is considered to have an interest in or signature or other authority over a financial account in a foreign country.

If "Yes" is checked for this question, file Form TD F 90-22.1 by June 30, 1998, with the Department of the Treasury at the address shown on the form. Because Form TD F 90-22.1 is not a tax return, do not file it with Form 1120 (or Form 1120-A).

You can get Form TD F 90-22.1 from an IRS Distribution Center or by calling 1–800–TAX–FORM (1–800–829–3676).

Also, if "Yes" is checked for this question, enter the name of the foreign country or countries. Attach a separate sheet if more space is needed.

Question 9
(Form 1120 Only)

The corporation may be required to file **Form 3520,** Annual Return To Report Transactions with Foreign Trusts and Receipt of Certain Foreign Gifts, if:

• It directly or indirectly transferred money or property to a foreign trust. For this purpose, any U.S. person who created a foreign trust is considered a transferor.

• It is treated as the owner of any part of the assets of a foreign trust under the grantor trust rules.

• It received a distribution from a foreign trust.

For more information, see the instructions for 3520.

Note: *An owner of a foreign trust must ensure that the trust files an annual information return on Form 3520-A, as well as U.S. owner and U.S. beneficiary statements. For details, see Notice 97–34, 1997–25 I.R.B. 22.*

The corporation may be required to file **Form 926,** Return by a U.S. Transferor of Property to a Foreign Corporation, Foreign Estate or Trust, or Foreign Partnership to:

• Pay any excise tax due under section 1491.

• Report information required under section 6038B.

• Report transfers of property to a foreign corporation, estate, trust or partnership, and

• Make elections under section 1492 with respect to those transfers.

For more information, see the instructions for Form 926.

Question 10
(Form 1120 Only)

Check the "Yes" box if one foreign person owned at least 25% of **(a)** the total voting power of all classes of stock of the corporation entitled to vote or **(b)** the total value of all classes of stock of the corporation.

The constructive ownership rules of section 318 apply in determining if a corporation is foreign owned. See section 6038A(c)(5) and the related regulations.

Enter on line 10a the percentage owned by the foreign person specified in question 10. On line 10b, write the name of the owner's country.

Note: *If there is more than one 25%-or-more foreign owner, complete lines 10a and 10b for the foreign person with the highest percentage of ownership.*

Foreign person.— The term "foreign person" means:

• A foreign citizen or nonresident alien.

• An individual who is a citizen of a U.S. possession (but who is not a U.S. citizen or resident).

• A foreign partnership.

• A foreign corporation.

• Any foreign estate or trust within the meaning of section 7701(a)(31).

• A foreign government (or one of its agencies or instrumentalities) to the extent that it is engaged in the conduct of a commercial activity as described in section 892.

Owner's country.— For individuals, the term "owner's country" means the country of residence. For all others, it is the country where incorporated, organized, created, or administered.

Requirement to file Form 5472.— If the corporation checked "Yes" to question 10, it may have to file Form 5472. Generally, a 25% foreign-owned corporation that had a reportable transaction with a foreign or domestic related party during the tax year must file Form 5472.

See Form 5472 for filing instructions and penalties for failure to file.

Question 12, Form 1120
(Question 3, Form 1120-A)

Show any tax-exempt interest received or accrued. Include any exempt-interest dividends received as a shareholder in a mutual fund or other regulated investment company.

Question 14
(Form 1120 Only)

Check the box on line 14 if the corporation elects under section 172(b)(3) to forego the carryback period for a net operating loss (NOL). If you check this box, do not attach the statement described in Temporary Regulations section 301.9100-12T(d).

Question 15
(Form 1120 Only)

Enter the amount of the net operating loss (NOL) carryover to the tax year from prior years, even if some of the loss is used to offset income on this return. The amount to enter is the total of all NOLs generated in prior years but not used to offset income (either as a carryback or carryover) to a tax year prior to 1997. Do not reduce the amount by any NOL deduction reported on line 29a.

Pub. 536 has a worksheet for figuring a corporation's NOL carryover.

Schedule L, Form 1120
(Part III, Form 1120-A)

Balance Sheets per Books

The balance sheet should agree with the corporation's books and records. Include

certificates of deposit as cash on line 1, Schedule L.

Line 5

Tax-Exempt Securities

Include on this line:

1. State and local government obligations, the interest on which is excludable from gross income under section 103(a), and

2. Stock in a mutual fund or other regulated investment company that distributed exempt-interest dividends during the tax year of the corporation.

Line 26, Form 1120
(Line 21, Form 1120–A)

Adjustments to Shareholders' Equity

Some examples of adjustments to report on this line include:

• Unrealized gains and losses on securities held "available for sale."

• Foreign currency translation adjustments.

• The excess of additional pension liability over unrecognized prior service cost.

• Guarantees of employee stock (ESOP) debt.

• Compensation related to employee stock award plans.

If the total adjustment to be entered on line 26 (line 21, Form 1120–A) is a negative amount, enter the amount in parentheses.

Schedule M-1, Form 1120
(Part IV, Form 1120-A)

Reconciliation of Income (Loss) per Books With Income per Return
Line 5c, Form 1120
(Line 5, Form 1120-A)

Travel and Entertainment

Include on line 5c (line 5, Form 1120-A) any of the following:

• 50% of the meals and entertainment not allowed under section 274(n).

• Expenses for the use of an entertainment facility.

• The part of business gifts over $25.

• Expenses of an individual over $2,000, which are allocable to conventions on cruise ships.

• Employee achievement awards over $400.

• The cost of entertainment tickets over face value (also subject to 50% disallowance under section 274(n)).

• The cost of skyboxes over the face value of nonluxury box seat tickets.

• The part of luxury water travel not allowed under section 274(m).

• Expenses for travel as a form of education.

• Other travel and entertainment expenses not allowed as a deduction.

For more information, see Pub. 542.

Line 7, Form 1120
(Line 6, Form 1120-A)

Tax-Exempt Interest

Include as interest on line 7 (line 6, Form 1120-A), any exempt-interest dividends received as a shareholder in a mutual fund or other regulated investment company.

Codes for Principal Business Activity

These codes for the Principal Business Activity are designed to classify enterprises by the type of activity in which they are engaged to facilitate the administration of the Internal Revenue Code. Though similar in format and structure to the Standard Industrial Classification (SIC) codes, they should not be used as SIC codes.

Using the list below, enter on Form 1120, Schedule K, line 2a (Form 1120-A, Part II, line 1a) the code number for the specific industry group from which the largest percentage of "total receipts" is derived. "Total receipts" means gross receipts (line 1a, page 1) plus all other income (lines 4 through 10, page 1).

On Form 1120, Schedule K, lines 2b and 2c (Form 1120-A, Part II, lines 1b and 1c), state the principal business activity and principal product or service that account for the largest percentage of total receipts. For example, if the principal business activity is "Grain mill products," the principal product or service may be "Cereal preparations."

If, as its principal business activity, the corporation: (1) purchases raw materials, (2) subcontracts out for labor to make a finished product from the raw materials, and (3) retains title to the goods, the corporation is considered to be a manufacturer and must enter one of the codes (2010-3998) under "Manufacturing."

Agriculture, Forestry, and Fishing
Code
0400 Agricultural production
0600 Agricultural services (except veterinarians), forestry, fishing, hunting, and trapping

Mining
Metal mining
1010 Iron ores
1070 Copper, lead and zinc, gold and silver ores
1098 Other metal mining
1150 Coal mining
Oil and gas extraction
1330 Crude petroleum, natural gas, and natural gas liquids
1380 Oil and gas field services
Nonmetallic minerals, except fuels
1430 Dimension, crushed and broken stone; sand and gravel
1498 Other nonmetallic minerals, except fuels

Construction
General building contractors and operative builders
1510 General building contractors
1531 Operative builders
1600 Heavy construction contractors
Special trade contractors
1711 Plumbing, heating, and air conditioning
1731 Electrical work
1798 Other special trade contractors

Manufacturing
Food and kindred products
2010 Meat products
2020 Dairy products
2030 Preserved fruits and vegetables
2040 Grain mill products
2050 Bakery products
2060 Sugar and confectionary products
2081 Malt liquors and malt
2088 Alcoholic beverages, except malt liquors and malt
2089 Bottled soft drinks, and flavorings
2096 Other food and kindred products
2100 Tobacco manufacturers
Textile mill products
2228 Weaving mills and textile finishing
2250 Knitting mills
2298 Other textile mill products
Apparel and other textile products
2315 Men's and boys' clothing
2345 Women's and children's clothing
2388 Other apparel and accessories
2390 Miscellaneous fabricated textile products
Lumber and wood products
2415 Logging, sawmills, and planing mills
2430 Millwork, plywood, and related products
2498 Other wood products, including wood buildings and mobile homes
2500 Furniture and fixtures

Code
Paper and allied products
2625 Pulp, paper, and board mills
2699 Other paper products
Printing and publishing
2710 Newspapers
2720 Periodicals
2735 Books, greeting cards, and miscellaneous publishing
2799 Commercial and other printing, and printing trade services
Chemicals and allied products
2815 Industrial chemicals, plastics materials, and synthetics
2830 Drugs
2840 Soap, cleaners, and toilet goods
2850 Paints and allied products
2898 Agricultural and other chemical products
Petroleum refining and related industries (including those integrated with extraction)
2910 Petroleum refining (including integrated)
2998 Other petroleum and coal products
Rubber and misc. plastics products
3050 Rubber products, plastics footwear, hose and belting
3070 Misc. plastics products
Leather and leather products
3140 Footwear, except rubber
3198 Other leather and leather products
Stone, clay, and glass products
3225 Glass products
3240 Cement, hydraulic
3270 Concrete, gypsum, and plaster products
3298 Other nonmetallic mineral products
Primary metal industries
3370 Ferrous metal industries; misc. primary metal products
3380 Nonferrous metal industries
Fabricated metal products
3410 Metal cans and shipping containers
3428 Cutlery, hand tools, and hardware; screw machine products, bolts, and similar products
3430 Plumbing and heating, except electric and warm air
3440 Fabricated structural metal products
3460 Metal forgings and stampings
3470 Coating, engraving, and allied services
3480 Ordnance and accessories, except vehicles and guided missiles
3490 Misc. fabricated metal products
Machinery, except electrical
3520 Farm machinery
3530 Construction and related machinery
3540 Metalworking machinery
3550 Special industry machinery
3560 General industrial machinery
3570 Office, computing, and accounting machines
3598 Other machinery except electrical

Code
Electrical and electronic equipment
3630 Household appliances
3665 Radio, television, and communication equipment
3670 Electronic components and accessories
3698 Other electrical equipment
3710 Motor vehicles and equipment
Transportation equipment, except motor vehicles
3725 Aircraft, guided missiles and parts
3730 Ship and boat building and repairing
3798 Other transportation equipment, except motor vehicles
Instruments and related products
3815 Scientific instruments and measuring devices; watches and clocks
3845 Optical, medical, and ophthalmic goods
3860 Photographic equipment and supplies
3998 Other manufacturing products

Transportation and Public Utilities
Transportation
4000 Railroad transportation
4100 Local and interurban passenger transit
4200 Trucking and warehousing
4400 Water transportation
4500 Transportation by air
4600 Pipe lines, except natural gas
4700 Miscellaneous transportation services
Communication
4825 Telephone, telegraph, and other communication services
4830 Radio and television broadcasting
Electric, gas, and sanitary services
4910 Electric services
4920 Gas production and distribution
4930 Combination utility services
4990 Water supply and other sanitary services

Wholesale Trade
Durable
5008 Machinery, equipment, and supplies
5010 Motor vehicles and automotive equipment
5020 Furniture and home furnishings
5030 Lumber and construction materials
5040 Sporting, recreational, photographic, and hobby goods, toys and supplies
5050 Metals and minerals, except petroleum and scrap
5060 Electrical goods
5070 Hardware, plumbing and heating equipment and supplies
5098 Other durable goods
Nondurable
5110 Paper and paper products
5129 Drugs, drug proprietaries, and druggists' sundries
5130 Apparel, piece goods, and notions
5140 Groceries and related products
5150 Farm-product raw materials
5160 Chemicals and allied products
5170 Petroleum and petroleum products
5180 Alcoholic beverages
5190 Misc. nondurable goods

Retail Trade
Building materials, garden supplies, and mobile home dealers
5220 Building materials dealers
5251 Hardware stores
5265 Garden supplies and mobile home dealers
5300 General merchandise stores
Food stores
5410 Grocery stores
5490 Other food stores
Automotive dealers and service stations
5515 Motor vehicle dealers
5541 Gasoline service stations
5598 Other automotive dealers
5600 Apparel and accessory stores
5700 Furniture and home furnishings stores

Code
5800 Eating and drinking places
Misc. retail stores
5912 Drug stores and proprietary stores
5921 Liquor stores
5995 Other retail stores

Finance, Insurance, and Real Estate
Banking
6030 Mutual savings banks
6060 Bank holding companies
6090 Banks, except mutual savings banks and bank holding companies
Credit agencies other than banks
6120 Savings and loan associations
6140 Personal credit institutions
6150 Business credit institutions
6199 Other credit agencies
Security, commodity brokers and services
6210 Security brokers, dealers, and flotation companies
6299 Commodity contracts brokers and dealers; security and commodity exchanges; and allied services
Insurance
6355 Life insurance
6356 Mutual insurance, except life or marine and certain fire or flood insurance companies
6359 Other insurance companies
6411 Insurance agents, brokers, and service
Real estate
6511 Real estate operators and lessors of buildings
6516 Lessors of mining, oil, and similar property
6518 Lessors of railroad property and other real property
6530 Condominium management and cooperative housing associations
6550 Subdividers and developers
6599 Other real estate
Holding and other investment companies, except bank holding companies
6744 Small business investment companies
6749 Other holding and investment companies except bank holding companies

Services
7000 Hotels and other lodging places
7200 Personal services
Business services
7310 Advertising
7389 Business services, except advertising
Auto repair; misc. repair services
7500 Auto repair and services
7600 Misc. repair services
Amusement and recreation services
7812 Motion picture production, distribution, and services
7830 Motion picture theaters
7900 Amusement and recreation services, except motion pictures
Other services
8015 Offices of physicians, including osteopathic physicians
8021 Offices of dentists
8040 Offices of other health practitioners
8050 Nursing and personal care facilities
8060 Hospitals
8071 Medical laboratories
8099 Other medical services
8111 Legal services
8200 Educational services
8300 Social services
8600 Membership organizations
8911 Architectural and engineering services
8930 Accounting, auditing, and bookkeeping
8980 Miscellaneous services (including veterinarians)

Other Forms That May Be Required

Use Form ▼	To ▼
1098, Mortgage Interest Statement	Report the receipt from any individual of $600 or more of mortgage interest and points in the course of the corporation's trade or business for any calendar year
1099-A	Report the following: • Acquisitions and abandonments of secured property through foreclosure
1099-B	• Proceeds from broker and barter exchange transactions
1099-C	• Cancellation of a debt
1099-DIV	• Certain dividends and distributions
1099-INT	• Interest income
1099-LTC	• Certain payments made on a per diem basis under a long-term care insurance contract, and certain accelerated death benefits
1099-MISC	• Miscellaneous income (e.g., payments to certain fishing boat crew members; payments to providers of health and medical services; miscellaneous income payments and nonemployee compensation)
1099-MSA	• Distributions from a medical savings account (MSA)
1099-OID	• Original issue discount
1099-PATR	• Distributions from cooperatives to their patrons
1099-R	• Distributions from retirement or profit-sharing plans, IRAs, SEPs, or SIMPLEs, and insurance contracts
1099-S	• Proceeds from real estate transactions
W-2, Wage and Tax Statement (and **Form W-3,** Transmittal of Wage and Tax Statements).	Report withheld income, social security, and Medicare taxes for an employee
W-2G, Certain Gambling Winnings	Report gambling winnings from horse racing, dog racing, jai alai, lotteries, keno, bingo, slot machines, sweepstakes, and wagering pools
5498, IRA, SEP, or SIMPLE Retirement Plan Information	Report contributions (including rollover contributions) to an IRA, SEP, or SIMPLE, and the value of an IRA, SEP or SIMPLE account.
8027, Employer's Annual Information Return of Tip Income and Allocated Tips	Report receipts from food or beverage operations and tips reported by employees (applies to large food and beverage establishments)
8281, Information Return for Publicly Offered Original Issue Discount Instruments	Report the issuance of public offerings of debt instruments
8300, Report of Cash Payments Over $10,000 Received in a Trade or Business	Report the receipt of more than $10,000 in cash or foreign currency in one transaction or a series of related transactions

The left margin of the above rows is labeled **Information Returns**.

Note: *To transmit Forms 1099, 1098, 5498, and W-2G, get* **Form 1096,** *Annual Summary and Transmittal of U.S. Information Returns.*

Use Form	To
940 or 940-EZ, Employer's Annual Federal Unemployment (FUTA) Tax Return	Report annual Federal unemployment (FUTA) tax. The tax applies if **either** of the following requirements are met: • You paid wages of $1,500 or more in any calendar quarter in 1996 or 1997, or • You had at least one employee who worked for the corporation for some part of a day in any 20 or more different weeks in 1996 or 20 or more different weeks in 1997.
941, Employer's Quarterly Federal Tax Return, or, for agricultural employers, **Form 943,** Employer's Annual Tax Return for Agricultural Employees	Report payroll income tax withheld and employer and employee social security and Medicare taxes (also see **Trust fund recovery penalty** in the instructions).
945, Annual Return of Withheld Federal Income Tax	Report income tax withholding from nonpayroll distributions (e.g., pensions, annuities, IRAs, military retirement, gambling winnings, Indian gaming profits, and backup withholding). Also see **Trust fund recovery penalty** in the instructions.
720, Quarterly Federal Excise Tax Return	Report and pay: • The luxury tax on passenger vehicles • Environmental excise taxes • Communications and air transportation taxes • Fuel taxes • Manufacturers' taxes • Ship passenger taxes • Certain other excise taxes
952, Consent to Extend Period of Limitation on Assessment of Income Taxes	Extend period of assessment of all income taxes of the receiving corporation on the complete liquidation of a subsidiary under section 332.

The left margin of the above rows is labeled **Employment Tax Returns**.

<table>
<tr><th colspan="2" style="text-align:center">Use Form ▼</th><th style="text-align:center">To ▼</th></tr>
<tr><td rowspan="11">Other Forms</td><td>966, Corporate Dissolution or Liquidation</td><td>Report the adoption of a resolution or plan to dissolve the corporation or liquidate any of its stock.</td></tr>
<tr><td>2553, Election by a Small Business Corporation</td><td>Elect S corporation status</td></tr>
<tr><td>5452, Corporate Report of Nondividend Distributions</td><td>Report nondividend distributions</td></tr>
<tr><td>8264, Application for Registration of a Tax Shelter</td><td>Apply for a tax shelter registration number (used by tax shelter organizers)</td></tr>
<tr><td>8271, Investor Reporting of Tax Shelter Registration Number</td><td>Report a registered tax shelter's registration number. This form must be filed with any return on which a deduction, loss, credit, or other tax benefit is claimed or reported (or any income is reported) from an interest in a tax shelter. The requirement applies to all returns, including applications for tentative refund (Form 1139) and amended returns (Form 1120X).</td></tr>
<tr><td>8275, Disclosure Statement, and Form 8275-R, Regulation Disclosure Statement</td><td>Disclose items or positions taken on a tax return that are not otherwise adequately disclosed on the tax return or that are contrary to Treasury regulations (to avoid parts of the accuracy-related penalty or certain preparer penalties).</td></tr>
<tr><td>8594, Asset Acquisition Statement Under Section 1060</td><td>Report the purchase or sale of a group of assets that constitute a trade or business if goodwill or going concern value attach to the assets.</td></tr>
<tr><td>8697, Interest Computation Under the Look-Back Method for Completed Long-Term Contracts</td><td>Figure the interest due or to be refunded under the look-back method of section 460(b)(2). The look-back method applies to certain long-term contracts accounted for under the percentage of completion or percentage of completion-capitalized cost methods).</td></tr>
<tr><td>8810, Corporate Passive Activity Loss and Credit Limitations</td><td>Figure allowable passive activity loss and credit for closely-held or personal service corporations.</td></tr>
<tr><td>8817, Allocation of Patronage and Nonpatronage Income and Deductions</td><td>Figure and report patronage and nonpatronage income and deductions (used by taxable cooperatives).</td></tr>
<tr><td>8842, Election To Use Different Annualization Periods for Corporate Estimated Tax</td><td>Elect one of the annualization periods in section 6655(e)(2) to figure estimated tax payments under the annualized installment method.</td></tr>
</table>

<table>
<tr><td>8849, Claim for Refund of Excise Taxes</td><td>Claim a refund of:
● Excise taxes reported on Form 720, 730, or 2290
● Excise taxes on fuels, chemicals, and other articles that are later used for nontaxable purposes, or for which there is a reduced rate of tax.</td></tr>
</table>

<table>
<tr><th colspan="2" style="text-align:center">Use Form ▼</th><th style="text-align:center">If the corporation ▼</th></tr>
<tr><td rowspan="7">International Forms</td><td>926, Return by a U.S. Transferor of Property to a Foreign Corporation, Foreign Estate or Trust, or Foreign Partnership</td><td>Is required to pay excise tax under section 1491, report information under section 6038B, report transfers of property to certain foreign entities (or make an election under section 1492 with respect to those transfers).</td></tr>
<tr><td>3520, Annual Return To Report Transactions With Foreign Trusts and Receipt of Certain Foreign Gifts</td><td>Received a distribution from a foreign trust; or, was the grantor of or transferor to a foreign trust that existed during the tax year. (See the instructions for Schedule K, Question 9.)</td></tr>
<tr><td>1042, Annual Withholding Tax Return for U.S. Source Income of Foreign Persons, and Form 1042-S, Foreign Person's U.S. Source Income Subject to Withholding. Also see Pub. 515, Withholding of Tax on Nonresident Aliens and Foreign Corporations, and sections 1441 and 1442.</td><td>Is required to report and send withheld tax on payments or distributions made to nonresident alien individuals, foreign partnerships, or foreign corporations.</td></tr>
<tr><td>5471, Information Return of U.S. Persons With Respect to Certain Foreign Corporations</td><td>Meets any of the following conditions:
● It controls a foreign corporation,
● It acquires, disposes of, or owns 5% or more in value of the outstanding stock of a foreign corporation, or
● It had control of a foreign corporation for an uninterrupted period of at least 30 days during the annual accounting period of the foreign corporation.</td></tr>
<tr><td>5472, Information Return of a 25% Foreign-Owned U.S. Corporation or a Foreign Corporation Engaged in a U.S. Trade or Business</td><td>Is 25% or more foreign-owned. (See the instructions for Schedule K, Question 10.)</td></tr>
<tr><td>5713, International Boycott Report</td><td>Has operations in, or related to, a "boycotting" country, company, or national of a country</td></tr>
<tr><td>8621, Return by a Shareholder in a Passive Foreign Investment Company or Qualified Electing Fund</td><td>Was a shareholder in a passive foreign investment company (under section 1296) at any time during the tax year</td></tr>
</table>

INSTRUCTIONS FOR FORM 1120S

U.S. Income Tax Return for an S Corporation

1997

Department of the Treasury
Internal Revenue Service

Instructions for Form 1120S

U.S. Income Tax Return for an S Corporation

Section references are to the Internal Revenue Code unless otherwise noted.

Paperwork Reduction Act Notice. We ask for the information on this form to carry out the Internal Revenue laws of the United States. You are required to give us the information. We need it to ensure that you are complying with these laws and to allow us to figure and collect the right amount of tax.

You are not required to provide the information requested on a form that is subject to the Paperwork Reduction Act unless the form displays a valid OMB control number. Books or records relating to a form or its instructions must be retained as long as their contents may become material in the administration of any Internal Revenue law. Generally, tax returns and return information are confidential, as required by section 6103.

The time needed to complete and file this form and related schedules will vary depending on individual circumstances. The estimated average times are:

Form	Recordkeeping	Learning about the law or the form	Preparing the form	Copying, assembling, and sending the form to the IRS
1120S	63 hr., 8 min.	20 hr., 37 min.	36 hr., 31 min.	4 hr., 1 min.
Sch. D (1120S)	10 hr., 31 min.	4 hr., 20 min.	9 hr., 20 min.	1 hr., 20 min.
Sch. K-1 (1120S)	15 hr., 4 min.	10 hr., 19 min.	14 hr., 44 min.	1 hr., 4 min.

If you have comments concerning the accuracy of these time estimates or suggestions for making these forms simpler, we would be happy to hear from you. You can write to the Tax Forms Committee, Western Area Distribution Center, Rancho Cordova, CA 95743-0001. **DO NOT** send the tax form to this address. Instead, see **Where To File** on page 3.

General Instructions

Changes To Note

The Small Business Job Protection Act of 1996 made the following changes that affect S corporations. Unless otherwise noted, the changes are effective for tax years beginning after 1996:

- The maximum number of permitted shareholders has been increased to 75.

- A new type of trust, an "electing small business trust," is permitted to be a shareholder. An electing small business trust is an eligible trust that has made an election in accordance with Notice 97-12, 1997-3 I.R.B. 11, and that does not have as a beneficiary any person other than an individual, an estate, or a charity that holds a contingent remainder interest.

- A financial institution that **does not** use the reserve method of accounting for bad debts under section 585 is eligible to be an S corporation.

- The period during which a testamentary trust may remain a shareholder following the death of the deemed owner is extended to 2 years.

- There is no longer any restriction on the percentage of another corporation's stock that an S corporation may hold. In addition, an S corporation may make an election to treat the assets, liabilities, income, deductions, and credits of a wholly-owned subsidiary as those of the parent S corporation. For details on making the election, see Notice 97-4, 1997-2 I.R.B. 24.

- For an election to be an S corporation for tax years beginning after 1982, the IRS has been given the authority to:

  1. Allow an S corporation that has inadvertently made an invalid election to be treated as an S corporation for a specified period if the corporation takes the steps needed to perfect the election. To obtain relief for an invalid election, the corporation generally must request a private letter ruling and pay a user fee.

  2. Treat late elections as timely made if the corporation demonstrates reasonable cause for being late. To obtain relief for a late election, the corporation generally must request a private letter ruling and pay a user fee. In certain cases, these requirements do not apply. For details, see Rev. Proc. 97-40, 1997-33 I.R.B. 50, and Rev. Proc. 97-48, 1997-43 I.R.B. 19.

- The election to close the corporation's books when a shareholder terminates his or her interest in the S corporation is made by the corporation and the affected shareholders rather than all shareholders.

Cat. No. 11515K

113

- The consolidated audit procedures at the corporate level that applied to certain corporations, including those with more than 5 shareholders, have been repealed. Instead, S corporation items will be determined in separate proceedings with the individual shareholders.

- Any net negative adjustment for the tax year (as defined in section 1368(e)(1)(C)(ii)) is disregarded when figuring the accumulated adjustments account for the purpose of determining the taxability of distributions for that tax year.

- For its first tax year beginning after 1996, an S corporation's accumulated earnings and profits (E&P) is reduced (as of the first day of that year) by the E&P accumulated from any tax year beginning before 1983 when the corporation was a subchapter S corporation. Thus, an S corporation's E&P after 1996 is solely attributable to tax years when the corporation did not have an S election in effect.

- For purposes of the 5-year waiting period that generally applies to an election to be an S corporation after a prior termination, any termination in a tax year beginning before 1997 is not taken into account.

The Taxpayer Relief Act of 1997 (the Act) made the following changes that affect S corporations:

- Employers that pay wages to long-term family assistance recipients may qualify for the welfare-to-work credit. This new credit is based on wages paid to qualified individuals who begin work after December 31, 1997, and is figured on **Form 8861,** Welfare-to-Work Credit.

- The penalty for failure to make electronic deposits of depository taxes using the Electronic Federal Tax Payment System (EFTPS), has been temporarily waived for filers who were first required to use EFTPS on or after July 1, 1997. For more information, see **Electronic Deposit Requirement** on page 4.

- For tax years ending after August 5, 1997, commodities dealers and traders of commodities and securities may make an election to use the mark-to-market accounting method. For more information, see Act section 1001.

- The Act imposed additional limitations on the deduction of premiums and interest on debt with respect to life insurance, annuity, or endowment contracts. The Act also reduces interest deductions that are allocable, under proration rules described in new section 264(f), to the unborrowed policy cash values of certain life insurance, endowment, or annuity contracts issued or deemed issued after June 8, 1997. For details, see section 264.

Unresolved Tax Problems

The Problem Resolution Program is for taxpayers that have been unable to resolve their problems with the IRS. If the corporation has a tax problem it cannot clear up through normal channels, write to the corporation's local IRS District Director or call the corporation's local IRS office and ask for Problem Resolution assistance. Persons who have access to TTY/TDD equipment may call 1-800-829-4059 to ask for help from Problem Resolution. This office cannot change the tax law or technical decisions. But it can help the corporation clear up problems that resulted from previous contacts.

How To Make a Contribution To Reduce the Public Debt

To make a contribution to reduce the public debt, send a check made payable to "Bureau of the Public Debt" to Bureau of the Public Debt, Department G, Washington, DC 20239-0601. Or, enclose a check with Form 1120S. Contributions to reduce the public debt are deductible, subject to the rules and limitations for charitable contributions.

How To Get Forms and Publications

Personal Computer

Visit the IRS's Internet Web Site at **www.irs.ustreas.gov** to get:
- Forms and instructions
- Publications
- IRS press releases and fact sheets.

You can also reach us using:
- Telnet at **iris.irs.ustreas.gov**
- File Transfer Protocol at **ftp.irs.ustreas.gov**
- Direct Dial (by modem). Dial direct to the Internal Revenue Information Services (IRIS) by calling **703-321-8020** using your modem. IRIS is an on-line information service on FedWorld.

CD-ROM

A CD-ROM containing over 2,000 tax products (including many prior year forms) can be purchased from the Government Printing Office (GPO). To order the CD-ROM, call the Superintendent of Documents at **202-512-1800** or go through GPO's Internet Web Site (**www.access.gpo.gov/su_docs**).

By Phone and in Person

To order forms and publications, call **1-800-TAX-FORM (1-800-829-3676)** between 7:30 a.m. and 5:30 p.m. on weekdays. You can also get most forms and publications at your local IRS office.

Purpose of Form

Form 1120S is used to report the income, deductions, gains, losses, etc., of a domestic corporation that has elected to be an S corporation by filing **Form 2553,** Election by a Small Business Corporation, and whose election is in effect for the tax year.

Who Must File

A corporation must file Form 1120S if **(a)** it elected to be an S corporation by filing Form 2553, **(b)** the IRS accepted the election, and **(c)** the election remains in effect. **Do not** file Form 1120S for any tax year before the year the election takes effect.

Termination of Election

Once the election is made, it stays in effect until it is terminated. If the election is terminated in a tax year beginning after 1996, the corporation (or a successor corporation) can make another election on Form 2553 only with IRS consent for any tax year before the 5th tax year after the first tax year in which the termination took effect. See Regulations section 1.1362-5 for more details.

An election terminates **automatically** in any of the following cases:

1. The corporation is no longer a small business corporation as defined in section 1361(b). The termination of an election in this manner is effective as of the day on which the corporation no longer meets the definition of a small business corporation. If the election terminates for this reason, attach to Form 1120S for the final year of the S corporation a statement notifying the IRS of the termination and the date it occurred.

2. The corporation, for each of three consecutive tax years, **(a)** has accumulated earnings and profits and **(b)** derives more than 25% of its gross receipts from passive investment income as defined in section 1362(d)(3)(C). The election terminates on the first day of the first tax year beginning after the third consecutive tax year. The corporation must pay a tax for each year it has excess net passive income. See the instructions for line 22a for details on how to figure the tax.

3. The election is revoked. An election may be revoked only with the consent of shareholders who, at the time the revocation is made, hold more than 50% of the number of issued and outstanding shares of stock (including non-voting stock). The revocation may specify an effective revocation date that is on or after the day the revocation is filed. If no date is specified, the revocation is effective at the start of a tax year if the revocation is made on or before the 15th day of the 3rd month of that tax year. If no date is specified and the revocation is made after the 15th day of the 3rd month of the tax year, the revocation is effective at the start of the next tax year.

To revoke the election, the corporation must file a statement with the service center where it filed its election to be an S corporation. In the statement, the corporation must notify the IRS that it is revoking its election to be an S corporation. The statement must be signed by each shareholder who consents to the revocation and contain the information required by Regulations section 1.1362-6(a)(3). A revocation may be rescinded before the revocation takes effect. See Regulations section 1.1362-6(a)(4) for details.

For rules on allocating income and deductions between an S short year and a C short year and other special rules that apply when an election is terminated, see section 1362(e) and Regulations section 1.1362-3.

If an election was terminated under **1** or **2** above, and the corporation believes the termination was inadvertent, the corporation may request permission from the IRS to continue to be treated as an S corporation. See Regulations section 1.1362-4 for the specific requirements that must be met to qualify for inadvertent termination relief.

When To File

In general, file Form 1120S by the 15th day of the 3rd month following the date the corporation's tax year ended as shown at the top of Form 1120S. For calendar year corporations, the due date is March 16, 1998. If the due date falls on a Saturday, Sunday, or legal holiday, file on the next business day. A business day is any day that is not a Saturday, Sunday, or legal holiday.

If the S election was terminated during the tax year, file Form 1120S for the S short year by the due date (including extensions) of the C short year return.

Private Delivery Services

You can use certain private delivery services designated by the IRS to meet the "timely filing as timely filing/paying" rule for tax returns and payments. The IRS publishes a list of designated private delivery services in September of each year. The list published in September 1997 includes only the following:

- Airborne Express (Airborne): Overnight Air Express Service, Next Afternoon Service, Second Day Service.
- DHL Worldwide Express (DHL): DHL "Same Day" Service, DHL USA Overnight.
- Federal Express (FedEx): FedEx Priority Overnight, FedEx Standard Overnight, FedEx 2Day.
- United Parcel Service (UPS): UPS Next Day Air, UPS Next Day Air Saver, UPS 2nd Day Air, UPS 2nd Day Air A.M.

The private delivery service can tell you how to get written proof of the mailing date.

Extension

Use **Form 7004,** Application for Automatic Extension of Time To File Corporation Income Tax Return, to request an automatic 6-month extension of time to file Form 1120S.

Period Covered

File the 1997 return for calendar year 1997 and fiscal years beginning in 1997 and ending in 1998. If the return is for a fiscal year or a short tax year, fill in the tax year space at the top of the form.

Note: *The 1997 Form 1120S may also be used if **(a)** the corporation has a tax year of less than 12 months that begins and ends in 1998 and **(b)** the 1998 Form 1120S is not available by the time the corporation is required to file its return. However, the corporation must show its 1998 tax year on the 1997 Form 1120S and incorporate any tax law changes that are effective for tax years beginning after December 31, 1997.*

Where To File

File your return at the applicable IRS address listed below.

If the corporation's principal business, office, or agency is located in	Use the following Internal Revenue Service Center address
New Jersey, New York (New York City and counties of Nassau, Rockland, Suffolk, and Westchester)	Holtsville, NY 00501-0013
New York (all other counties), Connecticut, Maine, Massachusetts, New Hampshire, Rhode Island, Vermont	Andover, MA 05501-0013
Florida, Georgia, South Carolina	Atlanta, GA 39901-0013
Indiana, Kentucky, Michigan, Ohio, West Virginia	Cincinnati, OH 45999-0013
Kansas, New Mexico, Oklahoma, Texas	Austin, TX 73301-0013
Illinois, Iowa, Minnesota, Missouri, Wisconsin	Kansas City, MO 64999-0013
Alabama, Arkansas, Louisiana, Mississippi, North Carolina, Tennessee	Memphis, TN 37501-0013
Alaska, Arizona, California (counties of Alpine, Amador, Butte, Calaveras, Colusa, Contra Costa, Del Norte, El Dorado, Glenn, Humboldt, Lake, Lassen, Marin, Mendocino, Modoc, Napa, Nevada, Placer, Plumas, Sacramento, San Joaquin, Shasta, Sierra, Siskiyou, Solano, Sonoma, Sutter, Tehama, Trinity, Yolo, and Yuba), Colorado, Idaho, Montana, Nebraska, Nevada, North Dakota, Oregon, South Dakota, Utah, Washington, Wyoming	Ogden, UT 84201-0013
California (all other counties), Hawaii	Fresno, CA 93888-0013
Delaware, District of Columbia, Maryland, Pennsylvania, Virginia	Philadelphia, PA 19255-0013

Who Must Sign

The return must be signed and dated by the president, vice president, treasurer, assistant treasurer, chief accounting officer, or any other corporate officer (such as tax officer) authorized to sign. A receiver, trustee, or assignee must sign and date any return he or she is required to file on behalf of a corporation.

If a corporate officer filled in Form 1120S, the Paid Preparer's space under "Signature of officer" should remain blank. If someone prepares Form 1120S and does not charge the corporation, that person should not sign the return. Certain others who prepare Form 1120S should not sign. For example, a regular, full-time employee of the corporation such as a clerk, secretary, etc., should not sign.

Generally, anyone paid to prepare Form 1120S must sign the return and fill in the other blanks in the Paid Preparer's Use Only area of the return.

The preparer required to sign the return MUST complete the required preparer information and:

- Sign it, by hand, in the space provided for the preparer's signature. (Signature stamps or labels are not acceptable.)
- Give a copy of Form 1120S to the taxpayer in addition to the copy filed with the IRS.

Accounting Methods

Figure ordinary income using the method of accounting regularly used in keeping the corporation's books and records. Generally, permissible methods include:

- Cash,
- Accrual, or
- Any other method permitted by the Internal Revenue Code.

In all cases, the method adopted must clearly reflect income.

Generally, an S corporation may not use the cash method of accounting if the corporation is a tax shelter (as defined in section 448(d)(3)). See section 448 for details.

Under the accrual method, an amount is includible in income when:

- All the events have occurred that fix the right to receive the income, and
- The amount can be determined with reasonable accuracy.

See Regulations section 1.451-1(a) for details.

Generally, an accrual basis taxpayer can deduct accrued expenses in the tax year in which:

- All events that determine liability have occurred,
- The amount of the liability can be figured with reasonable accuracy, and
- Economic performance takes place with respect to the expense. There are exceptions for certain items, including recurring expenses. See section 461(h) and the related regulations for the rules for determining when economic performance takes place.

Except for certain home construction contracts and other real property small construction contracts, long-term contracts must generally be accounted for using the percentage of completion method described in section 460.

Mark-to-Market Accounting Method for Dealers in Securities

Dealers in securities must use the "mark-to-market" accounting method described in section 475. Under this method, any security that is inventory to the dealer must be included in inventory at its fair market value. Any security that is not inventory and that is held at the close of the tax year is treated as sold at its fair market value on the last business day of the tax year, and any gain or loss must be taken into account in determining gross income. The gain or loss taken into account is generally treated as ordinary gain or loss. For details, including exceptions, see section 475 and the related regulations.

Note: *For tax years ending after August 5, 1997, dealers in commodities, and traders in securities and commodities, may make an election to use the mark-to-market accounting method. See sections 475(e) and (f) for details.*

Change in Accounting Method

Generally, the corporation may change its method of accounting used to report taxable income (for income as a whole or for any material item) only by getting consent on **Form 3115,** Application for Change in Accounting Method. For more information, see **Pub. 538,** Accounting Periods and Methods.

Accounting Periods

Generally, an S corporation may not change its accounting period to a tax year that is not a permitted year. A "permitted year" is a calendar year or any other accounting period for which the corporation can establish to the satisfaction of the IRS that there is a business purpose for the tax year.

To change an accounting period, see Regulations section 1.442-1 and **Form 1128,** Application To Adopt, Change, or Retain a Tax Year. Also see Pub. 538.

Election of a Tax Year Other Than a Required Year

Under the provisions of section 444, an S corporation may elect to have a tax year other than a permitted year, but only if the deferral period of the tax year is not longer than the shorter of 3 months or the deferral period of the tax year being changed. This election is made by filing **Form 8716,** Election To Have a Tax Year Other Than a Required Tax Year.

An S corporation may not make or continue an election under section 444 if it is a member of a tiered structure, other than a tiered structure that consists entirely of partnerships and S corporations that have the same tax year. For the S corporation to have a section

Page 3

444 election in effect, it must make the payments required by section 7519 and file **Form 8752,** Required Payment or Refund Under Section 7519.

A section 444 election ends if an S corporation changes its accounting period to a calendar year or some other permitted year; it is penalized for willfully failing to comply with the requirements of section 7519; or its S election is terminated (unless it immediately becomes a personal service corporation). If the termination results in a short tax year, type or legibly print at the top of the first page of Form 1120S for the short tax year, "SECTION 444 ELECTION TERMINATED."

Rounding Off to Whole Dollars

You may round off cents to whole dollars on your return and accompanying schedules. To do so, drop amounts under 50 cents and increase amounts from 50 to 99 cents to the next higher dollar.

Recordkeeping

The corporation's records must be kept as long as they may be needed for the administration of any provision of the Internal Revenue Code. Usually, records that support an item of income, deduction, or credit on the corporation's return must be kept for 3 years from the date each shareholder's return is due or is filed, whichever is later. Keep records that verify the corporation's basis in property for as long as they are needed to figure the basis of the original or replacement property.

The corporation should also keep copies of any returns it has filed. They help in preparing future returns and in making computations when filing an amended return.

Depository Method of Tax Payment

The corporation must pay the tax due in full no later than the 15th day of the 3rd month after the end of the tax year. Some corporations (described below) are required to electronically deposit all depository taxes, including corporation income tax payments.

Electronic Deposit Requirement

The corporation must make electronic deposits for all depository tax liabilities that occur after 1997 if:

- It was required to electronically deposit taxes in prior years,

- It deposited more than $50,000 in social security, Medicare, and withheld income taxes in 1996, or

- It **did not** deposit social security, Medicare, or withheld income taxes in 1995 or 1996, but deposited more than $50,000 in other taxes under section 6302 (such as corporate income taxes) in either year.

For details, see Regulations section 31.6302-1(h).

The Electronic Federal Tax Payment System (EFTPS) must be used to make electronic deposits. If the corporation is required to make electronic deposits and fails to do so, it may be subject to a 10% penalty.

Note: *A penalty will not be imposed prior to July 1, 1998, if the corporation was first required to use EFTPS on or after July 1, 1997.*

Corporations that are not required to make electronic deposits may voluntarily participate in EFTPS. To enroll in EFTPS, call 1-800-945-8400 or 1-800-555-4477. For general information on EFTPS, call 1-800-829-1040.

Deposits With Form 8109

If the corporation does not use EFTPS, deposit corporation income tax payments (and estimated tax payments) with **Form 8109,** Federal Tax Deposit Coupon. Do not submit deposits directly to an IRS office; otherwise, the corporation may have to pay a penalty. Mail or deliver the completed Form 8109 with the payment to a qualified depositary for Federal taxes or to the Federal Reserve bank (FRB) servicing your geographic area. Make your checks or money orders payable to that depositary or FRB.

To help ensure proper crediting, write the corporation's employer identification number, the tax period to which the deposit applies, and "Form 1120S" on your check or money order. Be sure to darken the "1120" box on the coupon. These records of deposit will be sent to the IRS.

For more information on deposits, see the instructions in the coupon booklet (Form 8109) and **Pub. 583,** Starting a Business and Keeping Records.

Estimated Tax

Generally, the corporation must make estimated tax payments for the following taxes if the total of these taxes is $500 or more: **(a)** the tax on certain capital gains, **(b)** the tax on built-in gains, **(c)** the excess net passive income tax, and **(d)** the investment credit recapture tax.

The amount of estimated tax required to be paid annually is the smaller of **(a)** the total of the above taxes shown on the return for the tax year (or if no return is filed, the total of these taxes for the year); or **(b)** the sum of *(i)* the investment credit recapture tax and the built-in gains tax (or the tax on certain capital gains) shown on the return for the tax year (or if no return is filed, the total of these taxes for the year), and *(ii)* any excess net passive income tax shown on the corporation's return for the preceding tax year. If the preceding tax year was less than 12 months, the estimated tax must be determined under **(a).**

The estimated tax is generally payable in four equal installments. However, the corporation may be able to lower the amount of one or more installments by using the annualized income installment method or adjusted seasonal installment method under section 6655(e).

For a calendar year corporation, the payments are due for 1998 by April 15, June 15, September 15, and December 15. For a fiscal year corporation, they are due by the 15th day of the 4th, 6th, 9th, and 12th months of the fiscal year.

The corporation must make the payments using the depository method described above.

Interest and Penalties

Interest

Interest is charged on taxes not paid by the due date, even if an extension of time to file is granted. Interest is also charged from the due date (including extensions) to the date of payment on the failure to file penalty, the accuracy-related penalty, and the fraud penalty. The interest charge is figured at a rate determined under section 6621.

Late Filing of Return

A corporation that does not file its tax return by the due date, including extensions, may have to pay a penalty of 5% a month, or part of a month, up to a maximum of 25%, for each month the return is not filed. The penalty is imposed on the net amount due. The minimum penalty for filing a return more than 60 days late is the smaller of the tax due or $100. The penalty will not be imposed if the corporation can show that the failure to file on time was due to reasonable cause. If the failure is due to reasonable cause, attach an explanation to the return.

Late Payment of Tax

A corporation that does not pay the tax when due generally may have to pay a penalty of ½ of 1% a month or part of a month, up to a maximum of 25%, for each month the tax is not paid. The penalty is imposed on the net amount due.

The penalty will not be imposed if the corporation can show that failure to pay on time was due to reasonable cause.

Failure To Furnish Information Timely

Section 6037(b) requires an S corporation to furnish to each shareholder a copy of the information shown on Schedule K-1 (Form 1120S) that is attached to Form 1120S. Provide Schedule K-1 to each shareholder on or before the day on which the corporation files Form 1120S.

For each failure to furnish Schedule K-1 to a shareholder when due and each failure to include on Schedule K-1 all the information required to be shown (or the inclusion of incorrect information), a $50 penalty may be imposed with regard to each Schedule K-1 for which a failure occurs. If the requirement to report correct information is intentionally disregarded, each $50 penalty is increased to $100 or, if greater, 10% of the aggregate amount of items required to be reported. See sections 6722 and 6724 for more information.

The penalty will not be imposed if the corporation can show that not furnishing information timely was due to reasonable cause and not due to willful neglect.

Trust Fund Recovery Penalty

This penalty may apply if certain excise, income, social security, and Medicare taxes that must be collected or withheld are not collected or withheld, or these taxes are not paid to the IRS. These taxes are generally reported on Forms 720, 941, 943, or 945. The trust fund recovery penalty may be imposed on all persons who are determined by the IRS to have been **responsible** for collecting, accounting for, and paying over these taxes, and who acted willfully in not doing so. The penalty is equal to the unpaid trust fund tax. See the instructions for Form 720, **Pub. 15 (Circular E),** Employer's Tax Guide, or **Pub. 51 (Circular A),** Agricultural Employer's Tax Guide, for more details, including the definition of responsible persons.

Other Forms and Statements That May Be Required

- **Forms W-2** and **W-3,** Wage and Tax Statement; and Transmittal of Wage and Tax Statements.

- **Form 720,** Quarterly Federal Excise Tax Return. Use Form 720 to report environmental excise taxes, communications and air transportation taxes, fuel taxes, luxury tax on passenger vehicles, manufacturers' taxes, ship passenger tax, and certain other excise taxes.
Caution: *See **Trust Fund Recovery Penalty** on page 4.*

- **Form 940** or **Form 940-EZ,** Employer's Annual Federal Unemployment (FUTA) Tax Return. The corporation may be liable for FUTA tax and may have to file Form 940 or 940-EZ if it paid wages of $1,500 or more in any calendar quarter during the calendar year (or the preceding calendar year) or one or more employees worked for the corporation for some part of a day in any 20 different weeks during the calendar year (or the preceding calendar year). A corporate officer who performs substantial services is considered an employee. Except as provided in section 3306(a), reasonable compensation for these services is subject to FUTA tax, no matter what the corporation calls the payments.

- **Form 941,** Employer's Quarterly Federal Tax Return. Employers must file this form quarterly to report income tax withheld on wages and employer and employee social security and Medicare taxes. A corporate officer who performs substantial services is considered an employee. Except as provided in sections 3121(a) and 3401(a), reasonable compensation for these services is subject to employer and employee social security and Medicare taxes and income tax withholding, no matter what the corporation calls the payments. Agricultural employers must file **Form 943,** Employer's Annual Tax Return for Agricultural Employees, instead of Form 941, to report income tax withheld and employer and employee social security and Medicare taxes on farmworkers.
Caution: *See **Trust Fund Recovery Penalty** on page 4.*

- **Form 945,** Annual Return of Withheld Federal Income Tax. Use this form to report income tax withheld from nonpayroll payments, including pensions, annuities, IRAs, gambling winnings, and backup withholding.
Caution: *See **Trust Fund Recovery Penalty** on page 4.*

- **Form 966,** Corporate Dissolution or Liquidation.

- **Forms 1042** and **1042-S,** Annual Withholding Tax Return for U.S. Source Income of Foreign Persons; and Foreign Person's U.S. Source Income Subject to Withholding. Use these forms to report and transmit withheld tax on payments made to nonresident alien individuals, foreign partnerships, or foreign corporations to the extent such payments constitute gross income from sources within the United States (see sections 861 through 865). For more information, see sections 1441 and 1442, and **Pub. 515,** Withholding of Tax on Nonresident Aliens and Foreign Corporations.

- **Form 1096,** Annual Summary and Transmittal of U.S. Information Returns.

- **Form 1098,** Mortgage Interest Statement. Use this form to report the receipt from any individual of $600 or more of mortgage interest and points in the course of the corporation's trade or business.

- **Forms 1099-A, B, C, DIV, INT, LTC, MISC, MSA, OID, PATR, R,** and **S.** You may have to file these information returns to report acquisitions or abandonments of secured property; proceeds from broker and barter exchange transactions; cancellation of debt; certain dividends and distributions; interest payments; payments of long-term care and accelerated death benefits; miscellaneous income payments; distributions from a medical savings account; original issue discount; distributions from cooperatives to their patrons; distributions from pensions, annuities, retirement or profit-sharing plans, IRAs, insurance contracts, etc.; and proceeds from real estate transactions. Also use certain of these returns to report amounts that were received as a nominee on behalf of another person.

Use Form 1099-DIV to report actual dividends paid by the corporation. Only distributions from accumulated earnings and profits are classified as dividends. **Do not** issue Form 1099-DIV for dividends received by the corporation that are allocated to shareholders on line 4b of Schedule K-1.

For more information, see the separate **Instructions for Forms 1099, 1098, 5498,** and **W-2G.**

Note: *Every corporation must file Forms 1099-MISC if it makes payments of rents, commissions, or other fixed or determinable income (see section 6041) totaling $600 or more to any one person in the course of its trade or business during the calendar year.*

- **Form 5471,** Information Return of U.S. Persons With Respect to Certain Foreign Corporations. A corporation may have to file Form 5471 if any of the following applies:

  1. It controls a foreign corporation.

  2. It acquires, disposes of, or owns 5% or more in value of the outstanding stock of a foreign corporation.

  3. It owns stock in a corporation that is a controlled foreign corporation for an uninterrupted period of 30 days or more during any tax year of the foreign corporation, and it owned that stock on the last day of that year.

- **Form 5713,** International Boycott Report. Every corporation that had operations in, or related to, a "boycotting" country, company, or national of a country must file Form 5713 to report those operations and figure the loss of certain tax benefits.

- **Form 8264,** Application for Registration of a Tax Shelter. Tax shelter organizers must file Form 8264 to register tax shelters with the IRS for the purpose of receiving a tax shelter registration number.

- **Form 8271,** Investor Reporting of Tax Shelter Registration Number. Corporations that have acquired an interest in a tax shelter that is required to be registered use Form 8271 to report the tax shelter's registration number. Attach Form 8271 to any return on which a deduction, credit, loss, or other tax benefit attributable to a tax shelter is taken or any income attributable to a tax shelter is reported.

- **Form 8275,** Disclosure Statement. File Form 8275 to disclose items or positions, except those contrary to a regulation, that are not otherwise adequately disclosed on a tax return. The disclosure is made to avoid the parts of the accuracy-related penalty imposed for disregard of rules or substantial understatement of tax. Form 8275 is also used for disclosures relating to preparer penalties for understatements due to unrealistic positions or disregard of rules.

- **Form 8275-R,** Regulation Disclosure Statement, is used to disclose any item on a tax return for which a position has been taken that is contrary to Treasury regulations.

- **Form 8281,** Information Return for Publicly Offered Original Issue Discount Instruments. This form is used by issuers of publicly offered debt instruments having OID to provide the information required by section 1275(c).

- **Forms 8288** and **8288-A,** U.S. Withholding Tax Return for Dispositions by Foreign Persons of U.S. Real Property Interests; and Statement of Withholding on Dispositions by Foreign Persons of U.S. Real Property Interests. Use these forms to report and transmit withheld tax on the sale of U.S. real property by a foreign person. See section 1445 and the related regulations for additional information.

- **Form 8300,** Report of Cash Payments Over $10,000 Received in a Trade or Business. File this form to report the receipt of more than $10,000 in cash or foreign currency in one transaction (or a series of related transactions).

- **Form 8594,** Asset Acquisition Statement. Both the purchaser and seller of a group of assets constituting a trade or business must file this form if section 197 intangibles attach, or could attach, to such assets and if the purchaser's basis in the assets is determined only by the amount paid for the assets.

- **Form 8697,** Interest Computation Under the Look-Back Method for Completed Long-Term Contracts. Certain S corporations that are not closely held may have to file Form 8697. Form 8697 is used to figure the interest due or to be refunded under the look-back method of section 460(b)(2) on certain long-term contracts that are accounted for under either the percentage of completion-capitalized cost method or the percentage of completion method. Closely held corporations should see the instructions on page 20 for line 23, item 10, of Schedule K-1 for details on the Form 8697 information they must provide to their shareholders.

Statements

Stock ownership in foreign corporations. If the corporation owned at least 5% in value of the outstanding stock of a foreign personal holding company, and the corporation was required to include in its gross income any undistributed foreign personal holding company income, attach the statement required by section 551(c).

Transfers to a corporation controlled by the transferor. If a person receives stock of a corporation in exchange for property, and no gain or loss is recognized under section 351, the transferor and transferee must each attach to their tax returns the information required by Regulations section 1.351-3.

Attachments

Attach **Form 4136,** Credit for Federal Tax Paid on Fuels, after page 4, Form 1120S. Attach schedules in alphabetical order and other forms in numerical order after Form 4136.

To assist us in processing the return, **please complete every applicable entry space on Form 1120S and Schedule K-1.** If you attach statements, do not write "See attached" instead of completing the entry spaces on Form 1120S and Schedule K-1.

Page 5

If you need more space on the forms or schedules, attach separate sheets. Use the same size and format as on the printed forms. **But show the totals on the printed forms.** Attach these separate sheets after all the schedules and forms. Be sure to put the corporation's name and employer identification number (EIN) on each sheet.

Amended Return

To correct an error on a Form 1120S already filed, file an amended Form 1120S and check box F(4). If the amended return results in a change to income, or a change in the distribution of any income or other information provided any shareholder, an amended Schedule K-1 (Form 1120S) must also be filed with the amended Form 1120S and given to that shareholder. Be sure to check box D(2) on each Schedule K-1 to indicate that it is an amended Schedule K-1.

A change to the corporation's Federal return may affect its state return. This includes changes made as the result of an IRS examination of Form 1120S. For more information, contact the state tax agency for the state in which the corporation's return was filed.

Passive Activity Limitations

In general, section 469 limits the amount of losses, deductions, and credits that shareholders may claim from "passive activities." The passive activity limitations do not apply to the corporation. Instead, they apply to each shareholder's share of any income or loss and credit attributable to a passive activity. Because the treatment of each shareholder's share of corporate income or loss and credit depends upon the nature of the activity that generated it, the corporation must report income or loss and credits separately for each activity.

The instructions below (pages 6 through 9) and the instructions for Schedules K and K-1 (pages 14 through 20) explain the applicable passive activity limitation rules and specify the type of information the corporation must provide to its shareholders for each activity. If the corporation had more than one activity, it must report information for each activity on an attachment to Schedules K and K-1.

Generally, passive activities include **(a)** activities that involve the conduct of a trade or business in which the shareholder does not materially participate and **(b)** any rental activity (defined below) even if the shareholder materially participates. For exceptions, see **Activities That Are Not Passive Activities** below. The level of each shareholder's participation in an activity must be determined by the shareholder.

The passive activity rules provide that losses and credits from passive activities can generally be applied only against income and tax from passive activities. Thus, passive losses and credits cannot be applied against income from salaries, wages, professional fees, or a business in which the shareholder materially participates; against "portfolio income" (defined on page 7); or against the tax related to any of these types of income.

Special rules require that net income from certain activities that would otherwise be treated as passive income must be recharacterized as nonpassive income for purposes of the passive activity limitations.

To allow each shareholder to apply the passive activity limitations at the individual level, the corporation must report income or loss and credits separately for each of the following: trade or business activities, rental real estate activities, rental activities other than rental real estate, and portfolio income.

Activities That Are Not Passive Activities

Passive activities do not include:

1. Trade or business activities in which the shareholder materially participated for the tax year.

2. Any rental real estate activity in which the shareholder materially participated and met both of the following conditions for the tax year:

a. More than half of the personal services the shareholder performed in trades or businesses were performed in real property trades or businesses in which he or she materially participated, and

b. The shareholder performed more than 750 hours of services in real property trades or businesses in which he or she materially participated.

For purposes of this rule, each interest in rental real estate is a separate activity unless the shareholder elects to treat all interests in rental real estate as one activity.

If the shareholder is married filing jointly, either the shareholder or his or her spouse must separately meet both of the above conditions, without taking into account services performed by the other spouse.

A real property trade or business is any real property development, redevelopment, construction, reconstruction, acquisition, conversion, rental, operation, management, leasing, or brokerage trade or business. Services the shareholder performed as an employee are not treated as performed in a real property trade or business unless he or she owned more than 5% of the stock in the employer.

3. The rental of a dwelling unit used by a shareholder for personal purposes during the year for more than the greater of 14 days or 10% of the number of days that the residence was rented at fair rental value.

4. An activity of trading personal property for the account of owners of interests in the activity. See Temporary Regulations section 1.469-1T(e)(6).

Note: *The section 469(c)(3) exception for a working interest in oil and gas properties is not applicable to an S corporation because state law generally limits the liability of corporate shareholders.*

Trade or Business Activities

A trade or business activity is an activity (other than a rental activity or an activity treated as incidental to an activity of holding property for investment) that—

1. Involves the conduct of a trade or business (within the meaning of section 162),

2. Is conducted in anticipation of starting a trade or business, or

3. Involves research or experimental expenditures deductible under section 174 (or that would be if you chose to deduct rather than capitalize them).

If the shareholder does not materially participate in the activity, a trade or business activity of the corporation is a passive activity for the shareholder.

Each shareholder must determine if he or she materially participated in an activity. As a result, while the corporation's overall trade or business income (loss) is reported on page 1 of Form 1120S, the specific income and deductions from each separate trade or business activity must be reported on attachments to Form 1120S. Similarly, while each shareholder's allocable share of the corporation's overall trade or business income (loss) is reported on line 1 of Schedule K-1, each shareholder's allocable share of the income and deductions from each trade or business activity must be reported on attachments to each Schedule K-1. See **Passive Activity Reporting Requirements** on page 8 for more information.

Rental Activities

Generally, except as noted below, if the gross income from an activity consists of amounts paid principally for the use of real or personal tangible property held by the corporation, the activity is a rental activity.

There are several exceptions to this general rule. Under these exceptions, an activity involving the use of real or personal tangible property is not a rental activity if any of the following apply:

- The average period of customer use (defined below) for such property is 7 days or less.

- The average period of customer use for such property is 30 days or less and significant personal services (defined below) are provided by or on behalf of the corporation.

- Extraordinary personal services (defined on page 7) are provided by or on behalf of the corporation.

- Rental of the property is treated as incidental to a nonrental activity of the corporation under Temporary Regulations section 1.469-1T(e)(3)(vi) and Regulations section 1.469-1(e)(3)(vi).

- The corporation customarily makes the property available during defined business hours for nonexclusive use by various customers.

- The corporation provides property for use in a nonrental activity of a partnership in its capacity as an owner of an interest in such partnership. Whether the corporation provides property used in an activity of a partnership in the corporation's capacity as an owner of an interest in the partnership is based on all the facts and circumstances.

In addition, a guaranteed payment described in section 707(c) is not income from a rental activity under any circumstances.

Average period of customer use. Figure the average period of customer use of property by dividing the total number of days in all rental periods by the number of rentals during the tax year. If the activity involves renting more than one class of property, multiply the average period of customer use of each class by the ratio of the gross rental income from that class to the activity's total gross rental income. The activity's average period of customer use equals the sum of these class-by-class average periods weighted by gross income. See Regulations section 1.469-1(e)(3)(iii).

Significant personal services. Personal services include only services performed by individuals. In determining whether personal services are significant personal services, consider all of the relevant facts and circumstances. Relevant facts and circumstances include how often the services are provided, the type and amount of labor required to perform the services, and the value of the services in relation to the amount charged for the use of the property.

The following services are not considered in determining whether personal services are significant:

● Services necessary to permit the lawful use of the rental property.

● Services performed in connection with improvements or repairs to the rental property that extend the useful life of the property substantially beyond the average rental period.

● Services provided in connection with the use of any improved real property that are similar to those commonly provided in connection with long-term rentals of high-grade commercial or residential property. Examples include cleaning and maintenance of common areas, routine repairs, trash collection, elevator service, and security at entrances.

Extraordinary personal services. Services provided in connection with making rental property available for customer use are extraordinary personal services only if the services are performed by individuals and the customers' use of the rental property is incidental to their receipt of the services. For example, a patient's use of a hospital room generally is incidental to the care that the patient receives from the hospital's medical staff. Similarly, a student's use of a dormitory room in a boarding school is incidental to the personal services provided by the school's teaching staff.

Rental property incidental to a nonrental activity. An activity is not a rental activity if the rental of the property is incidental to a nonrental activity, such as the activity of holding property for investment, a trade or business activity, or the activity of dealing in property.

Rental of property is incidental to an activity of holding property for investment if both of the following apply:

● The main purpose for holding the property is to realize a gain from the appreciation of the property.

● The gross rental income from such property for the tax year is less than 2% of the smaller of the property's unadjusted basis or its fair market value.

Rental of property is incidental to a trade or business activity if all of the following apply:

● The corporation owns an interest in the trade or business at all times during the year.

● The rental property was mainly used in the trade or business activity during the tax year or during at least 2 of the 5 preceding tax years.

● The gross rental income from the property is less than 2% of the smaller of the property's unadjusted basis or its fair market value.

The sale or exchange of property that is also rented during the tax year (where the gain or loss is recognized) is treated as incidental to the activity of dealing in property if, at the time of the sale or exchange, the property was held primarily for sale to customers in the ordinary course of the corporation's trade or business.

See Temporary Regulations section 1.469-1T(e)(3) and Regulations section 1.469-1(e)(3) for more information on the definition of rental activities for purposes of the passive activity limitations.

Reporting of rental activities. In reporting the corporation's income or losses and credits from rental activities, the corporation must separately report **(a)** rental real estate activities and **(b)** rental activities other than rental real estate activities.

Shareholders who actively participate in a rental real estate activity may be able to deduct part or all of their rental real estate losses (and the deduction equivalent of rental real estate credits) against income (or tax) from nonpassive activities. Generally, the combined amount of rental real estate losses and the deduction equivalent of rental real estate credits from all sources (including rental real estate activities not held through the corporation) that may be claimed is limited to $25,000.

Report rental real estate activity income (loss) on **Form 8825,** Rental Real Estate Income and Expenses of a Partnership or an S Corporation, and on line 2 of Schedules K and K-1 rather than on page 1 of Form 1120S. Report credits related to rental real estate activities on lines 12c and 12d and low-income housing credits on line 12b of Schedules K and K-1.

Report income (loss) from rental activities other than rental real estate on line 3 and credits related to rental activities other than rental real estate on line 12e of Schedules K and K-1.

Portfolio Income

Generally, portfolio income includes all gross income, other than income derived in the ordinary course of a trade or business, that is attributable to interest; dividends; royalties; income from a real estate investment trust, a regulated investment company, a real estate mortgage investment conduit, a common trust fund, a controlled foreign corporation, a qualified electing fund, or a cooperative; income from the disposition of property that produces income of a type defined as portfolio income; and income from the disposition of property held for investment.

Solely for purposes of the preceding paragraph, gross income derived in the ordinary course of a trade or business includes **(and portfolio income, therefore, does not include)** only the following types of income:

● Interest income on loans and investments made in the ordinary course of a trade or business of lending money.

● Interest on accounts receivable arising from the performance of services or the sale of property in the ordinary course of a trade or business of performing such services or selling such property, but only if credit is customarily offered to customers of the business.

● Income from investments made in the ordinary course of a trade or business of furnishing insurance or annuity contracts or reinsuring risks underwritten by insurance companies.

● Income or gain derived in the ordinary course of an activity of trading or dealing in any property if such activity constitutes a trade or business (unless the dealer held the property for investment at any time before such income or gain is recognized).

● Royalties derived by the taxpayer in the ordinary course of a trade or business of licensing intangible property.

● Amounts included in the gross income of a patron of a cooperative by reason of any payment or allocation to the patron based on patronage occurring with respect to a trade or business of the patron.

● Other income identified by the IRS as income derived by the taxpayer in the ordinary course of a trade or business.

See Temporary Regulations section 1.469-2T(c)(3) for more information on portfolio income.

Report portfolio income on line 4 of Schedules K and K-1, rather than on page 1 of Form 1120S.

Report deductions related to portfolio income on line 9 of Schedules K and K-1.

Grouping Activities

Generally, one or more trade or business activities or rental activities may be treated as a single activity if the activities make up an appropriate economic unit for measurement of gain or loss under the passive activity rules. Whether activities make up an appropriate economic unit depends on all the relevant facts and circumstances. The factors given the greatest weight in determining whether activities make up an appropriate economic unit are—

1. Similarities and differences in types of trades or businesses,

2. The extent of common control,

3. The extent of common ownership,

4. Geographical location, and

5. Reliance between or among the activities.

Example: The corporation has a significant ownership interest in a bakery and a movie theater in Baltimore and in a bakery and a movie theater in Philadelphia. Depending on the relevant facts and circumstances, there may be more than one reasonable method for grouping the corporation's activities. For instance, the following groupings may or may not be permissible: a single activity, a movie theater activity and a bakery activity, a Baltimore activity and a Philadelphia activity, or four separate activities.

Once the corporation chooses a grouping under these rules, it must continue using that grouping in later tax years unless a material change in the facts and circumstances makes it clearly inappropriate.

The IRS may regroup the corporation's activities if the corporation's grouping fails to reflect one or more appropriate economic units and one of the primary purposes for the grouping is to avoid the passive activity limitations.

Limitation on grouping certain activities. The following activities may not be grouped together—

1. A rental activity with a trade or business activity unless the activities being grouped together make up an appropriate economic unit, and

a. The rental activity is insubstantial relative to the trade or business activity or vice versa, or

b. Each owner of the trade or business activity has the same proportionate ownership interest in the rental activity. If so, the portion of the rental activity involving the rental of property to be used in the trade or business activity may be grouped with the trade or business activity.

2. An activity involving the rental of real property with an activity involving the rental of personal property (except for personal property provided in connection with real property), or vice versa.

3. Any activity with another activity in a different type of business and in which the corporation holds an interest as a limited partner or as a limited entrepreneur (as defined in section 464(e)(2)) if that other activity engages in holding, producing, or distributing motion picture films or videotapes; farming; leasing section 1245 property; or exploring for (or exploiting) oil and gas resources or geothermal deposits.

Activities conducted through partnerships. Once a partnership determines its activities under these rules, the corporation as a partner may use these rules to group those activities with each other, with activities conducted directly by the corporation, and with activities conducted through other partnerships. The corporation may not treat as separate activities those activities grouped together by the partnership.

Recharacterization of Passive Income

Under Temporary Regulations section 1.469-2T(f) and Regulations section 1.469-2(f), net passive income from certain passive activities must be treated as nonpassive income. Net passive income is the excess of an activity's passive activity gross income over its passive activity deductions (current year deductions and prior year unallowed losses).

Income from the following six sources is subject to recharacterization. Note that any net passive income recharacterized as nonpassive income is treated as investment income for purposes of figuring investment interest expense limitations if it is from **(a)** an activity of renting substantially nondepreciable property from an equity-financed lending activity or **(b)** an activity related to an interest in a pass-through entity that licenses intangible property.

1. Significant participation passive activities. A significant participation passive activity is any trade or business activity in which the shareholder both participates for more than 100 hours during the tax year and does not materially participate. Because each shareholder must determine his or her level of participation, the corporation will not be able to identify significant participation passive activities.

2. Certain nondepreciable rental property activities. Net passive income from a rental activity is nonpassive income if less than 30% of the unadjusted basis of the property used or held for use by customers in the activity is subject to depreciation under section 167.

3. Passive equity-financed lending activities. If the corporation has net income from a passive equity-financed lending activity, the smaller of the net passive income or equity-financed interest income from the activity is nonpassive income.

Note: *The amount of income from the activities in items 1 through 3 above that any shareholder will be required to recharacterize as nonpassive income may be limited under Temporary Regulations section 1.469-2T(f)(8). Because the corporation will not have information regarding all of a shareholder's activities, it must identify all corporate activities meeting the definitions in items 2 and 3 as activities that may be subject to recharacterization.*

4. Rental activities incidental to a development activity. Net rental activity income is nonpassive income for a shareholder if all of the following apply: **(a)** the corporation recognizes gain from the sale, exchange, or other disposition of the rental property during the tax year; **(b)** the use of the item of property in the rental activity started less than 12 months before the date of disposition (the use of an item of rental property begins on the first day on which *(i)* the corporation owns an interest in the property, *(ii)* substantially all of the property is either rented or held out for rent and ready to be rented, and *(iii)* no significant value-enhancing services remain to be performed); and **(c)** the shareholder materially participated or significantly participated for any tax year in an activity that involved the performance of services for the purpose of enhancing the value of the property (or any other item of property, if the basis of the property disposed of is determined in whole or in part by reference to the basis of that item of property). Net rental activity income is the excess of passive activity gross income from renting or disposing of property over passive activity deductions (current year deductions and prior year unallowed losses) that are reasonably allocable to the rented property.

Because the corporation cannot determine a shareholder's level of participation, the corporation must identify net income from property described in items **(a)** and **(b)** above as income that may be subject to recharacterization.

5. Activities involving property rented to a nonpassive activity. If a taxpayer rents property to a trade or business activity in which the taxpayer materially participates, the taxpayer's net rental activity income (defined above) from the property is nonpassive income.

6. Acquisition of an interest in a pass-through entity that licenses intangible property. Generally, net royalty income from intangible property is nonpassive income if the taxpayer acquired an interest in the pass-through entity after it created the intangible property or performed substantial services or incurred substantial costs in developing or marketing the intangible property. Net royalty income is the excess of passive activity gross income from licensing or transferring any right in intangible property over passive activity deductions (current year deductions and prior year unallowed losses) that are reasonably allocable to the intangible property.

See Temporary Regulations section 1.469-2T(f)(7)(iii) for exceptions to this rule.

Passive Activity Reporting Requirements

To allow shareholders to correctly apply the passive activity loss and credit limitation rules, any corporation that carries on more than one activity must:

1. Provide an attachment for each activity conducted through the corporation that identifies the type of activity conducted (trade or business, rental real estate, rental activity other than rental real estate, or investment).

2. On the attachment for each activity, provide a schedule, using the same line numbers as shown on Schedule K-1, detailing the net income (loss), credits, and all items required to be separately stated under section 1366(a)(1) from each trade or business activity, from each rental real estate activity, from each rental activity other than a rental real estate activity, and from investments.

3. Identify the net income (loss) and the shareholder's share of corporation interest expense from each activity of renting a dwelling unit that any shareholder uses for personal purposes during the year for more than the greater of 14 days or 10% of the number of days that the residence is rented at fair rental value.

4. Identify the net income (loss) and the shareholder's share of interest expense from each activity of trading personal property conducted through the corporation.

5. For any gain (loss) from the disposition of an interest in an activity or of an interest in property used in an activity (including dispositions before 1987 from which gain is being recognized after 1986):

a. Identify the activity in which the property was used at the time of disposition;

b. If the property was used in more than one activity during the 12 months preceding the disposition, identify the activities in which the property was used and the adjusted basis allocated to each activity; and

c. For gains only, if the property was substantially appreciated at the time of the disposition and the applicable holding period specified in Regulations section 1.469-2(c)(2)(iii)(A) was not satisfied, identify the amount of the nonpassive gain and indicate whether or not the gain is investment income under Regulations section 1.469-2(c)(2)(iii)(F).

6. Specify the amount of gross portfolio income, the interest expense properly allocable to portfolio income, and expenses other than interest expense that are clearly and directly allocable to portfolio income.

7. Identify the ratable portion of any section 481 adjustment (whether a net positive or a net negative adjustment) allocable to each corporate activity.

8. Identify any gross income from sources specifically excluded from passive activity gross income, including:

a. Income from intangible property, if the shareholder is an individual whose personal efforts significantly contributed to the creation of the property;

b. Income from state, local, or foreign income tax refunds; and

c. Income from a covenant not to compete, if the shareholder is an individual who contributed the covenant to the corporation.

9. Identify any deductions that are not passive activity deductions.

10. If the corporation makes a full or partial disposition of its interest in another entity, identify the gain (loss) allocable to each activity conducted through the entity, and the gain allocable to a passive activity that would have been recharacterized as nonpassive gain had the corporation disposed of its interest in property used in the activity (because the property was substantially appreciated at the time of the disposition, and the gain represented more than 10% of the shareholder's total gain from the disposition).

11. Identify the following items that may be subject to the recharacterization rules under Temporary Regulations section 1.469-2T(f) and Regulations section 1.469-2(f):

a. Net income from an activity of renting substantially nondepreciable property;

b. The smaller of equity-financed interest income or net passive income from an equity-financed lending activity;

c. Net rental activity income from property developed (by the shareholder or the corporation), rented, and sold within 12 months after the rental of the property commenced;

d. Net rental activity income from the rental of property by the corporation to a trade or business activity in which the shareholder had an interest (either directly or indirectly); and

e. Net royalty income from intangible property if the shareholder acquired the shareholder's interest in the corporation after the corporation created the intangible property or performed substantial services or incurred substantial costs in developing or marketing the intangible property.

12. Identify separately the credits from each activity conducted by or through the corporation.

Specific Instructions

General Information

Name, Address, and Employer Identification Number

Use the label that was mailed to the corporation. Cross out any errors and print the correct information on the label.

Name. If the corporation did not receive a label, print or type the corporation's true name (as set forth in the corporate charter or other legal document creating it).

Address. Include the suite, room, or other unit number after the street address. If a preaddressed label is used, please include the information on the label. If the Post Office does not deliver to the street address and the corporation has a P.O. box, show the box number instead of the street address.

If the corporation changes its mailing address after filing its return, it can notify the IRS by filing **Form 8822,** Change of Address.

Employer identification number (EIN). Show the correct EIN in item C on page 1 of Form 1120S.

Item B—Business Code No.

See **Codes for Principal Business Activity** on page 23 of these instructions.

Item E—Total Assets

Enter the corporation's total assets at the end of the tax year, as determined by the accounting method regularly used in maintaining the corporation's books and records. If there were no assets at the end of the tax year, enter the total assets as of the beginning of the tax year. If the S election terminated during the tax year, see the instructions for Schedule L on page 21 for special rules that may apply when figuring the corporation's year end assets.

Item F—Initial Return, Final Return, Change in Address, and Amended Return

If this is the corporation's first return, check box F(1). If the corporation has ceased to exist, check box F(2). Also check box D(1) on each Schedule K-1 to indicate that it is a final Schedule K-1. Indicate a change in address by checking box F(3). If this amends a previously filed return, check box F(4). If Schedules K-1 are also being amended, check box D(2) on each Schedule K-1.

Income

Caution: *Report only trade or business activity income or loss on lines 1a through 6.* **Do not report rental activity income or portfolio income or loss on these lines.** *(See the instructions on* **Passive Activity Limitations** *beginning on page 6 for definitions of rental income and portfolio income.) Rental activity income and portfolio income are reported on Schedules K and K-1 (rental real estate activities are also reported on Form 8825).*

Do not include any tax-exempt income on lines 1 through 5. A corporation that receives any exempt income other than interest, or holds any property or engages in an activity that produces exempt income, reports the amount of this income on line 18 of Schedules K and K-1.

Report tax-exempt interest income, including exempt-interest dividends received as a shareholder in a mutual fund or other regulated investment company, on line 17 of Schedules K and K-1.

See **Deductions** on page 10 for information on how to report expenses related to tax-exempt income.

If the S corporation has had debt discharged resulting from a title 11 bankruptcy proceeding, or while insolvent, see **Form 982,** Reduction of Tax Attributes Due to Discharge of Indebtedness, and **Pub. 908,** Bankruptcy Tax Guide.

Line 1—Gross Receipts or Sales

Enter gross receipts or sales from all trade or business operations except those you report on lines 4 and 5. For reporting advance payments, see Regulations section 1.451-5. To report income from long-term contracts, see section 460.

Installment sales. Generally, the installment method cannot be used for dealer dispositions of property. A dealer disposition is any disposition of personal property by a person who regularly sells or otherwise disposes of property of the same type on the installment plan or any disposition of real property held for sale to customers in the ordinary course of the taxpayer's trade or business. The disposition of property used or produced in the farming business is not included as a dealer disposition. See section 453(l) for details and exceptions.

Enter on line 1a the gross profit on collections from installment sales for any of the following:

- Dealer dispositions of property before March 1, 1986.
- Dispositions of property used or produced in the trade or business of farming.
- Certain dispositions of timeshares and residential lots reported under the installment method.

Attach a schedule showing the following information for the current and the 3 preceding years:

- Gross sales.
- Cost of goods sold.
- Gross profits.
- Percentage of gross profits to gross sales.
- Amount collected.
- Gross profit on the amount collected.

Line 2—Cost of Goods Sold

See the instructions for Schedule A.

Line 4—Net Gain (Loss) From Form 4797

Caution: *Include only ordinary gains or losses from the sale, exchange, or involuntary conversion of assets used in a trade or business activity. Ordinary gains or losses from the sale, exchange, or involuntary conversions of assets used in rental activities are reported separately on Schedule K as part of the net income (loss) from the rental activity in which the property was used.*

A corporation that is a partner in a partnership must include on **Form 4797,** Sales of Business Property, its share of ordinary gains (losses) from sales, exchanges, or involuntary or compulsory conversions (other than casualties or thefts) of the partnership's trade or business assets.

Do not include any recapture of the section 179 expense deduction. See the instructions on page 20 for Schedule K-1, line 23, item 3, and the Instructions for Form 4797 for more information.

Line 5—Other Income (Loss)

Enter on line 5 trade or business income (loss) that is not included on lines 1a through 4. Examples of such income include:

1. Interest income derived in the ordinary course of the corporation's trade or business, such as interest charged on receivable balances;

2. Recoveries of bad debts deducted in earlier years under the specific charge-off method;

3. Taxable income from insurance proceeds;

4. The amount of credit figured on **Form 6478,** Credit for Alcohol Used as Fuel;

5. All section 481 income adjustments resulting from changes in accounting methods (show the computation on an attached schedule); and

6. Ordinary income (loss) from trade or business activities of a partnership (from Schedule K-1 (Form 1065), line 1).

The corporation must include as other income the recapture amount for section 280F if the business use of listed property drops to 50% or less. To figure the recapture amount, the corporation must complete Part IV of Form 4797.

The corporation must also include in other income the amount of any deduction previously taken under section 179A that is subject to recapture. The S corporation may have to recapture the benefit of any allowable deduction for qualified clean-fuel vehicle property (or clean-fuel vehicle refueling property), if the property later ceases to qualify for the deduction. See **Pub. 535,** Business Expenses, for details on how to figure the recapture.

Do not include items requiring separate computations by shareholders that must be reported on Schedules K and K-1. See the instructions for Schedules K and K-1 beginning on page 14.

If "other income" consists of only one item, identify it by showing the account caption in parentheses on line 5. A separate schedule need not be attached to the return in this case.

Do not net any expense item (such as interest) with a similar income item. Report all trade or business expenses on lines 7 through 19.

Deductions

Caution: *Report **only** trade or business activity expenses on lines 7 through 19.*

Do not report rental activity expenses or deductions allocable to portfolio income on these lines. Rental activity expenses are separately reported on Form 8825 or line 3 of Schedules K and K-1. Deductions allocable to portfolio income are separately reported on line 9 of Schedules K and K-1. See **Passive Activity Limitations** beginning on page 6 for more information on rental activities and portfolio income.

Do not report any nondeductible amounts (such as expenses connected with the production of tax-exempt income) on lines 7 through 19. Instead, report nondeductible expenses on line 19 of Schedules K and K-1. If an expense is connected with both taxable income and nontaxable income, allocate a reasonable part of the expense to each kind of income.

Limitations on Deductions

Section 263A uniform capitalization rules. The uniform capitalization rules of section 263A require corporations to capitalize or include in inventory certain costs incurred in connection with:

- The production of real and tangible personal property held in inventory or held for sale in the ordinary course of business.
- Personal property (tangible and intangible) acquired for resale.
- The production of property constructed or improved by a corporation for use in its trade or business or in an activity engaged in for profit.

The costs required to be capitalized under section 263A are not deductible until the property to which the costs relate is sold, used, or otherwise disposed of by the corporation.

Exceptions. Section 263A **does not** apply to:

- Personal property acquired for resale if the taxpayer's average annual gross receipts for the 3 prior tax years are $10 million or less.
- Timber.
- Most property produced under a long-term contract.
- Certain property produced in a farming business. See below.

The corporation must report the following costs separately to the shareholders for purposes of determinations under section 59(e):

- Research and experimental costs under section 174.
- Intangible drilling costs for oil, gas, and geothermal property.
- Mining exploration and development costs.

Tangible personal property produced by a corporation includes a film, sound recording, video tape, book, or similar property.

Corporations subject to the rules are required to capitalize not only direct costs but an allocable portion of most indirect costs (including taxes) that benefit the assets produced or acquired for resale.

For inventory, some of the *indirect costs* that must be capitalized are:

- Administration expenses.
- Taxes.
- Depreciation.
- Insurance.
- Compensation paid to officers attributable to services.
- Rework labor.
- Contributions to pension, stock bonus, and certain profit-sharing, annuity, or deferred compensation plans.

Regulations section 1.263A-1(e)(3) specifies other indirect costs that relate to production or resale activities that must be capitalized and those that may be currently deducted.

Interest expense paid or incurred during the production period of certain property must be capitalized and is governed by special rules. For more details, see Regulations sections 1.263A-8 through 1.263A-15.

For more details on the uniform capitalization rules, see Regulations sections 1.263A-1 through 1.263A-3.

Special rules for certain corporations engaged in farming. For S corporations not required to use the accrual method of accounting, the rules of section 263A **do not** apply to expenses of raising any:

- Animal or
- Plant that has a preproductive period of 2 years or less.

Shareholders of S corporations not required to use the accrual method of accounting may elect to currently deduct the preproductive period expenses of certain plants that have a preproductive period of more than 2 years. Because each shareholder makes the election to deduct these expenses, the corporation should not capitalize them. Instead, the corporation should report the expenses separately on line 21 of Schedule K and each shareholder's pro rata share on line 23 of Schedule K-1.

See sections 263A(d) and (e) and Temporary Regulations section 1.263A-4T for definitions and other details.

Transactions between related taxpayers. Generally, an accrual basis S corporation may deduct business expenses and interest owed to a related party (including any shareholder) **only** in the tax year of the corporation that includes the day on which the payment is includible in the income of the related party. See section 267 for details.

Section 291 limitations. If the S corporation was a C corporation for any of the 3 immediately preceding years, the corporation may be required to adjust deductions allowed to the corporation for depletion of iron ore and coal, and the amortizable basis of pollution control facilities. See section 291 to determine the amount of the adjustment.

Business start-up expenses. Business start-up expenses must be capitalized. An election may be made to amortize them over a period of not less than 60 months. See section 195.

Reducing certain expenses for which credits are allowable. For each of the credits listed below, the corporation must reduce the otherwise allowable deductions for expenses used to figure the credit by the amount of the current year credit:

1. The work opportunity credit,
2. The welfare-to-work credit,
3. The credit for increasing research activities,
4. The enhanced oil recovery credit,
5. The disabled access credit,
6. The empowerment zone employment credit,
7. The Indian employment credit,
8. The credit for employer social security and Medicare taxes paid on certain employee tips, and
9. The orphan drug credit.

If the corporation has any of these credits, be sure to figure each current year credit before figuring the deductions for expenses on which the credit is based.

Line 7—Compensation of Officers

Enter on line 7 the total compensation of all officers paid or incurred in the trade or business activities of the corporation, including fringe benefit expenditures made on behalf of officers owning more than 2% of the corporation's stock. Also report these fringe benefits as wages in box 1 of Form W-2. Do not include on line 7 amounts paid or incurred for fringe benefits of officers owning 2% or less of the corporation's stock. These amounts are reported on line 18, page 1, of Form 1120S. See the instructions for that line for information on the types of expenditures that are treated as fringe benefits and for the stock ownership rules.

Report amounts paid for health insurance coverage for a more than 2% shareholder (including that shareholder's spouse and dependents) as an information item in box 14 of that shareholder's Form W-2. For 1997, a more than 2% shareholder may be allowed to deduct up to 40% of such amounts on Form 1040, line 27.

Do not include on line 7 compensation reported elsewhere on the return, such as amounts included in cost of goods sold, elective contributions to a section 401(k) cash or deferred arrangement, or amounts contributed under a salary reduction SEP agreement.

Line 8—Salaries and Wages

Enter on line 8 the amount of salaries and wages paid or incurred for the tax year, reduced by any applicable employment credits from **Form 5884,** Work Opportunity Credit, **Form 8861,** Welfare-to-Work Credit, **Form 8844,** Empowerment Zone Employment Credit, and **Form 8845,** Indian Employment Credit. See the instructions for these forms for more information. Include fringe benefit expenditures made on behalf of employees (other than officers) owning more than 2% of the corporation's stock. Also report these fringe benefits as wages in box 1 of Form W-2. Do not include on line 8 amounts paid or incurred for fringe benefits of employees owning 2% or less of the corporation's stock. These amounts are reported on line 18, page 1, of Form 1120S. See the instructions for that line for information on the types of expenditures that are treated as fringe benefits and for the stock ownership rules.

Report amounts paid for health insurance coverage for a more than 2% shareholder (including that shareholder's spouse and dependents) as an information item in box 14 of that shareholder's Form W-2. For 1997, a more than 2% shareholder may be allowed to deduct up to 40% of such amounts on Form 1040, line 27.

Do not include on line 8 salaries and wages reported elsewhere on the return, such as

Page 10

amounts included in cost of goods sold, elective contributions to a section 401(k) cash or deferred arrangement, or amounts contributed under a salary reduction SEP agreement.

If a shareholder or a member of the family of one or more shareholders of the corporation renders services or furnishes capital to the corporation for which reasonable compensation is not paid, the IRS may make adjustments in the items taken into account by such individuals and the value of such services or capital. See section 1366(e).

Line 9—Repairs and Maintenance

Enter the costs of incidental repairs and maintenance, such as labor and supplies, that do not add to the value of the property or appreciably prolong its life, but only to the extent that such costs relate to a trade or business activity and are not claimed elsewhere on the return. New buildings, machinery, or permanent improvements that increase the value of the property are not deductible. They are chargeable to capital accounts and may be depreciated or amortized.

Line 10—Bad Debts

Enter the total debts that became worthless in whole or in part during the year, but only to the extent such debts relate to a trade or business activity. Report deductible nonbusiness bad debts as a short-term capital loss on Schedule D (Form 1120S).

Caution: *Cash method taxpayers cannot take a bad debt deduction unless the amount was previously included in income.*

Line 11—Rents

If the corporation rented or leased a vehicle, enter the total annual rent or lease expense paid or incurred in the trade or business activities of the corporation. Also complete Part V of **Form 4562**, Depreciation and Amortization. If the corporation leased a vehicle for a term of 30 days or more, the deduction for vehicle lease expense may have to be reduced by an amount called the **inclusion amount.** The corporation may have an inclusion amount if—

The lease term began:	And the vehicle's fair market value on the first day of the lease exceeded:
After 12/31/96	$15,800
After 12/31/94 but before 1/1/97	$15,500
After 12/31/93 but before 1/1/95	$14,600
After 12/31/92 but before 1/1/94	$14,300
After 12/31/91 but before 1/1/93	$13,700

If the lease term began before January 1, 1992, see **Pub. 463,** Travel, Entertainment, Gift, and Car Expenses, to find out if the corporation has an inclusion amount.

See Pub. 463 for instructions on figuring the inclusion amount.

Line 12—Taxes and Licenses

Enter taxes and licenses paid or incurred in the trade or business activities of the corporation, if not reflected in cost of goods sold. Federal import duties and Federal excise and stamp taxes are deductible only if paid or incurred in carrying on the trade or business of the corporation.

Do not deduct the following taxes on line 12:
• State and local sales taxes, paid or incurred

in connection with the acquisition or disposition of business property. These taxes must be added to the cost of the property, or in the case of a disposition, subtracted from the amount realized.

• Taxes assessed against local benefits that increase the value of the property assessed, such as for paving, etc.

• Federal income taxes, or taxes reported elsewhere on the return.

• Section 901 foreign taxes. Report these taxes separately on line 15e, Schedule K.

• Taxes allocable to a rental activity. Taxes allocable to a rental real estate activity are reported on Form 8825. Taxes allocable to a rental activity other than a rental real estate activity are reported on line 3b of Schedule K.

• Taxes allocable to portfolio income. Report these taxes separately on line 9 of Schedules K and K-1.

• Taxes paid or incurred for the production or collection of income, or for the management, conservation, or maintenance of property held to produce income. Report these taxes separately on line 10 of Schedules K and K-1.

See section 263A(a) for information on capitalization of allocable costs (including taxes) for any property.

Line 13—Interest

Include on line 13 only interest incurred in the trade or business activities of the corporation that is not claimed elsewhere on the return.

Do not include interest expense on debt used to purchase rental property or debt used in a rental activity. Interest allocable to a rental real estate activity is reported on Form 8825 and is used in arriving at net income (loss) from rental real estate activities on line 2 of Schedules K and K-1. Interest allocable to a rental activity other than a rental real estate activity is included on line 3b of Schedule K and is used in arriving at net income (loss) from a rental activity (other than a rental real estate activity). This net amount is reported on line 3c of Schedule K and line 3 of Schedule K-1.

Do not include interest expense clearly and directly allocable to portfolio or investment income. This interest expense is reported separately on line 11a of Schedule K.

Do not include interest on debt proceeds allocated to distributions made to shareholders during the tax year. Instead, report such interest on line 10 of Schedules K and K-1. To determine the amount to allocate to distributions to shareholders, see Notice 89-35, 1989-1 C.B. 675.

Do not include interest expense on debt required to be allocated to the production of qualified property. Interest allocable to certain property produced by an S corporation for its own use or for sale must be capitalized. The corporation must also capitalize any interest on debt that is allocable to an asset used to produce the above property. A shareholder may have to capitalize interest that the shareholder incurs during the tax year for the production expenditures of the S corporation. Similarly, interest incurred by an S corporation may have to be capitalized by a shareholder for the shareholder's own production expenditures. The information required by the shareholder to properly capitalize interest for this purpose must be provided by the corporation on an attachment for line 23 of Schedule K-1. See section 263A(f) and Regulations sections 1.263A-8 through 1.263A-15 for additional information.

Temporary Regulations section 1.163-8T gives rules for allocating interest expense among activities so that the limitations on passive activity losses, investment interest, and personal interest can be properly figured. Generally, interest expense is allocated in the same manner as debt is allocated. Debt is allocated by tracing disbursements of the debt proceeds to specific expenditures. These regulations give rules for tracing debt proceeds to expenditures.

Generally, prepaid interest can only be deducted over the period to which the prepayment applies. See section 461(g) for details.

Note: *Additional limitations on interest deductions apply when the corporation is a policyholder or beneficiary with respect to a life insurance, endowment, or annuity contract issued after June 8, 1997. For details, see section 264. Attach a statement showing the computation of the deduction disallowed under section 264.*

Line 14—Depreciation

Enter on line 14a only the depreciation claimed on assets used in a trade or business activity. See the Instructions for Form 4562 or **Pub. 946,** How To Depreciate Property, to figure the amount of depreciation to enter on this line. Complete and attach Form 4562 only if the corporation placed property in service during 1997 or claims depreciation on any car or other listed property.

Do not include any section 179 expense deduction on this line. This amount is not deductible by the corporation. Instead, it is passed through to the shareholders on line 8 of Schedule K-1.

Line 15—Depletion

If the corporation claims a deduction for timber depletion, complete and attach **Form T,** Forest Activities Schedules.

Caution: *Do not deduct depletion for oil and gas properties. Each shareholder figures depletion on these properties under section 613A(c)(11). See the instructions on page 20 for Schedule K-1, line 23, item 2, for information on oil and gas depletion that must be supplied to the shareholders by the corporation.*

Line 17—Pension, Profit-Sharing, etc., Plans

Enter the deductible contributions not claimed elsewhere on the return made by the corporation for its employees under a qualified pension, profit-sharing, annuity, or simplified employee pension (SEP) or SIMPLE plan, and under any other deferred compensation plan.

If the corporation contributes to an individual retirement arrangement (IRA) for employees, include the contribution in salaries and wages on page 1, line 8, or Schedule A, line 3, and not on line 17.

Employers who maintain a pension, profit-sharing, or other funded deferred compensation plan, whether or not qualified under the Internal Revenue Code and whether or not a deduction is claimed for the current tax year, generally must file one of the forms listed below:

Form 5500, Annual Return/Report of Employee Benefit Plan (With 100 or more participants).

Form 5500-C/R, Return/Report of Employee Benefit Plan (With fewer than 100 participants).

Form 5500-EZ, Annual Return of One-Participant (Owners and Their Spouses) Retirement Plan.

There are penalties for failure to file these forms on time and for overstating the pension plan deduction.

Line 18—Employee Benefit Programs

Enter amounts for fringe benefits paid or incurred on behalf of employees owning 2% or less of the corporation's stock. These fringe benefits include **(a)** employer contributions to certain accident and health plans, **(b)** the cost of up to $50,000 of group-term life insurance on an employee's life, and **(c)** meals and lodging furnished for the employer's convenience.

Do not deduct amounts that are an incidental part of a pension, profit-sharing, etc., plan included on line 17 or amounts reported elsewhere on the return.

Report amounts paid on behalf of more than 2% shareholders on line 7 or 8, whichever applies. A shareholder is considered to own more than 2% of the corporation's stock if that person owns on any day during the tax year more than 2% of the outstanding stock of the corporation or stock possessing more than 2% of the combined voting power of all stock of the corporation. See section 318 for attribution rules.

Line 19—Other Deductions

Attach your own schedule listing by type and amount all allowable deductions related to a trade or business activity for which there is no separate line on page 1 of Form 1120S. Enter the total on this line. Do not include items that must be reported separately on Schedules K and K-1.

An S corporation may not take the deduction for net operating losses provided by section 172 or the special deductions in sections 241 through 249 (except the election to amortize organizational expenditures under section 248). Subject to limitations, the corporation's net operating loss is allowed as a deduction from the shareholders' gross income. See section 1366.

Do not include qualified expenditures to which an election under section 59(e) may apply. See the instructions on page 19 for lines 16a and 16b of Schedule K-1 for details on treatment of these items.

Include on line 19 the deduction taken for amortization. See the instructions for Form 4562 for more information. Complete and attach Form 4562 if the corporation is claiming amortization of costs that began during its 1997 tax year.

Section 464(f) limits the deduction for certain expenditures of S corporations engaged in farming that use the cash method of accounting, and whose prepaid farm supplies are more than 50% of other deductible farming expenses. Prepaid farm supplies include expenses for feed, seed, fertilizer, and similar farm supplies not used or consumed during the year. They also include the cost of poultry that would be allowable as a deduction in a later tax year if the corporation were to **(a)** capitalize the cost of poultry bought for use in its farm business and deduct it ratably over the lesser of 12 months or the useful life of the poultry, and **(b)** deduct the cost of poultry bought for resale in the year it sells or otherwise disposes of it. If the limit applies, the corporation can deduct prepaid farm supplies that do not exceed 50% of its other deductible farm expenses in the year of payment. The excess is deductible only in the year the corporation uses or consumes the supplies (other than poultry, which is deductible as explained above). For exceptions and more details on these rules, see **Pub. 225,** Farmer's Tax Guide.

Do not deduct amounts paid or incurred to participate or intervene in any political campaign on behalf of a candidate for public office, or to influence the general public regarding legislative matters, elections, or referendums. In addition, corporations generally cannot deduct expenses paid or incurred to influence Federal or state legislation, or to influence the actions or positions of certain Federal executive branch officials. However, certain in-house lobbying expenditures that do not exceed $2,000 are deductible. See section 162(e) for more details.

Do not deduct fines or penalties paid to a government for violating any law.

A deduction is allowed for part of the cost of qualified clean-fuel vehicle property and qualified clean-fuel vehicle refueling property. For more details, see section 179A.

Travel, meals, and entertainment. Subject to limitations and restrictions discussed below, a corporation can deduct ordinary and necessary travel, meals, and entertainment expenses paid or incurred in its trade or business. Special rules apply to deductions for gifts, skybox rentals, luxury water travel, convention expenses, and entertainment tickets. See section 274 and Pub. 463 for more details.

Travel. The corporation cannot deduct travel expenses of any individual accompanying a corporate officer or employee, including a spouse or dependent of the officer or employee, unless:

● That individual is an employee of the corporation, and

● His or her travel is for a bona fide business purpose and would otherwise be deductible by that individual.

Meals and entertainment. Generally, the corporation can deduct only 50% of the amount otherwise allowable for meals and entertainment expenses. In addition (subject to exceptions under section 274(k)(2)):

● Meals must not be lavish or extravagant,

● A bona fide business discussion must occur during, immediately before, or immediately after the meal; and

● An employee of the corporation must be present at the meal.

Membership dues. The corporation may deduct amounts paid or incurred for membership dues in civic or public service organizations, professional organizations (such as bar and medical associations), business leagues, trade associations, chambers of commerce, boards of trade, and real estate boards. However, no deduction is allowed if a principal purpose of the organization is to entertain, or provide entertainment facilities for, members or their guests. In addition, corporations may not deduct membership dues in any club organized for business, pleasure, recreation, or other social purpose. This includes country clubs, golf and athletic clubs, airline and hotel clubs, and clubs operated to provide meals under conditions favorable to business discussion.

Entertainment facilities. The corporation cannot deduct an expense paid or incurred for a facility (such as a yacht or hunting lodge) used for an activity usually considered entertainment, amusement, or recreation.

Note: *The corporation may be able to deduct otherwise nondeductible meals, travel, and entertainment expenses if the amounts are treated as compensation and reported on Form W-2 for an employee or on Form 1099-MISC for an independent contractor.*

Line 21—Ordinary Income (Loss)

Enter this income or loss on line 1 of Schedule K. Line 21 income is not used in figuring the tax on line 22a or 22b. See the instructions for line 22a for figuring taxable income for purposes of line 22a or 22b tax.

Tax and Payments

Line 22a—Excess Net Passive Income Tax

If the corporation has always been an S corporation, the excess net passive income tax does not apply. If the corporation has accumulated earnings and profits (E&P) at the close of its tax year, has passive investment income for the tax year that is in excess of 25% of gross receipts, **and** has taxable income at year end, the corporation must pay a tax on the excess net passive income. Complete lines 1 through 3 and line 9 of the worksheet on page 13 to make this determination. If line 2 is greater than line 3 and the corporation has taxable income (see instructions for line 9 of worksheet), it must pay the tax. Complete a separate schedule using the format of lines 1 through 11 of the worksheet on page 13 to figure the tax. Enter the tax on line 22a, page 1, Form 1120S, and attach the computation schedule to Form 1120S.

Reduce each item of passive income passed through to shareholders by its portion of tax on line 22a. See section 1366(f)(3).

Line 22b—Tax From Schedule D (Form 1120S)

If the corporation elected to be an S corporation before 1987 (or elected to be an S corporation during 1987 or 1988 and qualifies for transitional relief from the built-in gains tax), see instructions for Part III of Schedule D (Form 1120S) to determine if the corporation is liable for the capital gains tax.

If the corporation made its election to be an S corporation after 1986, see the instructions for Part IV of Schedule D to determine if the corporation is liable for the built-in gains tax.

Note: *For purposes of line 20 of Part III and line 26 of Part IV of Schedule D, taxable income is defined in section 1375(b)(1)(B) and is generally figured in the same manner as taxable income for line 9 of the line 22a worksheet on page 13.*

Line 22c

Include in the total for line 22c the following:

Investment credit recapture tax. The corporation is liable for investment credit recapture attributable to credits allowed for tax years for which the corporation was not an S corporation. Figure the corporation's investment credit recapture tax by completing **Form 4255,** Recapture of Investment Credit. Include the tax in the total amount to be entered on line 22c.

Write to the left of the line 22c total the amount of recapture tax and the words "Tax

From Form 4255," and attach Form 4255 to Form 1120S.

LIFO recapture tax. The corporation may be liable for the additional tax due to LIFO recapture under Regulations section 1.1363-2 if:

• The corporation used the LIFO inventory pricing method for its last tax year as a C corporation, or

• A C corporation transferred LIFO inventory to the corporation in a nonrecognition transaction in which those assets were transferred basis property.

The additional tax due to LIFO recapture is figured for the corporation's last tax year as a C corporation or for the tax year of the transfer, whichever applies. See the Instructions for Forms 1120 and 1120-A to figure the tax. The tax is paid in four equal installments. The C corporation must pay the first installment by the due date (not including extensions) of Form 1120 for the corporation's last tax year as a C corporation or for the tax year of the transfer, whichever applies. The S corporation must pay each of the remaining installments by the due date (not including extensions) of Form 1120S for the 3 succeeding tax years. Include this year's installment in the total amount to be entered on line 22c. Write to the left of the total on line 22c the installment amount and the words "LIFO tax."

Interest due under the look-back method for completed long-term contracts. If the corporation completed **Form 8697,** Interest Computation Under the Look-Back Method for Completed Long-Term Contracts, and owes interest, write to the left of the line 22c total the amount of interest and "From Form 8697." Attach the completed form to Form 1120S.

Line 23d

If the S corporation is a beneficiary of a trust and the trust makes a section 643(g) election to credit its estimated tax payments to its beneficiaries, include the corporation's share of the payment (reported to the corporation on Schedule K-1 (Form 1041)) in the total amount entered on line 23d. Also, to the left of line 23d, write "T" and the amount of the payment.

Line 24—Estimated Tax Penalty

A corporation that fails to make estimated tax payments when due may be subject to an underpayment penalty for the period of underpayment. Use **Form 2220,** Underpayment of Estimated Tax by

Corporations, to see if the corporation owes a penalty and to figure the amount of the penalty. If you attach Form 2220 to Form 1120S, be sure to check the box on line 24 and enter the amount of any penalty on this line.

Schedule A—Cost of Goods Sold

Inventories are required at the beginning and end of each tax year if the production, purchase, or sale of merchandise is an income-producing factor. See Regulations section 1.471-1.

Section 263A Uniform Capitalization Rules

The uniform capitalization rules of section 263A are discussed under **Limitations on Deductions** on page 10. See those instructions before completing Schedule A.

Line 4—Additional Section 263A Costs

An entry is required on this line only for corporations that have elected a simplified method of accounting.

For corporations that have elected the simplified production method, additional section 263A costs are generally those costs, other than interest, that were not capitalized under the corporation's method of accounting immediately prior to the effective date of section 263A that are required to be capitalized under section 263A. For new corporations, additional section 263A costs are the costs, other than interest, that must be capitalized under section 263A, but which the corporation would not have been required to capitalize if it had existed before the effective date of section 263A. For more details, see Regulations section 1.263A-2(b).

For corporations that have elected the simplified resale method, additional section 263A costs are generally those costs incurred with respect to the following categories:

• Off-site storage or warehousing.

• Purchasing.

• Handling, processing, assembly, and repackaging.

• General and administrative costs (mixed service costs).

For more details, see Regulations section 1.263A-3(d).

Enter on line 4 the balance of section 263A costs paid or incurred during the tax year not included on lines 2, 3, and 5.

Line 5—Other Costs

Enter on line 5 any other inventoriable costs paid or incurred during the tax year not entered on lines 2 through 4.

Line 7—Inventory at End of Year

See Regulations sections 1.263A-1 through 1.263A-3 for details on figuring the costs to be included in ending inventory.

Lines 9a through 9e—Inventory Valuation Methods

Inventories can be valued at:

• Cost.

• Cost or market value (whichever is lower).

• Any other method approved by the IRS that conforms to the requirements of the applicable regulations.

The average cost (rolling average) method of valuing inventories generally does not conform to the requirements of the regulations. See Rev. Rul. 71-234, 1971-1 C.B. 148.

Corporations that use erroneous valuation methods must change to a method permitted for Federal income tax purposes. To make this change, use Form 3115.

On line 9a, check the method(s) used for valuing inventories. Under "lower of cost or market," *market* (for normal goods) means the current bid price prevailing on the inventory valuation date for the particular merchandise in the volume usually purchased by the taxpayer. For a manufacturer, market applies to the basic elements of cost—raw materials, labor and burden. If section 263A applies to the taxpayer, the basic elements of cost must reflect the current bid price of all direct costs and all indirect costs properly allocable to goods on hand at the inventory date.

Inventory may be valued below cost when the merchandise is unsalable at normal prices or unusable in the normal way because the goods are "subnormal" due to damage, imperfections, shop wear, etc., within the meaning of Regulations section 1.471-2(c). These goods may be valued at a current bona fide selling price minus direct cost of disposition (but not less than scrap value) if such a price can be established.

If this is the first year the last-in, first-out (LIFO) inventory method was either adopted or extended to inventory goods not previously valued under the LIFO method provided in section 472, attach **Form 970,** Application To Use LIFO Inventory Method, or a statement with the information required by Form 970. Also

---

Worksheet for Line 22a

1. Enter gross receipts for the tax year (see section 1362(d)(3)(B) for gross receipts from the sale of capital assets)* . . . . ______

2. Enter passive investment income as defined in section 1362(d)(3)(C)* . . ______

3. Enter 25% of line 1 (If line 2 is less than line 3, stop here. You are not liable for this tax.) . . . . ______

4. Excess passive investment income—Subtract line 3 from line 2 . . . ______

5. Enter deductions directly connected with the production of income on line 2 (see section 1375(b)(2))* . . . ______

6. Net passive income—Subtract line 5 from line 2 . . . ______

7. Divide amount on line 4 by amount on line 2 . . . . ______ %

8. Excess net passive income—Multiply line 6 by line 7 . . . . ______

9. Enter taxable income (see instructions for taxable income below) . . . ______

10. Enter smaller of line 8 or line 9 . ______

11. Excess net passive income tax—Enter 35% of line 10. Enter here and on line 22a, page 1, Form 1120S . . . ______

*Income and deductions on lines 1, 2, and 5 are from total operations for the tax year. This includes applicable income and expenses from page 1, Form 1120S, as well as those reported separately on Schedule K. See section 1375(b)(4) for an exception regarding lines 2 and 5.

Line 9 of Worksheet—Taxable income

Line 9 taxable income is defined in Regulations section 1.1374-1(d). Figure this income by completing lines 1 through 28 of **Form 1120,** U.S. Corporation Income Tax Return. Include the Form 1120 computation with the worksheet computation you attach to Form 1120S. You do not have to attach the schedules, etc., called for on Form 1120. However, you may want to complete certain Form 1120 schedules, such as Schedule D (Form 1120) if you have capital gains or losses.

Page 13

check the LIFO box on line 9c. On line 9d, enter the amount or the percent of total closing inventories covered under section 472. Estimates are acceptable.

If the corporation has changed or extended its inventory method to LIFO and has had to "write up" its opening inventory to cost in the year of election, report the effect of this write-up as income (line 5, page 1) proportionately over a 3-year period that begins with the tax year of the election (section 472(d)).

See Pub. 538 for more information on inventory valuation methods.

Schedule B—Other Information

Be sure to answer the questions and provide other information in items 1 through 10.

Line 5—Foreign Financial Accounts

Answer "Yes" to question 5 if either **1** or **2** below applies to the corporation. Otherwise, check the "No" box.

1. At any time during calendar year 1997, the corporation had an interest in or signature or other authority over a bank account, securities account, or other financial account in a foreign country; AND

● The combined value of the accounts was more than $10,000 during the calendar year; AND

● The accounts were NOT with a U.S. military banking facility operated by a U.S. financial institution.

2. The corporation owns more than 50% of the stock in any corporation that would answer the question "Yes" based on item **1** above.

Get **Form TD F 90-22.1,** Report of Foreign Bank and Financial Accounts, to see if the corporation is considered to have an interest in or signature or other authority over a bank account, securities account, or other financial account in a foreign country.

If you answered "Yes" to question 5, file Form TD F 90-22.1 by June 30, 1998, with the Department of the Treasury at the address shown on the form. Form TD F 90-22.1 is not a tax return, so do not file it with Form 1120S. Form TD F 90-22.1 may be ordered by calling 1-800-TAX-FORM (1-800-829-3676).

Line 6

The corporation may be required to file **Form 3520,** Annual Return To Report Transactions With Foreign Trusts and Receipt of Certain Foreign Gifts, if:

● It directly or indirectly transferred property or money to a foreign trust. For this purpose, any U.S. person who created a foreign trust is considered a transferor.

● It is treated as the owner of any part of the assets of a foreign trust under the grantor trust rules.

● It received a distribution from a foreign trust.

For more information, see the Instructions for Form 3520.

Note: *An owner of a foreign trust must ensure that the trust files an annual information return on Form 3520-A, as well as U.S. owner and beneficiary statements. For details, see Notice 97-34, 1997-25 I.R.B. 22.*

The corporation may be required to file **Form 926,** Return by a U.S. Transferor of Property to a Foreign Corporation, Foreign Estate or Trust, or Foreign Partnership, to:

● Pay any excise tax due under section 1491.

● Report information required under section 6038B.

● Report transfers of property to a foreign corporation, estate, trust or partnership, and make elections under section 1492 with respect to those transfers.

For more information, see the Instructions for Form 926.

Line 9

Complete line 9 if the corporation **(a)** filed its election to be an S corporation after 1986; **(b)** was a C corporation before it elected to be an S corporation **or** the corporation acquired an asset with a basis determined by reference to its basis (or the basis of any other property) in the hands of a C corporation; and **(c)** has net unrealized built-in gain (defined below) in excess of the net recognized built-in gain from prior years.

The corporation is liable for section 1374 tax if **(a), (b),** and **(c)** above apply and it has a net recognized built-in gain (section 1374(d)(2)) for its tax year.

Section 633(d)(8) of the Tax Reform Act of 1986 provides transitional relief from the built-in gains tax for certain corporations that elected to be S corporations in 1987 or 1988. See the instructions for Part IV of Schedule D (Form 1120S) for more information.

The corporation's net unrealized built-in gain is the amount, if any, by which the fair market value of the assets of the corporation at the beginning of its first S corporation year (or as of the date the assets were acquired, for any asset with a basis determined by reference to its basis (or the basis of any other property) in the hands of a C corporation) exceeds the aggregate adjusted basis of such assets at that time.

Enter on line 9 the corporation's net unrealized built-in gain reduced by the net recognized built-in gain for prior years. See sections 1374(c)(2) and (d)(1).

Line 10

Check the box on line 10 if the corporation was a C corporation in a prior year and has accumulated earnings and profits (E&P) at the close of its 1997 tax year. For details on figuring accumulated E&P, see section 312. If the corporation has accumulated E&P, it may be liable for tax imposed on excess net passive income. See the instructions for line 22a, page 1, of Form 1120S for details on this tax.

General Instructions for Schedules K and K-1— Shareholders' Shares of Income, Credits, Deductions, etc.

Purpose of Schedules

The corporation is liable for taxes on lines 22a, 22b, and 22c, page 1, Form 1120S. Shareholders are liable for income tax on their shares of the corporation's income (reduced by any taxes paid by the corporation on income) and must include their share of the income on their tax return whether or not it is distributed to them. Unlike most partnership income, S corporation income is **not** self-employment income and is not subject to self-employment tax.

Schedule K is a summary schedule of all the shareholders' shares of the corporation's income, deductions, credits, etc. Schedule K-1 shows each shareholder's separate share. Attach a copy of each shareholder's Schedule K-1 to the Form 1120S filed with the IRS. Keep a copy as a part of the corporation's records, and give each shareholder a separate copy.

The total pro rata share items (column (b)) of all Schedules K-1 should equal the amount reported on the same line of Schedule K. Lines 1 through 20 of Schedule K correspond to lines 1 through 20 of Schedule K-1. Other lines do not correspond, but instructions explain the differences.

Be sure to give each shareholder a copy of the Shareholder's Instructions for Schedule K-1 (Form 1120S). These instructions are available separately from Schedule K-1 at most IRS offices.

Note: *Instructions that apply only to line items reported on Schedule K-1 may be prepared and given to each shareholder instead of the instructions printed by the IRS.*

Substitute Forms

The corporation **does not** need IRS approval to use a substitute Schedule K-1 if it is an exact copy of the IRS schedule, **or** if it contains only those lines the taxpayer is required to use, and the lines have the same numbers and titles and are in the same order as on the IRS Schedule K-1. In either case, the substitute schedule must include the OMB number and either **(a)** the Shareholder's Instructions for Schedule K-1 (Form 1120S) or **(b)** instructions that apply to the items reported on Schedule K-1 (Form 1120S).

The corporation must request IRS approval to use other substitute Schedules K-1. To request approval, write to Internal Revenue Service, Attention: Substitute Forms Program Coordinator, T:FP:S, 1111 Constitution Avenue, N.W., Washington, DC 20224.

The corporation may be subject to a penalty if it files a substitute Schedule K-1 that does not conform to the specifications of Rev. Proc. 96-48, 1996-2 C.B. 339.

Shareholder's Pro Rata Share Items

General Rule

Items of income, loss, deductions, etc., are allocated to a shareholder on a daily basis, according to the number of shares of stock held by the shareholder on each day during the tax year of the corporation. See the instructions for item A.

A shareholder who disposes of stock is treated as the shareholder for the day of disposition. A shareholder who dies is treated as the shareholder for the day of the shareholder's death.

Special Rules

Termination of shareholder's interest. If a shareholder terminates his or her interest in a corporation during the tax year, the corporation, with the consent of all affected shareholders (including the one whose interest is terminated), may elect to allocate income and expenses, etc., as if the corporation's tax year consisted of 2 separate tax years, the first of which ends on the date of the shareholder's termination.

To make the election, the corporation must attach a statement to a timely filed original or amended Form 1120S for the tax year for which the election is made. In the statement, the corporation must state that it is electing under section 1377(a)(2) and Regulations section 1.1377-1(b) to treat the tax year as if it consisted of 2 separate tax years. The statement must also explain how the shareholder's entire interest was terminated (e.g., sale or gift), and state that the corporation and each affected shareholder consent to the corporation making the election. A corporate officer must sign the statement under penalties of perjury on behalf of the corporation. A single statement may be filed for all terminating elections made for the tax year. If the election is made, write "Section 1377(a)(2) Election Made" at the top of each affected shareholder's Schedule K-1.

For more details on the election, see Regulations section 1.1377-1(b).

Qualifying dispositions. If a qualifying disposition takes place during the tax year, the corporation may make an irrevocable election to allocate income and expenses, etc., as if the corporation's tax year consisted of 2 tax years, the first of which ends on the close of the day on which the qualifying disposition occurs. A qualifying disposition is:

1. A disposition by a shareholder of at least 20% of the corporation's outstanding stock in one or more transactions in any 30-day period during the tax year,

2. A redemption treated as an exchange under section 302(a) or 303(a) of at least 20% of the corporation's outstanding stock in one or more transactions in any 30-day period during the tax year, or

3. An issuance of stock that equals at least 25% of the previously outstanding stock to one or more new shareholders in any 30-day period during the tax year.

To make the election, the corporation must attach a statement to a timely filed original or amended Form 1120S for the tax year for which the election is made. In the statement, the corporation must state that it is electing under Regulations section 1.1368-1(g)(2)(i) to treat the tax year as if it consisted of separate tax years. The statement must also give the facts relating to the qualifying disposition (e.g., sale, gift, stock issuance, or redemption), and state that each shareholder who held stock in the corporation during the tax year consents to the election. A corporate officer must sign the statement under penalties of perjury on behalf of the corporation. A single election statement may be filed for all elections made under this special rule for the tax year.

For more details on the election, see Regulations section 1.1368-1(g)(2).

Specific Instructions (Schedule K Only)

Enter the total pro rata share amount for each applicable line item on Schedule K.

Specific Instructions (Schedule K-1 Only)

General Information

On each Schedule K-1, complete the date spaces at the top; enter the names, addresses, and identifying numbers of the shareholder and corporation; complete items A through D; and enter the shareholder's pro rata share of each item. **Schedule K-1 must be prepared and given to each shareholder on or before the day on which Form 1120S is filed.**

Note: *Space has been provided on line 23 (Supplemental Information) of Schedule K-1 for the corporation to provide additional information to shareholders. This space, if sufficient, should be used in place of any attached schedules required for any lines on Schedule K-1, or other amounts not shown on lines 1 through 22 of Schedule K-1. Please be sure to identify the applicable line number next to the information entered below line 23.*

Special Reporting Requirements for Corporations With Multiple Activities

If items of income, loss, deduction, or credit from more than one activity (determined for purposes of the passive activity loss and credit limitations) are reported on lines 1, 2, or 3 of Schedule K-1, the corporation must provide information for each activity to its shareholders. See **Passive Activity Reporting Requirements** on page 8 for details on the reporting requirements.

Special Reporting Requirements for At-Risk Activities

If the corporation is involved in one or more at-risk activities for which a loss is reported on Schedule K-1, the corporation must report information separately for each at-risk activity. See section 465(c) for a definition of at-risk activities.

For each at-risk activity, the following information must be provided on an attachment to Schedule K-1:

1. A statement that the information is a breakdown of at-risk activity loss amounts.

2. The identity of the at-risk activity; the loss amount for the activity; other income and deductions; and other information that relates to the activity.

Specific Items

Item A

If there was no change in shareholders or in the relative interest in stock the shareholders owned during the tax year, enter the percentage of total stock owned by each shareholder during the tax year. For example, if shareholders X and Y each owned 50% for the entire tax year, enter 50% in item A for each shareholder. Each shareholder's pro rata share items (lines 1 through 20 of Schedule K-1) are figured by multiplying the Schedule K amount on the corresponding line of Schedule K by the percentage in item A.

If there was a change in shareholders or in the relative interest in stock the shareholders owned during the tax year, each shareholder's percentage of ownership is weighted for the number of days in the tax year that stock was owned. For example, A and B each held 50% for half the tax year and A, B, and C held 40%, 40%, and 20%, respectively, for the remaining half of the tax year. The percentage of ownership for the year for A, B, and C is figured as follows and is then entered in item A.

	a	b	c (a × b)	
	% of total stock owned	% of tax year held	% of ownership for the year	
A	50 40	50 50	25 +20	45
B	50 40	50 50	25 +20	45
C	20	50	10	10
Total 100%				

If there was a change in shareholders or in the relative interest in stock the shareholders owned during the tax year, each shareholder's pro rata share items generally are figured by multiplying the Schedule K amount by the percentage in item A. However, if a shareholder terminated his or her entire interest in the corporation during the year or a qualifying disposition took place, the corporation may elect to allocate income and expenses, etc., as if the tax year consisted of 2 tax years, the first of which ends on the day of the termination or qualifying disposition. See **Special Rules** on page 14 for more details. Each shareholder's pro rata share items are figured separately for each period on a daily basis, based on the percentage of stock held by the shareholder on each day.

Item B

Enter the Internal Revenue Service Center address where the Form 1120S, to which a copy of this K-1 was attached, was or will be filed.

Item C

If the corporation is a registration-required tax shelter or has invested in a registration-required tax shelter, it must enter its tax shelter registration number in item C. Also, a corporation that has invested in a registration-required shelter must furnish a copy of its Form 8271 to its shareholders. See Form 8271 for more details.

Specific Instructions (Schedules K and K-1, Except as Noted)

Income (Loss)

Reminder: Before entering income items on Schedule K or K-1, be sure to reduce the items of income for the following:

1. Built-in gains tax (Schedule D, Part IV, line 32). Each recognized built-in gain item (within the meaning of section 1374(d)(3)) is reduced by its proportionate share of the built-in gains tax.

2. Capital gains tax (Schedule D, Part III, line 24). The section 1231 gain included on line 5a, 5b, or 6 of Schedule K is reduced by this tax.

3. Excess net passive income tax (line 22a, page 1, Form 1120S). Each item of passive investment income (within the meaning of section 1362(d)(3)(C)) is reduced by its proportionate share of the net passive income tax.

Line 1—Ordinary Income (Loss) From Trade or Business Activities

Enter the amount from line 21, page 1. Enter the income or loss without reference to **(a)**

Page 15

shareholders' basis in the stock of the corporation and in any indebtedness of the corporation to the shareholders (section 1366(d)), **(b)** shareholders' at-risk limitations, and **(c)** shareholders' passive activity limitations. These limitations, if applicable, are determined at the shareholder level.

If the corporation is involved in more than one trade or business activity, see **Passive Activity Reporting Requirements** on page 8 for details on the information to be reported for each activity. If an at-risk activity loss is reported on line 1, see **Special Reporting Requirements for At-Risk Activities** on page 15.

Line 2—Net Income (Loss) From Rental Real Estate Activities

Enter the net income or loss from rental real estate activities of the corporation from **Form 8825,** Rental Real Estate Income and Expenses of a Partnership or an S Corporation. Each Form 8825 has space for reporting the income and expenses of up to eight properties.

If the corporation has income or loss from more than one rental real estate activity reported on line 2, see **Passive Activity Reporting Requirements** on page 8 for details on the information to be reported for each activity. If an at-risk activity loss is reported on line 2, see **Special Reporting Requirements for At-Risk Activities** on page 15.

Line 3—Income and Expenses of Other Rental Activities

Enter on lines 3a and 3b of Schedule K (line 3 of Schedule K-1) the income and expenses of rental activities other than the income and expenses reported on Form 8825. If the corporation has more than one rental activity reported on line 3, see **Passive Activity Reporting Requirements** on page 8 for details on the information to be reported for each activity. If an at-risk activity loss is reported on line 3, see **Special Reporting Requirements for At-Risk Activities** on page 15. Also see **Rental activities** on page 6 for a definition and other details on other rental activities.

Lines 4a Through 4f—Portfolio Income (Loss)

Enter portfolio income (loss) on lines 4a through 4f. See **Portfolio income** on page 7 for the definition of portfolio income. Do not reduce portfolio income by deductions allocated to it. Report such deductions (other than interest expense) on line 9 of Schedules K and K-1. Interest expense allocable to portfolio income is generally investment interest expense and is reported on line 11a of Schedules K and K-1.

Lines 4a and 4b. Enter only taxable interest and dividends that are portfolio income. Interest income derived in the ordinary course of the corporation's trade or business, such as interest charged on receivable balances, is reported on line 5, page 1, Form 1120S. See Temporary Regulations section 1.469-2T(c)(3).

Lines 4d, 4e(1), and 4e(2). Enter on line 4d the gain or loss that is portfolio income (loss) from Schedule D (Form 1120S), line 6. Enter on line 4e(1) the gain or loss that is portfolio income (loss) from Schedule D (Form 1120S), line 12. Enter on line 4e(2) the gain or loss that is portfolio income (loss) from Schedule D (Form 1120S), line 13.

If any gain or loss from lines 6, 12, and 13 of Schedule D is not portfolio income (e.g., gain or loss from the disposition of nondepreciable personal property used in a trade or business), do not report this income or loss on lines 4d(2), 4e(1), and 4e(2). Instead, report it on line 6 of Schedules K and K-1. If the income or loss is attributable to more than one activity, report the income or loss amount separately for each activity on an attachment to Schedule K-1 and identify the activity to which the income or loss relates.

Line 4f. Enter any other portfolio income not reported on lines 4a through 4e.

If the corporation holds a residual interest in a REMIC, report on an attachment for line 4f each shareholder's share of taxable income (net loss) from the REMIC (line 1b of Schedule Q (Form 1066)); excess inclusion (line 2c of Schedule Q (Form 1066)); and section 212 expenses (line 3b of Schedule Q (Form 1066)). Because Schedule Q (Form 1066) is a quarterly statement, the corporation must follow the Schedule Q (Form 1066) Instructions for Residual Interest Holder to figure the amounts to report to shareholders for the corporation's tax year.

Lines 5a and 5b—Net Section 1231 Gain (Loss) (Other Than Due to Casualty or Theft)

Enter on line 5a the 28% rate gain or loss (excluding net gain or loss from involuntary conversions due to casualty or theft) from Form 4797, line 7, column (h). Enter on line 5b the total net section 1231 gain or loss (excluding net gain from involuntary conversions due to casualty or theft) from Form 4797, line 7, column (g). Report net gain or loss from involuntary conversions due to casualty or theft on line 6.

If the corporation is involved in more than one trade or business or rental activity, see **Passive Activity Reporting Requirements** on page 8 for details on the information to be reported for each activity. If an at-risk activity loss is reported on line 5, see **Special Reporting Requirements for At-Risk Activities** on page 15.

Line 6—Other Income (Loss)

Enter any other item of income or loss not included on lines 1 through 5. Items to be reported on line 6 include:

- Recoveries of tax benefit items (section 111).
- Gambling gains and losses (section 165(d)).
- Net gain (loss) from involuntary conversions due to casualty or theft. The amount for this item is shown on **Form 4684,** Casualties and Thefts, line 38a or 38b. Also, separately report the 28% rate gain (loss), if any, from involuntary conversions due to casualty or theft.
- Any net gain or loss from section 1256 contracts from **Form 6781,** Gains and Losses From Section 1256 Contracts and Straddles.
- Eligible gain from the sale or exchange of qualified small business stock (as defined in section 1202(c)). Also report on an attachment to Schedules K and K-1 the name of the corporation that issued the stock and the adjusted basis of that stock.

If the corporation is involved in more than one trade or business or rental activity, see **Passive Activity Reporting Requirements** on page 8 for details on the information to be reported for each activity. If an at-risk activity loss is reported on line 6, see **Special Reporting Requirements for At-Risk Activities** on page 15.

Deductions

Line 7—Charitable Contributions

Enter the amount of charitable contributions paid by the corporation during its tax year. On an attachment to Schedules K and K-1, show separately the dollar amount of contributions subject to each of the 50%, 30%, and 20% of adjusted gross income limits. For additional information, see **Pub. 526,** Charitable Contributions.

Generally, no deduction is allowed for any contribution of $250 or more unless the corporation obtains a written acknowledgment from the charitable organization that shows the amount of cash contributed, describes any property contributed, and gives an estimate of the value of any goods or services provided in return for the contribution. The acknowledgment must be obtained by the due date (including extensions) of the corporation's return, or if earlier, the date the corporation files its return. Do not attach the acknowledgment to the tax return, but keep it with the corporation's records. These rules apply in addition to the filing requirements for Form 8283 described below.

Certain contributions made to an organization conducting lobbying activities are not deductible. See section 170(f)(9) for more details.

If the corporation contributes property other than cash and the deduction claimed for such property exceeds $500, complete **Form 8283,** Noncash Charitable Contributions, and attach it to Form 1120S. The corporation must give a copy of its Form 8283 to every shareholder if the deduction for any item or group of similar items of contributed property exceeds $5,000, even if the amount allocated to any shareholder is $5,000 or less.

If the deduction for an item or group of similar items of contributed property is $5,000 or less, the corporation must report each shareholder's pro rata share of the amount of noncash contributions to enable individual shareholders to complete their own Forms 8283. See the Instructions for Form 8283 for more information.

If the corporation made a qualified conservation contribution under section 170(h), also include the fair market value of the underlying property before and after the donation, as well as the type of legal interest contributed, and describe the conservation purpose furthered by the donation. Give a copy of this information to each shareholder.

Line 8—Section 179 Expense Deduction

An S corporation may elect to expense part of the cost of certain tangible property that the corporation purchased during the tax year for use in its trade or business or certain rental activities. See the Instructions for Form 4562 for more information.

Complete Part I of Form 4562 to figure the corporation's section 179 expense deduction. The corporation does not claim the deduction itself, but instead passes it through to the shareholders. Attach Form 4562 to Form 1120S and show the total section 179 expense deduction on Schedule K, line 8. Report each individual shareholder's pro rata share on Schedule K-1, line 8. Do not complete line 8 of Schedule K-1 for any shareholder that is an estate or trust.

If the corporation is an enterprise zone business, also report on an attachment to

Schedules K and K-1 the cost of section 179 property placed in service during the year that is qualified zone property.

See the instructions for line 23 of Schedule K-1, item 3, for any recapture of a section 179 amount.

Line 9—Deductions Related to Portfolio Income (Loss)

Enter on line 9 the deductions clearly and directly allocable to portfolio income (other than interest expense). Interest expense related to portfolio income is investment interest expense and is reported on line 11a of Schedules K and K-1. Generally, the line 9 expenses are section 212 expenses and are subject to section 212 limitations at the shareholder level.

Note: *No deduction is allowed under section 212 for expenses allocable to a convention, seminar, or similar meeting. Because these expenses are not deductible by shareholders, the corporation does not report these expenses on line 9 or line 10. The expenses are nondeductible and are reported as such on line 19 of Schedules K and K-1.*

Line 10—Other Deductions

Enter any other deductions not included on lines 7, 8, 9, and 15e. On an attachment, identify the deduction and amount, and if the corporation has more than one activity, the activity to which the deduction relates.

Examples of items to be reported on an attachment to line 10 include:

• Amounts (other than investment interest required to be reported on line 11a of Schedules K and K-1) paid by the corporation that would be allowed as itemized deductions on a shareholder's income tax return if they were paid directly by a shareholder for the same purpose. These amounts include, but are not limited to, expenses under section 212 for the production of income other than from the corporation's trade or business.

• Any penalty on early withdrawal of savings not reported on line 9 because the corporation withdrew funds from its time savings deposit before its maturity.

• Soil and water conservation expenditures (section 175).

• Expenditures paid or incurred for the removal of architectural and transportation barriers to the elderly and disabled that the corporation has elected to treat as a current expense. See section 190.

• Interest expense allocated to debt-financed distributions. See Notice 89-35, 1989-1 C.B. 675, for more information.

• If there was a gain (loss) from a casualty or theft to property not used in a trade or business or for income producing purposes, provide each shareholder with the needed information to complete Form 4684.

Investment Interest

Lines 11a and 11b must be completed for all shareholders.

Line 11a—Investment Interest Expense

Include on this line the interest properly allocable to debt on property held for investment purposes. Property held for investment includes property that produces income (unless derived in the ordinary course of a trade or business) from interest, dividends, annuities, or royalties; and gains from the disposition of property that produces those types of income or is held for investment.

Investment interest expense **does not** include interest expense allocable to a passive activity.

Report investment interest expense only on line 11a of Schedules K and K-1.

The amount on line 11a will be deducted by individual shareholders on Schedule A (Form 1040), line 13, after applying the investment interest expense limitations of section 163(d).

For more information, see **Form 4952,** Investment Interest Expense Deduction.

Lines 11b(1) and 11b(2)—Investment Income and Expenses

Enter on line 11b(1) only the investment income included on lines 4a, b, c, and f of Schedule K-1. Do not include other portfolio gains or losses on this line.

Enter on line 11b(2) only the investment expense included on line 9 of Schedule K-1.

If there are other items of investment income or expense included in the amounts that are required to be passed through separately to the shareholders on Schedule K-1, such as net short-term capital gain or loss, net long-term capital gain or loss, and other portfolio gains or losses, give each shareholder a schedule identifying these amounts.

Investment income includes gross income from property held for investment, the excess of net gain attributable to the disposition of property held for investment over net capital gain from the disposition of property held for investment, and any net capital gain from the disposition of property held for investment that each shareholder elects to include in investment income under section 163(d)(4)(B)(iii). Generally, investment income and investment expenses do not include any income or expenses from a passive activity. See Regulations section 1.469-2(f)(10) for exceptions.

Property subject to a net lease is not treated as investment property because it is subject to the passive loss rules. Do not reduce investment income by losses from passive activities.

Investment expenses are deductible expenses (other than interest) directly connected with the production of investment income. See the Instructions for Form 4952 for more information on investment income and expenses.

Credits

Note: *If the corporation has credits from more than one trade or business activity on line 12a or 13, or from more than one rental activity on line 12b, 12c, 12d, or 12e, it must report separately on an attachment to Schedule K-1, the amount of each credit and provide any other applicable activity information listed in* **Passive Activity Reporting Requirements** *on page 8.*

Line 12a—Credit for Alcohol Used as Fuel

Enter on line 12a of Schedule K the credit for alcohol used as fuel attributable to trade or business activities. Enter on line 12d or 12e the credit for alcohol used as fuel attributable to rental activities. Figure the credit on **Form 6478,** Credit for Alcohol Used as Fuel, and attach it to Form 1120S. The credit must be included in income on page 1, line 5, of Form 1120S. See section 40(f) for an election the corporation can make to have the credit not apply.

Enter each shareholder's share of the credit for alcohol used as fuel on line 12a, 12d, or 12e of Schedule K-1.

If this credit includes the small ethanol producer credit, identify on a statement attached to each Schedule K-1 **(a)** the amount of the small producer credit included in the total credit allocated to the shareholder, **(b)** the number of gallons of qualified ethanol fuel production allocated to the shareholder, and **(c)** the shareholder's pro rata share in gallons of the corporation's productive capacity for alcohol.

Line 12b—Low-Income Housing Credit

Section 42 provides for a credit that may be claimed by owners of low-income residential rental buildings. If shareholders are eligible to claim the low-income housing credit, complete the applicable parts of **Form 8586,** Low-Income Housing Credit, and attach it to Form 1120S. Enter the credit figured by the corporation on Form 8586, and any low-income housing credit received from other entities in which the corporation is allowed to invest, on the applicable line as explained below. The corporation must also complete and attach **Form 8609,** Low-Income Housing Credit Allocation Certification, and **Schedule A (Form 8609),** Annual Statement, to Form 1120S. See the Instructions for Form 8586 and Form 8609 for information on completing these forms.

Line 12b(1). If the corporation invested in a partnership to which the provisions of section 42(j)(5) apply, report on line 12b(1) the credit the partnership reported to the corporation on line 12a(1) of Schedule K-1 (Form 1065). If the corporation invested **before 1990** in a section 42(j)(5) partnership, also include on this line any credit the partnership reported to the corporation on line 12a(3) of Schedule K-1 (Form 1065).

Line 12b(2). Report on line 12b(2) any low-income housing credit for property placed in service before 1990 and not reported on line 12b(1). This includes any credit from a building placed in service before 1990 in a project owned by the corporation and any credit from a partnership reported to the corporation on line 12a(2) of Schedule K-1 (Form 1065). Also include on this line any credit from a partnership reported to the corporation on line 12a(4) of Schedule K-1 (Form 1065), if the corporation invested in that partnership **before 1990.**

Line 12b(3). If the corporation invested **after 1989** in a partnership to which the provisions of section 42(j)(5) apply, report on line 12b(3) the credit the partnership reported to the corporation on line 12a(3) of Schedule K-1 (Form 1065).

Line 12b(4). Report on line 12b(4) any low-income housing credit for property placed in service after 1989 and not reported on any other line. This includes any credit from a building placed in service after 1989 in a project owned by the corporation and any credit from a partnership reported to the corporation on line 12a(4) of Schedule K-1 (Form 1065), if the corporation invested in that partnership **after 1989.**

Line 12c—Qualified Rehabilitation Expenditures Related to Rental Real Estate Activities

Enter total qualified rehabilitation expenditures related to rental real estate activities of the corporation. For line 12c of Schedule K, complete the applicable lines of **Form 3468,**

Page 17

Investment Credit, that apply to qualified rehabilitation expenditures for property related to rental real estate activities of the corporation for which income or loss is reported on line 2 of Schedule K. See Form 3468 for details on qualified rehabilitation expenditures. Attach Form 3468 to Form 1120S.

For line 12c of Schedule K-1, enter each shareholder's pro rata share of the expenditures. On the dotted line to the left of the entry space for line 12c, enter the line number of Form 3468 on which the shareholder should report the expenditures. If there is more than one type of expenditure, or the expenditures are from more than one line 2 activity, report this information separately for each expenditure or activity on an attachment to Schedules K and K-1.

Note: *Qualified rehabilitation expenditures not related to rental real estate activities must be listed separately on line 23 of Schedule K-1.*

Line 12d—Credits (Other Than Credits Shown on Lines 12b and 12c) Related to Rental Real Estate Activities

Enter on line 12d any other credit (other than credits on lines 12b and 12c) related to rental real estate activities. On the dotted line to the left of the entry space for line 12d, identify the type of credit. If there is more than one type of credit or the credit is from more than one line 2 activity, report this information separately for each credit or activity on an attachment to Schedules K and K-1. These credits may include any type of credit listed in the instructions for line 13.

Line 12e—Credits Related to Other Rental Activities

Enter on line 12e any credit related to other rental activities for which income or loss is reported on line 3 of Schedules K and K-1. On the dotted line to the left of the entry space for line 12e, identify the type of credit. If there is more than one type of credit or the credit is from more than one line 3 activity, report this information separately for each credit or activity on an attachment to Schedules K and K-1. These credits may include any type of credit listed in the instructions for line 13.

Line 13—Other Credits

Enter on line 13 any other credit, except credits or expenditures shown or listed for lines 12a through 12e of Schedules K and K-1 or the credit for Federal tax paid on fuels (which is reported on line 23c of page 1). On the dotted line to the left of the entry space for line 13, identify the type of credit. If there is more than one type of credit or the credit is from more than one activity, report this information separately for each credit or activity on an attachment to Schedules K and K-1.

The credits to be reported on line 13 and other required attachments are as follows:

• Credit for backup withholding on dividends, interest, or patronage dividends.

• Nonconventional source fuel credit. Figure this credit on a separate schedule and attach it to Form 1120S. See section 29 for rules on figuring the credit.

• Qualified electric vehicle credit (Form 8834).

• Unused investment credit from cooperatives. If the corporation is a member of a cooperative that passes an unused investment credit through to its members, the credit is in turn passed through to the corporation's shareholders.

• Work opportunity credit (Form 5884).

• Welfare-to-work credit (Form 8861).

• Credit for increasing research activities (Form 6765).

• Enhanced oil recovery credit (Form 8830).

• Disabled access credit (Form 8826).

• Renewable electricity production credit (Form 8835).

• Empowerment zone employment credit (Form 8844).

• Indian employment credit (Form 8845).

• Credit for employer social security and Medicare taxes paid on certain employee tips (Form 8846).

• Orphan drug credit (Form 8820).

• Credit for contributions to selected community development corporations (Form 8847).

See the instructions on page 20 for line 21 (Schedule K) and line 23 (Schedule K-1) to report expenditures qualifying for the **(a)** rehabilitation credit not related to rental real estate activities, **(b)** energy credit, or **(c)** reforestation credit.

Adjustments and Tax Preference Items

Lines 14a through 14e must be completed for all shareholders.

Enter items of income and deductions that are adjustments or tax preference items. See **Form 6251,** Alternative Minimum Tax—Individuals, or Schedule I of **Form 1041,** U.S. Income Tax Return for Estates and Trusts, to determine the amounts to enter and for other information.

Do not include as a tax preference item any qualified expenditures to which an election under section 59(e) may apply. Because these expenditures are subject to an election by each shareholder, the corporation cannot figure the amount of any tax preference related to them. Instead, the corporation must pass through to each shareholder on lines 16a and 16b of Schedule K-1 the information needed to figure the deduction.

Line 14a—Depreciation Adjustment on Property Placed in Service After 1986

Figure the adjustment for line 14a based only on tangible property placed in service after 1986 (and tangible property placed in service after July 31, 1986, and before 1987 for which the corporation elected to use the General Depreciation System). **Do not** make an adjustment for motion picture films, videotapes, sound recordings, certain public utility property (as defined in section 168(f)(2)), or property depreciated under the unit-of-production method (or any other method not expressed in a term of years).

Using the same convention the corporation used for regular tax purposes, refigure depreciation as follows:

• For property that is neither real property nor property depreciated using the straight line method, use the 150% declining balance method over the property's class life (instead of the recovery period), switching to straight line for the first tax year that method gives a better result. See Pub. 946 for a table of class lives. For property having no class life, use 12 years.

• For property depreciated using the straight line method (other than real property), use the straight line method over the property's class life (instead of the recovery period). For property having no class life, use 12 years.

• For residential rental and nonresidential real property, use the straight line method over 40 years.

Determine the depreciation adjustment by subtracting the refigured depreciation from the depreciation claimed on Form 4562. If the refigured depreciation exceeds the depreciation claimed on Form 4562, enter the difference as a negative amount. See the instructions for Form 6251 and Form 4562 for more information.

Line 14b—Adjusted Gain or Loss

If the corporation disposed of any tangible property placed in service after 1986 (or after July 31, 1986, if an election was made to use the General Depreciation System), or if it disposed of a certified pollution control facility placed in service after 1986, refigure the gain or loss from the disposition using the adjusted basis for the alternative minimum tax (AMT). The property's adjusted basis for the AMT is its cost or other basis minus all depreciation or amortization deductions allowed or allowable for the AMT during the current tax year and previous tax years. Enter on this line the difference between the regular tax gain (loss) and the AMT gain (loss). If the AMT gain is less than the regular tax gain, OR the AMT loss is more than the regular tax loss, OR there is an AMT loss and a regular tax gain, enter the difference as a negative amount.

If any part of the adjustment is allocable to net short-term capital gain (loss), net long-term capital gain (loss), or net section 1231 gain (loss), attach a schedule that identifies the amount of the adjustment allocable to each type of gain or loss. For a net long-term capital gain (loss) or net section 1231 gain (loss), also identify the amount of adjustment that is 28% rate gain (loss) and unrecaptured section 1250 gain. No schedule is required if the adjustment is allocable solely to ordinary gain (loss).

Line 14c—Depletion (Other Than Oil and Gas)

Do not include any depletion on oil and gas wells. The shareholders must figure their depletion deductions and preference items separately under section 613A.

Refigure the depletion deduction under section 611 for mines, wells (other than oil and gas wells), and other natural deposits for the AMT. Percentage depletion is limited to 50% of the taxable income from the property as figured under section 613(a), using only income and deductions for the AMT. Also, the deduction is limited to the property's adjusted basis at the end of the year, as refigured for the AMT. Figure this limit separately for each property. When refiguring the property's adjusted basis, take into account any AMT adjustments made this year or in previous years that affect basis (other than the current year's depletion).

Enter the difference between the regular tax and AMT deduction. If the AMT deduction is greater, enter the difference as a negative amount.

Lines 14d(1) and 14d(2)

Generally, the amounts to be entered on these lines are only the income and deductions for oil, gas, and geothermal properties that are used to figure the amount on line 21, page 1, Form 1120S.

If there are any items of income or deductions for oil, gas, and geothermal properties included in the amounts that are

Page 18

required to be passed through separately to the shareholders on Schedule K-1, give each shareholder a schedule that shows, for the line on which the income or deduction is included, the amount of income or deductions included in the total amount for that line. Do not include any of these direct passthrough amounts on line 14d(1) or 14d(2). The shareholder is told in the Shareholder's Instructions for Schedule K-1 (Form 1120S) to adjust the amounts on lines 14d(1) and 14d(2) for any other income or deductions from oil, gas, or geothermal properties included on lines 2 through 10 and 23 of Schedule K-1 in order to determine the total income and deductions from oil, gas, and geothermal properties for the corporation.

Figure the amounts for lines 14d(1) and 14d(2) separately for oil and gas properties which are not geothermal deposits and for all properties that are geothermal deposits.

Give the shareholders a schedule that shows the separate amounts included in the computation of the amounts on lines 14d(1) and 14d(2).

Line 14d(1)—Gross income from oil, gas, and geothermal properties. Enter the total amount of gross income (within the meaning of section 613(a)) from all oil, gas, and geothermal properties received or accrued during the tax year and included on page 1, Form 1120S.

Line 14d(2)—Deductions allocable to oil, gas, and geothermal properties. Enter the amount of any deductions allowed for the AMT that are allocable to oil, gas, and geothermal properties.

Line 14e—Other Adjustments and Tax Preference Items

Attach a schedule that shows each shareholder's share of other items not shown on lines 14a through 14d(2) that are adjustments or tax preference items or that the shareholder needs to complete Form 6251 or Schedule I of Form 1041. See these forms and their instructions to determine the amount to enter. Other adjustments or tax preference items include the following:

- Accelerated depreciation of real property under pre-1987 rules.
- Accelerated depreciation of leased personal property under pre-1987 rules.
- Long-term contracts entered into after February 28, 1986. Except for certain home construction contracts, the taxable income from these contracts must be figured using the percentage of completion method of accounting for the AMT.
- Losses from tax shelter farm activities. No loss from any tax shelter farm activity is allowed for the AMT.

Foreign Taxes

Lines 15a through 15g must be completed whether or not a shareholder is eligible for the foreign tax credit, if the corporation has foreign income, deductions, or losses, or has paid or accrued foreign taxes.

In addition to the instructions below, see **Form 1116,** Foreign Tax Credit (Individual, Estate, Trust, or Nonresident Alien Individual), and the related instructions.

Line 15a—Type of Income

Enter the type of income from outside the United States as follows:
- Passive income.

- High withholding tax interest.
- Financial services income.
- Shipping income.
- Dividends from a DISC or former DISC.
- Certain distributions from a foreign sales corporation (FSC) or former FSC.
- Dividends from each noncontrolled section 902 corporation.
- Taxable income attributable to foreign trade income (within the meaning of section 923(b)).
- General limitation income (all other income from sources outside the United States, including income from sources within U.S. possessions).

If, for the country or U.S. possession shown on line 15b, the corporation had more than one type of income, enter "See attached" and attach a schedule for each type of income for lines 15c through 15g.

Line 15b—Foreign Country or U.S. Possession

Enter the name of the foreign country or U.S. possession. If, for the type of income shown on line 15a, the corporation had income from, or paid taxes to, more than one foreign country or U.S. possession, enter "See attached" and attach a schedule for each country for lines 15a and 15c through 15g.

Line 15c—Total Gross Income From Sources Outside the United States

Enter in U.S. dollars the total gross income from sources outside the United States. Attach a schedule that shows each type of income listed in the instructions for line 15a.

Line 15d—Total Applicable Deductions and Losses

Enter in U.S. dollars the total applicable deductions and losses attributable to income on line 15c. Attach a schedule that shows each type of deduction or loss as follows:
- Expenses directly allocable to each type of income listed above.
- Pro rata share of all other deductions not directly allocable to specific items of income.
- Pro rata share of losses from other separate limitation categories.

Line 15e—Total Foreign Taxes

Enter in U.S. dollars the total foreign taxes (described in section 901) paid or accrued by the corporation to foreign countries or U.S. possessions. Attach a schedule that shows the dates the taxes were paid or accrued, and the amount in both foreign currency and in U.S. dollars, as follows:
- Taxes withheld at source on dividends.
- Taxes withheld at source on rents and royalties.
- Other foreign taxes paid or accrued.

Line 15f—Reduction in Taxes Available for Credit

Enter in U.S. dollars the total reduction in taxes available for credit. Attach a schedule that shows separately the:
- Reduction for foreign mineral income.
- Reduction for failure to furnish returns required under section 6038.
- Reduction for taxes attributable to boycott operations (section 908)
- Reduction for foreign oil and gas extraction income (section 907(a)).

- Reduction for any other items (specify).

Line 15g—Other Foreign Tax Information

Enter in U.S. dollars any items not covered on lines 15c through 15f that shareholders need to complete Form 1116 (e.g., gross income from all sources).

Other

Lines 16a and 16b—Section 59(e)(2) Expenditures

Generally, section 59(e) allows each shareholder to make an election to deduct the shareholder's pro rata share of the corporation's otherwise deductible qualified expenditures ratably over 10 years (3 years for circulation expenditures), beginning with the tax year in which the expenditures were made (or for intangible drilling and development costs, over the 60-month period beginning with the month in which such costs were paid or incurred). The term "qualified expenditures" includes only the following types of expenditures paid or incurred during the tax year:
- Circulation expenditures.
- Research and experimental expenditures.
- Intangible drilling and development costs.
- Mining exploration and development costs.

If a shareholder makes the election, the above items are not treated as tax preference items.

Because the shareholders are generally allowed to make this election, the corporation cannot deduct these amounts or include them as adjustments or tax preference items on Schedule K-1. Instead, on lines 16a and 16b of Schedule K-1, the corporation passes through the information the shareholders need to figure their separate deductions.

On line 16a, enter the type of expenditures claimed on line 16b. Enter on line 16b the qualified expenditures paid or incurred during the tax year to which an election under section 59(e) may apply. Enter this amount for all shareholders whether or not any shareholder makes an election under section 59(e). If the expenditures are for intangible drilling and development costs, enter the month in which the expenditures were paid or incurred (after the type of expenditures on line 16a). If there is more than one type of expenditure included in the total shown on line 16b (or intangible drilling and development costs were paid or incurred for more than 1 month), report this information separately for each type of expenditure (or month) on an attachment to Schedules K and K-1.

Line 17—Tax-Exempt Interest Income

Enter on line 17 tax-exempt interest income, including any exempt-interest dividends received from a mutual fund or other regulated investment company. This information must be reported by individuals on line 8b of Form 1040. Generally, the basis of the shareholder's stock is increased by the amount shown on this line under section 1367(a)(1)(A).

Line 18—Other Tax-Exempt Income

Enter on line 18 all income of the corporation exempt from tax other than tax-exempt interest (e.g., life insurance proceeds). Generally, the basis of the shareholder's stock is increased by the amount shown on this line under section 1367(a)(1)(A).

Page 19

Line 19—Nondeductible Expenses

Enter on line 19 nondeductible expenses paid or incurred by the corporation. Do not include separately stated deductions shown elsewhere on Schedules K and K-1, capital expenditures, or items the deduction for which is deferred to a later tax year. Generally, the basis of the shareholder's stock is decreased by the amount shown on this line under section 1367(a)(2)(D).

Line 20

Enter total distributions made to each shareholder other than dividends reported on line 22 of Schedule K. Noncash distributions of appreciated property are valued at fair market value. See **Distributions** on page 21 for the ordering rules on distributions.

Line 21 (Schedule K Only)

Attach a statement to Schedule K to report the corporation's total income, expenditures, or other information for items 1 through 16 of the line 23 (Schedule K-1 Only) instruction below.

Line 22 (Schedule K Only)

Enter total dividends paid to shareholders from accumulated earnings and profits. Report these dividends to shareholders on Form 1099-DIV. Do not report them on Schedule K-1.

Lines 22a and 22b (Schedule K-1 Only)—Recapture of Low-Income Housing Credit

If recapture of part or all of the low-income housing credit is required because **(a)** prior year qualified basis of a building decreased or **(b)** the corporation disposed of a building or part of its interest in a building, see **Form 8611,** Recapture of Low-Income Housing Credit. The instructions for Form 8611 indicate when Form 8611 is completed by the corporation and what information is provided to shareholders when recapture is required.

Note: *If a shareholder's ownership interest in a building decreased because of a transaction at the shareholder level, the corporation must provide the necessary information to the shareholder to enable the shareholder to figure the recapture.*

If the corporation filed **Form 8693,** Low-Income Housing Credit Disposition Bond, to avoid recapture of the low-income housing credit, no entry should be made on line 22 of Schedule K-1.

See Form 8586, Form 8611, and section 42 for more information.

Supplemental Information

Line 23 (Schedule K-1 Only)

Enter in the line 23 Supplemental Information space of Schedule K-1, or on an attached schedule if more space is needed, each shareholder's share of any information asked for on lines 1 through 22 that is required to be reported in detail, and items **1** through **16** below. Please identify the applicable line number next to the information entered in the Supplemental Information space. Show income or gains as a positive number. Show losses in parentheses.

1. Taxes paid on undistributed capital gains by a regulated investment company or a real estate investment trust (REIT). As a shareholder of a regulated investment company or a REIT, the corporation will receive notice on **Form 2439,** Notice to Shareholder of Undistributed Long-Term Capital Gains, of the amount of tax paid on undistributed capital gains.

2. Gross income and other information relating to oil and gas well properties that are reported to shareholders to allow them to figure the depletion deduction for oil and gas well properties. See section 613A(c)(11) for details.

The corporation cannot deduct depletion on oil and gas wells. Each shareholder must determine the allowable amount to report on his or her return. See Pub. 535 for more information.

3. Recapture of section 179 expense deduction. For property placed in service after 1986, the section 179 deduction is recaptured at any time the business use of property drops to 50% or less. Enter the amount originally passed through and the corporation's tax year in which it was passed through. Inform the shareholder if the recapture amount was caused by the disposition of the section 179 property. See section 179(d)(10) for more information. Do not include this amount on line 4 or 5, page 1, Form 1120S.

4. Recapture of certain mining exploration expenditures (section 617).

5. Any information or statements the corporation is required to furnish to shareholders to allow them to comply with requirements under section 6111 (registration of tax shelters) or section 6662(d)(2)(B)(ii) (regarding adequate disclosure of items that may cause an understatement of income tax).

6. If the corporation is involved in farming or fishing activities, report the gross income from these activities to shareholders.

7. Any information needed by a shareholder to compute the interest due under section 453(l)(3). If the corporation elected to report the dispositions of certain timeshares and residential lots on the installment method, each shareholder's tax liability must be increased by the shareholder's pro rata share of the interest on tax attributable to the installment payments received during the tax year.

8. Any information needed by a shareholder to compute the interest due under section 453A(c). If an obligation arising from the disposition of property to which section 453A applies is outstanding at the close of the year, each shareholder's tax liability must be increased by the tax due under section 453A(c) on the shareholder's pro rata share of the tax deferred under the installment method.

9. Any information needed by a shareholder to properly capitalize interest as required by section 263A(f). See **Section 263A uniform capitalization rules** on page 10 for more information.

10. If the corporation is a closely held S corporation (defined in section 460(b)) and it entered into any long-term contracts after February 28, 1986, that are accounted for under either the percentage of completion-capitalized cost method or the percentage of completion method, it must attach a schedule to Form 1120S showing the information required in items (a) and (b) of the instructions for lines 1 and 3 of Part II for **Form 8697,** Interest Computation Under the Look-Back Method for Completed Long-Term Contracts. It must also report the amounts for Part II, lines 1 and 3, to its shareholders. See the instructions for Form 8697 for more information.

11. Expenditures qualifying for the **(a)** rehabilitation credit not related to rental real estate activities, **(b)** energy credit, or **(c)** reforestation credit. Complete and attach Form 3468 to Form 1120S. See Form 3468 and related instructions for information on eligible property and the lines on Form 3468 to complete. Do not include that part of the cost of the property the corporation has elected to expense under section 179. Attach to each Schedule K-1 a separate schedule in a format similar to that shown on Form 3468 detailing each shareholder's pro rata share of qualified expenditures. Also indicate the lines of Form 3468 on which the shareholders should report these amounts.

12. Recapture of investment credit. Complete and attach **Form 4255,** Recapture of Investment Credit, when investment credit property is disposed of, or it no longer qualifies for the credit, before the end of the recapture period or the useful life applicable to the property. State the type of property at the top of Form 4255, and complete lines 2, 4, and 5, whether or not any shareholder is subject to recapture of the credit. Attach to each Schedule K-1 a separate schedule providing the information the corporation is required to show on Form 4255, but list only the shareholder's pro rata share of the cost of the property subject to recapture. Also indicate the lines of Form 4255 on which the shareholders should report these amounts.

The corporation itself is liable for investment credit recapture in certain cases. See the instructions for line 22c, page 1, Form 1120S, for details.

13. Any information needed by a shareholder to compute the recapture of the qualified electric vehicle credit. See Pub. 535 for more information.

14. Any information a shareholder may need to figure recapture of the Indian employment credit. Generally, if the corporation terminates a qualified employee less than 1 year after the date of initial employment, any Indian employment credit allowed for a prior tax year by reason of wages paid or incurred to that employee must be recaptured. For details, see section 45A(d).

15. Unrecaptured section 1250 gain. Figure this amount for each section 1250 property in Part III of Form 4797 for which you had an entry in column (g), but not in column (h), of Part I of Form 4797 by subtracting line 26g of Form 4797 from the **smaller** of line 22 or line 24 of Form 4797. Figure the total of these amounts for all section 1250 properties. Report each shareholder's pro rata share of the total amount as "Unrecaptured section 1250 gain."

If the corporation also received a Schedule K-1 or Form 1099-DIV from an estate, a trust, a REIT, or a mutual fund reporting "unrecaptured section 1250 gain," **do not** add it to the corporation's own unrecaptured section 1250 gain. Instead, report it as a separate amount. For example, if the corporation received a Form 1099-DIV from a REIT with unrecaptured section 1250 gain, report it as "Unrecaptured section 1250 gain from a REIT."

16. Any other information the shareholders need to prepare their tax returns.

Schedule L—Balance Sheets per Books

The balance sheets should agree with the corporation's books and records. Include certificates of deposit as cash on line 1 of Schedule L.

If the S election terminated during the tax year, the year end balance sheet generally should agree with the books and records at the end of the C short year. However, if the corporation elected under section 1362(e)(3) to have items assigned to each short year under normal tax accounting rules, the year end balance sheet should agree with the books and records at the end of the S short year.

Line 5—Tax-Exempt Securities

Include on this line—

1. State and local government obligations, the interest on which is excludible from gross income under section 103(a), and

2. Stock in a mutual fund or other regulated investment company that distributed exempt-interest dividends during the tax year of the corporation.

Line 24—Retained Earnings

If the corporation maintains separate accounts for appropriated and unappropriated retained earnings, it may want to continue such accounting for purposes of preparing its financial balance sheet. Also, if the corporation converts to C corporation status in a subsequent year, it will be required to report its appropriated and unappropriated retained earnings on separate lines of Schedule L of Form 1120.

Schedule M-1—Reconciliation of Income (Loss) per Books With Income (Loss) per Return

Line 3b—Travel and Entertainment

Include on this line 50% of meals and entertainment not allowed under section 274(n); expenses for the use of an entertainment facility; the part of business gifts over $25; expenses of an individual allocable to conventions on cruise ships over $2,000; employee achievement awards over $400; the part of the cost of entertainment tickets that exceeds face value (also subject to 50% disallowance); the part of the cost of skyboxes that exceeds the face value of nonluxury box seat tickets; the part of the cost of luxury water travel not allowed under section 274(m); expenses for travel as a form of education; nondeductible club dues; and other travel and entertainment expenses not allowed as a deduction.

Schedule M-2—Analysis of Accumulated Adjustments Account, Other Adjustments Account, and Shareholders' Undistributed Taxable Income Previously Taxed

Column (a)—Accumulated Adjustments Account

The accumulated adjustments account (AAA) is an account of the S corporation that generally reflects the accumulated undistributed net income of the corporation for the corporation's post-1982 years. S corporations with accumulated E&P must maintain the AAA to determine the tax effect of distributions during S years and the post-termination transition period. An S corporation without accumulated E&P does not need to maintain the AAA in order to determine the tax effect of distributions. Nevertheless, if an S corporation without accumulated E&P engages in certain transactions to which section 381(a) applies, such as a merger into an S corporation with accumulated E&P, the S corporation must be able to calculate its AAA at the time of the merger for purposes of determining the tax effect of post-merger distributions. Therefore, it is recommended that the AAA be maintained by all S corporations.

At the end of the tax year, the AAA is determined by taking into account the taxable income, deductible losses and expenses, and nondeductible losses and expenses for the tax year (other than expenses related to tax-exempt income and Federal taxes attributable to a C corporation tax year). See Regulations section 1.1368-2. After the year-end income and expense adjustments are made, the AAA is reduced by distributions made during the tax year. See **Distributions** below for distribution rules. For adjustments to the AAA for redemptions, reorganizations, and corporate separations, see Regulations section 1.1368-2(d).

Note: *The AAA may have a negative balance at year end. See section 1368(e).*

Column (b)—Other Adjustments Account

The other adjustments account is adjusted for tax-exempt income (and related expenses) and Federal taxes attributable to a C corporation tax year. After these adjustments are made, the account is reduced for any distributions made during the year. See **Distributions** below.

Column (c)—Shareholders' Undistributed Taxable Income Previously Taxed

The shareholders' undistributed taxable income previously taxed account, also called previously taxed income (PTI), is maintained only if the corporation had a balance in this account at the start of its 1996 tax year. If there is a beginning balance for the 1996 tax year, no adjustments are made to the account except to reduce the account for distributions made under section 1375(d) (as in effect before the enactment of the Subchapter S Revision Act of 1982). See **Distributions** below for the order of distributions from the account.

Each shareholder's right to nontaxable distributions from PTI is personal and cannot be transferred to another person. The corporation is required to keep records of each shareholder's net share of PTI.

Distributions

General rule. Unless the corporation makes one of the elections described below, property distributions (including cash) are applied in the following order to reduce accounts of the S corporation that are used to figure the tax effect of distributions made by the corporation to its shareholders:

1. Reduce the AAA determined without regard to any net negative adjustment for the tax year (but not below zero). If distributions during the tax year exceed the AAA at the close of the tax year determined without regard to any net negative adjustment for the tax year, the AAA is allocated pro rata to each distribution made during the tax year. See section 1368(c). The term "net negative adjustment" means the excess, if any, of the reductions in the AAA for the tax year (other than distributions) over the increases in the AAA for the tax year.

2. Reduce shareholders' PTI account for any section 1375(d) (as in effect before 1983) distributions. A distribution from the PTI account is tax free to the extent of a shareholder's basis in his or her stock in the corporation.

3. Reduce accumulated E&P. Generally, the S corporation has accumulated E&P only if it has not distributed E&P accumulated in prior years when the S corporation was a C corporation (section 1361(a)(2)). See section 312 for information on E&P. The only adjustments that can be made to the accumulated E&P of an S corporation are **(a)** reductions for dividend distributions; **(b)** adjustments for redemptions, liquidations, reorganizations, etc.; and **(c)** reductions for investment credit recapture tax for which the corporation is liable. See sections 1371(c) and (d)(3).

Note: *For its first tax year beginning after 1996, an S corporation's accumulated E&P is reduced as of the first day of that year by the E&P accumulated from any tax year beginning before 1983 when the corporation was a subchapter S corporation.*

4. Reduce the other adjustments account.

5. Reduce any remaining shareholders' equity accounts.

Elections relating to source of distributions. The corporation may modify the above ordering rules by making one or more of the following elections:

1. *Election to distribute accumulated E&P first.* If the corporation has accumulated E&P and wants to distribute this E&P before making distributions from the AAA, it may elect to do so with the consent of all its affected shareholders (section 1368(e)(3)(B)). This election is irrevocable and applies only for the tax year for which it is made. For details on making the election, see **Statement regarding elections** on page 22.

2. *Election to make a deemed dividend.* If the corporation wants to distribute all or part of its accumulated E&P through a deemed dividend, it may elect to do so with the consent of all its affected shareholders (section 1368(e)(3)(B)). Under this election, the corporation will be treated as also having made the election to distribute accumulated E&P first. The amount of the deemed dividend cannot exceed the accumulated E&P at the end of the tax year, reduced by any actual distributions of accumulated E&P made during the tax year. A deemed dividend is treated as if it were a pro rata distribution of money to the shareholders, received by the shareholders, and immediately contributed back to the corporation, all on the last day of the tax year. This election is irrevocable and applies only for the tax year for which it is made. For details on making the election, see **Statement regarding elections** on page 22.

3. *Election to forego PTI.* If the corporation wants to forego distributions of PTI, it may elect to do so with the consent of all its affected shareholders (section 1368(e)(3)(B)). Under this election, paragraph 2 under the **General rule** above does not apply to any distribution made during the tax year. This election is irrevocable and applies only for the tax year for which it is made. For details on making the

election, see **Statement regarding elections** below.

Statement regarding elections. To make any of the above elections, the corporation must attach a statement to a timely filed original or amended Form 1120S for the tax year for which the election is made. In the statement, the corporation must identify the election it is making and must state that each shareholder consents to the election. A corporate officer must sign the statement under penalties of perjury on behalf of the corporation. The statement of election to make a deemed dividend must include the amount of the deemed dividend distributed to each shareholder.

Example

The following example shows how the Schedule M-2 accounts are adjusted for items of income (loss), deductions, and distributions reported on Form 1120S.

Items per return are:

  1. Page 1, line 21 income—$219,000

  2. Schedule K, line 2 loss—($3,000)

  3. Schedule K, line 4a income—$4,000

  4. Schedule K, line 4b income—$16,000

  5. Schedule K, line 7 deduction—$24,000

  6. Schedule K, line 8 deduction—$3,000

  7. Schedule K, line 13 work opportunity credit—$6,000

  8. Schedule K, line 17 tax-exempt interest—$5,000

  9. Schedule K, line 19 nondeductible expenses—$6,000 (reduction in salaries and wages for work opportunity credit), and

  10. Schedule K, line 20 distributions—$65,000.

Based on return items 1 through 10 and starting balances of zero, the columns for the AAA and the other adjustments account are completed as shown in the Schedule M-2 Worksheet below.

Note: *For the AAA account, the worksheet line 3—$20,000 amount is the total of the Schedule K, lines 4a and 4b incomes of $4,000 and $16,000. The worksheet line 5—$36,000 amount is the total of the Schedule K, line 2 loss of ($3,000), line 7 deduction of $24,000, line 8 deduction of $3,000, and the line 19 nondeductible expenses of $6,000. For the other adjustments account, the worksheet line 3 amount is the Schedule K, line 17, tax-exempt interest income of $5,000. Other worksheet amounts are self-explanatory.*

Schedule M-2   **Worksheet**

		(a) Accumulated adjustments account	(b) Other adjustments account	(c) Shareholders' undistributed taxable income previously taxed
1	Balance at beginning of tax year	-0-	-0-	
2	Ordinary income from page 1, line 21	219,000		
3	Other additions	20,000	5,000	
4	Loss from page 1, line 21	( )		
5	Other reductions	(36,000)	( )	
6	Combine lines 1 through 5	203,000	5,000	
7	Distributions other than dividend distributions	65,000	-0-	
8	Balance at end of tax year. Subtract line 7 from line 6	138,000	5,000	

Codes for Principal Business Activity

These codes for the Principal Business Activity are designed to classify enterprises by the type of activity in which they are engaged to facilitate the administration of the Internal Revenue Code. Though similar in format and structure to the Standard Industrial Classification (SIC) codes, they should not be used as SIC codes.

Using the list below, enter on page 1, under B, the code number for the specific industry group from which the largest percentage of

"total receipts" is derived. Total receipts means the total of: gross receipts on line 1a, page 1; all other income on lines 4 and 5, page 1; all income on lines 2, 19, and 20a of Form 8825; and income (receipts only) on lines 3a and 4a through 4f of Schedule K.

On page 2, Schedule B, line 2, state the principal business activity and principal product or service that account for the largest percentage of total receipts. For example, if the

principal business activity is "Grain mill products," the principal product or service may be "Cereal preparations."

If, as its principal business activity, the corporation: (1) purchases raw materials, (2) subcontracts out for labor to make a finished product from the raw materials, and (3) retains title to the goods, the corporation is considered to be a manufacturer and must enter one of the codes (2010–3998) under "Manufacturing."

Agriculture, Forestry, and Fishing
Code
- 0400 Agricultural production.
- 0600 Agricultural services (except veterinarians), forestry, fishing, hunting, and trapping.

Mining
Metal mining:
- 1010 Iron ores.
- 1070 Copper, lead and zinc, gold and silver ores.
- 1098 Other metal mining.
- 1150 Coal mining.

Oil and gas extraction:
- 1330 Crude petroleum, natural gas, and natural gas liquids.
- 1380 Oil and gas field services.

Nonmetallic minerals, except fuels:
- 1430 Dimension, crushed and broken stone; sand and gravel.
- 1498 Other nonmetallic minerals, except fuels.

Construction
General building contractors and operative builders:
- 1510 General building contractors.
- 1531 Operative builders.

- 1600 **Heavy construction contractors.**

Special trade contractors:
- 1711 Plumbing, heating, and air conditioning.
- 1731 Electrical work.
- 1798 Other special trade contractors.

Manufacturing
Food and kindred products:
- 2010 Meat products.
- 2020 Dairy products.
- 2030 Preserved fruits and vegetables.
- 2040 Grain mill products.
- 2050 Bakery products.
- 2060 Sugar and confectionery products.
- 2081 Malt liquors and malt.
- 2088 Alcoholic beverages, except malt liquors and malt.
- 2089 Bottled soft drinks, and flavorings.
- 2096 Other food and kindred products.

- 2100 **Tobacco manufacturers.**

Textile mill products:
- 2228 Weaving mills and textile finishing.
- 2250 Knitting mills.
- 2298 Other textile mill products.

Apparel and other textile products:
- 2315 Men's and boys' clothing.
- 2345 Women's and children's clothing.
- 2388 Other apparel and accessories.
- 2390 Miscellaneous fabricated textile products.

Lumber and wood products:
- 2415 Logging, sawmills, and planing mills.
- 2430 Millwork, plywood, and related products.
- 2498 Other wood products, including wood buildings and mobile homes.

- 2500 **Furniture and fixtures.**

Paper and allied products:
- 2625 Pulp, paper, and board mills.
- 2699 Other paper products.

Printing and publishing:
- 2710 Newspapers.
- 2720 Periodicals.
- 2735 Books, greeting cards, and miscellaneous publishing.
- 2790 Commercial and other printing, and printing trade services.

Code

Chemicals and allied products:
- 2815 Industrial chemicals, plastics materials and synthetics.
- 2830 Drugs.
- 2840 Soap, cleaners, and toilet goods.
- 2850 Paints and allied products.
- 2898 Agricultural and other chemical products.

Petroleum refining and related industries (including those integrated with extraction):
- 2910 Petroleum refining (including integrated).
- 2998 Other petroleum and coal products.

Rubber and misc. plastics products:
- 3050 Rubber products: plastics footwear, hose, and belting.
- 3070 Misc. plastics products.

Leather and leather products:
- 3140 Footwear, except rubber.
- 3198 Other leather and leather products.

Stone, clay, and glass products:
- 3225 Glass products.
- 3240 Cement, hydraulic.
- 3270 Concrete, gypsum, and plaster products.
- 3298 Other nonmetallic mineral products.

Primary metal industries:
- 3370 Ferrous metal industries; misc. primary metal products.
- 3380 Nonferrous metal industries.

Fabricated metal products:
- 3410 Metal cans and shipping containers.
- 3428 Cutlery, hand tools, and hardware; screw machine products, bolts, and similar products.
- 3430 Plumbing and heating, except electric and warm air.
- 3440 Fabricated structural metal products.
- 3460 Metal forgings and stampings.
- 3470 Coating, engraving, and allied services.
- 3480 Ordnance and accessories, except vehicles and guided missiles.
- 3490 Misc. fabricated metal products.

Machinery, except electrical:
- 3520 Farm machinery.
- 3530 Construction and related machinery.
- 3540 Metalworking machinery.
- 3550 Special industry machinery.
- 3560 General industrial machinery.
- 3570 Office, computing, and accounting machines.
- 3598 Other machinery except electrical.

Electrical and electronic equipment:
- 3630 Household appliances.
- 3665 Radio, television, and communications equipment.
- 3670 Electronic components and accessories.
- 3698 Other electrical equipment.

- 3710 **Motor vehicles and equipment.**

Transportation equipment, except motor vehicles:
- 3725 Aircraft, guided missiles and parts.
- 3730 Ship and boat building and repairing.
- 3798 Other transportation equipment, except motor vehicles.

Instruments and related products:
- 3815 Scientific instruments and measuring devices; watches and clocks.
- 3845 Optical, medical, and ophthalmic goods.
- 3860 Photographic equipment and supplies.

- 3998 **Other manufacturing products.**

Transportation and Public Utilities
Code

Transportation:
- 4000 Railroad transportation.
- 4100 Local and interurban passenger transit.
- 4200 Trucking and warehousing.
- 4400 Water transportation.
- 4500 Transportation by air.
- 4600 Pipe lines, except natural gas.
- 4700 Miscellaneous transportation services.

Communication:
- 4825 Telephone, telegraph, and other communication services.
- 4830 Radio and television broadcasting.

Electric, gas, and sanitary services:
- 4910 Electric services.
- 4920 Gas production and distribution.
- 4930 Combination utility services.
- 4990 Water supply and other sanitary services.

Wholesale Trade
Durable:
- 5008 Machinery, equipment, and supplies.
- 5010 Motor vehicles and automotive equipment.
- 5020 Furniture and home furnishings.
- 5030 Lumber and construction materials.
- 5040 Sporting, recreational, photographic, and hobby goods, toys and supplies.
- 5050 Metals and minerals, except petroleum and scrap.
- 5060 Electrical goods.
- 5070 Hardware, plumbing and heating equipment and supplies.
- 5098 Other durable goods.

Nondurable:
- 5110 Paper and paper products.
- 5129 Drugs, drug proprietaries, and druggists' sundries.
- 5130 Apparel, piece goods, and notions.
- 5140 Groceries and related products.
- 5150 Farm-product raw materials.
- 5160 Chemicals and allied products.
- 5170 Petroleum and petroleum products.
- 5180 Alcoholic beverages.
- 5190 Misc. nondurable goods.

Retail Trade
Building materials, garden supplies, and mobile home dealers:
- 5220 Building materials dealers.
- 5251 Hardware stores.
- 5265 Garden supplies and mobile home dealers.

- 5300 **General merchandise stores.**

Food stores:
- 5410 Grocery stores.
- 5490 Other food stores.

Automotive dealers and service stations:
- 5515 Motor vehicle dealers.
- 5541 Gasoline service stations.
- 5598 Other automotive dealers.

- 5600 **Apparel and accessory stores.**

- 5700 **Furniture and home furnishings stores.**

- 5800 **Eating and drinking places.**

Misc. retail stores:
- 5912 Drug stores and proprietary stores.
- 5921 Liquor stores.
- 5995 Other retail stores.

Finance, Insurance, and Real Estate
Code

Banking:
- 6030 Mutual savings banks.
- 6060 Bank holding companies.
- 6090 Banks, except mutual savings banks and bank holding companies.

Credit agencies other than banks:
- 6120 Savings and loan associations.
- 6140 Personal credit institutions.
- 6150 Business credit institutions.
- 6199 Other credit agencies.

Security, commodity brokers and services:
- 6210 Security brokers, dealers, and flotation companies.
- 6299 Commodity contracts brokers and dealers; security and commodity exchanges; and allied services.

Insurance:
- 6355 Life Insurance.
- 6356 Mutual insurance, except life or marine and certain fire or flood insurance companies.
- 6359 Other insurance companies.
- 6411 Insurance agents, brokers, and service.

Real estate:
- 6511 Real estate operators and lessors of buildings.
- 6516 Lessors of mining, oil, and similar property.
- 6518 Lessors of railroad property and other real property.
- 6530 Condominium management and cooperative housing associations.
- 6550 Subdividers and developers.
- 6599 Other real estate.

Holding and other investment companies, except bank holding companies:
- 6744 Small business investment companies.
- 6749 Other holding and investment companies, except bank holding companies.

Services
- 7000 **Hotels and other lodging places.**
- 7200 **Personal services.**

Business services:
- 7310 Advertising.
- 7389 Business services, except advertising.

Auto repair; miscellaneous repair services:
- 7500 Auto repair and services.
- 7600 Misc. repair services.

Amusement and recreation services:
- 7812 Motion picture production, distribution, and services.
- 7830 Motion picture theaters.
- 7900 Amusement and recreation services, except motion pictures.

Other services:
- 8015 Offices of physicians, including osteopathic physicians.
- 8021 Offices of dentists.
- 8040 Offices of other health practitioners.
- 8050 Nursing and personal care facilities.
- 8060 Hospitals.
- 8071 Medical laboratories.
- 8099 Other medical services.
- 8111 Legal services.
- 8200 Educational services.
- 8300 Social services.
- 8600 Membership organizations.
- 8911 Architectural and engineering services.
- 8930 Accounting, auditing, and bookkeeping.
- 8980 Miscellaneous services (including veterinarians).

INSTRUCTIONS FOR SCHEDULE D (FORM 1120S)

Capital Gains and Losses and Built-in Gains of an S Corporation

1997

Instructions for Schedule D (Form 1120S)

Capital Gains and Losses and Built-In Gains

Department of the Treasury
Internal Revenue Service

Section references are to the Internal Revenue Code unless otherwise noted.

General Instructions

Changes To Note

Real estate subdivided for sale. For tax years beginning after 1996, the Small Business Job Protection Act of 1996 extends capital asset treatment to certain lots or parcels that are part of a tract of real estate subdivided for sale. See section 1237.

Capital gains reporting revised to reflect reduced tax rates. The Taxpayer Relief Act of 1997 (the Act) generally reduced the tax rates for individuals, estates, and trusts that apply to net capital gain for sales, exchanges, and conversions of assets (including installment payments received) after May 6, 1997. Schedule D, and Schedules K and K-1, have been revised to reflect the reporting of capital gains to shareholders under the new law.

Constructive sales treatment for certain appreciated positions. Under the Act, the corporation may have to recognize gain if it enters into a constructive sale after June 8, 1997, of property in which it held an appreciated position (such as a "short sale against the box").

Purpose of Schedule

Schedule D is used by all S corporations to report:

- Sales or exchanges of capital assets.
- Gains on distributions to shareholders of appreciated capital assets (referred to here as distributions).
- Nonbusiness bad debts.

If the corporation filed its election to be an S corporation before 1987 (or filed its election during 1987 or 1988 and qualifies for the transitional relief from the built-in gains tax described in Part IV on page 3), and had net capital gain (line 16) of more than $25,000, it may be liable for a capital gains tax on the gain in excess of $25,000. The tax is figured in Part III of Schedule D.

Generally, if the corporation filed an election to be an S corporation after 1986, was a C corporation at the time it made the election, **and** has net recognized built-in gain as defined in section 1374(d)(2), **it is liable** for the built-in gains tax. The tax is figured in Part IV of Schedule D.

Other Forms That May Be Required

Use **Form 4797,** Sales of Business Property, to report:

- Sales, exchanges, and distributions of property other than capital assets, including property used in a trade or business.
- Involuntary conversions (other than from casualties or thefts).
- Gain from the disposition of an interest in oil, gas, or geothermal property.

Use **Form 4684,** Casualties and Thefts, to report involuntarily conversions of property due to casualty or theft.

Use **Form 6781,** Gains and Losses From Section 1256 Contracts and Straddles, to report gains and losses from section 1256 contracts and straddles.

Use **Form 8824,** Like-Kind Exchanges, if the corporation made one or more like-kind exchange. A "like-kind exchange" occurs when business or investment property is exchanged for property of a like kind. For exchanges of capital assets, enter the gain or loss from Form 8824, if any, on line 3 or line 9 in column (f), and in column (g) if required.

Capital Asset

Each item of property the corporation held (whether or not connected with its trade or business) is a capital asset **except:**

1. Assets that can be inventoried or property held mainly for sale to customers.

2. Depreciable or real property used in the trade or business.

3. Certain copyrights; literary, musical, or artistic compositions; letters or memorandums; or similar property.

4. Accounts or notes receivable acquired in the ordinary course of trade or business for services rendered or from the sale of property described in **1** above.

5. U.S. Government publications, including the Congressional Record, that the corporation received from the Government, other than by purchase at the normal sales price, or that the corporation got from another taxpayer who had received it in a similar way, if the corporation's basis is determined by reference to the previous owner.

Items for Special Treatment

Note: *For more information, see **Pub. 544,** Sales and Other Dispositions of Assets.*

Loss from a sale or exchange between the corporation and a related person. Except for distributions in complete liquidation of a corporation, no loss is allowed from the sale or exchange of property between the corporation and certain related persons. See section 267 for details.

Loss from a wash sale. The corporation cannot deduct a loss from a wash sale of stock or securities (including contracts or options to acquire or sell stock or securities) unless the corporation is a dealer in stock or securities and the loss was sustained in a transaction made in the ordinary course of the corporation's trade or business. A wash sale occurs if the corporation acquires (by purchase or exchange), or has a contract or option to acquire, substantially identical stock or securities within 30 days before or after the date of the sale or exchange. See section 1091 for more information.

Gain on distribution of appreciated property. Generally, gain (but not loss) is recognized on a nonliquidating distribution of appreciated property to the extent that the property's fair market value exceeds its adjusted basis. See section 311 for more information.

Gain or loss on distribution of property in complete liquidation. Generally, gain or loss is recognized by a corporation upon the liquidating distribution of property as if it had sold the property at its fair market value. See section 336 for details and exceptions.

Gain or loss on certain short-term Federal, state, and municipal obligations. Such obligations are treated as capital assets in determining gain or loss. On any gain realized, a portion is treated as ordinary income and the balance is considered as a short-term capital gain. See section 1271.

Gain from installment sales. If a corporation has a gain this year from the sale of real property or a casual sale of personal property other than inventory and is to receive any payment in a later year, it must use the installment method (unless it elects not to) and file **Form 6252,** Installment Sale Income. Also use Form 6252 if a payment is received this year from a sale made in an earlier year on the installment basis.

The corporation may elect out of the installment method by reporting the full amount of the gain on a timely filed return (including extensions).

The installment method may not be used for sales of stock or securities (or certain other property described in the regulations) traded on an established securities market. See section 453(k).

Gain or loss on an option to buy or sell property. See sections 1032 and 1234 for the rules that apply to a purchaser or grantor of an option.

Gain or loss from a short sale of property. Report the gain or loss to the extent that the property used to close the short sale is considered a capital asset in the hands of the taxpayer.

Loss from securities that are capital assets that become worthless during the year. Except for securities held by a bank, treat the loss as a capital loss as of the last day of the tax year. See section 582 for the rules on treatment of securities held by a bank.

Cat. No. 64419L

Nonrecognition of gain on sale of stock to an ESOP. See section 1042 and Temporary Regulations section 1.1042-1T for rules under which a taxpayer may elect not to recognize gain from the sale of certain stock to an employee stock ownership plan (ESOP).

Disposition of market discount bonds. See section 1276 for rules on the disposition of any market discount bonds.

Capital gain distributions. Report the **total** capital gain distributions as long-term capital gain on line 7, column (f), regardless of how long the corporation held the investment. Enter on line 7, column (g), the total amounts reported by the funds as the 28% rate gain portion of your total capital gain distributions.

Nonbusiness bad debts. A nonbusiness bad debt must be treated as a short-term capital loss and can be deducted only in the year the debt becomes totally worthless. For each bad debt, enter the name of the debtor and "schedule attached" in column (a) of line 1 and the amount of the bad debt as a loss in column (f). Also attach a statement of facts to support each bad debt deduction.

Real estate subdivided for sale. Certain lots or parcels that are part of a tract of real estate subdivided for sale may be treated as capital assets. See section 1237.

Constructive sales treatment for certain appreciated positions. Generally, the corporation must recognize gain (but not loss) on the date it enters into a constructive sale of any appreciated interest in stock, a partnership interest, or certain debt instruments as if the position were disposed of at fair market value on that date. In most cases, this new rule applies to constructive sales after June 8, 1997.

The corporation is treated as making a constructive sale of an appreciated position if it (or a related person, in some cases) does one of the following:

● Enters into a short sale of the same or substantially identical property (i.e., a "short sale against the box").

● Enters into an offsetting notional principal contract relating to the same or substantially identical property.

● Enters into a futures or forward contract to deliver the same or substantially identical property.

● Acquires the same or substantially identical property (if the appreciated position is a short sale, offsetting notional principal contract, or a futures or forward contract).

Generally, constructive sales treatment **does not** apply to the corporation if:

● The transaction was closed before the end of the 30th day after the end of the year in which it was entered into,

● The appreciated position to which the transaction relates was held throughout the 60-day period starting on the date the transaction was closed, **and**

● At no time during that 60-day period was the corporation's risk of loss reduced by holding certain other positions.

For details and exceptions to these rules, see **Pub. 550,** Investment Income and Expenses.

Specific Instructions

Parts I and II

Generally, report sales or exchanges (including like-kind exchanges) even if there is no gain or loss. In Part I, report the sale, exchange, or distribution of capital assets held 1 year or less. In Part II, report the sale, exchange, or distribution of capital assets held more than 1 year. Use the trade dates for the dates of acquisition and sale of stocks and bonds on an exchange or over-the-counter market.

Column (e)—Cost or other basis. In determining gain or loss, the basis of property is generally its cost (see section 1012 and related regulations). The exceptions to the general rule are provided in sections contained in subchapters C, K, O, and P of the Code. For example, if the corporation acquired the property by dividend, liquidation of another corporation, transfer from a shareholder, reorganization, bequest, contribution or gift, tax-free exchange, involuntary conversion, certain asset acquisitions, or wash sale of stock, see sections 301 (or 1059), 334, 362 (or 358), 1014, 1015, 1031, 1033, 1060, and 1091, respectively. Attach an explanation if you use a basis other than actual cash cost of the property.

If the corporation is allowed a charitable contribution deduction because it sold property to a charitable organization, figure the adjusted basis for determining gain from the sale by dividing the amount realized by the fair market value and multiplying that result by the adjusted basis.

See section 852(f) for the treatment of certain load charges incurred in acquiring stock in a mutual fund with a reinvestment right.

Before making an entry in column (e), increase the cost or other basis by any expense of sale, such as broker's fees, commissions, option premiums, and state and local transfer taxes, unless the net sales price was reported in column (d).

Column (f)—Gain or (loss) for entire year. Make a separate entry in this column for each transaction reported on lines 1 and 7 and any other line(s) that apply to the corporation. For lines 1 and 7, subtract the amount in column (e) from the amount in column (d). Enter negative amounts in parentheses.

Column (g)—28% rate gain or (loss). Enter the amount, if any, from Part II, column (f), that is from a sale, exchange, or conversion (or installment payment received):

● Before May 7, 1997, OR

● After July 28, 1997, for assets held more than 1 year but not more than 18 months.

Also include collectibles gains and losses. A **collectibles gain or loss** is any gain or loss from the sale or exchange of a collectible that is a capital asset but **only** if that asset was held **either:**

● More than 18 months, OR

● More than 1 year but not more than 18 months if sold or exchanged after May 6, 1997, but before July 29, 1997.

Collectibles gain also includes gain from the sale of an interest in a partnership or trust attributable to unrealized appreciation of collectibles.

Collectibles include works of art, rugs, antiques, metals (such as gold, silver, and platinum bullion), gems, stamps, coins, alcoholic beverages, and certain other tangible property.

Enter negative amounts in parentheses.

Part III—Capital Gains Tax

If the net long-term capital gain is more than the net short-term capital loss, there is a net capital gain. If this gain exceeds $25,000, **and** the corporation elected to be an S corporation before 1987 (or filed its election during 1987 or 1988 and qualifies for the transitional relief from the built-in gains tax described in Part IV below), the corporation may be liable for income tax on the gain.

Determine if the corporation is liable for the tax by answering questions A, B, and C below. If all the answers are "Yes," the tax applies and Part III of Schedule D must be completed. Otherwise, the corporation is not liable for the tax.

If net capital gain is more than $25,000, and the corporation is not liable for the tax, attach the Part III instructions to Schedule D with questions A, B, and C answered to show why the tax does not apply.

A. Is net capital gain (line 16, Schedule D) more than $25,000, and more than 50% of taxable income (see the instructions for line 20, Schedule D)? . . . . . ☐ Yes ☐ No

B. Is taxable income (see the instructions for line 20, Schedule D) more than $25,000? . . . . . ☐ Yes ☐ No

C. Does any long-term capital gain (line 15, Schedule D) represent gain from substituted basis property (defined below)? . . . . ☐ Yes ☐ No

For purposes of the capital gains tax, **substituted basis property** is property that:

● Was acquired by the S corporation during the period that began 36 months before the first day of the tax year and ended on the last day of the tax year, and

● Has a basis determined by reference to the basis of any property in the hands of another corporation, if the other corporation was **not** an S corporation throughout the period that, **began** the later of:

1. 36 months before the first day of the tax year, or

2. The time the other corporation came into existence,

and **ended** on the date the other corporation transferred the property used to determine the basis of the property acquired by the S corporation.

Line 16. If the corporation is liable for the tax on excess net passive income (line 22a, page 1, Form 1120S) or the built-in gains tax (see Part IV below), and capital gain or loss was included in the computation of either tax, figure the amount to enter on line 16 as follows:

Step 1. Refigure lines 1 through 3, 7 through 9 in column (f), and 14 of Schedule D by:

● Excluding the portion of any recognized built-in capital gain or loss that does not qualify for transitional relief, and

● Reducing any capital gain taken into account in determining passive investment income (line 2 of the worksheet for line 22a, page 1 of Form 1120S) by the portion of excess net passive income attributable to such gain. The attributable portion is figured by multiplying excess net passive income by a fraction, the numerator of which is the capital gain (less any expenses attributable to such gain), and the denominator of which is net passive income.

Step 2. Refigure lines 4, 10, 15, and 16 of Schedule D using the amounts determined in step 1.

Line 20. Figure taxable income by completing lines 1 through 28 of **Form 1120,** U.S. Corporation Income Tax Return. Follow the instructions for Form 1120. Enter the amount from line 28 of Form 1120 on line 20 of Schedule D. Attach to Schedule D the Form 1120 computation or other worksheet used to figure taxable income.

Line 21. Figure the tax under section 11 on the taxable income shown on line 20 as if the corporation were not an S corporation. You may use Schedule J of Form 1120 to figure the tax. Attach your tax computation to Schedule D.

Line 22. Figure the excess of the net long-term capital gain over the net short-term capital loss from substituted basis property (defined above). Reduce this amount by any excess net passive income attributable to this gain (see the instructions for line 16). Attach to Schedule D your computation of the line 22 amount.

Part IV—Built-In Gains Tax

Section 1374 provides for a tax on built-in gains that applies to certain corporations that made the election to be an S corporation after 1986. This tax does not apply to any corporation that has been an S corporation for each of its tax years, unless the corporation acquired an asset with a basis determined by reference to its basis (or the basis of any other property) in the hands of a C corporation.

Transitional relief from built-in gains tax. Section 633(d)(8) of the Tax Reform Act of 1986 provides special transitional relief from the built-in gains tax for qualified corporations that elected to be S corporations during 1987 or 1988. A qualified corporation is any corporation, the stock of which:

• Was more than 50% owned (by value) by a qualified group (defined below) on August 1, 1986, and at all times thereafter before the corporation is completely liquidated, and

• Had a fair market value of less than $10 million on both the date the corporation made a valid S election and on August 1, 1986. However, if the fair market value of the stock on either date was between $5 million and $10 million, the corporation is given only partial relief from the built-in gains tax. The portion of

the built-in gain **not** eligible for relief is a fraction, the numerator of which is the amount by which the fair market value of the corporation on the date it made a valid S election (or on August 1, 1986, if higher) exceeds $5 million and the denominator of which is $5 million.

A qualified group is a group of 10 or fewer qualified persons. A qualified person is:

• An individual,

• An estate, or

• A trust described in section 1361(c)(2)(A)(ii) or (iii).

For any corporation that elected to be an S corporation after March 30, 1988, the qualified group must have owned (or be treated as having owned) more than 50% (by value) of the corporation's stock at all times during the 5-year period ending on the date of adoption of a plan of complete liquidation.

Transitional relief **does not** apply to:

• Ordinary gains or losses (determined without regard to section 1239),

• Gains or losses from the disposition of capital assets held for 6 months or less, and

• Gains from the disposition of any asset acquired by the corporation with a substituted basis, if a principal purpose for acquiring the asset was to secure transitional relief from the built-in gains tax.

Line 25. Enter the amount that would be the taxable income of the corporation for the tax year if only recognized built-in gains (including any carryover of gain under section 1374(d)(2)(B)) and recognized built-in losses were taken into account.

Section 1374(d)(3) defines a **recognized built-in gain** as any gain recognized during the recognition period (the 10-year period beginning on the first day of the first tax year for which the corporation is an S corporation, or beginning the date the asset was acquired by the S corporation, for an asset with a basis determined by reference to its basis (or the basis of any other property) in the hands of a C corporation) on the sale or distribution (disposition) of any asset, except to the extent the corporation establishes that—

• The asset was not held by the corporation as of the beginning of the first tax year the corporation was an S corporation (except this does not apply to an asset acquired by the S corporation with a basis determined by reference to its basis (or the basis of any other property) in the hands of a C corporation), or

• The gain exceeds the excess of the fair market value of the asset as of the start of the first tax year (or as of the date the asset was

acquired by the S corporation, for an asset with a basis determined by reference to its basis (or the basis of any other property) in the hands of a C corporation) over the adjusted basis of the asset at that time.

Section 1374(d)(4) defines a **recognized built-in loss** as any loss recognized during the recognition period (stated above) on the disposition of any asset to the extent the corporation establishes that—

• The asset was held by the corporation as of the beginning of the 1st tax year the corporation was an S corporation (except that this does not apply to an asset acquired by the S corporation with a basis determined by reference to its basis (or the basis of any other property) in the hands of a C corporation), and

• The loss does not exceed the excess of the adjusted basis of the asset as of the beginning of the first tax year (or as of the date the asset was acquired by the S corporation, for an asset with a basis determined by reference to its basis (or the basis of any other property) in the hands of a C corporation), over the fair market value of the asset as of that time.

A qualified corporation must show on an attachment to Schedule D its total net recognized built-in gain and also list separately the gain or loss that is from:

• Capital assets held 6 months or less, and

• Assets for which the disposition results in ordinary income or loss.

A nonqualified corporation must show on an attachment its total net recognized built-in gain and list separately any capital gain or loss and ordinary gain or loss.

Line 26. Figure taxable income by completing lines 1 through 28 of Form 1120. Follow the instructions for Form 1120. Enter the amount from line 28 of Form 1120 on line 26 of Schedule D. Attach to Schedule D the Form 1120 computation or other worksheet used to figure taxable income.

Line 27. If for any tax year the amount on line 25 exceeds the taxable income on line 26, the excess is treated as a recognized built-in gain in the succeeding tax year. This carryover provision applies only in the case of an S corporation that made its election to be an S corporation after March 30, 1988. See section 1374(d)(2)(B).

Line 28. Enter the section 1374(b)(2) deduction. Generally, this is any net operating loss carryforward or capital loss carryforward (to the extent of net capital gain included in recognized built-in gain for the tax year) arising in tax years for which the corporation was a C corporation. See section 1374(b)(2) for details.

Page 3

INSTRUCTIONS FOR FORM 4562

Depreciation and Amortization

1997

Department of the Treasury
Internal Revenue Service

Instructions for Form 4562

Depreciation and Amortization
(Including Information on Listed Property)

Section references are to the Internal Revenue Code unless otherwise noted.

Changes To Note

• For tax years beginning in 1997, the maximum section 179 expense deduction has been increased to $18,000 ($38,000 for enterprise zone businesses).

• Any qualified rent-to-own property placed in service after August 5, 1997, is classified as 3-year property under the General Depreciation System and has a 4-year class life under the Alternative Depreciation System. Generally, qualified rent-to-own property is tangible personal property of a type used within the home for personal use and held by a dealer for lease to customers under a rent-to-own agreement. See section 168(i)(14) for more details.

• For property placed in service after August 5, 1997, the use of the income forecast method is limited to motion picture films, video tapes, sound recordings, copyrights, books, and patents. You cannot use this method to depreciate any amortizable section 197 intangible.

• For property placed in service after August 5, 1997, the limits on depreciation and the section 179 expense deduction that apply solely to passenger automobiles have been **(a)** eliminated for the cost of installed qualified clean-fuel vehicle property and **(b)** tripled for certain electric vehicles. See page 8 for more details.

General Instructions

Purpose of Form

Use Form 4562 to claim your deduction for depreciation and amortization; to make the election to expense certain tangible property (section 179); and to provide information on the business/investment use of automobiles and other listed property.

Who Must File

Except as otherwise noted, complete and file Form 4562 if you are claiming any of the following.

• Depreciation for property placed in service during the 1997 tax year.

• A section 179 expense deduction (which may include a carryover from a previous year).

• Depreciation on any vehicle or other listed property (regardless of when it was placed in service).

• A deduction for any vehicle reported on a form other than **Schedule C (Form 1040),** Profit or Loss From Business, or **Schedule C-EZ (Form 1040),** Net Profit From Business.

• Any depreciation on a corporate income tax return (other than Form 1120S).

• Amortization of costs that begins during the 1997 tax year.

However, **do not** file Form 4562 to report depreciation and information on the use of vehicles if you are an employee deducting job-related vehicle expenses using either the standard mileage rate or actual expenses. Instead, use **Form 2106,** Employee Business Expenses, or **Form 2106-EZ,** Unreimbursed Employee Business Expenses, for this purpose.

Submit a separate Form 4562 for each business or activity on your return. If you need more space, attach additional sheets. However, complete only one Part I in its entirety when computing your allowable section 179 expense deduction.

Definitions

Depreciation

Depreciation is the annual deduction allowed to recover the cost or other basis of business or income-producing property with a determinable useful life of more than 1 year. However, land is not depreciable.

Depreciation starts when you first use the property in your business or for the production of income. It ends when you take the property out of service, deduct all your depreciable cost or other basis, or no longer use the property in your business or for the production of income.

Amortization

Amortization is similar to the straight line method of depreciation in that an annual deduction is allowed to recover certain costs over a fixed time period. You can amortize such items as the costs of starting a business, goodwill and certain other intangibles, reforestation, and pollution control facilities. For additional information, get **Pub. 535,** Business Expenses.

Listed Property

Listed property generally includes:

• Passenger automobiles weighing 6,000 pounds or less.

• Any other property used for transportation if the nature of the property lends itself to personal use, such as motorcycles, pick-up trucks, etc.

• Any property used for entertainment or recreational purposes (such as photographic, phonographic, communication, and video recording equipment).

• Cellular telephones (or other similar telecommunications equipment).

• Computers or peripheral equipment.

Exception. Listed property does not include **(a)** photographic, phonographic, communication, or video equipment used exclusively in a taxpayer's trade or business or at the taxpayer's regular business establishment; **(b)** any computer or peripheral equipment used exclusively at a regular business establishment and owned or leased by the person operating the establishment; or **(c)** an ambulance, hearse, or vehicle used for transporting persons or property for

Cat. No. 12907Y

hire. For purposes of the preceding sentence, a portion of the taxpayer's home is treated as a regular business establishment only if that portion meets the requirements under section 280A(c)(1) for deducting expenses attributable to the business use of a home. However, for any property listed under **(a)** above, the regular business establishment of an employee is his or her employer's regular business establishment.

Recordkeeping

Except for Part V (relating to listed property), the IRS does not require you to submit detailed information with your return on the depreciation of assets placed in service in previous tax years. However, the information needed to compute your depreciation deduction (basis, method, etc.) must be part of your permanent records.

Because Form 4562 does not provide for permanent recordkeeping, you may use the depreciation worksheet on page 12 to assist you in maintaining depreciation records. However, the worksheet is designed only for Federal income tax purposes. You may need to keep additional records for accounting and state income tax purposes.

Specific Instructions

Part I

Caution: *An estate or trust cannot make this election.*

You may elect to expense part of the cost of certain tangible personal property used in your trade or business and certain other property described in section 1245(a)(3). To do so, you must have:

• Purchased the property (as defined in section 179(d)(2)) and

• Placed it in service during the 1997 tax year.

You must make the election with:

1. The original return you file for the tax year the property was placed in service (whether or not you file your return on time), or

2. An amended return filed no later than the due date (including extensions) for your return for the tax year the property was placed in service.

Once made, the election (and the selection of the property you elect to expense) may not be revoked without IRS consent.

If you elect this deduction, reduce the amount on which you figure your depreciation or amortization deduction by the section 179 expense deduction.

Section 179 property does **not** include:

1. Property used 50% or less in your trade or business.

2. Property held for investment (section 212 property).

3. Property you lease to others as a noncorporate lessor **unless (a)** you manufactured or produced the property or **(b)** the term of the lease is less than 50% of the property's class life, and for the first 12 months after the property is transferred to the lessee, the sum of the deductions related to the property that are allowed to you **solely** under section 162 (except rents and reimbursed amounts) is more than 15% of the rental income from the property.

4. Property used mainly outside the United States (except for property described in section 168(g)(4)).

5. Property used for lodging or for furnishing the lodging (except as provided in section 50(b)(2)).

6. Property used by a tax-exempt organization (other than a section 521 farmers' cooperative) unless the property is used mainly in a taxable unrelated trade or business.

7. Property used by a governmental unit or foreign person or entity (except for property used under a lease with a term of less than 6 months).

8. Air conditioning or heating units.

The section 179 expense deduction is subject to two separate limitations: a dollar limitation and a taxable income limitation. Both limitations are figured in Part I.

For a partnership, these limitations apply to the partnership and each partner. For an S corporation, these limitations apply to the S corporation and each shareholder. For a controlled group, all component members are treated as one taxpayer.

For more details on the section 179 expense deduction, see **Pub. 946,** How To Depreciate Property.

Line 1

For an enterprise zone business, the maximum section 179 expense deduction of $18,000 is increased by the **smaller** of:

• $20,000 or

• The cost of section 179 property that is also qualified zone property (including such property placed in service by your spouse, even if you are filing a separate return).

Cross out the preprinted entry on line 1 and enter in the margin the larger amount if your business is an enterprise zone business. For the definitions of enterprise zone business and qualified zone property, see sections 1397B and 1397C.

Recapture Rule: *If any qualified zone property placed in service during the current year ceases to be used in an empowerment zone by an enterprise zone business in a later year, the benefit of the increased section 179 expense deduction must be reported as "other income" on your return.*

Line 2

Enter the cost of all section 179 property placed in service during the tax year. Include amounts from any listed property from Part V. Also include any section 179 property placed in service by your spouse, even if you are filing a separate return.

For an enterprise zone business, include on this line only 50% of the cost of section 179 property that is also qualified zone property.

Line 5

If line 5 is zero, you cannot elect to expense any property. Skip lines 6 through 11, enter zero on line 12, and enter the carryover of any disallowed deduction from 1996 on line 13.

If you are married filing separately, you and your spouse must allocate the dollar limitation for the tax year. To do so, multiply the total limitation that you would otherwise enter on line 5 by 50%, unless you both elect a different allocation. If you both elect a different allocation, multiply the total limitation by the percentage elected. The sum of the percentages you and your spouse elect must equal 100%. **Do not** enter on line 5 more than your share of the total dollar limitation.

Line 6

Caution: *Do not include any listed property on line 6.*

Column (a). Enter a brief description of the property for which you are making the election (e.g., truck, office furniture, etc.).

Column (b). Enter the cost of the property. If you acquired the property through a trade-in, **do not** include any undepreciated basis of the assets you traded in. See **Pub. 551,** Basis of Assets, for more details.

Column (c). Enter the amount you elect to expense. You do not have to expense the entire cost of the property. You can depreciate the amount you do not expense. See the line 15 and line 16 instructions.

To report your share of a section 179 expense deduction from a partnership or an S corporation, write "from Schedule K-1 (Form 1065)" or "from Schedule K-1 (Form 1120S)" across columns (a) and (b).

Line 10

The carryover of disallowed deduction from 1996 is the amount of section 179 property, if any, you elected to expense in previous years, but not allowed as a deduction due to the business income limitation. If you filed Form 4562 for 1996, enter the amount from line 13 of your 1996 Form 4562. For additional details, see Pub. 946.

Line 11

The section 179 expense deduction is further limited to the "business income" limitation under section 179(b)(3).

For purposes of the rules that follow:

- If you have to apply another Code section that has a limitation based on taxable income, see Regulations section 1.179-2(c)(5) for rules on how to apply the business income limitation under section 179 in such a case.
- You are considered to **actively conduct** a trade or business if you meaningfully participate in its management or operations. A mere passive investor is not considered to actively conduct a trade or business.

Individuals. Enter the smaller of line 5 or the aggregate taxable income from any trade or business you actively conducted, computed without regard to any section 179 expense deduction, the deduction for one-half of self-employment taxes under section 164(f), or any net operating loss deduction. Include in aggregate taxable income the wages, salaries, tips, and other compensation you earned as an employee (not reduced by unreimbursed employee business expenses). If you are married filing a joint return, combine the aggregate taxable incomes for you and your spouse.

Partnerships. Enter the smaller of line 5 or the aggregate of the partnership's items of income and expense described in section 702(a) from any trade or business the partnership actively conducted (other than credits, tax-exempt income, the section 179 expense deduction, and guaranteed payments under section 707(c)).

S corporations. Enter the smaller of line 5 or the aggregate of the corporation's items of income and expense described in section 1366(a) from any trade or business the corporation actively conducted (other than credits, tax-exempt income, the section 179 expense deduction, and the deduction for compensation paid to the corporation's shareholder-employees).

Corporations other than S corporations. Enter the smaller of line 5 or the corporation's taxable income before the section 179 expense deduction, net operating loss deduction, and special deductions (excluding items not derived from a trade or business actively conducted by the corporation).

Line 12

The limitations on lines 5 and 11 apply to the taxpayer, and not to each separate business or activity. Therefore, if you have more than one business or activity, you may allocate your allowable section 179 expense deduction among them.

To do so, write "Summary" at the top of Part I of the separate Form 4562 you are completing for the aggregate amounts from all businesses or activities. **Do not** complete the rest of that form. On line 12 of the Form 4562 you prepare for each separate business or activity, enter the amount allocated to the business or activity from the "Summary." No other entry is required in Part I of the separate Form 4562 prepared for each business or activity.

Part II

The term "Modified Accelerated Cost Recovery System" (MACRS) includes the General Depreciation System and the Alternative Depreciation System. Generally, MACRS is used to depreciate any tangible property placed in service after 1986. However, MACRS does not apply to films, videotapes, and sound recordings. See section 168(f) for other exceptions. For more details on MACRS, see Pub. 946. For information on other methods of depreciation, see **Pub. 534,** Depreciating Property Placed in Service Before 1987.

Depreciation may be an adjustment for alternative minimum tax purposes. For details, see **Form 4626,** Alternative Minimum Tax—Corporations; **Form 6251,** Alternative Minimum Tax—Individuals; or Schedule I of **Form 1041,** U.S. Income Tax Return for Estates and Trusts.

Section A

Line 14

To simplify the computation of MACRS depreciation, you may elect to group assets into one or more general asset accounts under section 168(i)(4). The assets in each general asset account are depreciated as a single asset.

Each account must include only assets that were placed in service during the same tax year with the same asset class (if any), depreciation method, recovery period, and convention. However, an asset cannot be included in a general asset account if the asset is used both for personal purposes and business/investment purposes.

When an asset in an account is disposed of, the amount realized generally must be recognized as ordinary income. The unadjusted depreciable basis and depreciation reserve of the general asset account are not affected as a result of a disposition.

Special rules apply to passenger automobiles, assets generating foreign source income, assets converted to personal use, and certain asset dispositions. For more details, see Regulations section 1.168(i)-1.

To make the election, check the box on line 14. You must make the election on your return filed no later than the due date (including extensions) for the tax year in which the assets included in the general asset account were placed in service. Once made, the election is irrevocable and applies to the tax year for which the election is made and all later tax years.

Section B

Lines 15a Through 15i

Use lines 15a through 15i only for assets placed in service during the

Page 3

tax year beginning in 1997 and depreciated under the General Depreciation System, except for automobiles and other listed property (which are reported in Part V).

Column (a). Determine which property you acquired and placed in service during the tax year beginning in 1997. Then, sort that property according to its classification (3-year property, 5-year property, etc.) as shown in column (a) of lines 15a through 15i. The classifications for some property are shown below. For property not shown, see **Determining the classification** on this page.

3-year property includes:
- A race horse that is more than 2 years old at the time it is placed in service.
- Any horse (other than a race horse) that is more than 12 years old at the time it is placed in service.
- Any qualified rent-to-own property (as defined in section 168(i)(14)) placed in service after August 5, 1997.

5-year property includes:
- Automobiles.
- Light general purpose trucks.
- Typewriters, calculators, copiers, and duplicating equipment.
- Any semi-conductor manufacturing equipment.
- Any computer or peripheral equipment.
- Any section 1245 property used in connection with research and experimentation.
- Certain energy property specified in section 168(e)(3)(B)(vi).

7-year property includes:
- Office furniture and equipment.
- Appliances, carpets, furniture, etc., used in residential rental property.
- Railroad track.
- Any property that does not have a class life and is not otherwise classified.

10-year property includes:
- Vessels, barges, tugs, and similar water transportation equipment.
- Any single purpose agricultural or horticultural structure (see section 168(i)(13)).
- Any tree or vine bearing fruit or nuts.

15-year property includes:
- Any municipal wastewater treatment plant.
- Any telephone distribution plant and comparable equipment used for 2-way exchange of voice and data communications.
- Any section 1250 property that is a retail motor fuels outlet (whether or not food or other convenience items are sold there).

20-year property includes:
- Farm buildings (other than single purpose agricultural or horticultural structures).
- Municipal sewers not classified as 25-year property.

25-year property is water utility property, which is:
- Property that is an integral part of the gathering, treatment, or commercial distribution of water, that, without regard to this classification, would be 20-year property.
- Municipal sewers. This classification applies to property placed in service after June 12, 1996, except for property placed in service under a binding contract in effect at all times since June 9, 1996.

Residential rental property is a building in which 80% or more of the total rent is from dwelling units.

Nonresidential real property is any real property that is neither residential rental property nor property with a class life of less than 27.5 years.

50-year property includes any improvements necessary to construct or improve a roadbed or right-of-way for railroad track that qualifies as a railroad grading or tunnel bore under section 168(e)(4).

There is no separate line to report 50-year property. Therefore, attach a statement showing the same information as required in columns (a) through (g). Include the deduction in the line 21 "Total" and write "See attachment" in the bottom margin of the form.

Determining the classification. If your depreciable property is **not** listed above, determine the classification as follows.

1. Find the property's class life. See the Table of Class Lives and Recovery Periods in Pub. 946.

2. Use the following table to find the classification in column (b) that corresponds to the class life of the property in column (a).

(a) Class life (in years) (See Pub. 946)	(b) Classification
4 or less	3-year property
More than 4 but less than 10.	5-year property
10 or more but less than 16 ..	7-year property
16 or more but less than 20 ..	10-year property
20 or more but less than 25 ..	15-year property
25 or more	20-year property

Column (b). For lines 15h and 15i, enter the month and year you placed the property in service. If you converted property held for personal use to use in a trade or business or for the production of income, treat the property as being placed in service on the conversion date.

Column (c). To find the basis for depreciation, multiply the cost or other basis of the property by the percentage of business/investment use. From that result, subtract any section 179 expense deduction, deduction for removal of barriers to the disabled and the elderly, disabled access credit, and enhanced oil recovery credit. See section 50(c) to determine the basis adjustment for investment credit property.

Column (d). Determine the recovery period from the table on page 5, unless either **1** or **2** below applies.

1. You make an irrevocable election to use the 150% declining balance method of depreciation for 3-, 5-, 7-, or 10-year property (excluding any tree or vine bearing fruit or nuts). The election applies to all property within the classification for which it is made that was placed in service during the tax year. If you elect this method, you must use the recovery period under the Alternative Depreciation System (ADS) discussed in the line 16 instructions. You will not have an adjustment for alternative minimum tax purposes on the property for which you make this election.

2. You acquired qualified Indian reservation property (as defined in section 168(j)(4)). Qualified Indian reservation property does not include property placed in service to conduct class I, II, or III gaming activities. The table for qualified Indian reservation property can be found in Pub. 946.

Page 4

Recovery Period for Most Property

In the case of:	The recovery period is:
3-year property	3 yrs.
5-year property	5 yrs.
7-year property	7 yrs.
10-year property	10 yrs.
15-year property	15 yrs.
20-year property	20 yrs.
25-year property	25 yrs.
Residential rental property	27.5 yrs.
Nonresidential real property placed in service before May 13, 1993	31.5 yrs.
Nonresidential real property placed in service after May 12, 1993	* 39 yrs.
Railroad gradings and tunnel bores	50 yrs.

* The recovery period is 31.5 years for property you placed in service before 1994, if you started construction on the property before May 13, 1993, or you had a binding written contract to buy or build it before that date.

Column (e). The applicable convention determines the portion of the tax year for which depreciation is allowable during a year property is either placed in service or disposed of. There are three types of conventions. To select the correct convention, you must know when you placed the property in service and the type of property.

Half-year convention (HY). This convention applies to all property reported on lines 15a through 15g, unless the mid-quarter convention applies. It does not apply to residential rental property, nonresidential real property, and railroad gradings and tunnel bores. It treats all property placed in service (or disposed of) during any tax year as placed in service (or disposed of) on the midpoint of that tax year.

Mid-quarter convention (MQ). If the aggregate bases of property subject to depreciation under section 168 and placed in service during the last 3 months of your tax year exceed 40% of the aggregate bases of property subject to depreciation under section 168 and placed in service during the entire tax year, the mid-quarter, instead of the half-year, convention applies.

In determining whether the mid-quarter convention applies, **do not** take into account the following:

● Property that is being depreciated under the pre-1987 rules.

● Any residential rental property, nonresidential real property, or railroad gradings and tunnel bores.

● Property that is placed in service and disposed of within the same tax year.

The mid-quarter convention treats all property placed in service (or disposed of) during any quarter as placed in service (or disposed of) on the midpoint of that quarter. However, no depreciation is allowed under this convention for property that is placed in service and disposed of within the same tax year.

Mid-month convention (MM). This convention applies ONLY to residential rental property, nonresidential real property (lines 15h or 15i), and railroad gradings and tunnel bores. It treats all property placed in service (or disposed of) during any month as placed in service (or disposed of) on the midpoint of that month.

Enter "HY" for half-year, "MQ" for mid-quarter, or "MM" for mid-month convention.

Column (f). Applicable depreciation methods are prescribed for each classification of property. Except as otherwise stated below, the applicable method for 3-, 5-, 7-, and 10-year property is the 200% declining balance method, switching to the straight line method in the first tax year that maximizes the depreciation allowance.

For 15- and 20-year property, property used in a farming business, and property for which you elected to use the 150% declining balance method, the applicable method is the 150% declining balance method, switching to the straight line method in the first tax year that maximizes the depreciation allowance.

For water utility property, residential rental property, nonresidential real property, any railroad grading or tunnel bore, or any tree or vine bearing fruit or nuts, the only applicable method is the straight line method.

You may also make an irrevocable election to use the straight line method for all property within a classification that is placed in service during the tax year.

Enter "200 DB" for 200% declining balance, "150 DB" for 150% declining balance, or "S/L" for straight line.

Column (g). To compute the depreciation deduction you may use optional Tables A through E, starting on page 10. To do this, multiply the applicable rate from the appropriate table by the property's **unadjusted** basis (column (c)). See Pub. 946 for complete tables. If you disposed of the property during the current tax year, multiply the result by the applicable decimal amount from the tables in step 3 below. Or you may compute the deduction yourself by completing the following steps:

Step 1. Determine the depreciation rate as follows.

● If you are using the 200% or 150% declining balance method in column (f), divide the declining balance rate (use 2.00 for 200 DB or 1.50 for 150 DB) by the number of years in the recovery period in column (d). For example, for property depreciated using the 200 DB method over a recovery period of 5 years, divide 2.00 by 5 for a rate of 40%.

You must switch to the straight line rate in the first year that the straight line rate exceeds the declining balance rate.

● If you are using the straight line method, divide 1.00 by the remaining number of years in the recovery period as of the beginning of the tax year (but not less than one). For example, if there are 6½ years remaining in the recovery period as of the beginning of the year, divide 1.00 by 6.5 for a rate of 15.38%.

Step 2. Multiply the percentage rate determined in Step 1 by the property's unrecovered basis (basis for depreciation (as defined in column (c)) reduced by all prior year's depreciation).

Step 3. For property placed in service or disposed of during the current tax year, multiply the result from Step 2 by the applicable decimal amount from the tables below (based on the convention shown in column (e)).

Half-year (HY) convention	0.5

Mid-quarter (MQ) convention

Placed in service (or disposed of) during the:	Placed in service	Disposed of
1st quarter	0.875	0.125
2nd quarter	0.625	0.375
3rd quarter	0.375	0.625
4th quarter	0.125	0.875

Mid-month (MM) convention

Placed in service (or disposed of) during the:	Placed in service	Disposed of
1st month	0.9583	0.0417
2nd month	0.8750	0.1250
3rd month	0.7917	0.2083
4th month	0.7083	0.2917
5th month	0.6250	0.3750
6th month	0.5417	0.4583
7th month	0.4583	0.5417
8th month	0.3750	0.6250
9th month	0.2917	0.7083
10th month	0.2083	0.7917
11th month	0.1250	0.8750
12th month	0.0417	0.9583

Short tax years. See Pub. 946 for rules on how to compute the depreciation deduction for property placed in service in a short tax year.

Section C

Lines 16a Through 16c

Complete lines 16a through 16c for assets, other than automobiles and other listed property, placed in service ONLY during the tax year beginning in 1997 and depreciated under the Alternative Depreciation System. Report on line 17 depreciation on assets placed in service in prior years.

Under ADS, use the applicable depreciation method, the applicable recovery period, and the applicable convention to compute depreciation.

The following types of property **must** be depreciated under ADS:
- Tangible property used predominantly outside the United States.
- Tax-exempt use property.
- Tax-exempt bond financed property.
- Imported property covered by an executive order of the President of the United States.
- Property used predominantly in a farming business and placed in service during any tax year in which you made an election under section 263A(d)(3).

Instead of depreciating property under GDS (line 15), you may make an irrevocable election with respect to any classification of property for any tax year to use ADS. For residential rental and nonresidential real property, you may make this election separately for each property.

Column (a). Use the following rules to determine the classification of the property under ADS.

Class life. Under ADS, the depreciation deduction for most property is based on the property's class life. See the Table of Class Lives and Recovery Periods in Pub. 946. Use line 16a for all property depreciated under ADS, except property that does not have a class life, residential rental and nonresidential real property, water utility property, and railroad gradings and tunnel bores.

See section 168(g)(3) for special rules for determining the class life for certain property.

12-year property. Use line 16b for property that does not have a class life.

40-year property. Use line 16c for residential rental and nonresidential real property.

Water utility property and railroad gradings and tunnel bores. These assets are 50-year property under ADS. There is no separate line to report 50-year property. Therefore, attach a statement showing the same information required in columns (a) through (g). Include the deduction in the line 21 "Total" and write "See attachment" in the bottom margin of the form.

Column (b). For 40-year property, enter the month and year placed in service or converted to use in a trade or business or for the production of income.

Column (c). See the instructions for line 15, column (c).

Column (d). On line 16a, enter the property's class life.

Column (e). Under ADS, the applicable conventions are the same as those used under GDS. See the instructions for line 15, column (e).

Column (g). Compute the depreciation deduction in the same manner as under GDS, except use the straight line method over the ADS recovery period and use the applicable convention.

Part III

Do not use Part III for automobiles and other listed property. Instead, report this property in Part V on page 2 of Form 4562.

Line 17

For tangible property depreciated under MACRS, enter the GDS and ADS deductions for the current year. To compute the deductions, see the instructions for column (g), line 15.

Line 18

Report property that you elect, under section 168(f)(1), to depreciate under the unit-of-production method or any other method not based on a term of years (other than the retirement-replacement-betterment method).

Attach a separate sheet showing:
- A description of the property and the depreciation method you elect that excludes the property from ACRS or MACRS.
- The depreciable basis (cost or other basis reduced, if applicable, by salvage value, any section 179 expense deduction, deduction for removal of barriers to the disabled and the elderly, disabled access credit, and enhanced oil recovery credit).

See section 50(c) to determine the basis adjustment for investment credit property.

Line 19

Enter the total depreciation you are claiming for the following types of property (except listed property and property subject to a section 168(f)(1) election):
- Accelerated cost recovery system (ACRS) property (pre-1987 rules). See Pub. 534.
- Property placed in service before 1981.
- Certain public utility property, which does not meet certain normalization requirements.
- Certain property acquired from related persons.
- Property acquired in certain nonrecognition transactions.
- Certain sound recordings, movies, and videotapes.
- Property depreciated under the income forecast method. For property placed in service after August 5, 1997, the use of the income forecast method is limited to motion picture films, video tapes, sound recordings, copyrights, books, and patents. You cannot use this method to depreciate any amortizable section 197 intangible. See page 9 for more details on section 197 intangibles.
- Intangible property, other than section 197 intangibles, including:

1. Computer software. Use the straight line method over 36 months.

2. Any right to receive tangible property or services under a contract or granted by a governmental unit (not acquired as part of a business).

3. Any interest in a patent or copyright not acquired as part of a business.

4. Residential mortgage servicing rights. Use the straight line method over 108 months.

See section 167(f) for more details.

Prior years' depreciation, plus current year's depreciation, can never exceed the depreciable basis of the property.

The basis and amounts claimed for depreciation should be part of your permanent books and records. **No attachment is necessary.**

Part IV

Line 21

A partnership or S corporation does not include any section 179 expense deduction (line 12) on this line. Any section 179 expense deduction is passed through separately to the partners and shareholders on the appropriate line of their Schedules K-1.

Line 22

If you are subject to the uniform capitalization rules of section 263A, enter the increase in basis from costs you must capitalize. For a detailed discussion of who is subject to these rules, which costs must be capitalized, and allocation of costs among activities, see Regulations section 1.263A-1.

Part V

If you claim the standard mileage rate, actual vehicle expenses (including depreciation), or depreciation on other listed property, you must provide the information requested in Part V, regardless of the tax year the property was placed in service. However, if you file Form 2106, 2106-EZ, or Schedule C-EZ (Form 1040), report this information on that form and not in Part V. Also, if you file Schedule C (Form 1040) and are claiming the standard mileage rate or actual vehicle expenses (except depreciation), and you are not required to file Form 4562 for any other reason, report vehicle information in Part IV of Schedule C and not on Form 4562.

Section A

Lines 24 and 25

Qualified business use. To determine whether to use line 24 or line 25 to report your listed property, you must first determine the percentage of qualified business use for each property. Generally, a qualified business use is any use in your trade or business. However, it does not include any of the following:

- Investment use.
- Leasing the property to a 5% owner or related person.
- The use of the property as compensation for services performed by a 5% owner or related person.
- The use of the property as compensation for services performed by any person (who is not a 5% owner or related person), unless an amount is included in that person's income for the use of the property and, if required, income tax was withheld on that amount.

Exception. If at least 25% of the total use of any aircraft during the tax year is for a qualified business use, the leasing or compensatory use of the aircraft by a 5% owner or related person is treated as a qualified business use.

Determine your percentage of qualified business use similar to the method used to figure the business/investment use percentage in column (c). Your percentage of qualified business use may be smaller than the business/investment use percentage.

For more information, see Pub. 946.

Column (a). List on a property-by-property basis all your listed property in the following order:

1. Automobiles and other vehicles; and

2. Other listed property (computers and peripheral equipment, etc.).

In column (a), list the make and model of automobiles, and give a general description of other listed property.

If you have more than five vehicles used 100% for business/investment purposes, you may group them by tax year. Otherwise, list each vehicle separately.

Column (b). Enter the date the property was placed in service. If property held for personal use is converted to business/investment use, treat the property as placed in service on the date of conversion.

Column (c). Enter the percentage of business/investment use. For automobiles and other vehicles, determine this percentage by dividing the number of miles the vehicle is driven for trade or business purposes or for the production of income during the year (not to include any commuting mileage) by the total number of miles the vehicle is driven for all purposes. Treat vehicles used by employees as being used 100% for business/investment purposes if the value of personal use is included in the employees' gross income, or the employees reimburse the employer for the personal use.

Employers who report the amount of personal use of the vehicle in the employee's gross income, and withhold the appropriate taxes, should enter "100%" for the percentage of business/investment use. For more information, see **Pub. 463,** Travel, Entertainment, Gift, and Car Expenses.

For listed property (such as computers or video equipment), allocate the use based on the most appropriate unit of time the property is actually used. See Temporary Regulations section 1.280F-6T.

If during the tax year you convert property used solely for personal purposes to business/investment use, figure the percentage of business/investment use only for the number of months you use the property in your business or for the production of income. Multiply that percentage by the number of months you use the property in your business or for the production of income, and divide the result by 12.

Column (d). Enter the property's actual cost (including sales tax) or other basis (unadjusted for prior years' depreciation). If you traded in old property, your basis is the adjusted basis of the old property (figured as if 100% of the property's use had been for business/investment purposes) plus any additional amount you paid for the new property.

For a vehicle, reduce your basis by any diesel-powered highway vehicle credit, qualified electric vehicle credit, or deduction for clean-fuel vehicles you claimed.

If you converted the property from personal use to business/investment use, your basis for depreciation is the smaller of the property's adjusted basis or its fair market value on the date of conversion.

Column (e). Multiply column (d) by the percentage in column (c). From that result, subtract any section 179 expense deduction and half of any investment credit taken before 1986 (unless you took the reduced credit).

For automobiles and other listed property placed in service after 1985 (i.e., transition property), reduce the depreciable basis by the entire investment credit.

Column (f). Enter the recovery period. For property placed in service after 1986 and used more than 50% in a qualified business use, use the table in the line 15, column (d) instructions. For property placed in service after 1986 and used 50% or less in a qualified business use, depreciate the property using the straight line method over its ADS recovery period. The ADS recovery period is 5 years for automobiles and computers.

Column (g). Enter the method and convention used to figure your depreciation deduction. See the instructions for line 15, columns (e) and (f). Write "200 DB," "150 DB," or "S/L," for the depreciation method, and "HY," "MM," or "MQ," for half-year, mid-month, or mid-quarter conventions, respectively. For property placed in service before 1987, write "PRE" if you used the prescribed percentages under ACRS. If you elected an alternate percentage, enter "S/L."

Column (h). See **Limits for passenger automobiles** below before entering an amount in column (h).

For property used more than 50% in a qualified business use (line 24) and placed in service after 1986, figure column (h) by following the instructions for line 15, column (g). If placed in service before 1987, multiply column (e) by the applicable percentage given in Pub. 534 for ACRS property. If the recovery period for an automobile ended before your tax year beginning in 1997, enter your unrecovered basis, if any, in column (h).

For property used 50% or less in a qualified business use (line 25) and placed in service after 1986, figure column (h) by dividing column (e) by column (f) and using the same conventions as discussed in the instructions for line 15, column (e). The amount in column (h) cannot exceed the property's unrecovered basis. If the recovery period for an automobile ended before your tax year beginning in 1997, enter your unrecovered basis, if any, in column (h).

For computers placed in service in a tax year beginning in 1985, multiply column (e) by 4.167%. For computers placed in service in a tax year beginning in 1986, multiply column (e) by 8.333%.

For property placed in service before 1987 that was disposed of during the year, enter zero.

Limits for passenger automobiles. The depreciation deduction plus section 179 expense deduction for passenger automobiles is limited for any tax year.

Definition. "Passenger automobiles" are 4-wheeled vehicles manufactured primarily for use on public roads that are rated at 6,000 pounds unloaded gross vehicle weight or less. For a truck or van, gross vehicle weight is substituted for unloaded gross vehicle weight.

Exception. The following vehicles are not considered passenger automobiles:

• An ambulance, hearse, or combination ambulance-hearse used in your trade or business.

• A vehicle used in your trade or business of transporting persons or property for compensation or hire.

For any passenger automobile you list on line 24 or line 25, the total of columns (h) and (i) for that automobile cannot exceed the limit shown in the tables below. The limit is further reduced when the business/investment use percentage is less than 100%.

Example. If an automobile placed in service in 1997 is used 60% for business/investment purposes, the limit generally is figured as follows: $3,160 × 60% = $1,896. However, the $3,160 limit is increased for certain clean-fuel and electric vehicles. See the footnote below.

For help in figuring the limit, use the **Worksheet for Passenger Automobiles** in Pub. 946.

Limits for Passenger Automobiles Placed in Service Before 1995

IF you placed your automobile in service:	THEN the limit on your depreciation and section 179 expense deduction is:
June 19–Dec. 31, 1984	$6,000
Jan. 1–Apr. 2, 1985	$6,200
Apr. 3, 1985–Dec. 31, 1986	$4,800
Jan. 1. 1987–Dec. 31, 1990	$1,475
Jan. 1, 1991–Dec. 31, 1992	$1,575
Jan. 1, 1993–Dec. 31, 1994	$1,675

Limits for Passenger Automobiles Placed in Service After 1994

IF you placed your automobile in service:	AND the number of tax years in which this automobile has been in service is:	THEN the limit on your depreciation and section 179 expense deduction is:
Jan. 1, 1995–Dec. 31, 1996	1	$3,060
	2	$4,900
	3	$2,950
	4 or more	$1,775
Jan. 1–Dec. 31, 1997	1	$3,160 *
	2	$5,000 *
After Dec. 31, 1997	1	*,**

*For vehicles placed in service after August 5, 1997:

• This limit does not apply to the cost of any qualified clean-fuel vehicle property (such as retrofit parts and components) installed on a vehicle for the purpose of permitting that vehicle to run on a clean-burning fuel. See section 179A for definitions.

• This limit is **tripled** for vehicles produced by an original equipment manufacturer and designed to run primarily on electricity.

**The limit for automobiles placed in service after Dec. 31, 1997, will be published in the Internal Revenue Bulletin. This amount was not available at the time these instructions were printed.

Column (i). Enter the amount you choose to expense for section 179 property used more than 50% in a qualified business use (subject to the limits for passenger automobiles noted above). Refer to the Part I instructions to determine if the property qualifies under section 179. Be sure to include the total cost of such property (50% of the cost if qualified zone property placed in service by an enterprise zone business) on line 2, page 1.

Recapture of depreciation and section 179 expense deduction. For listed property used more than 50% in a qualified business use in the year placed in service and used 50% or less in a later year, you may have to recapture in the later year part of the depreciation and section 179 expense deduction. Use **Form 4797,** Sales of Business Property, to figure the recapture amount.

Section B

Except as noted below, you must complete items 28 through 34 for each vehicle identified in Section A. Employees must provide their employers with the information requested in items 28 through 34 for each automobile or vehicle provided for their use.

Exception. Employers are not required to complete items 28 through 34 for vehicles used by employees who are not more than 5% owners or related persons and for which question 35, 36, 37, 38, or 39 is answered "Yes."

Section C

For employers providing vehicles to their employees, two types of written policy statements will satisfy the employer's substantiation requirements under section 274(d):

• A policy statement that prohibits personal use including commuting, and

• A policy statement that prohibits personal use except for commuting.

An employee does not need to keep a separate set of records for any vehicle that satisfies these written policy statement rules.

Line 35

A policy statement that prohibits personal use (including commuting) must meet **all** of the following conditions:

• The employer owns or leases the vehicle and provides it to one or more employees for use in the employer's trade or business.

• When the vehicle is not used in the employer's trade or business, it is kept on the employer's business premises, unless it is temporarily located elsewhere (e.g., for maintenance or because of a mechanical failure).

• No employee using the vehicle lives at the employer's business premises.

• No employee may use the vehicle for personal purposes, other than de minimis personal use (e.g., a stop for lunch between two business deliveries).

• Except for de minimis use, the employer reasonably believes that no employee uses the vehicle for any personal purpose.

Line 36

A policy statement that prohibits personal use (except for commuting) is **not** available if the commuting employee is an officer, director, or 1% or more owner. This policy must meet **all** of the following conditions:

• The employer owns or leases the vehicle and provides it to one or more employees for use in the employer's trade or business, and it is used in the employer's trade or business.

• For bona fide noncompensatory business reasons, the employer requires the employee to commute to and/or from work in the vehicle.

• The employer establishes a written policy under which the employee may not use the vehicle for personal purposes, other than commuting or de minimis personal use (e.g., a stop for a personal errand between a business delivery and the employee's home).

• Except for de minimis use, the employer reasonably believes that the employee does not use the vehicle for any personal purpose other than commuting.

• The employer accounts for the commuting use by including an appropriate amount in the employee's gross income.

For both written policy statements, there must be evidence that would enable the IRS to determine whether use of the vehicle meets the conditions stated above.

Line 38

An employer that provides more than five vehicles to its employees who are not 5% owners or related persons need not complete Section B for such vehicles. Instead, the employer must obtain the information from its employees and retain the information received.

Line 39

An automobile meets the requirements for qualified demonstration use if the employer maintains a written policy statement that:

• Prohibits its use by individuals other than full-time automobile salesmen.

• Prohibits its use for personal vacation trips.

• Prohibits storage of personal possessions in the automobile.

• Limits the total mileage outside the salesmen's normal working hours.

Part VI

Each year you may elect to deduct part of certain capital costs over a fixed period. If you amortize property, the part you amortize does not qualify for the election to expense certain tangible property or for depreciation.

For individuals reporting amortization of bond premium for bonds acquired before October 23, 1986, **do not** report the deduction here. See the instructions for Schedule A (Form 1040), line 27.

For taxpayers (other than corporations) claiming a deduction for amortization of bond premium for bonds acquired after October 22, 1986, but before January 1, 1988, the deduction is treated as interest expense and is subject to the investment interest limitations. Use **Form 4952**, Investment Interest Expense Deduction, to compute the allowable deduction.

For taxable bonds acquired after 1987, the amortization offsets the interest income. See **Pub. 550**, Investment Income and Expenses.

Line 40

Complete line 40 only for those costs for which the amortization period begins during your tax year beginning in 1997.

Column (a). Describe the costs you are amortizing. You may amortize:

• Pollution control facilities (section 169, limited by section 291 for corporations).

• Certain bond premiums (section 171).

• Research and experimental expenditures (section 174).

• The cost of acquiring a lease (section 178).

• Qualified forestation and reforestation costs (section 194).

• Business start-up expenditures (section 195).

• Organizational expenditures for a corporation (section 248) or partnership (section 709).

• Optional write-off of certain tax preferences over the period specified in section 59(e).

• Certain section 197 intangibles, which generally include the following:

    1. Goodwill.

    2. Going concern value.

    3. Workforce in place.

    4. Business books and records, operating systems, or any other information base.

    5. Any patent, copyright, formula, process, design, pattern, knowhow, format, or similar item.

    6. Any customer-based intangible (e.g., composition of market or market share).

    7. Any supplier-based intangible.

    8. Any license, permit, or other right granted by a governmental unit.

    9. Any covenant not to compete entered into in connection with the acquisition of a business.

    10. Any franchise (other than a sports franchise), trademark, or trade name.

Section 197 intangibles must be amortized over 15 years starting with the month the intangibles were acquired.

Column (b). Enter the date the amortization period begins under the applicable Code section.

Column (c). Enter the total amount you are amortizing. See the applicable Code section for limits on the amortizable amount.

Column (d). Enter the Code section under which you amortize the costs.

Column (f). Compute the amortization deduction by:

1. Dividing column (c) by the number of months over which the costs are to be amortized, and multiplying the result by the number of months in the amortization period included in your tax year beginning in 1997; or

2. Multiplying column (c) by the percentage in column (e).

Attach any other information the Code and regulations may require to make a valid election. See Pub. 535 for more information.

Paperwork Reduction Act Notice. We ask for the information on this form to carry out the Internal Revenue laws of the United States. You are required to give us the information. We need it to ensure that you are complying with these laws and to allow us to figure and collect the right amount of tax.

You are not required to provide the information requested on a form that is subject to the Paperwork Reduction Act unless the form displays a valid OMB control number. Books or records relating to a form or its instructions must be retained as long as their contents may become material in the administration of any Internal Revenue law. Generally, tax returns and return information are confidential, as required by section 6103.

The time needed to complete and file this form will vary depending on individual circumstances. The estimated average time is:

Recordkeeping .... 34 hr., 41 min.

Learning about the law or the form .... 5 hr., 4 min.

Preparing and sending the form to the IRS .... 5 hr., 51 min.

If you have comments concerning the accuracy of these time estimates or suggestions for making this form simpler, we would be happy to hear from you. See the instructions for the tax return with which this form is filed.

Table A—General Depreciation System

Method: 200% declining balance switching to straight line
Convention: Half-year

Year	If the recovery period is:			
	3 years	5 years	7 years	10 years
1	33.33%	20.00%	14.29%	10.00%
2	44.45%	32.00%	24.49%	18.00%
3	14.81%	19.20%	17.49%	14.40%
4	7.41%	11.52%	12.49%	11.52%
5		11.52%	8.93%	9.22%
6		5.76%	8.92%	7.37%
7			8.93%	6.55%
8			4.46%	6.55%
9				6.56%
10				6.55%
11				3.28%

Table B—General and Alternative Depreciation System

Method: 150% declining balance switching to straight line
Convention: Half-year

Year	If the recovery period is:					
	5 years	7 years	10 years	12 years	15 years	20 years
1	15.00%	10.71%	7.50%	6.25%	5.00%	3.750%
2	25.50%	19.13%	13.88%	11.72%	9.50%	7.219%
3	17.85%	15.03%	11.79%	10.25%	8.55%	6.677%
4	16.66%	12.25%	10.02%	8.97%	7.70%	6.177%
5	16.66%	12.25%	8.74%	7.85%	6.93%	5.713%
6	8.33%	12.25%	8.74%	7.33%	6.23%	5.285%
7		12.25%	8.74%	7.33%	5.90%	4.888%
8		6.13%	8.74%	7.33%	5.90%	4.522%
9			8.74%	7.33%	5.91%	4.462%
10			8.74%	7.33%	5.90%	4.461%
11			4.37%	7.32%	5.91%	4.462%
12				7.33%	5.90%	4.461%

Page 10

Table C—General Depreciation System
Method: Straight line
Convention: Mid-month
Recovery period: 27.5 years

Year	The month in the 1st recovery year the property is placed in service:											
	1	2	3	4	5	6	7	8	9	10	11	12
1	3.485%	3.182%	2.879%	2.576%	2.273%	1.970%	1.667%	1.364%	1.061%	0.758%	0.455%	0.152%
2–9	3.636%	3.636%	3.636%	3.636%	3.636%	3.636%	3.636%	3.636%	3.636%	3.636%	3.636%	3.636%
10, 12	3.637%	3.637%	3.637%	3.637%	3.637%	3.637%	3.636%	3.636%	3.636%	3.636%	3.636%	3.636%
11	3.636%	3.636%	3.636%	3.636%	3.636%	3.636%	3.637%	3.637%	3.637%	3.637%	3.637%	3.637%

Table D—General Depreciation System
Method: Straight line
Convention: Mid-month
Recovery period: 31.5 years

Year	The month in the 1st recovery year the property is placed in service:											
	1	2	3	4	5	6	7	8	9	10	11	12
4–7	3.175%	3.175%	3.175%	3.175%	3.175%	3.175%	3.175%	3.175%	3.175%	3.175%	3.175%	3.175%
8	3.175%	3.174%	3.175%	3.174%	3.175%	3.174%	3.175%	3.175%	3.175%	3.175%	3.175%	3.175%
9, 11	3.174%	3.175%	3.174%	3.175%	3.174%	3.175%	3.174%	3.175%	3.174%	3.175%	3.174%	3.175%
10, 12	3.175%	3.174%	3.175%	3.174%	3.175%	3.174%	3.175%	3.174%	3.175%	3.174%	3.175%	3.174%

Table E—General Depreciation System
Method: Straight line
Convention: Mid-month
Recovery period: 39 years

Year	The month in the 1st recovery year the property is placed in service:											
	1	2	3	4	5	6	7	8	9	10	11	12
1	2.461%	2.247%	2.033%	1.819%	1.605%	1.391%	1.177%	0.963%	0.749%	0.535%	0.321%	0.107%
2–39	2.564%	2.564%	2.564%	2.564%	2.564%	2.564%	2.564%	2.564%	2.564%	2.564%	2.564%	2.564%

Depreciation Worksheet

Description of Property	Date Placed in Service	Cost or Other Basis	Business/ Investment Use %	Section 179 Deduction	Depreciation Prior Years	Basis for Depreciation	Method/ Convention	Recovery Period	Rate or Table %	Depreciation Deduction

INSTRUCTIONS FOR FORM 4626

Alternative Minimum Tax—Corporations

Instructions for Form 4626

Alternative Minimum Tax—Corporations

Section references are to the Internal Revenue Code unless otherwise noted.

Changes To Note

The Taxpayer Relief Act of 1997 made the following changes that affect the alternative minimum tax (AMT):

- For tax years beginning after 1986, the installment method is allowed for both the regular tax and the AMT for dispositions of property used or produced in a farming business and held primarily for sale to customers. No adjustment should be made on line 2g for these sales. An amended return should be filed to correct any prior year income tax return affected by this retroactive change. However, the corporation generally must file an amended return within 3 years after the date it filed its original return or within 2 years after the date it paid the tax, whichever is later.
- For tax years beginning after August 5, 1997, all corporations are subject to the 90% limitation on the use of the foreign tax credit for AMT purposes. The special exception under section 59(a)(2)(C) has been repealed.

General Instructions

Purpose of Form

Use Form 4626 to figure the AMT imposed on a corporation by section 55.
Note: *For an affiliated group filing a consolidated return under the rules of section 1501, AMT must be figured on a consolidated basis.*

Who Must File

File Form 4626 if the corporation's taxable income or (loss) before the net operating loss **(NOL)** deduction plus its adjustments and preferences total more than $40,000 or, if smaller, its allowable exemption amount.

Recordkeeping

Certain items of income, deductions, credits, etc., receive different tax treatment for the AMT than for the regular tax. The corporation should keep adequate records to support items refigured for the AMT. Examples include:

- Tax forms completed a second time to refigure the AMT.
- The computation of a carryback or carryforward to other tax years of certain deductions or credits (e.g., net operating loss, capital loss, and foreign tax credit) if the AMT amount is different from the regular tax amount.

- The computation of a carryforward of a passive loss or tax shelter farm activity loss if the AMT amount is different from the regular tax amount.
- A "running balance" of the excess of the corporation's total increases in alternative minimum taxable income (AMTI) from prior year adjusted current earnings (ACE) adjustments over the total reductions in AMTI from prior year ACE adjustments (line 4d). See the instructions for line 4d.

Short Period Return

If the corporation is filing for a period of less than 12 months, AMTI must be placed on an annual basis and the AMT prorated based on the number of months in the short period. Complete Form 4626 as follows.

Step 1. Complete lines 1 through 6 in the normal manner. Also subtract line 6 from lilne 5 to figure AMTI for the short period, but do not enter it on line 7.

Step 2. Multiply AMTI for the short period by 12. Divide the result by the number of months in the short period. Enter this result on line 7 and write "Sec. 443(d)(1)" on the dotted line to the left of the entry space.

Step 3. Complete lines 8 through 12.

Step 4. Subtract line 12 from line 11. Multiply the result by a fraction, the numerator of which is the number of months in the short period and the denominator of which is 12. Enter the result on line 13 and write "Sec. 443(d)(2)" on the dotted line to the left of the entry space.

Step 5. Complete the rest of the form in the normal manner.

Allocating Differently Treated Items Between Certain Entities and Their Investors

For a regulated investment company, a real estate investment trust, or a common trust fund, see section 59(d) for details on allocating certain differently treated items between the entity and its investors.

Credit for Prior Year Minimum Tax

A corporation may be able to take a minimum tax credit against the regular tax for AMT incurred in prior years. See **Form 8827,** Credit for Prior Year Minimum Tax—Corporations, for details.

Specific Instructions

Line 1—Taxable Income or (Loss) Before Net Operating Loss Deduction

Enter the corporation's taxable income or (loss) before the NOL deduction and after the special deductions and without regard to any excess inclusion (e.g., if filing Form 1120, subtract line 29b from line 28 of that form).

Line 2—Adjustments and Preferences

Caution: *To avoid duplication, do not include any AMT adjustment or preference taken into account on line 2j, 2k, 2l, or 2s in the amounts to be entered on any other line of this form.*

Line 2a—Depreciation of Post-1986 Property

This section describes when depreciation must be refigured for the AMT and how to figure the adjustment to enter on line 2a.

DO NOT make a depreciation adjustment on line 2a for:

- **Passive activities.** Take this adjustment into account on line 2k.
- **An activity for which the corporation is NOT at risk OR income or loss from a partnership if the base limitations apply.** Take this adjustment into account on line 2l.
- **A tax shelter farm activity.** Take this adjustment into account on line 2j.

What Depreciation MUST Be Refigured for the AMT?

Generally, depreciation must be refigured for the AMT if, for the regular tax, it is either:

- Claimed for tangible property placed in service after 1986, or
- Capitalized to inventory.

Transitional election. If the transitional election was made under section 203(a)(1)(B) of the Tax Reform Act of 1986, this rule applies to property placed in service after July 31, 1986.

What Depreciation Is NOT Refigured for the AMT?

Depreciation is not refigured for the AMT for:

Cat. No. 64443L

- Property for which the corporation made an election to use the alternative depreciation system (ADS) for the regular tax.
- Property expensed under section 179 for the regular tax.
- Property described in sections 168(f)(1) through (4).

How Is Depreciation Refigured for the AMT?

For the AMT, depreciation must be refigured using ADS. The following table summarizes the rules for using ADS to refigure depreciation.

IF the property is...	THEN figure AMT depreciation using the...
Section 1250(c) real property (generally nonresidential real and residential rental property).	Straight line method over 40 years, with the same mid-month convention used for the regular tax.
Tangible property (other than section 1250(c) real property) that was depreciated under straight line for the regular tax.	Straight line method over the property's class life with the same convention used for the regular tax.
Any other tangible property.	150% declining balance method, switching to the straight line method for the first tax year it gives a larger deduction, over the property's class life. Use the same convention used for the regular tax.

How Is the AMT Class Life Determined?

The class life used for the AMT is not necessarily the same as the recovery period used for the regular tax. The class lives for the AMT are listed in Rev. Proc. 87–56, 1987–2, C.B. 674, and in **Pub. 946,** How to Depreciate Property. Use 12 years for any tangible personal property not assigned a class life.

TIP. *See Rev. Proc. 87–57, 1987–2 C.B. 687, for optional tables (14 through 18) that can be used to figure AMT depreciation. These optional tables also appear in Pub. 946. Rev. Proc. 89–15, 1989–1 C.B. 816, has special rules for applying Rev. Proc. 87–57 to short years and for property disposed of before the end of the recovery period.*

Special rules for transition property and public utility property. Be sure to consider the transitional rules (described in section 56(a)(1)(C)) and the normalization rules (described in section 56(a)(1)(D)).

How Is the Line 2a Adjustment Figured?

Subtract the AMT depreciation from the regular tax depreciation. If the AMT depreciation is more than the regular tax depreciation, enter the difference as a negative amount.

Line 2b—Amortization of Certified Pollution Control Facilities

For facilities placed in service after 1986, figure the amortization deduction for the AMT using the ADS described in section 168(g) (i.e., the straight line method over the facility's class life). Section 168(g) applies to 100% of the asset's amortizable basis. Do not reduce the corporation's AMT basis by the 20% section 291 adjustment that applied for the regular tax

Subtract the AMT deduction from the regular tax deduction. Enter the result on line 2b. If the AMT deduction is more than the regular tax deduction, enter the difference as a negative amount.

Line 2c—Amortization of Mining Exploration and Development Costs

Important: **Do not** *make this adjustment for costs for which the corporation elected the optional 10-year writeoff under section 59(e) for the regular tax.*

For the AMT, the regular tax deductions under sections 616(a) and 617(a) for costs paid or incurred after 1986 are not allowed. Instead, capitalize these costs and amortize them ratably over a 10-year period beginning with the tax year in which the corporation paid or incurred them. The 10-year amortization applies to 100% of the mining development and exploration costs paid or incurred during the tax year. Do not reduce the corporation's AMT basis by the 30% section 291 adjustment that applied for the regular tax.

If the corporation had a loss on property for which mining exploration and development costs have not been fully amortized for the AMT, the AMT deduction is the smaller of **(a)** the loss allowable for the costs had they remained capitalized, or **(b)** the remaining costs to be amortized for the AMT.

Subtract the AMT deduction from the regular tax deduction. Enter the result on line 2c. If the AMT deduction is more than the regular tax deduction, enter the difference as a negative amount.

Line 2d—Amortization of Circulation Expenditures

This adjustment applies **only** to personal holding companies.

Important: **Do not** *make this adjustment for costs for which the corporation elected the optional 3-year writeoff under section 59(e) for the regular tax.*

For the regular tax, circulation expenditures may be deducted in full when paid or incurred. For the AMT, these expenditures must be capitalized and amortized over 3 years.

If the corporation had a loss on property for which the circulation expenditures have not been fully amortized for the AMT, the AMT deduction is the smaller of **(a)** the loss allowable for the costs had they remained capitalized, or **(b)** the remaining costs to be amortized for the AMT.

Subtract the AMT deduction from the regular tax deduction. Enter the result on line 2d. If the AMT deduction is more than the regular tax deduction, enter the difference as a negative amount.

Line 2e—Adjusted Gain or Loss

If, during the tax year, the corporation disposed of property for which it is making (or previously made) any of the adjustments described on lines 2a through 2d above, refigure the property's adjusted basis for the AMT. Then refigure the gain or loss on the disposition.

The property's adjusted basis for the AMT is its cost minus all applicable depreciation or amortization deductions allowed for the AMT during the current tax year and previous tax years. Subtract this AMT basis from the sales price to get the AMT gain or loss.

Important: *The corporation may also have gains or losses from lines 2j, 2k, and 2l that must be considered on line 2e. For example, if for the regular tax the corporation reports a loss from the disposition of an asset used in a passive activity, include the loss in the computations for line 2k to determine if any passive activity loss is limited for the AMT. Then, include the AMT passive activity loss allowed that relates to the disposition of the asset on line 2e in determining the corporation's AMT basis adjustment. It may be helpful to refigure Form 8810 and related worksheets and Schedule D (Form 1120), Form 4684 (Section B), or Form 4797 for the AMT.*

Enter the difference between the regular tax gain or loss and the AMT gain or loss. Enter the difference as a negative amount if:

- The AMT gain is less than the regular tax gain, OR
- The AMT loss exceeds the regular tax loss, OR
- The corporation has an AMT loss and a regular tax gain.

Line 2f—Long-Term Contracts

For the AMT, the corporation generally must use the percentage-of-completion method described in section 460(b) to determine the taxable income from any long-term contract (defined in section 460(f)). However, this rule does not apply to any home construction contract (as defined in section 460(e)(6)).

For contracts excepted from the percentage-of-completion method for the regular tax by section 460(e)(1), determine the percentage of completion using the simplified procedures for allocating costs outlined in section 460(b)(3).

Subtract the regular tax income from the AMT income. Enter the difference on line 2f. If the AMT income is less than the regular tax income, enter the difference as a negative amount.

Line 2g—Installment Sales

The installment method does not apply for the AMT to any nondealer disposition of property that occurred after August 16, 1986, but before the first day of the corporation's tax year that began in 1987, if an installment obligation to which the proportionate disallowance rule applied arose from the disposition.

Enter as a negative adjustment on line 2g the amount of installment sale income reported for the regular tax.

Line 2h—Merchant Marine Capital Construction Funds

Amounts deposited in these funds (established under section 607 of the Merchant Marine Act of 1936) are not deductible for the AMT. Earnings on these funds are not excludable from gross income for the AMT. If the corporation deducted these amounts or excluded them from income for the regular tax, add them back on line 2h. See section 56(c)(2) for more details.

Line 2i—Section 833(b) Deduction

This deduction is not allowed for the AMT. If the corporation took this deduction for the regular tax, add it back on line 2i.

Line 2j—Tax Shelter Farm Activities

Important: *Complete this line only if the corporation is a personal service corporation and it has a gain or loss from a tax shelter farm activity (as defined in section 58(a)(2)) that is* **not** *a passive activity. If the tax shelter farm activity* **is** *a passive activity, include the gain or loss in the computations for line 2k below.*

Refigure all gains and losses reported for the regular tax from tax shelter farm activities by taking into account any AMT adjustments and preferences. Determine the AMT gain or loss using the rules for the regular tax with the following modifications:

● No loss is allowed except to the extent the personal service corporation is insolvent (see section 58(c)(1)).

● Do not use a loss in the current tax year to offset gains from other tax shelter farm activities. Instead, suspend any loss and carry it forward indefinitely until the corporation has a gain in a subsequent tax year from that same tax shelter farm activity OR it disposes of the activity.

Note: *Keep adequate records for losses that are not deductible (and therefore carried forward) for both the AMT and regular tax.*

Enter on line 2j the difference between the AMT gain or loss and the regular tax gain or loss. Enter the difference as a negative amount if the corporation had:

● An AMT loss and a regular tax gain, OR

● An AMT loss that exceeds the regular tax loss, OR

● A regular tax gain that exceeds the AMT gain.

Line 2k—Passive Activities

This adjustment applies **only** to closely held corporations and personal service corporations. Refigure all passive activity gains and losses reported for the regular tax by taking into account the corporation's AMT adjustments, preferences, and AMT prior year unallowed losses.

Determine the corporation's AMT passive activity gain or loss using the same rules used for the regular tax. If the corporation is insolvent, see section 58(c)(1).

Disallowed losses of a personal service corporation are suspended until the corporation has income from that (or any other) passive activity or until the passive activity is disposed of (i.e., its passive losses cannot offset "net active income" (defined in section 469(e)(2)(B)) or "portfolio income"). Disallowed losses of a closely held corporation that is not a personal service corporation are treated the same except that, in addition, they may be used to offset "net active income."

Note: *Keep adequate records for losses that are not deductible (and therefore carried forward) for both the AMT and regular tax.*

Enter on line 2k the difference between the AMT gain or loss and the regular tax gain or loss. Enter the difference as a negative amount if the corporation had:

● An AMT loss and a regular tax gain, OR

● An AMT loss that exceeds the regular tax loss, OR

● A regular tax gain that exceeds the AMT gain.

Tax Shelter Farm Activities That Are Passive Activities

Refigure all gains and losses reported for the regular tax by taking into account the corporation's AMT adjustments and preferences and AMT prior year unallowed losses.

Use the same rules as outlined above for other passive assets, with the following modifications:

● AMT gains from tax shelter farm activities that are passive activities may be used to offset AMT losses from other passive activities.

● AMT losses from tax shelter farm activities that are passive activities may not be used to offset AMT gains from other passive activities. These losses must be suspended and carried forward indefinitely until the corporation has a gain in a subsequent year from that same activity or it disposes of the activity.

Line 2l—Loss Limitations

Refigure gains and losses reported for the regular tax from at-risk activities and partnerships by taking into account the corporation's AMT adjustments and preferences. If the corporation has recomputed losses that must be limited for the AMT (under section 59(h)) by

section 465 or by section 704(d) OR if, for the regular tax, the corporation reported losses from at-risk activities or partnerships that were limited by those sections, figure the difference between the loss limited for the AMT and the loss limited for the regular tax for each applicable at-risk activity or partnership. "Loss limited" means the amount of loss that is not allowable for the year because of the limitation of section 465 or 704(d).

Enter on line 2l the excess of the loss limited for the AMT over the loss limited for the regular tax. If the loss limited for the regular tax is more than the loss limited for the AMT, enter the difference as a negative amount.

Line 2m—Depletion

Refigure depletion using only income and deductions allowed for the AMT when refiguring the limit based on taxable income from the property under section 613(a) and the limit based on taxable income, with certain adjustments, under section 613A(d)(1). Also, the depletion deduction for mines, wells, and other natural deposits under section 611 is limited to the property's adjusted basis at the end of the year, as refigured for the AMT, unless the corporation is an independent producer or royalty owner claiming percentage depletion for oil and gas wells under section 613A(c). Figure this limit separately for each property. When refiguring the property's adjusted basis, take into account any AMT adjustments the corporation made this year or in previous years that affect basis (other than the current year's depletion). Do not include in the property's adjusted basis any unrecovered costs of depreciable tangible property used to exploit the deposits (e.g., machinery, tools, pipes, etc.).

For iron ore and coal (including lignite), apply the section 291 adjustment before figuring this preference.

Enter on line 2m the difference between the regular tax and the AMT deduction. If the AMT deduction is more than the regular tax deduction, enter the difference as a negative amount.

Line 2n—Tax-Exempt Interest From Specified Private Activity Bonds

Enter interest earned on specified private activity bonds reduced by any deduction that would have been allowable if the interest were includible in gross income for the regular tax. Generally, a specified private activity bond is any private activity bond (as defined in section 141) issued after August 7, 1986. See section 57(a)(5) for exceptions and for more details.

Line 2o—Charitable Contributions

Refigure this deduction using only income and deductions allowed for the AMT when refiguring the limit based on taxable income under section 170(b)(2). Also, any AMT carryover of charitable contributions is limited to the cost or other basis (instead of fair market value) for any contribution of capital gain or section 1231 property for which the preference for charitable contributions of appreciated property applied. The preference for charitable contributions of appreciated property does not apply to:

- Contributions made after 1992;
- Contributions of tangible personal property made in a tax year beginning after 1990; or
- Contributions of property for which the corporation elected under section 170(b)(1)(C)(iii) to figure the deduction using the property's adjusted basis rather than its fair market value.

Enter on line 2o the difference between the regular tax and the AMT deduction. If the AMT deduction is more than the regular tax deduction, enter the difference as a negative amount.

Line 2p—Intangible Drilling Costs

Important: **Do not** *make this adjustment for cost for which the corporation elected the optional 60-month writeoff under section 59(e) for the regular tax.*

Intangible drilling costs **(IDCs)** from oil, gas, and geothermal properties are a preference to the extent excess IDCs exceed 65% of the net income from the properties. Figure the preference for all geothermal deposits separately from the preference for all oil and gas properties that are not geothermal deposits.

Excess IDCs are the excess of:

1. The amount of IDCs the corporation paid or incurred for oil, gas, or geothermal properties that it elected to expense for the regular tax under section 263(c) (not including any section 263(c) deduction for nonproductive wells) reduced by the section 291(b)(1) adjustment for integrated oil companies and increased by any amortization of IDCs allowed under section 291(b)(2); over

2. The amount that would have been allowed if the corporation had amortized that amount over a 120-month period starting with the month the well was placed in production.

Note: *If the corporation prefers not to use the 120-month period, it can elect any method that is permissible in determining cost depletion.*

Net income is the gross income the corporation received or accrued from all oil, gas, and geothermal wells minus the deductions allocable to these properties (reduced by the excess IDCs). When refiguring net income, use only income and deductions allowed for the AMT.

Exception. The preference for IDCs from oil and gas wells does not apply to corporations that are independent producers (i.e., not integrated oil companies as defined in section 291(b)(4)). However, this benefit may be limited. First, figure the IDC preference as if this exception did not apply. Then, for purposes of this exception, complete a second Form 4626 through line 5,

including the IDC preference. If the amount of the IDC preference exceeds 40% of the amount figured for line 5, enter the excess on line 2p (the benefit of this exception is limited). If the amount of the IDC preference is equal to or less than 40% of the amount figured for line 5, do not enter an amount on line 2p (the benefit of this exception is not limited).

Line 2q—Accelerated Depreciation of Real Property (Pre-1987)

Refigure depreciation for the AMT using the straight line method for real property for which accelerated depreciation was determined for the regular tax using pre-1987 rules. Use a recovery period of 19 years for 19-year real property and 15 years for low-income housing property. Figure the excess of the regular tax deduction over the AMT depreciation separately for each property and include only positive adjustments on line 2q.

Line 2r—Accelerated Depreciation of Leased Personal Property (Pre-1987)

This preference applies **only** to personal holding companies.

For leased personal property other than recovery property, enter the excess of the depreciation claimed for the property for the regular tax using the pre-1987 rules over the depreciation allowable for the AMT as refigured using the straight line method.

For leased 10-year recovery property and leased 15-year public utility property, enter the amount by which the regular tax depreciation exceeds the depreciation allowable using the straight line method with a half-year convention, no salvage value, and a recovery period of 15 years (22 years for 15-year public utility property).

Figure this amount separately for each property and include only positive adjustments on line 2r.

Line 2s—Other Adjustments

Include the following adjustments on this line:

- **Income eligible for the possessions tax credit.** If this income was included in the corporation's taxable income for the regular tax, include this amount on line 2s as a negative amount.
- **Income from the alcohol fuel credit.** If this income was included in the corporation's income for the regular tax, include this amount on line 2s as a negative amount.
- **Income as the beneficiary of an estate or trust.** If the corporation is the beneficiary of an estate or trust, include the minimum tax adjustment from Schedule K-1 (Form 1041), line 9.
- **Patron's AMT adjustment.** Distributions the corporation received from a cooperative may be includible in income. Unless the distributions are nontaxable, include on line 2s the total AMT patronage dividend adjustment

reported to the corporation from the cooperative.
- **Cooperative's AMT adjustment.** If the corporation is a cooperative, refigure the cooperative's deduction for patronage dividends by taking into account the cooperative's AMT adjustments and preferences. Subtract the cooperative's AMT deduction for patronage dividends from its regular tax deduction for patronage dividends. If the AMT deduction is more than the regular tax deduction, enter the difference as a negative amount.
- **Related adjustments.** AMT adjustments and preferences may affect deductions that are based on an income limit. Refigure these deductions using the income limit as modified for the AMT. Include on line 2s an adjustment for the difference between the regular tax and AMT amounts for all such deductions. If the AMT deduction is more than the regular tax deduction, enter the difference as a negative amount.

Line 4—Adjusted Current Earnings (ACE) Adjustment

Note: *The ACE adjustment does not apply to a regulated investment company or a real estate investment trust.*

Line 4b.

Important: *For an affiliated group filing a consolidated return under the rules of section 1501, figure line 4b on a consolidated basis.*

The following examples illustrate the manner in which line 3 is subtracted from line 4a to get the amount to enter on line 4b.

Example 1. Corporation A has line 4a ACE of $25,000. If Corporation A has line 3 pre-adjustment AMTI in the amounts shown below, its line 3 pre-adjustment AMTI and line 4a ACE would be combined as follows to determine the amount to enter on line 4b:

Line 4a ACE	$25,000	$25,000	$25,000
Line 3 pre-adjustment AMTI	10,000	30,000	(50,000)
Amount to enter on line 4b	$15,000	$(5,000)	$75,000

Example 2. Corporation B has line 4a ACE of $(25,000). If Corporation B has line 3 pre-adjustment AMTI in the amounts shown below, its line 3 pre-adjustment AMTI and line 4a ACE would be combined as shown below to determine the amount to enter on line 4b:

Line 4a ACE	$(25,000)	$(25,000)	$(25,000)
Line 3 pre-adjustment AMTI	(10,000)	(30,000)	50,000
Amount to enter on line 4b	$(15,000)	$5,000	$(75,000)

Line 4d. A potential negative ACE adjustment (i.e., a negative amount on line 4b multiplied by 75%) is allowed as a negative ACE adjustment on line 4e only if the corporation's total increases in

AMTI from prior year ACE adjustments exceed its total reductions in AMTI from prior year ACE adjustments (line 4d). The purpose of line 4d is to provide a "running balance" of this limitation amount. As such, the corporation must keep adequate records (e.g., a copy of Form 4626 completed at least through line 5) from year to year (even in years in which it does not owe any AMT).

Any potential negative ACE adjustment that is not allowed as a negative ACE adjustment in a tax year because of the line 4d limitation may not be used to reduce a positive ACE adjustment in any other tax year.

Combine lines 4d and 4e of the 1996 Form 4626 and enter the result on line 4d of the 1997 form. Do not enter a negative amount on line 4d for the reason given in the preceding paragraph.

Example. Corporation C, a calendar-year corporation, was incorporated January 1, 1993. Its ACE and pre-adjustment AMTI for 1993 through 1997 were as follows:

Year	ACE	Pre-adjustment AMTI
1993	$700,000	$800,000
1994	900,000	600,000
1995	400,000	500,000
1996	(100,000)	300,000
1997	250,000	100,000

Corporation C subtracts its pre-adjustment AMTI from its ACE in each of the years and then multiplies the result by 75% to get the following potential ACE adjustments for 1993 through 1997:

Year	ACE minus pre-adjustment AMTI	Potential ACE adjustment
1993	$(100,000)	$ (75,000)
1994	300,000	225,000
1995	(100,000)	(75,000)
1996	(400,000)	(300,000)
1997	150,000	112,500

Under these facts, Corporation C has the following increases or reductions in AMTI for 1993 through 1997:

Year	Increase or (reduction) in AMTI from ACE adjustment
1993	$0
1994	225,000
1995	(75,000)
1996	(150,000)
1997	112,500

In 1993, Corporation C was not allowed to reduce its AMTI by any part of the potential negative ACE adjustment because it had no increases in AMTI from prior year ACE adjustments.

In 1994, Corporation C had to increase its AMTI by the full amount of its potential ACE adjustment. It was not allowed to use any part of its 1993 unallowed potential negative ACE adjustment of $75,000 to reduce its 1994 positive ACE adjustment of $225,000.

In 1995, Corporation C was allowed to reduce its AMTI by the full amount of its potential negative ACE adjustment because that amount is less than its line 4d limit of $225,000.

In 1996, Corporation C was allowed to reduce its AMTI by only $150,000. Its potential negative ACE adjustment of $300,000 was limited to its 1994 increase in AMTI of $225,000 minus its 1995 reduction in AMTI of $75,000.

In 1997, Corporation C must increase its AMTI by the full amount of its potential ACE adjustment. It may not use any part of its 1996 unallowed potential negative ACE adjustment of $150,000 to reduce its 1997 positive ACE adjustment of $112,500. Corporation C would complete the relevant portion of its 1997 Form 4626 as follows:

Line	Amount
4a	$250,000
4b	150,000
4c	112,500
4d	-0-
4e	112,500

Line 6—Alternative Tax Net Operating Loss Deduction (ATNOLD)

The alternative tax net operating loss deduction is the aggregate of the alternative tax net operating loss (ATNOL) carrybacks and carryovers to the tax year, subject to the limitation explained below. For a corporation that held a residual interest in a real estate mortgage investment conduit (REMIC), figure the ATNOLD without regard to any excess inclusion.

For a loss year that began after 1986, the ATNOL is the excess of the deductions allowed in figuring AMTI (excluding the ATNOLD) over the income included in AMTI. This excess is figured with the modifications in section 172(d), taking into account the adjustments in sections 56 and 58 and preferences in section 57 (i.e., the section 172(d) modifications must be separately computed in figuring the ATNOL).

In applying the rules relating to the determination of the amount of carrybacks and carryovers, use the modification to those rules described in section 56(d)(1)(B)(ii).

If, for any tax year that began before 1987, the corporation had minimum tax that was deferred under section 56(b) (as in effect before the enactment of the Tax Reform Act of 1986) and that deferred tax has not been paid, reduce the amount of ATNOL carryovers that may be carried over to this year by the corporation's preferences that caused the deferred add-on minimum tax. (Section 701(f)(2)(B) of the Tax Reform Act of 1986.)

The corporation's ATNOLD is limited. To figure the ATNOLD limitation, first figure AMTI without the ATNOLD. To do this, use a second Form 4626 as a worksheet. Complete the form through line 5, but when figuring lines 2m, 2o, and 2s, treat line 6 as if it were zero. Multiply line 5 of the second Form 4626 used as a worksheet by 90%. This is the corporation's ATNOLD limitation.

The amount of any ATNOL that is not deductible may be carried back or carried over using the rules outlined in section 172(b). An election under section 172(b)(3) to forego the carryback period for the regular tax also applies for the AMT. The ATNOL carried back or carried over may differ from the NOL (if any) that is carried back or carried over for the regular tax. Keep adequate records for both the AMT and the regular tax.

Line 7—Alternative Minimum Taxable Income

For a corporation that held a residual interest in a REMIC and is not a thrift institution, line 7 may not be less than the total of the amounts shown on line 2c of **Schedule(s) Q (Form 1066),** Quarterly Notice to Residual Interest Holder of REMIC Taxable Income or Net Loss Allocation, for the periods included in the corporation's tax year. If the total of the line 2c amounts is larger than the amount the corporation would otherwise enter on line 7, enter that total and write "Sch. Q" on the dotted line next to line 7.

Line 9—Exemption Phase-out Computation

Line 9a. If this Form 4626 is for a member of a controlled group of corporations, subtract $150,000 from the combined AMTI of all members of the controlled group. Divide the result among the members of the group in the same manner as the $40,000 tentative exemption is divided among the members. Enter this member's share on line 9a. The tentative exemption must be divided equally among the members, unless all members consent to a different allocation. See section 1561 for more details.

Line 9c. If this Form 4626 is for a member of a controlled group of corporations, reduce the member's share of the $40,000 tentative exemption by the amount entered on line 9b.

Line 12—Alternative Minimum Tax Foreign Tax Credit

Refigure the regular tax foreign tax credit claimed for each separate limitation category of income as follows:

Step 1. Refigure both the numerator (foreign source taxable income) and the denominator (worldwide taxable income) of the limitation fraction by considering the corporation's AMT adjustments and preferences.

Step 2. Substitute line 11 of Form 4626 for the "total U.S. income tax against which credit is allowed."

Step 3. Multiply the fraction in **Step 1** above by the amount in **Step 2** above to determine the refigured limitation.

Step 4. Subtract the smaller of the total foreign taxes paid for that separate limitation category and the refigured limitation from **Step 3** above.

Step 5. Add the credits you refigured for each separate limitation. Enter the result on line 12.

In determining if any income is "high-taxed" in applying the separate limitation categories for the AMT foreign tax credit, use the AMT rate instead of the regular rate.

The AMT foreign tax credit is subject to a 90% limit (i.e., the credit cannot be more than the amount on line 11 minus 10% of the amount that would be on that line if Form 4626 were refigured using zero on line 6 and if the exception for intangible drilling costs under section 57(a)(2)(E) did not apply). For tax years beginning **before** August 6, 1997, the 90% limit does not apply to certain corporations that meet the requirements of section 59(a)(2)(C).

Any AMT foreign tax credit the corporation cannot claim (because of the limitation fraction or the 90% limit discussed above) may be carried back or carried over according to the rules in section 904(c). Also, any foreign tax credit that the corporation cannot claim (and can therefore be carried back or carried over) for the AMT may differ from the amount (if any) that is carried back or carried over for the regular tax. Keep adequate records for both the AMT and the regular tax.

Line 14

Enter the corporation's regular tax liability (as defined in section 26(b)) minus any foreign tax credit and possessions tax credit (e.g., for Form 1120, Schedule J, line 3, minus the sum of Schedule J, lines 4a and 4b). **Do not** include any:
- Tax on accumulation distribution of trusts from Form 4970.
- Recapture of investment credit (under section 49(b) or 50(a)) from Form 4255.
- Recapture of low-income housing credit (under section 42(j) or (k)) from Form 8611.

ACE Worksheet Instructions

Treatment of Certain Ownership Changes

If a corporation with a net unrealized built-in loss (within the meaning of section 382(h)) undergoes an ownership change (within the meaning of Regulations section 1.56(g)-1(k)(2)), refigure the adjusted basis of each asset of the corporation (immediately after the ownership change). The new adjusted basis of each asset is its proportionate share (based on respective fair market values) of the fair market value of the corporation's assets (determined under section 382(h)) immediately before the ownership change.

To determine if the corporation has a net unrealized built-in loss, use the aggregate adjusted basis of its assets used for computing its ACE.

Note: *Use these new adjusted bases for all future ACE calculations (such as depreciation and gain or loss on disposition of an asset).*

Line 2—ACE Depreciation Adjustment

Line 2a. Generally, the amount entered on this line is: **(a)** the depreciation the corporation claimed for the regular tax (Form 4562, line 21), modified by **(b)** the AMT depreciation adjustments reported on lines 2a, 2q, and 2r of Form 4626.

Line 2b(1). For property placed in service after 1993, the ACE depreciation is the same as the AMT depreciation. Therefore, enter on line 2b(1) the same depreciation expense you entered on line 2a for such property.

Line 2b(2). For property placed in service in a tax year that began after 1989, and before 1994, use the ADS described in section 168(g). However, for property **(a)** placed in service in a tax year that began after 1989, and **(b)** described in sections 168(f)(1) through (4), use the same depreciation claimed for the regular tax and enter it on line 2b(5).

Line 2b(3). For property placed in service in a tax year that began after 1986 and before 1990 (MACRS property), use the straight line method over the remainder of the recovery period for the property under the ADS of section 168(g). In doing so, use the convention that would have applied to the property under section 168(d). For more information (including an example that illustrates the application of these rules), see Regulations section 1.56(g)-1(b)(2).

Line 2b(4). For property placed in service in a tax year that began after 1980 and before 1987 (to which the original ACRS applies), use the straight line method over the remainder of the recovery period for the property under ADS. In doing so, use the convention that would have applied to the property under section 168(d) (without regard to section 168(d)(3)). For more information (including an example that illustrates the application of these rules), see Regulations section 1.56(g)-1(b)(3).

Line 2b(5). For property described in sections 168(f)(1) through (4), use the regular tax depreciation, regardless of when the property was placed in service.

Important: *Line 2b(5) takes priority over lines 2b(1), 2b(2), 2b(3), and 2b(4) (i.e., for property that is described in sections 168(f)(1) through (4), use line 2b(5) instead of the line (2b(1), 2b(2), 2b(3), or 2b(4)) that would otherwise apply).*

Line 2b(6). Use the regular tax depreciation for **(a)** property placed in service before 1981 AND **(b)** property placed in service after 1980, in a tax year that began before 1990, that is excluded from MACRS by section 168(f)(5)(A)(i) or original ACRS by section 168(e)(4), as in effect before the Tax Reform Act of 1986.

Line 2c. Subtract line 2b(7) from line 2a and enter the result on line 2c. If line 2b(7) exceeds line 2a, enter the difference as a negative amount.

Line 3—Inclusion in ACE of Items Included in Earnings and Profits (E&P)

In general, any income item that is not taken into account (see below) in determining the corporation's pre-adjustment AMTI but that is taken into account in determining its E&P must be included in ACE. Any such income item may be reduced by all items related to that income item and that would be deductible when figuring pre-adjustment AMTI if the income items to which they relate were included in the corporation's pre-adjustment AMTI for the tax year. Examples of adjustments for these income items include: **(a)** interest income from tax-exempt obligations excluded under section 103 minus any costs incurred in carrying these tax-exempt obligations; and **(b)** proceeds of life insurance contracts excluded under section 101 minus the basis in the contract for purposes of ACE.

Note: *Do not make an adjustment for any income from discharge of indebtedness excluded from gross income under section 108 or any corresponding provision of prior law.*

An income item is considered taken into account without regard to the timing of its inclusion in a corporation's pre-adjustment AMTI or its E&P. Only income items that are permanently excluded from pre-adjustment AMTI are included in ACE. An income item will not be considered taken into account merely because the proceeds from that item might eventually be reflected in a corporation's pre-adjustment AMTI (e.g., that of a shareholder) on the liquidation or disposal of a business.

Line 3d. Include in ACE the income on life insurance contracts (as determined under section 7702(g)) for the tax year minus the part of any premium attributable to insurance coverage.

Line 3e. Do not include any adjustment related to the E&P effects of any charitable contribution (section 56(g)(4)(I)).

Line 4—Disallowance of Items Not Deductible From E&P

Generally, no deduction is allowed when figuring ACE for items not taken into account (see below) in computing E&P for the tax year. These amounts increase ACE if they are deductible in computing pre-adjustment AMTI (i.e., they would be positive adjustments). However, there are exceptions. **Do not** add back: **(a)** any deduction allowable under section 243 or 245 for any dividend that qualifies for a 100% dividends-received deduction under section 243(a), 245(b), or 245(c); and **(b)** any dividend received from a 20%-owned corporation (see section 243(c)(2)), but only if the dividend is from income of the paying corporation that is subject to

Federal income tax. See sections 56(g)(4)(C)(iii) and (iv) for special rules for dividends from section 936 corporations (including section 30A corporations) and certain dividends received by certain cooperatives.

An item is considered taken into account without regard to the timing of its deductibility in computing pre-adjustment AMTI or E&P. Therefore, only deduction items that are permanently disallowed in figuring E&P are disallowed in figuring ACE.

Items described in Regulations section 1.56(g)-1(e) for which no adjustment is necessary. Generally, no deduction is allowed for an item in figuring ACE if the item is not deductible in figuring pre-adjustment AMTI (even if the item is deductible in figuring E&P). The only exceptions to this general rule are the related reductions to an income item described in the second sentence of the instructions for line 3 on page 6. Deductions that are not allowed in figuring ACE include:

- Capital losses that exceed capital gains;
- Bribes, fines, and penalties disallowed under section 162;
- Charitable contributions that exceed the limitations of section 170;
- Meals and entertainment expenses that exceed the limitations of section 274;
- Federal taxes disallowed under section 275; and
- Golden parachute payments that exceed the limitation of section 280G.

Note: *No adjustment is necessary for these items since they were not allowed in figuring pre-adjustment AMTI.*

Line 4e. Do not include any adjustment related to the E&P effects of any charitable contribution (section 56(g)(4)(I)).

Line 5—Other Adjustments

Line 5a. Except as noted below, in figuring ACE, determine the deduction for intangible drilling costs (section 263(c)) under section 312(n)(2)(A). Subtract the ACE expense (if any) from the AMT expense (used to figure line 2p of Form 4626) and enter the result on line 5a. If the ACE expense exceeds the AMT amount, enter the result as a negative amount.

Exception. The above rule does not apply to amounts paid or incurred in a tax year that began after 1992 for any oil and gas well by corporations other than integrated oil companies (as defined in section 291(b)(4)). If this exception applies, do not enter an amount on line 5a.

Line 5b.

Note: Do not *make this adjustment for expenditures for which the corporation elected the optional 3-year writeoff under section 59(e) for the regular tax.*

When figuring ACE, the current year deduction for circulation expenditures under section 173 does not apply.

Therefore, treat circulation expenditures using the case law that existed before section 173 was enacted. Subtract the ACE expense (if any) from the regular tax expense (for a personal holding company, from the AMT expense used to figure line 2d of Form 4626) and enter the result on line 5b. If the ACE expense exceeds the regular tax amount (for a personal holding company, the AMT amount), enter the result as a negative amount.

Line 5c. When figuring ACE, the amortization provisions of section 248 do not apply. Therefore, charge all organizational expenditures to a capital account and do not take them into account when figuring ACE until the corporation is sold or otherwise disposed of. Enter on line 5c all amortization deductions for organizational expenditures that were taken for the regular tax during the tax year.

Line 5d. The adjustments provided in section 312(n)(4) apply in figuring ACE. See Regulations section 1.56(g)-1(f)(3) for more details.

Line 5e. For any installment sale in a tax year that began after 1989, the corporation generally cannot use the installment method to figure ACE. However, it may use the installment method for the applicable percentage (as determined under section 453A) of the gain from any installment sale to which section 453A(a)(1) applies. Subtract the installment sale income reported for AMT from the ACE income from the sales and enter the result on line 5e. If the ACE income from the sales is less than the AMT amount, enter the difference as a negative amount.

Line 6—Disallowance of Loss on Exchange of Debt Pools

When figuring ACE, the corporation may not recognize any loss on the exchange of any pool of debt obligations for any other pool of debt obligations having substantially the same effective interest rates and maturities. Add back (i.e., enter as a positive adjustment) on line 6 any such loss to the extent recognized for the regular tax.

Line 7—Acquisition Expenses of Life Insurance Companies for Qualified Foreign Contracts

For ACE, acquisition expenses of life insurance companies for qualified foreign contracts (as defined in section 807(e)(4) without regard to the treatment of reinsurance contract rules of section 848(e)(5)) must be capitalized and amortized by applying the treatment generally required under generally accepted accounting principles (and as if this rule applied to such contracts for all applicable tax years). Subtract the ACE expense (if any) from the regular tax expense and enter the result on line 7. If the ACE expense is more than the regular tax expense, enter the result as a negative amount.

Line 8—Depletion

When figuring ACE, the allowance for depletion for any property placed in service in a tax year that began after 1989 generally must be determined under the cost depletion method of section 611.

Subtract the ACE expense (if any) from the AMT expense (used to figure line 2m of Form 4626) and enter the result on line 8 of the worksheet. If the ACE expense is more than the AMT amount, enter the result as a negative amount.

Exception. Independent oil and gas producers and royalty owners that figured their regular tax depletion deduction under section 613A(c) do not have an adjustment for ACE purposes.

Line 9—Basis Adjustments in Determining Gain or Loss From Sale or Exchange of Pre-1994 Property

If, during the tax year, the corporation disposed of property for which it is making (or previously made) any of the section 56(g) ACE adjustments, refigure the property's adjusted basis for ACE. Then refigure the property's gain or loss.

Enter the difference between the AMT gain or loss (used to figure line 2e of Form 4626) and the ACE gain or loss. Enter the difference as a negative amount if: **(1)** the ACE gain is less than the AMT gain, OR **(2)** the ACE loss is more than the AMT loss, OR **(3)** the corporation had an ACE loss and an AMT gain.

Paperwork Reduction Act Notice. We ask for the information on this form to carry out the Internal Revenue laws of the United States. You are required to give us the information. We need it to ensure that you are complying with these laws and to allow us to figure and collect the right amount of tax.

You are not required to provide the information requested on a form that is subject to the Paperwork Reduction Act unless the form displays a valid OMB control number. Books or records relating to a form or its instructions must be retained as long as their contents may become material in the administration of any Internal Revenue law. Generally, tax returns and return information are confidential, as required by section 6103.

The time needed to complete and file this form will vary depending on individual circumstances. The estimated average time is:

Recordkeeping .... 18 hr., 25 min.

Learning about the law or the form .... 14 hr., 42 min.

Preparing and sending the form to the IRS .... 15 hr., 39 min.

If you have comments concerning the accuracy of these time estimates or suggestions for making this form simpler, we would be happy to hear from you. See the instructions for the tax return with which this form is filed.

Page 7

Adjusted Current Earnings Worksheet

▶ See ACE Worksheet Instructions (which begin on page 6).

1	Pre-adjustment AMTI. Enter the amount from line 3 of Form 4626		**1**
2	ACE depreciation adjustment:		
a	AMT depreciation	**2a**	
b	ACE depreciation:		
	(1) Post-1993 property	**2b(1)**	
	(2) Post-1989, pre-1994 property . .	**2b(2)**	
	(3) Pre-1990 MACRS property . . .	**2b(3)**	
	(4) Pre-1990 original ACRS property .	**2b(4)**	
	(5) Property described in sections 168(f)(1) through (4).	**2b(5)**	
	(6) Other property	**2b(6)**	
	(7) Total ACE depreciation. Add lines 2b(1) through 2b(6) . . .	**2b(7)**	
c	ACE depreciation adjustment. Subtract line 2b(7) from line 2a		**2c**
3	Inclusion in ACE of items included in earnings and profits (E&P):		
a	Tax-exempt interest income	**3a**	
b	Death benefits from life insurance contracts	**3b**	
c	All other distributions from life insurance contracts (including surrenders)	**3c**	
d	Inside buildup of undistributed income in life insurance contracts .	**3d**	
e	Other items (see Regulations sections 1.56(g)-1(c)(6)(iii) through (ix) for a partial list)	**3e**	
f	Total increase to ACE from inclusion in ACE of items included in E&P. Add lines 3a through 3e		**3f**
4	Disallowance of items not deductible from E&P:		
a	Certain dividends received	**4a**	
b	Dividends paid on certain preferred stock of public utilities that are deductible under section 247	**4b**	
c	Dividends paid to an ESOP that are deductible under section 404(k)	**4c**	
d	Nonpatronage dividends that are paid and deductible under section 1382(c)	**4d**	
e	Other items (see Regulations sections 1.56(g)-1(d)(3)(i) and (ii) for a partial list)	**4e**	
f	Total increase to ACE because of disallowance of items not deductible from E&P. Add lines 4a through 4e		**4f**
5	Other adjustments based on rules for figuring E&P:		
a	Intangible drilling costs	**5a**	
b	Circulation expenditures.	**5b**	
c	Organizational expenditures	**5c**	
d	LIFO inventory adjustments	**5d**	
e	Installment sales	**5e**	
f	Total other E&P adjustments. Combine lines 5a through 5e		**5f**
6	Disallowance of loss on exchange of debt pools		**6**
7	Acquisition expenses of life insurance companies for qualified foreign contracts		**7**
8	Depletion.		**8**
9	Basis adjustments in determining gain or loss from sale or exchange of pre-1994 property .		**9**
10	**Adjusted current earnings.** Combine lines 1, 2c, 3f, 4f, and 5f through 9. Enter the result here and on line 4a of Form 4626		**10**

Page 8

166

INSTRUCTIONS FOR FORM 4797

Sales of Business Property

1997

Department of the Treasury
Internal Revenue Service

Instructions for Form 4797

Sales of Business Property
(Also Involuntary Conversions and Recapture Amounts Under Sections 179 and 280F(b)(2))

Section references are to the Internal Revenue Code unless otherwise noted.

General Instructions

A Change To Note

The Taxpayer Relief Act of 1997 generally reduced the tax rates that apply to the net capital gain of noncorporate taxpayers for sales, exchanges, or conversions of assets (including installment payments received) after May 6, 1997. Because the change in the capital gains rates may affect the tax treatment of section 1231 gains and losses, noncorporate taxpayers (and S corporations) with a net section 1231 gain should use column (h) in Part I to report 28% rate gains and losses (as defined in the footnote on Form 4797, Part I).

Purpose of Form

Use Form 4797 to report:
- The sale or exchange of property used in your trade or business; depreciable and amortizable property; oil, gas, geothermal, or other mineral properties; and section 126 property.
- The involuntary conversion (from other than casualty or theft) of property used in your trade or business and capital assets held in connection with a trade or business or a transaction entered into for profit.
- The disposition of noncapital assets (other than inventory or property held primarily for sale to customers in the ordinary course of your trade or business).
- The recapture of section 179 expense deductions for partners and S corporation shareholders from property dispositions by partnerships and S corporations.
- The computation of recapture amounts under sections 179 and 280F(b)(2), when the business use of section 179 or listed property drops to 50% or less.

Other Forms To Use

- Use **Form 4684**, Casualties and Thefts, to report involuntary conversions from casualties and thefts.
- Use **Form 8824**, Like-Kind Exchanges, for each exchange of qualifying business or investment property for property of a like kind. For exchanges of property used in a trade or business (and other noncapital assets), enter the gain or (loss) from Form 8824, if any, on line 5 or 16.
- If you sold property on which you claimed investment credit, get **Form 4255**, Recapture of Investment Credit, to see if you must recapture some or all of the credit.

Special Rules

At-risk rules. If you report a loss on an asset used in an activity for which you are not at risk, in whole or in part, see the instructions for **Form 6198**, At-Risk Limitations. Also, get **Pub.**

925, Passive Activity and At-Risk Rules. Losses from passive activities are first subject to the at-risk rules and then to the passive activity rules.

Depreciable property and other property disposed of in the same transaction. If you disposed of both depreciable property and other property (e.g., a building and land) in the same transaction and realized a gain, you must allocate the amount realized between the two types of property based on their respective fair market values to figure the part of the gain to be recaptured as ordinary income because of depreciation. The disposition of each type of property is reported separately in the appropriate part of Form 4797 (e.g., for property held more than 1 year, report the sale of a building in Part III and land in Part I).

Disposition of assets that constitute a trade or business. For such a disposition, the buyer and seller must allocate the total purchase price using the residual method and file **Form 8594**, Asset Acquisition Statement.

Installment sales. If you sold property at a gain and you will receive a payment in a tax year after the year of sale, you generally must report the sale on the installment method unless you elect not to do so.

Use **Form 6252**, Installment Sale Income, to report the sale on the installment method. Also use Form 6252 to report any payment received in 1997 from a sale made in an earlier year that you reported on the installment method.

To elect out of the installment method, report the full amount of the gain on a timely filed return (including extensions).

Get **Pub. 537**, Installment Sales. for more details.

Involuntary conversion of property. You may not have to pay tax on a gain from an involuntary or compulsory conversion of property. Get **Pub. 544**, Sales and Other Dispositions of Assets, for details.

Exclusion of gain on sale of a home used for business. If you rented or used part of your home for business and meet certain requirements, you may be able to exclude part or all of the gain figured on Form 4797. For details on the exclusion and allocating the sales price, expenses of sale, and the adjusted basis of the home, see the instructions for **Form 2119**, Sale of Your Home, and **Pub. 523**, Selling Your Home.

If the home was held more than 1 year, complete Part III to figure the gain on the part that was rented or used for business. **Do not** take the business part of the exclusion into account when figuring the gain on line 24. If you qualify for and are claiming the one-time exclusion for people age 55 or older, take the business part of that exclusion into account when figuring any section 1250 recapture on line 26g. If you qualify for and are claiming the exclusion for sales after May 6, 1997, and line 22 includes depreciation for periods after that date, you **cannot** exclude gain to the extent of

	(a) Type of property	(b) Held 1 year or less	(c) Held more than 1 year
1	Depreciable trade or business property:		
a	Sold or exchanged at a gain	Part II	Part III (1245, 1250)
b	Sold or exchanged at a loss	Part II	Part I
2	Depreciable residential rental property:		
a	Sold or exchanged at a gain	Part II	Part III (1250)
b	Sold or exchanged at a loss	Part II	Part I
3	Farmland held less than 10 years upon which soil, water, or land clearing expenses were deducted:		
a	Sold at a gain	Part II	Part III (1252)
b	Sold at a loss	Part II	Part I
4	Disposition of cost-sharing payment property described in section 126	Part II	Part III (1255)
		Held less than 24 months	**Held 24 months or more**
5	Cattle and horses used in a trade or business for draft, breeding, dairy, or sporting purposes:		
a	Sold at a gain	Part II	Part III (1245)
b	Sold at a loss	Part II	Part I
c	Raised cattle and horses sold at a gain	Part II	Part I
		Held less than 12 months	**Held 12 months or more**
6	Livestock other than cattle and horses used in a trade or business for draft, breeding, dairy, or sporting purposes:		
a	Sold at a gain	Part II	Part III (1245)
b	Sold at a loss	Part II	Part I
c	Raised livestock sold at a gain	Part II	Part I

Cat. No. 13087T

that depreciation. On line 2 of Form 4797, write "Section 121 exclusion" and enter the business part of the exclusion as a (loss) in column (g) and, if applicable, as a (loss) in column (h). Complete Part II or IV of Form 2119 and attach it and Form 4797 to your return.

If the home was held for 1 year or less, report the sale and business part of the exclusion in a similar manner on line 10 of Form 4797.

Passive loss limitations. If you have an overall loss from passive activities, and you report a loss on an asset used in a passive activity, use **Form 8582,** Passive Activity Loss Limitations, to see how much loss is allowed before entering it on Form 4797.

You cannot claim unused passive activity credits when you dispose of your interest in an activity. However, if you dispose of your entire interest in an activity, you may elect to increase the basis of the credit property by the original basis reduction of the property to the extent that the credit has not been allowed because of the passive activity rules. Make the election on **Form 8582-CR,** Passive Activity Credit Limitations, or **Form 8810,** Corporate Passive Activity Loss and Credit Limitations. No basis adjustment may be elected on a partial disposition of your interest in an activity.

Recapture of preproductive expenses. If you elected out of the uniform capitalization rules of section 263A, any plant that you produce is treated as section 1245 property. For dispositions of plants reportable on Form 4797, enter the recapture amount taxed as ordinary income on line 22 of Form 4797. Get **Pub. 225,** Farmer's Tax Guide, for details.

Section 197(f)(9)(B)(ii) election. If you elected under section 197(f)(9)(B)(ii) to recognize gain on the disposition of a section 197 intangible and to pay a tax on that gain at the highest tax rate, include the additional tax on Form 1040, line 39 (or the appropriate line of other income tax returns). On the dotted line next to that line, write "197." The additional tax is the amount that, when added to any other income tax on the gain, equals the gain multiplied by the highest tax rate.

Specific Instructions

To show losses, enclose figures in (parentheses).

Part I

Section 1231 transactions are:
• Sales or exchanges of real or depreciable property used in a trade or business and held for more than 1 year. To figure the holding period, begin counting on the day after you received the property and include the day you disposed of it.
• Cutting of timber that the taxpayer elects to treat as a sale or exchange under section 631(a).
• Disposal of timber with a retained economic interest that is treated as a sale under section 631(b).
• Disposal of coal (including lignite) or domestic iron ore with a retained economic interest that is treated as a sale under section 631(c).
• Sales or exchanges of cattle and horses, regardless of age, used in a trade or business by the taxpayer for draft, breeding, dairy, or sporting purposes and held for 24 months or more from acquisition date.
• Sales or exchanges of livestock other than cattle and horses, regardless of age, used by the taxpayer for draft, breeding, dairy, or

sporting purposes and held for 12 months or more from acquisition date.

Note: *Livestock does not include poultry, chickens, turkeys, pigeons, geese, other birds, fish, frogs, reptiles, etc.*
• Sales or exchanges of unharvested crops. See section 1231(b)(4).
• Involuntary conversions of trade or business property or capital assets held more than 1 year in connection with a trade or business or a transaction entered into for profit.

These conversions may result from **(a)** part or total destruction, **(b)** theft or seizure, or **(c)** requisition or condemnation (whether threatened or carried out). If any recognized losses were from involuntary conversions from fire, storm, shipwreck, or other casualty, or from theft, and they exceed the recognized gains from the conversions, do not include them when figuring your net section 1231 losses.

Section 1231 transactions **do not** include sales or exchanges of:
• Inventory or property held primarily for sale to customers.
• Copyrights, literary, musical, or artistic compositions, letters or memoranda, or similar property **(a)** created by your personal efforts, **(b)** prepared or produced for you (in the case of letters, memoranda, or similar property), or **(c)** received from someone who created them or for whom they were created, as mentioned in **(a)** or **(b)**, in a way that entitled you to the basis of the previous owner (such as by gift).
• U.S. Government publications, including the Congressional Record, that you received from the Government, other than by purchase at the normal sales price, or that you got from someone who had received it in a similar way, if your basis is determined by reference to the previous owner's basis.

Lines 2 through 6, column (g). You must make a separate entry in this column for each transaction reported on line 2 and any other line(s) that apply to you.

Tip: *If you are required to complete column (h), complete column (g) before you begin column (h).*

Line 8, column (g). Part or all of your section 1231 gains on line 7, column (g) may be taxed as ordinary income instead of receiving long-term capital gain treatment. These net section 1231 gains are treated as ordinary income to the extent of the "nonrecaptured section 1231 losses." The nonrecaptured losses are net section 1231 losses deducted during the 5 preceding tax years that have not yet been applied against any net section 1231 gain for determining how much gain is ordinary income under these rules.

Example. If you had net section 1231 losses of $4,000 and $6,000 in 1992 and 1993 and net section 1231 gains of $3,000 and $2,000 in 1996 and 1997, line 7, column (g) would show the 1997 gain of $2,000, and line 8, column (g) would show nonrecaptured net section 1231 losses of $7,000 ($10,000 net section 1231 losses minus the $3,000 that was recaptured because of the 1996 gain). The $2,000 gain on line 7, column (g) is all ordinary income and would be entered on line 12 of Form 4797. For recordkeeping purposes, the $4,000 loss from 1992 is all recaptured ($3,000 in 1996 and $1,000 in 1997) and you have $5,000 left to recapture from 1993 ($6,000 minus the $1,000 recaptured this year).

Figuring the prior year losses. You had a net section 1231 loss if section 1231 losses exceeded section 1231 gains. Gains are included only to the extent taken into account in figuring gross income. Losses are included only to the extent taken into account in figuring

taxable income except that the limitation on capital losses does not apply.

Line 8, column (h). Make an entry on line 8, column (h) **only** if line 9, column (g) is more than zero. Figure the amount to enter as follows:
• If line 7, column (h) is zero or less, enter zero on line 8, column (h).
• If line 7, column (h) is more than zero, enter on line 8, column (h) the **smaller** of line 7, column (h) or line 8, column (g).

Line 9, column (g). For recordkeeping purposes, if line 9, column (g) is zero, the amount on line 7, column (g) is the amount of net section 1231 loss recaptured in 1997. If line 9, column (g) is more than zero, you have recaptured in 1997 all your net section 1231 losses from prior years.

Part II

If a transaction is not reportable in Part I or Part III and the property is not a capital asset reportable on Schedule D, report the transaction in Part II.

If you receive ordinary income from a sale or other disposition of your interest in a partnership, get **Pub. 541,** Partnerships.

Line 10. Report other ordinary gains and losses, including property held 1 year or less, on this line.

Small business investment company stock. Report on line 10 ordinary losses from the sale or exchange (including worthlessness) of stock in a small business investment company operating under the Small Business Investment Act of 1958. See section 1242.

Section 1244 (small business) stock. Individuals report ordinary losses from the sale or exchange (including worthlessness) of section 1244 (small business) stock on line 10.

To qualify as section 1244 stock, all of the following requirements must be met:

1. You acquired the stock after June 30, 1958, upon original issuance from a domestic corporation (or the stock was acquired by a partnership in which you were a partner continuously from the date the stock was issued until the time of the loss).

2. If the stock was issued before November 7, 1978, it was issued under a written plan that met the requirements of Regulations section 1.1244(c)-1(f), and when that plan was adopted, the corporation was treated as a small business corporation under Regulations section 1.1244(c)-2(c).

3. If the stock was issued after November 6, 1978, the corporation was treated as a small business corporation, at the time the stock was issued, under Regulations section 1.1244(c)-2(b). To be treated as a small business corporation, the total amount of money and other property received by the corporation for its stock as a contribution to capital and paid-in surplus generally may not exceed $1 million.

4. The stock was issued for money or other property (excluding stock or securities).

5. The corporation, for its 5 most recent tax years ending before the loss, derived more than 50% of its gross receipts from sources **other than** royalties, rents, dividends, interest, annuities, and gains from sales and exchanges of stocks or securities. (If the corporation was in existence for at least 1 tax year but fewer than 5 tax years ending before the loss, the 50% test applies for the tax years ending before the loss. If the corporation was not in existence for at least 1 tax year ending before the loss, the 50% test applies for the entire period ending before the loss.) However, the 50% test does not apply if the corporation's deductions (other than the net operating loss and dividends-received deductions) exceeded its gross income during that period.

6. If the stock was issued before July 19, 1984, it must have been common stock.

The maximum amount that may be treated as an ordinary loss is $50,000 ($100,000 if married filing jointly). Special rules may limit the amount of your ordinary loss if **(a)** you received section 1244 stock in exchange for property with a basis in excess of its fair market value or **(b)** your stock basis increased from contributions to capital or otherwise. See **Pub. 550,** Investment Income and Expenses, for more details. Report on Schedule D losses in excess of the maximum amount that may be treated as an ordinary loss (and gains from the sale or exchange of section 1244 stock).

Keep adequate records to distinguish section 1244 stock from any other stock owned in the same corporation.

Line 17. Enter any recapture of section 179 expense deduction included on Schedule K-1 (Form 1065), line 25, and on Schedule K-1 (Form 1120S), line 23, but only if it is due to a disposition. Include it only to the extent that you took a deduction for it in an earlier year. See the instructions for Part IV if you have section 179 recapture when the business use percentage of the property dropped to 50% or less.

Line 18b(1). You must complete this line if there is a gain on Form 4797, line 3, column (g); a loss on Form 4797, line 11; **and** a loss on Form 4684, line 35, column (b)(ii). Enter on this line and on Schedule A (Form 1040), line 22, the **smaller** of the loss on Form 4797, line 11; or the loss on Form 4684, line 35, column (b)(ii). To figure which loss is smaller, treat both losses as positive numbers.

Part III

Generally, **do not** complete Part III for property held 1 year or less; use Part II instead. For exceptions, see the chart on page 1.

Part III is used to figure recapture of depreciation and certain other items that must be reported as ordinary income on the disposition of property. Fill out lines 19 through 24 to determine the gain on the disposition of the property. If you have more than four properties to report, use additional forms. For more details on depreciation recapture, see Pub. 544.

Note: If the property was sold on the installment sale basis, see the Instructions for Form 6252 before completing this part. Also, if you have both installment sales and noninstallment sales, you may want to use a separate Form 4797, Part III, for each installment sale and one Form 4797, Part III, for the noninstallment sales.

Line 20. The gross sales price includes money, the fair market value of other property received, and any existing mortgage or other debt the buyer assumes or takes the property subject to. For casualty or theft gains, include insurance or other reimbursement you received or expect to receive for each item. Include on this line your insurance coverage, whether or not you are submitting a claim for reimbursement.

For section 1255 property disposed of in a sale, exchange, or involuntary conversion, enter the amount realized. For section 1255 property disposed of in any other way, enter the fair market value.

Line 21. Reduce the cost or other basis of the property by the amount of any qualified electric vehicle credit, diesel-powered highway vehicle credit, enhanced oil recovery credit, or disabled access credit.

However, **do not** reduce the cost or other basis on this line by any of the following amounts:

1. Deductions allowed or allowable for depreciation, amortization, depletion, or preproductive expenses;

2. The section 179 expense deduction;

3. The downward basis adjustment under section 50(c) (or the corresponding provision of prior law);

4. The deduction for qualified clean-fuel vehicle property or refueling property; or

5. Deductions claimed under section 190, 193, or 1253(d)(2) or (3) (as in effect before the enactment of P.L. 103-66).

Instead, include these amounts on line 22. They will be used to determine the property's adjusted basis on line 23.

Increase the cost or other basis by any qualified electric vehicle credit recapture amount.

Line 22. For a taxpayer other than a partnership or an S corporation, complete the following steps to figure the amount to enter on line 22:

Step 1. Add the following amounts:

1. Deductions allowed or allowable for depreciation, amortization, depletion, or preproductive expenses;

2. The section 179 expense deduction;

3. The downward basis adjustment under section 50(c) (or the corresponding provision of prior law);

4. The deduction for qualified clean-fuel vehicle property or refueling property; and

5. Deductions claimed under section 190, 193, or 1253(d)(2) or (3) (as in effect before the enactment of P.L. 103-66).

Step 2. From the step 1 total, **subtract** the following amounts:

1. Any investment credit recapture amount if the basis of the property was reduced for the tax year the property was placed in service under section 50(c)(1) (or the corresponding provision of prior law). See section 50(c)(2) (or the corresponding provision of prior law).

2. Any section 179 or 280F(b)(2) recapture amount included in gross income in a prior tax year because the business use of the property dropped to 50% or less.

3. Any qualified clean-fuel vehicle property or refueling property deduction you were required to recapture because the property ceased to be eligible for the deduction.

You may have to include depreciation allowed or allowable on another asset (and refigure the basis amount for line 21) if you use its adjusted basis in determining the adjusted basis of the property described on line 19. An example is property acquired by a trade-in. See Regulations section 1.1245-2(a)(4).

Partnerships should enter the deductions allowed or allowable for depreciation, amortization, or depletion on line 22. Enter the section 179 expense deduction on Form 1065, Schedule K, line 24. Partnerships should make the basis adjustment required under section 50(c) (or the corresponding provision of prior law). Partners adjust the basis of their interest in the partnership to take into account the basis adjustments made at the partnership level.

S corporations should enter the deductions allowed or allowable for depreciation, amortization, or depletion on line 22. Enter the section 179 expense deduction on Form 1120S, Schedule K, line 24, but only if the corporation disposed of property acquired in a tax year beginning after 1982. S corporations should make the basis adjustment required under section 50(c) (or the corresponding provision of prior law). Shareholders adjust the basis in their stock in the corporation to take

into account the basis adjustments made at the S corporation level under section 50(c) (or the corresponding provision of prior law).

Line 23. For section 1255 property, enter the adjusted basis of the section 126 property disposed of.

Line 25. Section 1245 property is depreciable (or amortizable under section 185 (repealed), 197, or 1253(d)(2) or (3) (as in effect before the enactment of P.L. 103-66)) and is one of the following:

● Personal property.

● Elevators and escalators placed in service before 1987.

● Real property (other than property described under tangible real property below) subject to amortization or deductions under section 169, 179, 185 (repealed), 188 (repealed), 190, 193, or 194.

● Tangible real property (except buildings and their structural components) if it is used in any of the following ways:

1. As an integral part of manufacturing, production, extraction, or furnishing transportation, communications, or certain public utility services.

2. As a research facility in these activities.

3. For the bulk storage of fungible commodities (including commodities in a liquid or gaseous state) used in these activities.

● A single purpose agricultural or horticultural structure (as defined in section 168(i)(13)).

● A storage facility (not including a building or its structural components) used in connection with the distribution of petroleum or any primary petroleum product.

● Any railroad grading or tunnel bore (as defined in section 168(e)(4)).

See section 1245(b) for exceptions and limits involving:

● Gifts.

● Transfers at death.

● Certain tax-free transactions.

● Certain like-kind exchanges, involuntary conversions, etc.

● Exchanges to comply with SEC orders.

● Property distributed by a partnership to a partner.

● Transfers to tax-exempt organizations where the property will be used in an unrelated business.

● Timber property.

See the following sections for special rules:

● Section 1245(a)(4) for player contracts and section 1056(c) for information required from the transferor of a franchise of any sports enterprise if the sale or exchange involves the transfer of player contracts.

● Section 1245(a)(5) (repealed) for property placed in service before 1987, when only a portion of a building is section 1245 recovery property.

● Section 1245(a)(6) (repealed) for qualified leased property placed in service before 1987.

Line 26. Section 1250 property is depreciable real property (other than section 1245 property). Section 1250 recapture applies when an accelerated depreciation method was used.

Section 1250 recapture does not apply to dispositions of the following property placed in service after 1986 (or after July 31, 1986, if elected).

1. 27.5-year (or 40-year, if elected) residential rental property.

2. 22-, 31.5-, or 39-year (or 40-year, if elected) nonresidential real property.

Real property depreciable under ACRS (pre-1987 rules) is subject to recapture under section 1245, except for the following, which are treated as section 1250 property:

Page 3

• 15-, 18-, or 19-year real property and low-income housing that is residential rental property.

• 15-, 18-, or 19-year real property and low-income housing that is used mostly outside the United States.

• 15-, 18-, or 19-year real property and low-income housing for which a straight line election was made.

• Low-income rental housing described in clause (i), (ii), (iii), or (iv) of section 1250(a)(1)(B). See instructions for line 26b.

See section 1250(d) for exceptions and limits involving:
• Gifts.
• Transfers at death.
• Certain tax-free transactions.
• Certain like-kind exchanges, involuntary conversions, etc.
• Exchanges to comply with SEC orders.
• Property distributed by a partnership to a partner.
• Disposition of a main home before May 7, 1997.
• Disposition of qualified low-income housing.
• Transfers of property to tax-exempt organizations where the property will be used in an unrelated business.
• Dispositions of property as a result of foreclosure proceedings.

Special rules:
• For additional depreciation attributable to rehabilitation expenditures, see section 1250(b)(4).
• If substantial improvements have been made, see section 1250(f).

Line 26a. Enter the additional depreciation for the period after 1975. **Additional depreciation** is the excess of actual depreciation over depreciation figured using the straight line method. For this purpose, do not reduce the basis under section 50(c)(1) (or the corresponding provision of prior law) in figuring straight line depreciation.

Line 26b. Use 100% as the percentage for this line, except for low-income rental housing described in clause (i), (ii), (iii), or (iv) of section 1250(a)(1)(B). For this type of low-income rental housing, see section 1250(a)(1)(B) for the percentage to use.

Line 26d. Enter the additional depreciation after 1969 and before 1976. If straight line depreciation exceeds the actual depreciation for the period after 1975, reduce line 26d by the excess. Do not enter less than zero on line 26d.

Line 26f. The amount the corporation treats as ordinary income under section 291 is 20% of the excess, if any, of the amount that would be treated as ordinary income if such property were section 1245 property, over the amount treated as ordinary income under section 1250. If the corporation used the straight line method of depreciation, the ordinary income under section 291 is 20% of the amount figured under section 1245.

Line 27. Partnerships should skip this section. Partners should enter on the applicable lines of Part III amounts subject to section 1252 according to instructions from the partnership.

You may have ordinary income on the disposition of certain farmland held more than 1 year but less than 10 years.

Refer to section 1252 to determine if there is ordinary income on the disposition of certain farmland for which deductions were allowed under sections 175 (soil and water conservation) and 182 (land clearing) (repealed). Skip line 27 if you dispose of such farmland during the 10th or later year after you acquired it.

Gain from disposition of certain farmland is subject to ordinary income rules under section 1252 before being considered under section 1231 (Part I).

When filling out line 27b, enter 100% of line 27a on line 27b, except as follows:
• 80% if the farmland was disposed of within the 6th year after it was acquired.
• 60% if disposed of within the 7th year.
• 40% if disposed of within the 8th year.
• 20% if disposed of within the 9th year.

Line 28. If you had a gain on the disposition of oil, gas, or geothermal property placed in service before 1987, you must treat all or part of the gain as ordinary income. Include on line 22 of Form 4797 any depletion allowed (or allowable) in determining the adjusted basis of the property.

If you had a gain on the disposition of oil, gas, geothermal, or other mineral properties (section 1254 property) placed in service after 1986, you must recapture all expenses that were deducted as intangible drilling costs, depletion, mine exploration costs, and development costs, under sections 263, 616, and 617.

Exception. Property placed in service after 1986 and acquired under a written contract entered into before September 26, 1985, and binding at all times thereafter is treated as placed in service before 1987.

Note: *In the case of a corporation that is an integrated oil company, amounts amortized under section 291(b)(2) are treated as a deduction under section 263(c) when completing line 28a.*

Line 28a. If the property was placed in service before 1987, enter the total expenses after 1975 that:
• Were deducted by the taxpayer or any other person as intangible drilling and development costs under section 263(c). (Previously expensed mining costs that have been included in income upon reaching the producing state are not taken into account in determining recapture.); and
• Would have been reflected in the adjusted basis of the property if they had not been deducted.

If the property was placed in service after 1986, enter the total expenses that:
• Were deducted under section 263, 616, or 617 by the taxpayer or any other person; and
• Which, but for such deduction, would have been included in the basis of the property; plus
• The deduction under section 611 that reduced the adjusted basis of such property.

If you disposed of a portion of section 1254 property or an undivided interest in it, see section 1254(a)(2).

Line 29a. Use 100% if the property is disposed of less than 10 years after receipt of payments excluded from income. Use 100% minus 10% for each year, or part of a year, that the property was held over 10 years after receipt of the excluded payments. Use zero if 20 years or more.

Line 29b. If any part of the gain shown on line 24 is treated as ordinary income under sections 1231 through 1254 (e.g., section 1252), enter the smaller of **(a)** line 24 reduced by the part of the gain treated as ordinary income under the other provision or **(b)** line 29a.

Part IV

Column (a). If you took a section 179 expense deduction for property placed in service after 1986 (other than listed property, as defined in section 280F(d)(4)), and the business use of the property was reduced to 50% or less this

year, complete column (a) of lines 33 through 35 to figure the recapture amount.

Column (b). If you have listed property that you placed in service in a prior year and the business use dropped to 50% or less this year, figure the amount to be recaptured under section 280F(b)(2). Complete column (b), lines 33 through 35. Get **Pub. 463,** Travel, Entertainment, Gift, and Car Expenses, for more details on recapture of excess depreciation.

Note: *If you have more than one property subject to the recapture rules, use separate statements to figure the recapture amounts and attach the statements to your tax return.*

Line 33. In column (a), enter the section 179 expense deduction claimed when the property was placed in service. In column (b), enter the depreciation allowable on the property in prior tax years. Include any section 179 expense deduction you took as depreciation.

Line 34. In column (a), enter the depreciation that would have been allowable on the section 179 amount from the year it was placed in service through the current year. Get **Pub. 946,** How To Depreciate Property. In column (b), enter the depreciation that would have been allowable if the property had not been used more than 50% in a qualified business. Figure the depreciation from the year it was placed in service until the current year. See Pub. 463 and Pub. 946.

Line 35. Subtract line 34 from line 33 and enter the recapture amount as "other income" on the same form or schedule on which you took the deduction. For example, if you took the deduction on Schedule C (Form 1040), report the recapture amount as other income on Schedule C (Form 1040).

Note: *If you filed Schedule C or F (Form 1040) and the property was used in both your trade or business and for the production of income, the portion attributable to your trade or business is subject to self-employment tax. Allocate the amount on line 35 before entering the recapture amount on the appropriate schedule.*

Be sure to increase the basis of the property by the recapture amount.

Paperwork Reduction Act Notice. We ask for the information on this form to carry out the Internal Revenue laws of the United States. You are required to give us the information. We need it to ensure that you are complying with these laws and to allow us to figure and collect the right amount of tax.

You are not required to provide the information requested on a form that is subject to the Paperwork Reduction Act unless the form displays a valid OMB control number. Books or records relating to a form or its instructions must be retained as long as their contents may become material in the administration of any Internal Revenue law. Generally, tax returns and return information are confidential, as required by section 6103.

The time needed to complete and file this form will vary depending on individual circumstances. The estimated average time is: **Recordkeeping,** 29 hr., 53 min.; **Learning about the law or the form,** 13 hr., 4 min.; **Preparing the form,** 18 hr., 47 min.; **Copying, assembling, and sending the form to the IRS,** 1 hr., 20 min.

If you have comments concerning the accuracy of these time estimates or suggestions for making this form simpler, we would be happy to hear from you. See the instructions for the tax return with which this form is filed.

Page 4